AF898522

Second Edition

MUSIC LAW

FOR THE GENERAL PRACTITIONER

THOMAS R. LEAVENS AND JOSEPH J. BOGDAN

AMERICAN BAR ASSOCIATION

Solo, Small Firm and
General Practice Division

Cover design by Sara Wadford/ABA Design

Printed in the United States of America.

30 29 28 27 26   5 4 3 2 1

Library of Congress Cataloging-in-Publication Data

Names: Leavens, Thomas R. author | Bogdan, Joseph J. author | American Bar Association. Solo, Small Firm and General Practice Division issuing body
Title: Music law for the general practicioner / Thomas R. Leavens and Joseph J. Bogdan.
Description: Second edition. | Chicago : American Bar Association, Solo, Small Firm and General Practice Division, 2026. | Includes bibliographical references and index. | Summary: "This is a guide for the general or non-music specialist practitioner to learn about the legal and business issues that they are likely to encounter when representing someone who has a current music-related issue"— Provided by publisher.
Identifiers: LCCN 2026022832 (print) | LCCN 2026022833 (ebook) | ISBN 9781639057771 paperback | ISBN 9781639057788 epub
Subjects: LCSH: Music trade—Law and legislation—United States | Musicians' contracts—United States
Classification: LCC KF4291 .L43 2026 (print) | LCC KF4291 (ebook)
LC record available at https://lccn.loc.gov/2026022832
LC ebook record available at https://lccn.loc.gov/2026022833

Dedication

Tom Leavens dedicates this book to Justin, Mary, Emily, and Molly, with the hope they will better understand what their father does with music when he is not listening to it, reading about it, or playing it.

Joe Bogdan—after pondering the long list of those who *deserve* this book dedicated to them, including family, friends, business colleagues, legal colleagues, higher-education colleagues, and more—dedicates this book to his hundreds of students across time from Columbia College Chicago, IIT Chicago-Kent College of Law, Oklahoma City University School of Law, The Illinois Institute of Technology, The School of American Law (in association with Bahçeşehir University Beşiktaş, Bar Association of Advocacy of Kyrgyz Republic, Chamber of Advocates of the Republic of Uzbekistan, Istanbul Arbitration Center, Ivan Franko National University, Odesa National Law Academy, University of Gdansk, and University of Wrocław), UC Davis School of Law, University of Connecticut School of Law, and University of Dayton School of Law.

Teaching you in California, Connecticut, Illinois, Ohio, and Oklahoma, and the countries of Azerbaijan, Georgia, Greece, Kazakhstan, Kyrgyzstan, Poland, Turkey, Ukraine, and Uzbekistan has truly been a joy, an inspiration, and always—always—an adventure.

Contents

About the Authors

Thomas R. Leavens is of counsel with the law firm Mandell PC in Chicago. Tom's career as an attorney has involved transactions, counseling, and litigation in all areas of performing, visual, and literary expression, new media, intellectual property, and technology.

Prior to joining Mandell PC, Tom practiced as a partner in Leavens, Strand, & Glover, LLC, a law firm in Chicago and Nashville focused on entertainment, media, and intellectual property. Prior to forming Leavens, Strand, & Glover, LLC, Tom was General Counsel for LRSmedia, LLC, a media production and brand development company, whose initial project was the PBS television series *Legends of Jazz* with Ramsey Lewis. His responsibilities there included general business management, development of business models, artist and other talent agreements, publishing and record company clearance, distribution agreements, business development, union agreements, and intellectual property protection. Prior to joining LRS, Tom was General Counsel for MusicNow LLC, a pioneer digital music company that commercially launched a subscription music service, webcasting, and the sale of music downloads in 2002.

Tom has also served as General Counsel and Senior Vice President of Platinum Entertainment, Inc., a public company that grew from its formation in 1992 to become at one point the largest U.S.-based independent record company. While there he also served as executive producer of various recording and television projects, and compiled and produced 16 House of Blues Essential Blues recordings released by the company under its joint venture with HOB Entertainment. Prior to Platinum, Tom was a partner with the law firm McBride, Baker & Coles in Chicago, where he chaired the firm's intellectual property department.

Tom was the first recipient of the Thomas R. Leavens Award, presented by Lawyers for the Creative Arts, for contributions to law and the arts in

Chicago; was the recipient of the David C. Hilliard Award, presented by the Chicago Bar Association for Outstanding Committee Service to the Legal Profession and Community; and has served as an elected member of the Board of Managers of the Chicago Bar Association, the Board of Directors of the Digital Media Association, and the National Recording Preservation Board of the Library of Congress. Tom is also an Adjunct Professor at Northwestern University School of Law; an Associate with The Henry Lydiate Partnership in London, the premiere arts consultancy in the U.K.; and a member of the Authors Guild. Tom has also served as an expert witness in litigation concerning issues pertaining to the music industry. Tom has also received the highest AV Peer Review Rating from the Martindale-Hubbell Law Directory, is included in The Best Lawyers in America, and is ranked in Band 1 in Media & Entertainment: Transactional by Chambers and Partners. He is a graduate of the University of Michigan (AB) and Wayne State University Law School (JD) and is admitted in Illinois and Utah (active) and Michigan (inactive).

Joe Bogdan is a partner in Rimon, PC, and a serial General Counsel to technology, entertainment, and technology/entertainment companies. He is also tenured faculty in the School of Business and Entrepreneurship at Columbia College Chicago, where he coordinates and teaches a variety of live entertainment, music business, and intellectual property programs and courses. Joe's portfolio career has involved legal work in all areas of entertainment and the arts, intellectual property, technology, and business. It has also involved a significant business component alongside its legal component, with his full-time General Counsel positions doubled by concurrent roles as Executive Vice President Business Affairs (OnAir Streaming Networks, a media streaming company Joe describes as "Spotify . . . ten years before Spotify"), Chief Operating Officer (Cognitive Concepts, a video game technology and publishing company), Senior Vice President, Business Affairs (World Wrestling Entertainment, an international media and entertainment company), and Executive Vice President, Business Affairs (PlanetArt, a make-on-demand, personalized products e-tailer).

While the cornerstone of Joe's practice has long been licensing, entertainment, and technology–industry transactions, he also has expertise in corporate, mergers and acquisitions, commercial transactions, compliance, international law, and commercial real estate. It is in all these areas that he provides services to clients, and teaches, currently.

Joe is admitted to practice in Illinois (active) and California (inactive). He obtained his JD from USC Gould School of Law and an MA in Communications Technologies from the USC Annenberg School of Communications. He also holds a bachelor of arts degree in English Literature with a Government Law minor from the University of Illinois at Urbana-Champaign.

Heather Liberman VanDyke is the founder and principal attorney at Javelina Legal, focusing on live/experiential events, entertainment/music-related transactions, content licensing, copyright, trademark, outside General Counsel services, and more. Heather started solo practice after seven years as General Counsel of South by Southwest (SXSW), where she was responsible for all legal matters, including intellectual property protection and enforcement, licensing, contracts, insurance, managing litigation, and privacy.

In 2017, Heather designed and began adjunct teaching the course Law of Music Festivals & Live Events at the University of Texas School of Law. Prior to joining SXSW, Heather worked at an entertainment and IP boutique law firm in Chicago, Illinois.

Before becoming an attorney, Heather was a professional modern dancer on the off-off (off) Broadway stages in NYC. Heather lives in Austin, Texas, with her husband, daughter, and corgi.

Thomas J. Kliebhan is Senior Counsel in the Chicago office of Gordon & Rees. He practices entertainment law and includes Grammy-Award winning artists, managers, producers, record labels, film directors, and models among his clients, and counsels them on a variety of issues in the entertainment industry, including management agreements, producer agreements, recording agreements, contract negotiation, trademark work, and business formation.

Thomas is an associate board member of the Lawyers for the Creative Arts (LCA), a pro bono legal service organization in Chicago where he has served as the associate board's President, Vice President, and Social Media Chair. Through the LCA, he provides pro bono legal services to clients in the Illinois arts and entertainment world. He is also the associate editor of the American Bar Association Entertainment and Sports Lawyer Journal and is a member of the Recording Academy's Chicago chapter.

Prior to law school, Thomas interned at Polyvinyl Records and worked extensively as a freelance music journalist. His writing has been published in the Chicago Reader, Noisey, Law360, Consequence of Sound, The Outline, A.V. Club, Vinyl Me Please, and others. He has also contributed to the Illinois State Bar Association Intellectual Property Section Newsletter and the American Bar Association Entertainment and Sports Lawyer Journal. He received his bachelor's degree in history and secondary education from the University of Illinois at Urbana-Champaign and his juris doctorate from DePaul University College of Law.

Acknowledgments

Tom Leavens: I first want to thank Joe Bogdan—my good friend and co-author of this second edition—who I have been trying for many years to convince to join me in some form of legal endeavor. This second edition of *Music Law for the General Practitioner* is the reward for those efforts—thank you Joe. Thanks also to Heather Liberman VanDyke and Thomas Kliebhan for their dedication and excellent work in co-authoring two of its chapters. Above all, thank you to my music clients, who through the years have taught me so much about not only the business of music but also the rewards of finding passion in your work. And, finally, thanks to Sarah for her always steadfast understanding and support while this project drew our time and attention.

Joe Bogdan: My thanks first go out to my co-author and friend Tom Leavens, who humbled and honored me by entrusting to me my co-author role for this, the second edition of *Music Law for the General Practitioner*. Then also to Heather Liberman VanDyke and Thomas "T.J." Kliebhan for their impressive work on portions this book, both the first edition (Heather) and the second (T.J.). Next, to the intelligent, diligent, and patient research assistants who helped me over time with the second edition of this book: Grace Branson, Deanna Hall, Cameron Henry, and Xin (Stella) Huang. My clients over the years also deserve thanks, since my work for them comprised on-the-job education that instilled the knowledge reflected in these pages. Finally, and most strongly, my family, friends, business colleagues, legal colleagues, and higher-education colleagues who have tolerated my idiosyncrasies, including many relevant to this book (e.g., "fire is not your friend" lol).

Preface

Music law is the collection of laws and business customs that affect those who make, market, and use music in all its forms. Music law involves several key substantive areas of law—copyrights, trademarks, identity rights, First Amendment rights, contractual rights that shape competition (non-competes, exclusivity, rights of first refusal, etc.), and data protections. It is also the body of law that is drawn into play by the transactions that take place between those who market or otherwise use music. Music law also involves technology, customs and practices, and the values our culture has given to music, which sculpt the landscape for the users of music. The intersections of these topics are the subject areas for this book.

The traditional players in the music industry are well known: songwriters, singers, instrumentalists, record companies, managers, agents, lawyers, music publishing companies, record stores, radio and television broadcasters, and venue owners. While these players remain key in the industry, technological advances in the digital distribution of music and recordings brought important new players into the mix over the years, such as computer and other device manufacturers, big data concerns, and telecommunications companies, and created new political constituencies of individuals concerned about their rights to use digital music. Disruptors continue to interlude, most recently, those involved with artificial intelligence. Such advances have also drawn masses of ordinary businesses and ordinary people into music-related issues. For example, many businesses have discovered that music is critical to branding or otherwise bringing attention to their products or services because music helps convene an audience that can be receptive to a commercial appeal; and many individuals have discovered that they, too, might be creators of music notwithstanding limitations on the talents traditionally required to do so.

Businesses and individuals alike have found that the emergence of inexpensive duplication technology, the portability and ubiquity of mobile music devices, and the ease of transmitting digital music files have brought music into their lives in unexpected but pervasive ways. Music law is not just a specialized area of practice devoted to creative individuals, if it ever was. It affects an expanding range of commercial activities that many general practitioners are likely to encounter with their clients.

The goal of *Music Law for the General Practitioner* is found in its title. This is a guide for the general or non-music specialist practitioner to learn about the legal and business issues that they are likely to encounter when representing someone who has a current music-related issue. The developments in and relating to the music industry in the thirteen years between the first edition and this second edition are many and vast, and they deserve the new treatment we have attempted to provide here. We have not prepared this book for the expert, although we hope experts find value in these pages. Our intent is for it to be a point of entry, with guidance on where additional information may be found for deeper analysis. We have tried to provide background, context, insights, and strategies as a means of introduction. The content of this book is not meant to be the final word on any of its topics; nor is it meant to replace any of the excellent in-depth publications available for the expert.

Chapter 1
What Is Music?

Before we launch our exploration of how the law intersects with music creation, performance, distribution, and sales, we should first understand what music is.

Music is the most abstract of creative works. You can't see or touch it—it exists solely as a sound wave that, unless recorded, dissipates within moments.[1] Despite this abstraction (or perhaps because of it), music enjoys an elevated role in our development as human beings. Many researchers and writers believe that music played an adaptive/evolutionary role in the development of speech, other cognitive functions, mate selection, and social development. Neuroscientists have traced the activities in our brains as music is heard to demonstrate the multiple areas involved in listening and reacting to music, physically and emotionally, and have connected multiple psychological mechanisms through which emotions may be produced when the brain reacts to music;[2] and they are using music to treat certain brain malfunctions.[3]

---

1. Early efforts to document audio, both for playback and visually, are explored in Patrick Feaster, *Pictures of Sound: One Thousand Years of Educed Audio, 980–1980* (Atlanta: Dust-to-Digital, 2012).

2. Amplifon, *The Impact of Sound on the Brain* (Milan: Amplifon, 2018).

3. See generally Daniel J. Levitin, *This Is Your Brain on Music: The Science of a Human Obsession* (New York: Plume, 2006); Daniel J. Levitin, *The World in Six Songs: How the Musical Brain Created Human Nature* (New York: Viking, 2008); Oliver Sacks, *Musicophilia:*

Research has also suggested that the music that moves humans most is that which was the most popular when they were in their early teens (age thirteen for females, fourteen for males)[4] and that music and sex stimulate the same part of the brain.[5] Music is not just something with a good beat that you can dance to (although that is believed by many to be important itself).

Music has a particularly wide commercial application and is generally shaped by commercial interests. Music is used to catch and hold attention for the delivery of commercial messages and is a productivity tool in various environments. It can be strategic to the shifting and shaping of mental states and the regulation of stress. Music is also shaped in ways meant to conform to the demands of music users, such as hook-based writing meant to capture attention and hold it for the thirty-second minimum needed to qualify as a royalty bearing performance on streaming services. Music can be used to inspire resilience and defiance, each as a force in support of political action and social change. Music can also provide solace. While music is mathematical, it is also art and a thing of beauty.

What music actually consists of is not something we tend to think too much about. Daniel J. Levitin, in his fascinating book *This Is Your Brain on Music*, identifies the following as the fundamental elements that comprise musical expression:

(1) Pitch, or the tone of the sound and its relative position in the musical scale;
(2) Rhythm, or the duration of notes and the units into which they are formed;

Tales of Music and the Brain (New York: Vintage Books, 2008); Andrew E. Budson, "Why Is Music Good for the Brain?" *Harvard Health Publishing*, October 7, 2020, https://www.health.harvard.edu/blog/why-is-music-good-for-the-brain-2020100721062; Michael Trimble and Dale Hesdorffer, "Music and the Brain: The Neuroscience of Music and Musical Appreciation," *BJPsych International* 14, no. 2 (May 2017): 28–31, https://doi.org/10.1192/s2056474000001720; Ronald Kotulak, "Rhythm, Melody, Life," *Chicago Tribune*, September 21, 2003.

4. Seth Stephens-Davidowitz, "The Songs That Bind," *The New York Times*, February 10, 2018, https://www.nytimes.com/2018/02/10/opinion/sunday/favorite-songs.html.

5. Ian Johnston, "Music and Sex Stimulate the Same Part of the Brain," *The Independent*, February 8, 2017, https://www.independent.co.uk/news/science/music-sex-stimulate-same-part-brain-opioid-drugs-rock-n-roll-mcgill-university-scientific-reports-neurological-science-a7568606.html.

(3) Tempo, or the overall speed or pace of a musical piece;
(4) Contour, or the overall shape of a melody;
(5) Timbre, or tonal color of a voice or an instrument;
(6) Loudness, or the energy created by a voice or an instrument; and
(7) Reverberation, or the sense of distance or spaciousness of a sound.[6]

To that list we would add velocity, or the speed at which any of the foregoing elements are accelerating or decelerating.

None of these items in and of themselves are legally protectable—they are the basic building blocks of musical expression, and no single person can claim rights to control any of them individually. The ability to protect them emerges with the way these elements are combined to form higher-order musical features, such as melody and harmony.[7] As we shall see, some of these higher-order features are protectable and others are not.

The combinations of these elements to create music are limited by what we consider pleasing in Western culture, and that is due to physiological reasons (more specifically, dopamine release).[8] Indeed, music accounts for nearly 75 percent of audio content consumed by users in the United States according to one recent study.[9]

These physical limits are a consideration whenever a claim is being weighed that a certain piece of music wrongfully copies other music. The following quotation from 1930 reflects the limitations generally expressed in Western music:

> The average composer who indulges in songs has a limited number of tones at his disposal. The combinations and permutations of the thirteen tones give the amazing total of 6,227,020,800 combinations,

6. Levitin, *This Is Your Brain on Music*, 15–16.
7. Ibid., 17–18.
8. Mitchel Benovoy et al., "Anatomically Distinct Dopamine Release During Anticipation and Experience of Peak Emotion to Music," *Nature Neuroscience*, January 9, 2011, https://doi.org/10.1038/nn.2726.
9. Edison Reports, *How Music Is Listened to in the U.S.* (December 4, 2024), https://www.edisonresearch.com/how-music-is-listened-to-in-the-u-s/; Ashley King, "Podcasts Keep Growing, But Music Still Takes the Cake by an Enormous Margin," *Digital Music News*, December 4, 2024, https://www.digitalmusicnews.com/2024/12/04/how-music-is-listened-to-in-the-united-states/.

of which only a small fraction may be used ordinarily. Popular songs, in particular, lie within a very small radius. In a confined space, similarity of tone construction is inevitable. Practically every original idea the composer can think of has appeared somewhere before; it is a matter of probabilities, and every day the number of new possibilities grows less.

Since it is generally agreed that the original fount of melodic ideas was long-ago exhausted, serious composers and others have turned to the other important elements of music—harmony and rhythm. In the use and treatment of these there is a certain originality to be attained; but even that is necessarily limited by obvious physical limitations.

Of the three essential elements—rhythm, harmony, and melody—the first two are usually emphasized, whereas the third is taken as a matter of course; and when it is impossible to invent new melodic ideas, the composer may display his skill in the means he uses to develop what theme he has.[10]

What Is Digital Music?

When dealing with music today in a commercial way, it is not enough to understand the artistic components that comprise musical expression. Since digital technology generally governs how music is created, recorded, distributed, and sold, the general practitioner must also have at least a basic understanding of some of the components of digital music formats and files.

Technology has always been put to the demands of the creative impulse. Like photography, sound recordings are an art form that would not exist without supporting technology. And this technology has always had an effect on musical expression. For instance, the three-minute song reflects the upper limit of the recording capabilities of early wax acoustic recording technology; and the twelve-song LP reflects the upper limit of the recording capabilities of vinyl LPs assuming three to four minutes per song. To this end, some artists' creative needs, and the desire to release live recordings of (or emulating)

---

10. Alfred M. Shafter, *Musical Copyright*, 2d ed. (1930), reprinted in A. Latman and R. Gorman, *Copyright for the Eighties* (1981), 328.

an entire concert, resulted in the well-known "double album" format. Early acoustic recording technology also favored certain sounds over others and, for example, elevated the clarinet to a featured role in klezmer orchestras.[11] Electrical recording technology permitted more intimate forms of singing to be captured, which helped make Bing Crosby a star.[12] LPs, and then CDs, begat longer performances, and boom boxes played a key role in the development of hip-hop culture.[13] Electronic instruments and sound processors such as synthesizers, Linn drum machines, MIDIs,[14] and Auto-Tune have created new sounds and compositional possibilities, making new forms of expression possible, such as "mashups."[15] The emergence of digital streaming as the dominant method of recorded music consumption and revenue generation has caused recordings to be shorter, even if mostly for no reason other than to increase the possible number of revenue-bearing performances.

When digital music is referenced, it is often referred to in a shorthand way as an MP3. The term "MP3" refers to a format for compressing and then decompressing a digital file representing a sound recording. There are many formats used for the distribution and sale of digital music, but MP3 is the most popular. The MP3 compression format was developed by the Moving Pictures Experts Group in 1988 as part of that group's effort to develop a format for compressing television video and soundtracks generally. The part of the format that described sound compression was Layer 3, which became known as MP3.[16] The specifications for the MP3 standard were developed under the auspices of the International Organization

11. Mark Katz, *Capturing Sound: How Technology Has Changed Music* (Berkeley: University of California Press, 2004), 39.

12. Gary Giddins, *Bing Crosby: A Pocketful of Dreams—The Early Years, 1903–1940* (Boston: Little, Brown, 2001), 117–18.

13. Lyle Owerko, *The Boombox Project: The Machines, the Music, and the Urban Underground* (New York: Abrams Image, 2010); "The History of the Boombox," *National Public Radio*, April 22, 2009, http://www.youtube.com/watch?v=e84hf5aUmNA.

14. MIDI is an acronym for Musical Instrumental Digital Interface; see MIDI Manufacturers Association, www.midi.org (last accessed September 2025).

15. Sunidhi Bansal and Shruti Agarwal, "Fair Use in Context of Mashups: Comparative Analysis of US, UK and India" (July 2018), *The Law Brigade*, https://thelawbrigade.com/wp-content/uploads/2019/05/Sunidhi.pdf; Elina Lae, "Mashups—A Protected Form of Appropriation Art or a Blatant Copyright Infringement?" (December 2011), *SSRN*, https://doi.org/10.2139/ssrn.2003854.

16. Library of Congress, *Sustainability of Digital Formats: Planning for Library of Congress Collections. MP3 (MPEG Layer III Audio Encoding)*, April 21, 2023, https://www.loc.gov/preservation/digital/formats/fdd/fdd000012.shtml.

for Standardization (IOS),[17] unlike the proprietary compression formats such as ALAC or WMA developed by Apple and Microsoft, respectively.

When sound is recorded digitally for ultimate sale to consumers, the analog sound wave is sampled 44,100 times per second. The sound is recorded for the left channel and for the right channel (stereo), and each sample is stored as sixteen bits for frequency (pitch) and amplitude (loudness). As a result, one second of digitally recorded music is made up of 1,411,220 bits. This is what is generally known as a WAV or AIFF file—the raw data from which the recording can then be processed. An MP3-formatted version of the raw data file is created by sampling the bits in the file at certain rates. The higher the "bit rate," the more information contained in the MP3 file and, thus, the greater fidelity to the original file. The "art" of the compression format is in how the format decides which bits to include and which to leave out. The format uses psychoacoustics (how people perceive sounds) to discard quieter or non-perceptible sounds and arrive at a playback that is acceptable to the listener. The advantage is a smaller file size. Early compressed digital files were reduced to 128,000 bits per second (128 Kbps), but higher bit rates reproducing recordings with greater fidelity are more common today as file size storage and electronic transmission capabilities increase. There are also other file formats in use today, such as FLAC, ALAC, WAV, and MQA, which do not lose data and thus can more accurately reproduce the sound of the original file.

Since digital files long ago overtook physical products as the means by which music is delivered to and consumed by people, the formats in which such digital products are offered and the interoperability of the devices with which such digital products may be used becomes more important to understand. This is due to the fact that file or format distinctions may implicate different rights for the owners of the recordings and compositions that are featured in such files.

---

17. Fraunhofer Institute for Integrated Circuits IIS, *The MP3 History*, October 16, 2019, https://www.mp3-history.com/.

Chapter 2

How Value in Musical Properties Is Created

It is no secret that the music industry had a downturn after the internet explosion of the late 1990s and early 2000s. Revenue from the sale of prerecorded music declined almost 40 percent between 2004 and 2012,[1] as new methods of digital distribution did not initially produce sufficient income to overcome the loss of revenue caused by the decline in the sale of physical media. The U.S. Department of Labor also reported that there were 41 percent fewer paid musicians in the United States in 2011 than there were twelve years prior, in 1999.[2] Finally, it took time for the internet and digital-age business models for the distribution, sale, and consumption of music to emerge through traditional music business models and legacy contractual relationships and terms and become fully sorted.

1. Robert Andrews, "Music Industry Can See the Light After 'Least Negative' Sales Since 2004," *PaidContent*, March 26, 2012, http://paidcontent.org/2012/03/26/419-music-industry-can-see-the-light-after-least-negative-sales-since-2004/.

2. Paul Resnikoff, "Updated: Recording Sales Declines & Musician Employment, 1999–2011 . . . ," *Digital Music News*, August 25, 2012, https://www.digitalmusicnews.com/2012/08/25/recording/.

In the years since the early 2010s, however, the decline, by most measures, rebounded hardily. For example, revenue from music streaming in the United States increased by a factor of 28 (2,800 percent) between 2010 and 2023, from ~$500,000 in 2010 to more than $14 billion in 2023; revenue from music publishing experienced a ten-year period of double-digit growth between 2015 and 2024;[3] and live music ticket sales revenue in the United States increased by more than 70 percent between 2017 and 2023.[4] While the U.S. Department of Labor statistics still show a decline in paid musicians in the United States, between 2011 and 2023 the government-measured decline was only 15 percent, as compared to the 41 percent decline in the twelve years prior.[5] Finally, ongoing research suggests that the music industry's contribution to the U.S. gross domestic product to be nearly 1 percent and its contribution to domestic jobs to be in excess of 2.5 million annually, with each of those numbers growing at an accelerating rate.[6] Those things said, it is interesting to note slowdowns were reported for 2024 in both music streaming and touring revenues.[7]

While value certainly remained in music properties and transactions during the downturn time, it has since remerged beyond. This chapter touches

---

3. Dylan Smith, "NMPA Head David Israelite Says U.S. Publishing Revenue Cracked $7 Billion in 2024—The 10th Consecutive Year of Double-Digit Growth," *Digital Music News* (June 23, 2025), https://www.digitalmusicnews.com/2025/06/23/nmpa-publishing-revenue-2024/.

4. Statista, "Revenue from Music Streaming in the United States from 2010 to 2023," https://www.statista.com/statistics/437717/music-streaming-revenue-usa/ (last accessed September 2025); Statista, "Live Music Ticket Sales—United States," https://www.statista.com/outlook/amo/media/music-radio-podcasts/traditional-music/live-music-ticket-sales/united-states#revenue (last accessed September 2025).

5. U.S. Department of Labor, Bureau of Labor Statistics, "Occupational Employment and Wage Statistics," https://www.bls.gov/oes/current/oes272042.htm (last updated July 23, 2025).

6. Robert Stoner and Jessica Dutra, *The U.S. Music Industries: Jobs & Benefits—The 2024 Report*, prepared for the Recording Industry Association of America (RIAA), October 2024, https://www.riaa.com.

7. See Ashley King, "Goldman Sachs Wildly Misses the Mark on 2024 Recorded Music & Streaming Revenues—Downgrades Forecast After a 'Marked Slowdown' and Streaming Plateau," *Digital Music News*, June 4, 2025, https://www.digitalmusicnews.com/2025/06/04/goldman-sachs-report-streaming-plateau/; see Ashley King, "Study Shows 'Steep Decline' in Touring for Artists of All Sizes over the Past Few Years," *Digital Music News*, May 21, 2025, https://www.digitalmusicnews.com/2025/05/21/study-shows-steep-decline-in-touring-for-artists-of-all-sizes/.

on the topic of value in a transaction, including copyrights, trademarks, rights of identity, domain names, social media platforms, data, and contractual competitive rights. These rights and properties form the basis for the transactions that will be discussed throughout this book.

Copyrights

Copyright Basics

Copyright is the most important source of value in a musical property. Copyright protects creative expression, which includes music, lyrics, and sound recordings. Copyright also protects the photographs, text, drawings, and other works of visual art that are used in the packaging, advertising, and promotion of musical properties. It is important to understand that each recording of a musical composition is protected by a claim to copyright that is separate from the copyright to the underlying musical composition performed in the recording and to every other recording of that composition. For example, there is only one copyright claim to the composition of the Beatles' song "Yesterday," but there are separate copyright claims to each of the hundreds of recordings of that composition.

The United States Copyright Act[8] has exclusive jurisdiction for the rights in creative expression that are included in the Act. The exclusive rights of a copyright owner of a musical composition or sound recording are set forth in § 106 of the Copyright Act, which are as follows:

(1) to reproduce the copyrighted work in copies or phonorecords;[9]
(2) to prepare derivative works based upon the copyrighted work;
(3) to distribute copies or phonorecords of the copyright work to the public by sale or other transfer of ownership, or by rental, lease, or lending;

8. United States Copyright Act, 17 U.S.C. §§ 101–1332 (2011).

9. A "phonorecord" is a material object in which sounds are fixed and from which the sounds can be perceived, reproduced, or otherwise communicated, either directly or with the aid of a machine or device. United States Copyright Act, 17 U.S.C. § 101 (2011). Examples include a cassette tape, a vinyl disc, or a compact disc. A phonorecord does not include sounds accompanying a motion picture or other audiovisual work.

(4) in the case of literary, musical, dramatic, and choreographic works, pantomimes, and motion picture and other audiovisual works, to perform the copyrighted work publicly;
(5) in the case of literary, musical, dramatic, and choreographic works, pantomimes, and pictorial, graphic, or sculptural works, including the individual images of a motion picture or other audiovisual work, to display the copyrighted work publicly; and
(6) in the case of sound recordings, to perform the copyrighted work publicly by means of a digital audio transmission.

In addition, the anti-bootlegging provisions of the Uruguay Round Agreements Act of 1994,[10] which are found at § 1101(a) of the Copyright Act, bar the unconsented recording, transmission, sale, or rental of copies of live musical performances. We will revisit these rights throughout this book as we discuss the various ways these rights are implicated and exercised.

Federal copyright protection in a musical composition or sound recording arises immediately and automatically upon the creation of that work.[11] A work is "created" when it is fixed for the first time in a tangible medium of expression (i.e., a copy for a composition or "phonorecord" for a sound recording).[12] A work is "fixed" in a tangible medium when its embodiment in a copy or phonorecord, by or under the authority of the author, is sufficiently permanent or stable to permit it to be perceived, reproduced, or otherwise communicated for a period of more than transitory duration.[13] This means that an artist or an author has federal copyright protection in any musical or lyrical work that is original to the author immediately after the work is fixed in some way, such as by writing it down or capturing it by some method of recording. The same principle holds true for sound recordings. Note that registration of one's claim to copyright with the United States Copyright Office of any claim to a copyright in a composition or sound recording is not a condition to copyright protection.[14]

10. Uruguay Round Agreements Act, Pub. L. No. 103–465, § 512, 108 Stat. 4809 (1994).
11. 17 U.S.C. § 302(a) (2011).
12. 17 U.S.C. § 101 (2011).
13. Ibid.
14. 17 U.S.C. § 408(a) (2011).

Nevertheless, and even though registration with the Copyright Office of one's claim to copyright is not required, it is available for purposes of perfecting and putting the world on notice of the copyright the author (or other owner) already has. This is important to understand because from a transactional point of view, the person creating the work starts by holding all the enumerated rights set forth earlier, and can in subsequent transactions only give away rights. However, registration of one's copyright claim is a prerequisite to the commencement of any claim in federal court for infringement.[15] Also, registration provides the availability of important remedies to a copyright owner that are not available for claims against an infringer who commenced before the registration became effective.[16] These remedies are the right to an award of the owner's attorney fees incurred in pursuing the infringement claim[17] and the right to elect to receive damages in an amount defined by the Copyright Act in lieu of proving actual damages. The latter remedy—known as statutory damages—is beneficial since actual damages may be either very difficult to establish or of a lesser amount than the statutory range. Consequently, registration of one's claim to copyright is always recommended.[18]

Registration of one's copyright claim is a relatively straightforward process and has been made easy and simple through the online process found at the Copyright Office website: www.copyright.gov. The process has been developed with the goal of encouraging copyright claimants to register their works with minimum obstacles or need for specialized advice. Registration requires a relatively modest registration fee of $65 for applications made through the Copyright Office's online system. While registration can still be conducted via the traditional method of submitting completed paper forms through the mail, online registration is highly encouraged not only because it is nearly half the $125 cost to file on paper but also to avoid lengthy delays caused by the security requirements of processing governmental filings. (As of this writing, the Copyright Office's estimated processing

---

15. 17 U.S.C. § 411 (2011); *Fourth Estate Public Benefit Corp. v. Wall-Street.com*, 586 U.S. (2019).
16. 17 U.S.C. § 412 (2011).
17. 17 U.S.C. § 505 (2011).
18. 17 U.S.C. § 504(c) (2011).

time for copyright applications is 1.2 months for online and 4.1 months for paper.[19]) Registration also requires submission of deposit copies of the work for which registration is sought.

When a musical property is published, it should bear a proper copyright notice. Since March 1, 1989, failure to include the notice does not invalidate the copyright claim. However, failure to include the notice may allow an infringement defendant to interpose a defense that their infringement was innocent, in mitigation of damages.[20]

The notice of copyright for musical properties takes one of two forms. For lyrics or music appearing in print form, or for any artistic or text work used in connection with the packaging, advertising, or promotion of a work or performer, the notice is comprised of either the word "Copyright" or the copyright symbol ©, the name of the copyright owner, and the year the work was first published. An example of the notice on printed lyrics first published in 2025 would be: © Thomas R. Leavens and Joseph J. Bogdan 2025. Publication is like a birth year—it does not change unless the work with which it appears changes (i.e., is "reborn"), in which case the changed (i.e., "reborn") work gets its own new birth year.

For sound recordings, the notice is comprised of either the word "Copyright" or the copyright symbol ℗, the name of the copyright owner, and the year the sound recording was first published. An example of the notice on a compact disc of a sound recording first published in 2025 would be: ℗ Thomas R. Leavens and Joseph J. Bogdan 2025. When you look at a commercially released sound recording, you will see both these notices. The notice with the © is for the artwork and text of the materials accompanying the sound recording. The ℗ will be for the sound recording itself.

The term of copyright protection for works created by human authors after January 1, 1978, is the life of the author, plus seventy years.[21] In the case of a work that was prepared by two or more human authors (a "joint work"), the period is the life of the last surviving human author, plus seventy

19. U.S. Copyright Office, *Registration Processing Times*, https://www.copyright.gov/registration/docs/processing-times-faqs.pdf (last accessed September 24, 2025).

20. 17 U.S.C. § 405(b) (2011).

21. 17 U.S.C. § 302(a) (2011).

years.[22] Works created by entity authors, or by individual "authors" who did not themselves provide creative input but nevertheless employed the one(s) who did (works for hire), are discussed later in the chapter.

Sound recordings have some special rules that apply only to them. Federal copyright protection was first extended to sound recordings in the United States starting in 1972, under the Copyright Act of 1976. At that time, protection was accorded only to sound recordings fixed on or after February 15, 1972. Pre-1972 recordings were and remain protected under state law, which varies from jurisdiction to jurisdiction. In 2018, the Classics Protection and Access Act, Title II of the Music Modernization Act, brought pre-1972 sound recordings into the federal copyright system, creating a new chapter under the copyright law, which, among other things, extends limited remedies for copyright infringement to owners of eligible pre-1972 sound recordings. To be eligible for statutory damages and attorney's fees, rights holders need to file schedules with the U.S. Copyright Office listing their pre-1972 recordings.[23] This situation will continue until February 15, 2067, when pre-1972 sound recordings will enter the public domain.[24]

The Music Modernization Act (MMA) is an overhauling U.S. copyright law passed in 2018 to update how music is licensed and paid for in the digital age. The MMA modernized music licensing by creating modern systems for identifying rights holders, paying royalties, and protecting both parties and sound recordings that had previously fallen into legal gray areas. It is widely regarded as the biggest change in U.S. music law in a generation. Its enactment touches a number of sections of this book, and is referenced throughout. Because a summary of the MMA in one place can be helpful, one is provided here.

The MMA solved several long-standing problems created by outdated copyright rules, namely those regarding mechanical licensing, protection for pre-1972 sound recordings, application to producers and engineers, and royalty rates for songwriters, as follows.

22. 17 U.S.C. § 302(b) (2011).
23. Music Modernization Act, Pub. L. No. 115–264, 132 Stat. 3676 (2018).
24. 17 U.S.C. § 301(c) (2011).

First, before the MMA, each digital platform reproducing musical works (songs) was required to locate and license individual songwriters one by one, even when songwriter information was incomplete or missing. This led to significant unpaid royalties and lawsuits claiming services were failing to license properly. The MMA created a single, blanket mechanical license covering all musical-work reproductions made by streaming platforms, which dramatically reduces administrative burdens and makes it easier for services to operate legally and efficiently. Related, the MMA also created the Mechanical Licensing Collective, an independent, not-for-profit organization responsible for administering the blanket license by maintaining a public musical-works database, collecting mechanical royalties from streaming services, paying songwriters and publishers directly, processing mismatched and unmatched royalties, and offering dispute-resolution procedures for identifying rightful owners.

Second, because federal copyright law historically covered only recordings made after 1972, pre-1972 sound recordings were handled by inconsistent and often incomplete state laws. This made it difficult for digital services to know how to legally stream classics. The MMA brought pre-1972 sound recordings under federal copyright protection, eliminating the confusing patchwork of state laws.

Third, historically, producers, mixers, and engineers had uncertain royalty rights for their part in the recording process due to their uncertain status as authors among the recording musicians. The MMA provided a clear path for producers, mixers, and sound engineers to receive their share of digital performance royalties for sound recordings by allowing them a way to claim through SoundExchange.

Fourth, and finally, royalty-rate calculation for songwriters had lagged behind the market because judges had been forced to use standards that tended to undervalue the songwriter's contribution, leading many in the industry to argue that songwriter royalties were artificially low. The MMA updated how the Copyright Royalty Board sets mechanical royalty rates so that judges can now consider market-based evidence, which generally helps to raise songwriter royalties. The MMA also rotates the judges who hear royalty-rate cases, instead of assigning them all to the same judge, which improves fairness and consistency.

While the MMA is far from perfect, it implemented changes that touch, and generally improve, nearly every part of the modern music ecosystem. Songwriters benefit from more accurate royalty payments, better royalty rates, and a centralized database that helps ensure they receive the money they are owed. Streaming services have a single, clear licensing system, reducing legal risk and simplifying compliance. Performers of pre-1972 recordings—many of whom never received digital royalties before—now receive federal protection and compensation. And producers, mixers, and engineers have formal recognition of their creative contributions and not only a right but also a way to collect digital royalties.

Work for Hire

While ordinarily the human creator of a musical work will be the copyright owner, there are circumstances under which someone other than the human creator will be considered the author and, therefore, own the copyright and be considered the "author" thereof from its inception. Those circumstances occur when a work is created in what is called a work-for-hire situation, which can occur under two scenarios. First, musical works created within the scope of a person's employment are works for hire,[25] and the person's human or entity employer is deemed to be the creator (i.e., the author) of those works. For example, if you are regularly employed in the marketing department of a company and it is your job to write music and lyrics for advertisements for your company, then your employer is deemed to be the author of those music and lyrics, and the copyright in them will belong to your employer. Whether one is an "employee" will depend principally on the general common law test of agency and control.[26] A person may be an employee even if their payment is in the form of royalties (or an advance on royalties).[27]

The second work-for-hire scenario involves independent contractors who are commissioned to create a musical work, and the person or entity that commissioned the work is deemed to be the creator (i.e., the author) of those works if (1) the parties so agree in writing signed by the human

25. 17 U.S.C. §§ 101(b), 201 (2011).
26. *Community for Creative Non-Violence v. Reid*, 490 U.S. 730 (1989).
27. *Fred Fisher Music Co. v. Leo Feist, Inc.*, 55 F. Supp. 359 (S.D.N.Y. 1944).

creator and (2) the work that is created falls within one of the following categories of works:

> A work specially ordered or commissioned for use as a contribution to a collective work, as a part of a motion picture or other audiovisual work, as a translation, as a supplementary work, as a compilation, as an instructional text, as a test, as answer material for a test, or as an atlas, if the parties expressly agree in a written instrument signed by them that the work shall be considered a work made for hire. For the purpose of the foregoing sentence, a "supplementary work" is a work prepared for publication as a secondary adjunct to a work by another author for the purpose of introducing, concluding, illustrating, explaining, revising, commenting upon, or assisting in the use of the other work, such as forewords, afterwords, pictorial illustrations, maps, charts, tables, editorial notes, musical arrangements, answer material for tests, bibliographies, appendixes, and indexes, and an "instructional text" is a literary, pictorial, or graphic work prepared for publication and with the purpose of use in systematic instructional activities.[28]

For example, if the authors request that you write a foreword to this book, and you and we agree in writing signed by you that the foreword is a work for hire, then we are deemed to be the authors of that foreword notwithstanding that you are not employed by us in the traditional sense.

In the absence of such a signed written agreement, or with respect to works that do not fall within the specifically identified categories of the preceding works, the copyright will remain with the human creator.[29] The term of copyright protection for a work made for hire is the shorter of ninety-five years from publication or 120 years from creation.[30]

---

28. 17 U.S.C. § 101 (2011).

29. Note, however, that under some circumstances a court may find that, while ownership of a copyright has not been established as a work for hire, the employer may nevertheless have acquired rights by means of a nonexclusive implied license; see, e.g., *Kolton v. Universal Studios, Inc.*, 73 U.S.P.Q.2d 1603 (C.D. Cal. 2004); *Karlson v. Red Door Homes, LLC*, 18 F. Supp. 3d 1301 (N.D. Ala. 2014).

30. 17 U.S.C. § 302(c) (2011).

Assignments

As with other forms of property, ownership of a copyright may be assigned from one party to another. However, to be effective, a copyright assignment must be documented (i.e., in writing and signed by the assigning copyright owner). Undocumented assignments are not effective. For example, an endorsed check written in payment for the purchase of a copyright interest is invalid as written assignment of the copyright that is the subject of the transaction.[31] Also, mere reference to the assignment of compositions in an otherwise valid recording agreement is not sufficient to pass title to compositions that might be recorded under the recording agreement.[32]

Scope of Copyright

Copyright ownership attaches to what is *original* with an author.[33] It is irrelevant whether an author's contribution to a composition or recording is new, novel, or unique.[34] The test is only whether the contribution originated with the author. If the author's effort to create a work is independent, the work will be accorded copyright protection no matter how similar it may be to a prior work. As stated by one court many years ago, "[I]f by some magic a man who had never known it were to compose anew Keats's 'Ode on a Grecian Urn,' he would be an 'author,' and . . . others might not copy that poem, though they might of course copy Keats's."[35] Also, copyright protection extends only to the particular *expression* fixed in a work, which is original with the author. Copyright does not protect any idea, concept, plan, or discovery that might be revealed in the expression.[36] Further, an author who has rearranged or adapted a particular composition or created a compilation of separate works, such as a song folio or revue, gains copyright protection only in the original material, such as the selection and

31. *Papa's-June Music, Inc. v. McLean*, 921 F. Supp. 1154 (S.D.N.Y. 1996).
32. *Pamfiloff v. Giant Records, Inc.*, 794 F. Supp. 933 (N.D. Cal. 1992).
33. 17 U.S.C. § 102(a) (2011).
34. *Vargas v. Pfizer, Inc.*, 418 F. Supp. 2d 369 (S.D.N.Y. 2005).
35. *Sheldon v. Metro Goldwyn Pictures Corp.*, 81 F.2d 49, 54 (2d Cir. 1936).
36. 17 U.S.C. § 102(b) (2011).

sequence of compositions, contributed by the author to the rearrangement, adaptation, or compilation.[37]

Technologists and musicians have been working for some time on the prospect of music written and/or performed by "robots."[38] For example, as early as the 1950s, experimental composers were writing music using randomized statistical models.[39] Nevertheless, the exponentially growing mass popularity of generative artificial intelligence (GAI),[40] raises questions on the topic of originality, more particularly whether GAI compositions or sound recordings are subject to copyright protection.[41] To this point, The U.S. Copyright Office (USCO) has stated that works of authorship that qualify for copyright protection must have a human author (although that author may be aided by GAI, provided there is a "sufficient" amount of human expression in their (the human's) contribution).[42] At least U.S. Court

---

37. 17 U.S.C. § 103(b) (2011).

38. William Hochberg, "When Robots Write Songs," *The Atlantic*, April 16, 2025, https://www.theatlantic.com/entertainment/archive/2014/08/computers-that-compose/374916/; Amir Mizroch and Juhana Rossi, "This Rapper's Machine," *The Wall Street Journal*, May 22, 2015, https://www.wsj.com/articles/BL-DGB-41906.

39. Cherie Hu, "How Music Generated by Artificial Intelligence Is Reshaping—Not Destroying—the Industry," *Billboard*, April 19, 2018, https://www.billboard.com/pro/artificial-intelligence-music-reshaping-destroying-industry/.

40. The streaming platform Deezer stated in early 2025 that nearly 20 percent of its content was AI generated; see Ashley King, "Deezer Says 20,000 AI-Generated Songs Are Uploaded Onto Its Platform Daily—Roughly 18% of All Tracks," *Digital Music News*, April 16, 2025, https://www.digitalmusicnews.com/2025/04/16/deezer-ai-generated-songs-stats/.

41. See Chapter 11 for a discussion on whether GAI music infringes the material upon which the GAI system was trained for purposes of creating new works.

42. U.S. Copyright Office, *Copyright and Artificial Intelligence: Part 2 Copyrightability* (2025), https://www.copyright.gov/ai/Copyright-and-Artificial-Intelligence-Part-2-Copyrightability-Report.pdf.

In its Report, the USCO considered multiple different examples of GAI usage and stated its position on each.

- With respect to *using prompts to get a particular result from a GAI engine*, the USCO said definitively that the output is unprotectable (and the corollary to this is, of course, once it exists it can't be infringed). The rationale provided by the USCO was that prompts themselves are ideas, and if the human's only contribution to a creation is an unprotectable idea, they cannot claim copyright. The USCO left open that there may come a time when prompts can sufficiently control expressive elements in GAI outputs to reflect human authorship.
- With respect to *inputting a human-created work, and asking the GAI to alter it in some way*, the USCO said that only those parts of the work that a human created are subject to copyright protection (and those parts created by GAI are not).

of Appeal (the D.C. Circuit) has already agreed.[43] As the issue is addressed by lawmakers worldwide, note that at least one country, South Korea, has adopted a "0 percent" standard (i.e., work not subject to copyright protection if human creator used artificial intelligence at all).[44] Within the industry, as distinguished from the government sector, ASCAP, BMI, and SOCAN began accepting registrations of partially GAI works in October 2025.[45]

As a result of this originality test, more than one author can compose their own song about a certain event or idea,[46] use a common word or phrase[47] or rhyme scheme,[48] or take a melody or verse from the public domain and express it in their own original fashion.[49] However, to gain protection in an arrangement of a work already in the public domain, the author's contribution must be more than a trivial addition or variation.[50] Originality is generally viewed as a low bar, and to give you an example of how low that bar might go, copyright protection has been extended to a single note "melody,"[51] to stage makeup,[52] to certain distinctive vocal effects (although in the context of the appropriation of other performance features),[53] and to the use of the word "dog" as musical punctuation and rhythmic panting.[54] Copyright protection, however, does not extend to the conventions and

---

- With respect to modifying or arranging GAI content, the USCO said that the output is subject to copyright protection if the human creator has modified those elements "in a sufficiently creative way."

43. *Thaler v. Perlmutter*, No. 1:22-cv-01564, 2025 WL 839178 (D.C. Cir. Mar. 18, 2025).

44. Ashley King, "Korea Music Copyright Association Bans Registration of AI-Generated Musical Works—0% AI Policy Starts Now," *Digital Music News*, April 2, 2025, https://www.digitalmusicnews.com/2025/04/02/korea-music-copyright-bans-registration-ai-works/.

45. ASCAP, "ASCAP, BMI and SOCAN Announce Alignment on AI Registration Policies," October 28, 2025, https://www.ascap.com/press/2025/10/10-28-ai-registration-policies.

46. *Stratchborneo v. Arc Music Corp.*, 357 F. Supp. 1393 (S.D.N.Y. 1973).

47. *Currin v. Arista Records, Inc.*, 724 F. Supp. 2d 286 (D. Conn. 2010); *Apps v. Universal Music Group et al.*, No. 17–17122 (9th Cir. 2019).

48. *Peters v. West*, 692 F.3d 629 (7th Cir. 2012); *Lil' Joe Wein Music, Inc. v. Jackson*, 245 Fed. Appx. 873 (11th Cir. 2007).

49. *Scott v. Paramount Pictures Corp.*, 449 F. Supp. 518 (D.D.C. 1978), aff'd, 607 F.2d 494 (D.C. Cir. 1979); *Withol v. Wells*, 231 F.2d 550 (7th Cir. 1956); *Plymouth Music Co. v. Magnus Organ Corp.*, 456 F. Supp. 676 (S.D.N.Y. 1978); *Newcomb v. Young*, 43 F. Supp. 744 (S.D.N.Y. 1960); *Whitney v. Ross Jungnickel, Inc.*, 43 F. Supp. 744 (S.D.N.Y. 1960).

50. *Smith v. George Muelebach Brewing Co.*, 140 F. Supp. 729 (W.D. Mo. 1956).

51. *Levine v. McDonald's Corp.*, 735 F. Supp. 92 (S.D.N.Y. 1990).

52. *Carrell v. Shubert Org., Inc.*, 104 F. Supp. 2d 236 (S.D.N.Y. 2000).

53. *Tin Pan Apple v. Miller Brewing Co.*, 1994 WL62360 (S.D.N.Y. 1994).

54. *Bridgeport Music, Inc. v. UMG Recording, Inc.*, 585 F.3d 267 (6th Cir. 2009).

tools of printed musical expression, such as scales, keys,[55] chords, notations, markings, and symbols, nor does it extend to chord progressions or standard "licks" in and of themselves. If the latter were the case, hundreds of performers and composers would be paying royalties to early blues performers or to Chuck Berry, or both. Where unprotectable ideas leave off and original expression begins is not always a bright line.

With respect to sound recordings, the scope of copyright protection is limited to the actual sounds fixed in the recording. Therefore, while so-called sound-alike recordings may give rise to a variety of legal claims (e.g., right of publicity, passing off, trademark), if they are independently fixed they do not infringe the copyright in prior recordings no matter how closely the prior recordings are imitated or simulated.[56]

Collaboration

The creation of music and recordings of music is often a collaborative process. Whether co-authors will separately own or control their respective contributions to a song or recording (e.g., the words contributed by one author and the music contributed by another) or whether they will co-own the entire song or recording as a single unitary work is a question of intent. If their intent is that their contributions be merged, or they have worked in furtherance of a preconcerted common design, the composition or recording will be considered a joint work that they own as co-owners.[57] This intent must be present at the time the work is co-authored or at the time an author makes their contribution, not later.[58] Lyricists and composers involved with musical-dramatic productions for the stage often expressly agree that their respective contributions to a musical stage play will not merge into

55. *Velez v. Sony Discos*, 2007 WL 120686 (S.D.N.Y. 2007).

56. 17 U.S.C. § 114(b) (2011); *Griffin v. J-Records*, 398 F. Supp. 2d 1137, 1142 n.14 (E.D. Wash. 2005); *Zany Toys, LLC v. Pearl Enters., LLC*, D.N.J. Civil Action No. 13-5262 (JAP) (TJB), 2014 U.S. Dist. LEXIS 70852 (May 23, 2014).

57. 17 U.S.C. §§ 101, 201(a) (2011).

58. *Janky v. Lake County Convention & Visitors Bureau*, 576 F.3d 356 (7th Cir. 2009); see also *Shapiro, Bernstein & Co. v. Jerry Vogel Music Co.*, 161 F.2d 406 (2d Cir. 1946); H. Rep. No. 1476, 94th Cong., 2d Sess. 120 (1976).

one until the play has been performed for a certain minimum number of performances, thereby permitting each contributor to use their material in another situation if the play is not produced or is produced unsuccessfully.

Moral Rights

Artist moral rights do not refer to questions of ethics but to the rights of an artist (among others) to control works of authorship they create even after they sell or otherwise divest control of the physical embodiment thereof. In the world outside the United States, moral rights are generally comprised of the following six inalienable rights personal to the author: (1) the right to create (cannot be compelled to create a work); (2) the right of disclosure (the right to determine whether or when to make a work public); (3) the right of withdrawal (the right to withdraw a work from a publisher, provided the author indemnifies the publisher); (4) the right of attribution (the right to be known as the author of a work, or to be pseudonymous or anonymous); (5) the right of integrity (the right to alter, distort or destroy a work); and (6) the right to reply (the right to reply to criticism the author feels is unjustified).

In the United States, the Copyright Act addresses the moral rights only of visual artists (not *all* artists), and even as to visual artists only lightly, as the result of the Visual Artists Rights Act of 1990.[59] Although the moral rights of composers and performers are not recognized in the United States,[60] moral rights may extend to the visual artists who create album cover artwork

59. 17 U.S.C. § 106A (2011). Note that, even as to visual artists, moral rights are quite limited in the United States. For example, VARA applies only to visual artists of certain kinds of works (e.g., paintings and drawings), and expressly excludes others (e.g., posters and art that applies design or decoration to everyday and essentially practical objects in order to make them aesthetically pleasing). Further, when moral rights *are* available to a visual artist under VARA, they are narrower than European moral rights, in that the VARA rights comprise only the right to claim authorship, prevent use of the artist's name in association with a work, prevent intentional distortion, mutilation, or other objectionable modification, and prevent destruction, those rights are waivable and, in any event, those rights mostly end with the life of the author.

60. *Shostakovich v. 20th Century-Fox*, 80 N.Y.S.2d 575, aff'd, 87 N.Y.S.2d 430 (1949); *Fahmy v. Jay-Z*, No. 16–55213 (9th Cir. 2018).

unless such rights have been waived by the visual artist.[61] Moreover, moral rights, conceptually, are at least partially available to composers and performers in the United States through other laws. For example, the moral right to create (cannot be compelled to create) is reflected in the Thirteenth Amendment to the United States Constitution, the moral right of disclosure is reflected as a part of the bundle or rights afforded to the author under the Copyright Act, and the moral right to reply is reflected in the state laws of defamation and trade libel.

Fair Use

The exclusive rights that the Copyright Act grants to the owner of a copyright are not absolute. Instead, the rights of the copyright holder are always balanced against the rights of other parties, particularly the First Amendment rights of someone using a work protected by copyright without the owner's consent. The doctrine that provides this balance is called the fair use doctrine, which began as a court-created, equitable defense to a claim of copyright infringement that permitted unconsented uses of a copyrighted work on certain public policy grounds. Fair use, as now codified in the Copyright Act, permits unconsented but otherwise infringing uses "for purposes such as criticism, comment, news reporting, teaching, . . . scholarship, or research."[62]

The following four factors set forth in § 107 must be analyzed to determine if a use is fair and thus not an infringement:

(1) the purpose and character of the use, including whether such use is of a commercial nature or is for nonprofit educational purposes;
(2) the nature of the copyrighted work;
(3) the amount and substantiality of the portion used in relation to the copyrighted work as a whole; and
(4) the effect of the use upon the potential market for or value of the copyrighted work.[63]

61. 17 U.S.C. § 106A (2011).
62. 17 U.S.C. § 107 (2011).
63. Ibid.

It is important to understand that fair use is a defense. Whether one's fair use defense is valid is not conclusively known unless and until there is a judicial determination—it is not fair use unless and until the trier of fact (judge or jury) says it is fair use. As a result, reliance upon fair use to justify an unconsented use comes with the risk of uncertainty and an acceptance of the proposition that if the use is not a fair use then the use is infringing.

Also, the fair use defense must be assessed on a case-by-case basis. There are no absolute rules that either permit or bar the defense in all cases. The most useful general rule could be characterized as the Fair Use Golden Rule—take only what you would be comfortable with others taking from you, and use only what you need to use and no more. That is not the expression of any legal doctrine, but it is generally a good initial measure to assess in association with the fair use factors set out in the Copyright Act.

The following are examples of cases involving music in which the fair use defense was successfully interposed:

(1) *Estate of James Oscar Smith v. Aubrey Drake Graham p/k/a Drake, personally known as Drake*[64] (Licensed sample of sound recording was fair as to unlicensed underlying composition, despite 35-second length of sample, primarily because use was held transformative.)
(2) *SOFA Entertainment, Inc. v. Dodger Productions, Inc.*[65] (Use of seven-second clip from The Ed Sullivan Show in the musical *Jersey Boys* was fair because use of the clip as a "biographical anchor" to mark an historical point in the Four Seasons' career was held transformative.)
(3) *Seltzer v. Green Day, Inc.* (Band's use in stage show video backdrop of artist's illustration was fair because use of the illustration as "raw material" in the four-minute video backdrop was held transformative.)[66]
(4) *Brownmark Films v. Comedy Partners*[67] (Animated television series *South Park*'s animated version of plaintiff's popular music video was fair since it was meant to "lampoon the recent craze in our society of watching video clips on the internet.")

64. *Estate of James Oscar Smith v. Aubrey Drake Graham p/k/a Drake*, No. 19–28 (2d Cir. 2020).
65. *SOFA Ent., Inc. v. Dodger Prods., Inc.*, 709 F.3d 1273 (9th Cir. 2013).
66. *Seltzer v. Green Day, Inc.*, 725 F.3d 1170 (9th Cir. 2013).
67. *Brownmark Films v. Comedy Partners*, 682 F.3d 687 (7th Cir. 2012).

(5) *Red Label Music Publishing, Inc. v. Chila Productions*[68] (Use of the song *Superbowl Shuffle* in documentary about the 1985 Chicago Bears held fair because the use was transformative and there was no effect on the market for the original.)
(6) *Lennon v. Premise Media Corp. L.P.*[69] (Fifteen-second use of song *Imagine* held fair principally on the basis that such use was critical of song's message and did not usurp market for licensing the song for non-transformative uses.)
(7) *Bill Graham Archives LLC v. Dorling Kindersley Ltd.*[70] (Use of photographs of posters and tickets in book held fair principally on the basis that such use was transformative of the original work and not financially harmful.)
(8) *Italian Book Corp. v. American Broadcasting Cos.*[71] (Television broadcast of film and sound recording of parade band performing plaintiff's composition held fair on the basis of no harm to plaintiff.)
(9) *Karll v. Curtis Publishing Co.*[72] (Publication of plaintiff's composition held fair on the basis of implied consent.)
(10) *Keep Thomson Governor Committee v. Citizens for Gallen Committee*[73] (Use of song identified with one candidate in political campaign by their opponent in the opponent's responding commercials held fair.)
(11) *Shapiro, Bernstein & Co. v. P.F. Collier & Son Co.*[74] (Reprinting of lyrics from play in fictional serial in which characters in serial hear performances of the play while listening to radio broadcast.)
(12) *Broadway Music Corp. v. F-R Publishing Corp.*[75] (Publication of portions of song in article about death of actress with whom song was associated.)

---

68. *Red Label Music Publ'g, Inc. v. Chila Prods.*, 388 F. Supp. 3d 975 (N.D. Ill. 2019).
69. *Lennon v. Premise Media Corp. L.P.*, 556 F. Supp. 2d 310 (S.D.N.Y. 2008).
70. *Bill Graham Archives LLC v. Dorling Kindersley Ltd.*, 386 F. Supp. 2d 324 (S.D.N.Y. 2005).
71. *Italian Book Corp. v. American Broadcasting Cos.*, 458 F. Supp. 65 (S.D.N.Y. 1978).
72. *Karll v. Curtis Publ'g Co.*, 39 F. Supp. 836 (E.D. Wis. 1941).
73. *Keep Thomson Governor Comm. v. Citizens for Gallen Comm.*, 457 F. Supp. 957 (D.N.H. 1978).
74. *Shapiro, Bernstein & Co. v. P.F. Collier & Son Co.*, 26 U.S.P.Q. 40 (S.D.N.Y. 1934).
75. *Broadway Music Corp. v. F-R Publ'g Corp.*, 31 F. Supp. 817 (S.D.N.Y. 1940).

The fair use defense has often been cited by politicians who have used musical compositions in political campaigns without consent, but the defense in such cases has generally been found to be unavailing.[76] In response to songwriters' fervor with respect to the use of their music in live settings at political rallies, where the premises at which the rallies are held typically hold blanket licenses from composers' performing rights organizations, the performing rights organizations ASCAP and BMI in 2012 added a "political opt-out clause" to their blanket licenses, purportedly giving composers the right to opt out of the license with respect to their music for performance by all or any particular political campaigns.[77] It remains to be seen whether those opt-out clauses are enforceable (i.e., whether artists can opt out of the blanket license for political purposes) because ASCAP and BMI have long been subject to antitrust consent decrees that govern the terms of their licensing, including prohibiting composers from selectively removing their works for some licensees while using the blanket license for those same works to other licensees.

Parody

Parody is a form of fair use. The success of a parody depends upon its perceived relation to a familiar object, person, or work, so parodists are permitted a somewhat greater freedom to borrow in order to "recall or conjure up" the original work as needed to link conceptually the parodist's work to the work being copied. However, to be defensible as a parody, the work being copied must be the work being parodied. For example, a parody defense interposed in a case involving use of a musical composition in a political ad was unsuccessful, as the "parody" took as its subject the user's opponent, rather than the song or those associated with the song.[78]

---

76. *Grant v. Trump*, 563 F. Supp. 3d 278 (S.D.N.Y. 2021); *Browne v. McCain*, 612 F. Supp. 2d 1125 (C.D. Cal. 2009). For a general discussion of the tension between copyright and the First Amendment where political campaigns are concerned, see also Danwill D. Schwender, "The Copyright Conflict Between Musicians and Political Campaigns Spins Around Again," *American Music* 35, no. 4 (Winter 2017): 490–500.

77. Schwender, "Copyright Conflict," 490–500.

78. *Henley v. DeVore*, 733 F. Supp. 2d 1144 (C.D. Cal. 2010).

The same result occurred when a salacious reworking of a popular song from the 1940s was included in a musical stage play and unsuccessfully defended as comment on the original composition.[79]

In the case of *Campbell v. Acuff-Rose Music, Inc.*,[80] the Supreme Court stated that, to the extent a parody does not take as the object of its criticism the work being copied, it diminishes the fairness of the borrowing but held that "parody, like other use, has to work its way through the relevant fair use factors, and to be judged case-by-case, in light of the end of copyright law."[81] The Court ruled that "it was error for the Court of Appeals to conclude that the commercial nature of 2 Live Crew's parody of 'Oh, Pretty Woman' rendered it presumptively unfair."[82] The following are other examples of cases involving music in which the parody defense was successfully interposed:

(1) *Elsmere Music, Inc. v. National Broadcasting Co.*[83] (Use of "I Love New York" advertising jingle in NBC *Saturday Night Live* sketch as "I Love Sodom")
(2) *Berlin v. E.C. Publications, Inc.*[84] (Publication of satirical lyrics that copied the meter of plaintiff's songs with directions to the reader to mentally supply the melodies)
(3) *Brownmark Films, LLC v. Comedy Partners*[85] (Parody of popular music video in episode of television series *South Park*)
(4) Mattel, Inc. v. MCA Records, Inc.[86] (Musical parody of the fictional character, Barbie, held fair use despite the subject's status as a cultural icon).

79. *MCA Music v. Earl Wilson*, 425 F. Supp. 443 (S.D.N.Y. 1976).
80. *Campbell v. Acuff-Rose Music, Inc.*, 510 U.S. 569 (1994).
81. Ibid., 581.
82. Ibid., 594.
83. *Elsmere Music, Inc. v. National Broadcasting Co.*, 482 F. Supp. 741 (S.D.N.Y. 1980), aff'd, 623 F.2d 252 (2d Cir. 1980).
84. *Berlin v. E.C. Publications, Inc.*, 329 F.2d 541 (2d Cir. 1964), cert. denied, 379 U.S. 822 (1964).
85. *Brownmark Films, LLC v. Comedy Partners*, 682 F.3d 687 (7th Cir. 2012).
86. *Mattel, Inc. v. MCA Records, Inc.*, 296 F.3d 894 (9th Cir. 2002).

Copyright Myths

The rules of copyright law are often the subject of myth—there are some ideas that seem hard to put to rest, notwithstanding the efforts of many to dispel the errors in the myths. Here are some often-heard misconceptions:

(1) "It is okay to use someone's music if . . .
  - you do not use more than [fill a number in the blank] seconds of it; or
  - you make at least [fill a number in the blank] changes to its melody or words; or
  - you make fewer than [fill a number in the blank] copies of it; or
  - you take less than [fill a number in the blank] percent of it."

  The only rule of thumb with respect to the use of musical compositions is that there is no rule of thumb, except that if you start with someone else's music and reproduce, distribute, publicly perform, publicly display, or change (i.e., create a derivative work of) any of it, then you are in a position of infringement. The myth described in this paragraph may arise as a result of the use of preview samples authorized by some copyright owners as a tool to increase actual sales. These samples are possible because a license to use them accompanies the right to sell the intellectual property being offered and do not exist independently as a general right to use thirty seconds (or some lesser period) of a composition. And there is neither any minimum number of changes, any minimum number of copies nor any minimum percentage of taking that one can make to a melody, words, or a sound recording to construct a shield against liability against a claim of copyright infringement. The legal test for liability is substantial similarity, which may not be absolutely escaped through the device of any of the minimum numbers set forth earlier constituting fair use. Each use of a composition or a recording has to be considered on a case-by-case basis, and while some uses of even greater duration, greater number of copies, or greater percentage of taking may be permitted without consent, even lesser uses may require permission.

(2) "To save yourself the cost of registering your work with the United States Copyright Office, just send a copy of your work to yourself by

certified or registered mail and do not open the package." This myth has persisted for decades despite equally persistent efforts to debunk it. There is no value, from a copyright perspective, in such a process as it is easily corruptible (just mail yourself an empty, unsealed envelope every day or every week or every month, then at a later date seal within it whatever you want). Standing to enforce a copyright in litigation requires a registration. Further, just from a practical point of view, the difference in price is immaterial given the relatively low cost of an application with the Copyright Office. While it may seem odd that some people still have this belief, the myth of the registered letter is like a vampire that will not die.

(3) "The work I want to use does not have a copyright notice on it, and I could not find it registered in the Copyright Office, so it must be in the public domain." This myth falls in the "it depends" category. It may be true that a work published without a copyright notice prior to January 1, 1978, or a work published between 1978 and March 1, 1989, without a notice and not registered within five years thereafter, is in the public domain. However, works published after March 1, 1989, do not require a copyright notice or a registration in order to remain protectable—it's just that a registration needs to be undertaken before a lawsuit is commenced. The upshot is that whether a work is in the public domain is a complex question that cannot be answered on the basis of these two simple factors.

(4) "It is okay to use another person's work because I am not charging people for what I am producing, I have given the original creator credit, and the original creator will benefit from the promotion I am giving to their work." Whether one charges for a work that incorporates the work of others is not relevant to whether an infringement has occurred—it is only one factor in assessing either a fair use defense or how damages will be determined (or both). Further, while giving credit is a recommended practice, it is not a shield to liability. An unconsented use remains actionable, whether the borrowing is acknowledged or not. Finally, the owner of a copyright interest in a work is the sole person entitled to determine whether a proposed use

of that work will provide a promotional incentive strong enough to forego more customary methods of compensation. No matter how strongly the second person may believe their use of a work will help create value in the work being used, the copyright owner has the right to be wrong about that. To conceptualize, consider that you take one of the author's cars from his driveway, solely for the purpose of taking it to the local detail shop, and on the way there you pronounce to every passerby that it is his car, not yours—in such case you still will have committed theft.

(5) "Even if my use is infringing, merely stopping if/when I receive a cease and desist letter will make the claim go away." While this is sometimes true as a practical matter, since some owners take satisfaction from the mere cessation of infringement and prefer to not engage in further disputes or litigation, again, an unconsented use remains actionable, even after the wrongful action of taking ceases.

(6) "I can always get a license later if my unconsented use is discovered, so why get a license in the first place?" An owner of a copyrighted work is under no obligation to issue a license, especially to a party they view as an infringer. If a license requested by an infringer is refused by the owner of a copyright, it may be expensive and inconvenient to withdraw the infringing material from the market, which could also trigger, against the infringer, indemnification claims from parties who used the infringing material in some manner in reliance on their expectation that the material was usable for its intended purpose. Finally, the fee for a license, if one is available, will invariably be a multiple of the normal fee—this is often referred to as the license fee for a "carrot" license (for a license the copyright owner wants to entice the licensee to take) versus for a "stick" license (given to an infringer, under threat of the infringement action "stick").

(7) "I didn't mean to copy the claimant's work—I thought my work was sufficiently different." Intent is not an element of copyright infringement—you can be an infringer even if your copying is subconscious. Your deliberateness though, or your lack thereof, will be a favorable consideration in determining damages.

Trademarks

Acquisition of Trademark Rights

Trademarks are usually thought of as words or logos used to identify the products or services of a person or company. However, trademarks go beyond simple words and logos—trademarks can comprise anything that has source-identifying significance, including such things such as color, sound, and scent.[87] Trademarks represent the goodwill of their owners and, in the music industry, make possible merchandising, packaging, licensing, and sponsorship opportunities that are important to musicians and musical performing groups. Trademarks are to be distinguished from trade names, which are simply the names of the business entities that use the trademark or services marks.

Trademark rights are acquired in one of two ways in the United States. The first is simply by adoption and use of a mark with a product or service. The trademark owner's rights will be measured by the following factors: (1) strength of the mark in relation to the goods or services with which it is used, (2) the territory in which the mark is used, (3) the channels of trade in which the mark is used to market goods or services, and (4) the success the mark owner has in creating an association in the public mind between the mark and the owner's goods or services. The owner's rights will begin as of the date the mark is first used in commerce with the product or service. Federal registration of the owner's mark under the Lanham Act[88] after the mark has been used in commerce is not a prerequisite to trademark protection, but it will give nationwide rights to the mark and certain remedies for the owner in the event of an infringement.

The second way trademark rights are obtained in the United States is by an application to register a proposed mark under the intent-to-use provisions

---

87. For a discussion concerning the protectability of nonconventional trademarks, see Irene Calboli and Martin Senftleben, *The Protection of Non-Traditional Trademarks: Critical Perspectives* (Oxford, 2018; online ed., Oxford Academic, February 21, 2019); Shaista Kahkeshani and Mohd Juned Ansar, "Non-Conventional Trademarks: The Spectrum of Distinctiveness in the Era of Globalization," *International Journal of Law, Management & Humanities* 5, no. 1 (2022): 117. For an interesting case concerning a claim to protect a performer's "costume," see *Naked Cowboy v. CBS*, 844 F. Supp. 2d 510 (S.D.N.Y. 2012).

88. 15 U.S.C. §§ 1051–1141n (2012).

of the Lanham Act.[89] An intent-to-use application, or ITU, permits the filing of an application to register a mark prior to the actual use of a mark in commerce, based on the applicant's sworn, bona fide intention to adopt the mark with the goods or services identified in the application. Under an ITU, rights in a proposed mark can be obtained as of the filing date of the application for registration, as long as the applicant thereafter files evidence within the time limits proscribed by the Lanham Act that they have commenced use of the mark in commerce in association with the goods or services identified in the application. This process protects the efforts of a trademark owner during the interim period between conceptualization of the mark and the actual use of the mark in commerce, which is the prerequisite event for a registration.

Registration of one's trademark or service mark creates a (rebuttable) legal presumption of one's ownership and exclusive right to use the mark nationwide on or in connection with the goods or services listed in the registration. A registration may also be recorded with the U.S. Customs and Border Protection Service to prevent the importation of infringing goods and may be used as a basis for obtaining registrations in foreign countries. The registration symbol ® may be used only in connection with a mark that has been registered. It is highly recommended to use the registration symbol for a mark that has been registered, because failure to give such notice of registration means no profits and no damages may be recovered in a suit under the Lanham Act unless it is proven that the defendant had actual notice of the registration.[90] Absent a registration, one may use "TM" or "SM" next to a mark to designate a claim of ownership, but such use provides only notice of the user's contention that it possesses trademark rights, and does not confer legal rights comparable to those arising from a registration.

Performing Group Names

Trademark rights are important for music industry companies such as record companies, publishing companies, production companies, event

89. 15 U.S.C. § 1051(b) (2012).
90. 15 U.S.C. § 1111 (2012).

promoters, and merchandising companies. However, some of the most interesting trademark issues arise in connection with the names of musical performing groups.[91]

The first trademark issue an emerging group faces is what the group is going to call itself. This is not an easy issue to address, given the number of performing groups in the United States and the longevity of the careers of some groups. Additionally, the international online platforms available for groups to promote themselves, such as TikTok, Instagram, X, and Facebook, mean that concurrent users of the same name cannot carve out separate geographic regions for themselves as they may have done in the past. The satirical publication, *The Onion*, made the observation in 2007 that there were only seven good band names left.[92] The best group names convey a sense of the creative output of the group, such as Metallica, Funkadelic, Insane Clown Posse, or the Clash. But the availability of such names has grown increasingly scarce, leading to the emergence of many names consisting of absurd non sequiturs, approaching narrative sentences, or reflecting a very low level of aspiration. One of the benefits of online social media platforms as a promotional tool for musical performers is the greater ability to search the availability of proposed names, as most names already being used are detectable through conventional online search methods.

The test for infringement under trademark law is whether use of a mark for a particular good or service is likely to cause confusion as to source, sponsorship, or approval of such goods or services with a prior user of a mark.[93] A group that presents itself with the same name as a different prior group would in many cases certainly cause people to believe that the new

---

91. While we generally think of musical performing groups as the owners of the names of the groups, the names may be actually owned by others, such as the record company for which the group records. For a case where the party enforcing rights in the name and "persona" of the musical group The Supremes was the record company, see, e.g., *Motown Record Corp. v. Hormel & Co.*, 657 F. Supp. 1236 (C.D. Cal. 1987); see also Juna Moon and Fan Wang, "The Row That Rocked K-pop: NewJeans Tell BBC Why They Spoke Out," *BBC*, March 26, 2025, https://www.bbc.com/news/articles/cdxq309kexeo; see also *Bell v. Streetwise Records, Inc.*, 640 F. Supp. 575 (D. Mass. 1986) (record company's claim of group name ownership rejected).

92. "Report: Only 7 Band Names Remaining," *The Onion*, May 17, 2007, https://theonion.com/report-only-7-band-names-remaining-1819569107/.

93. 15 U.S.C. §§ 1114, 1125 (2012).

group is either the original group or a group that had the approval of the original group.

Beyond use of identical names, the question of whether one name for a musical performing group is likely to be confused with the name of another musical performing group must be determined on a case-by-case basis, generally taking into account the following factors applicable to all trademark cases: (1) similarity of the marks, (2) strength of plaintiff's mark, (3) sophistication of consumers when making a purchase, (4) intent of defendant in adopting the mark, (5) evidence of actual confusion (or lack thereof), (6) similarity of marketing and advertising channels, (7) similarity between the targets of the parties' sales efforts, (8) product similarity, and (9) other factors suggesting that consumers might expect the prior owner to be involved with the defendant's product, service, or market.[94] With respect to music groups, the most important factors are the strength of the original user's mark and the similarity or dissimilarity of the marks in their entireties as to appearance, sound, connotation, and commercial impression.[95]

Whatever the name a group might select, it should be guided by at least two goals. First, the name should be selected with the goal of having offensive rights as opposed to defensive rights. The goal should not be to see what the group might be able to get away with, which is the defensive approach. The goal should be to select a name distinctive enough that it will enable the group to keep other groups from adopting names that are

---

94 *Interpace Corp. v. Lapp, Inc.*, 721 F.2d 460 (3d Cir. 1983).

95. Notwithstanding the rights trademark law provides to a mark's owner, the commercial music market seems to tolerate similar names for performers that might be more problematic in other commercial situations. For example, two groups with the name "Nirvana" agreed to coexist, two acts with the name "Lady A" agreed to coexist, and the group "fun." was able to distinguish itself from the group "Fun" by lowercasing the first letter and adding a period. Some other groups adopt certain modifications to their names, depending on the territory in which they are appearing or releasing recordings. For example, The Raconteurs in the United States are known as The Saboteurs in Australia, The English Beat in the United States is The Beat in the rest of the world, and the Spinners in the United States were the Detroit Spinners in the United Kingdom. The passage of time also sometimes permits tolerance of names that would otherwise be confusingly similar. For example, the eighties country music supergroup featuring Johnny Cash, Willie Nelson, Waylon Jennings, and Kris Kristofferson called The Highwaymen was able to reach an arrangement to coexist with the sixties folk group The Highwaymen.

close in meaning—then the group will have offensive rights against others. The second goal is to verify whether the name (or a suitable alternative) is available as a URL for the group's website and on social media platforms that will support the group's marketing efforts.[96]

Assuming the name a group selected does not run afoul of the rights of a prior user, conveys the values the group wants associated with its music, and is available on the platforms that will be critical for marketing efforts, the next step is to seek protection of the name selected. This is often a moment of truth for many groups. If the group wisely elects to seek a federal registration of its name (perhaps under the intent-to-use provisions of the Lanham Act if use in interstate commerce has not yet occurred), the application requires the identification of the owner of the mark. Is the owner the group as an entity, and if so, what is the form of that entity? Or is the owner of the name one of the group members (or less than all, in some configuration)? Or is the owner the manager of the group?[97] Or the company producing and releasing the group's performances?[98] Each of these options is a viable election—the application requires that the issue be resolved before filing.

Issues relating to a group name do not end with adoption. Given how fragile and fluid the makeup of many musical groups can turn out to be, the ownership and use of a group's name as members come and go has caused many interesting dustups in the past.[99] How to deal with these issues is considered in Chapter 4.

---

96. One good resource for checking the availability of a proposed name across multiple platforms, or monitoring how one's selected name might be in use by others, is www.namechk.com.

97. *Rick v. Buchansky*, 609 F. Supp. 1522 (S.D.N.Y. 1985) (manager found to be the owner of group name Vito and the Salutations).

98. See footnote 89.

99. See, e.g., *Crystal Entertainment & Filmworks, Inc. v. Jurado*, 643 F.3d 1313 (11th Cir. 2011) (Expose); *Marshak v. Treadwell*, 240 F.3d 184 (3d Cir. 2001) (The Platters); *Kassbaum v. Steppenwolf Productions, Inc.*, 236 F.3d 487 (9th Cir. 2000) (Steppenwolf); *Robi v. Reed*, 173 F.3d 736 (9th Cir. 1999) (The Platters); *Marshak v. Schaffner*, 2012 WL 1658393 (S.D.N.Y. 2012) (The Marvelettes); *Densmore v. Manzarek*, 2008 WL 2209993 (Cal. App. 2d Dist. 2008) (DOORS); *Grondin v. Rossington*, 690 F. Supp. 200 (S.D.N.Y. 1988) (Lynyrd Skynyrd); *Kingsmen v. K-Tel Int'l Ltd.*, 557 F. Supp. 178 (S.D.N.Y. 1983) (The Kingsmen); *HEC Enterprises, Ltd. v. Deep Purple, Inc.*, 213 U.S.P.Q. 991 (C.D. Cal. 1980) (Deep Purple); *Griffin v. Gates*, 205 U.S.P.Q. 1150 (N.D. Ill. 1979) (Bread); *Giammarese v. Delfino*,

Trademark Fair Use

Like copyright ownership, trademark rights do not convey an absolute ability to prevent others from using a mark. Under the doctrine of nominative fair use, performers' names can be used without liability to editorially refer to the performers themselves. For example, a newspaper used the name of the group New Kids On The Block (NKOTB) without the group's consent in a promotion asking young readers to vote for their favorite member of the group by means of a telephone number that produced revenue for the newspaper. The court hearing NKOTB's claim held that the newspaper's use met the following three requirements for a nominative fair use defense: "First, the product or service in question must be one not readily identifiable without use of the trademark; second, only so much of the mark or marks may be used as is reasonably necessary to identify the product or service; and third, the user must do nothing that would, in conjunction with the mark, suggest sponsorship or endorsement by the trademark owner."[100]

Titles

While trademark protection extends to products and services, it does not apply to either song or record titles. From the perspective of the U.S. Patent and Trademark Office, titles as a general matter are descriptive of an individual item and thus may not be registered.[101] However, while song or record titles will not be protected under trademark principles, they may be protected under theories of unfair competition if they have achieved secondary meaning, which means that the public principally associates the

197 U.S.P.Q. 162 (N.D. Ill. 1977) (Buckinghams); *Noone v. Banner Talent Assocs., Inc.*, 398 F. Supp. 260 (S.D.N.Y. 1975) (Herman's Hermits); *Rare Earth, Inc. v. Hoorelbeke*, 401 F. Supp. 26 (S.D.N.Y. 1975) (Rare Earth); *Tate v. Jackson*, Case No. 12–2-21829–3 (King Co. Sup. Ct.) (Queensrÿche).

100. *New Kids on the Block v. News America Publ'g*, 971 F.2d 302 (9th Cir. 1992).

101. *Herbko Int'l, Inc. v. Kappa Books, Inc.*, 308 F.3d 1156 (Fed. Cir. 2002).

title with a particular work.[102] Courts have noted, however, that a musical composition could not serve as a trademark for itself.[103]

Online Presence

Accompanying the need to develop and protect trademarks and service marks for a performer or company is the need to build a strong online presence with associated domain names and social media identifiers. By itself, a domain name, or uniform resource locator (URL), offers its owner control only of activity implemented by means of the URL. Variations on an established URL may be obtained—perhaps with a different extension (.net instead of .com, for example)—without any formal review or examination process to determine whether the second URL infringes the rights of an existing URL owner. If a trademark owner finds that a third party has obtained a URL that features the owner's mark, or that comprises a name that is confusingly similar to the owner's mark, and the trademark owner is also able to establish that the registrant has no legitimate interest in the domain name and that the name has been obtained and used in bad faith, then in addition to possible litigation the owner can initiate an arbitration proceeding to recover the offending URL under the Uniform Domain-Name Dispute Resolution Policy of ICANN.[104] Mere similarity of URLs will not be enough to obtain relief, which is why savvy website owners obtain multiple versions of their URLs as a defensive move against cyber squatters. While it is not practical to obtain all variations of a particular URL, the cost of maintaining at least a portfolio of the more common extensions, together

---

102. *Robert Stigwood Group Ltd v. Sperber*, 457 F.2d 50, 56 (2d Cir. 1972); *Jubilee Industries, Inc. v. Roulette Records, Inc.*, 153 U.S.P.Q. 431 (N.Y. Sup. Ct. 1967); *Glory Records, Inc. v. RCA*, 213 N.Y.2d 875 (1961); see also *Life Music, Inc. v. Wonderland Music Co.*, 241 F. Supp. 653 (S.D.N.Y. 1965) (protection of word "supercalafrajalisticexpialidocious" against use in dissimilar song denied).

103. *EMI Catalogue Partnership v. Hill, Holliday, Connors, Cosmopulos Inc.*, 228 F.3d 56 (2d Cir. 2000); see also *Mattel, Inc. v. MCA Records, Inc.*, 296 F.3d 894 (9th Cir. 2002), cert. denied, 537 U.S. 1171 (2003) (use of "Barbie" doll character name in title and lyrics of composition and recording protected fair use).

104. Internet Corporation for Assigned Names and Numbers, http://www.icann.org/en/help/dndr/udrp (last accessed September 2025).

with some other predictable variations,[105] is insignificant in comparison to the cost of pursuing an infringer.

With respect to infringing addresses and sites on social media services such as TikTok, Instagram, X, or Facebook, a recommended first step is to provide notice of the infringement as a violation of the terms of use of the service through the service's complaint procedure. It has been our experience that the services are generally cooperative in disabling sites and addresses that make unauthorized use of prior owners' names and marks, which provides effective relief with minimal expense.

Right of Publicity

The right of publicity is the right of an individual to control the commercial exploitation of their identity. This right is the foundation for many of the same sources of revenue for a performer as provided by trademarks, including merchandising, touring, licensing, fan clubs, sponsorships, and packaging.

The right of publicity originally developed out of the common law protection of the right of privacy but assumed its own standing as a right protected under both common law and in many states by statute. The right protects any element of an individual's identity—likeness, name, biography, voice—from unconsented commercial exploitation. The U.S. Supreme Court famously recognized this right in *Zacchini v. Scripps-Howard Broadcasting Co.*[106] In *Zacchini*, the plaintiff was "The Human Cannonball," whose entire performance of being propelled through the air as he was shot from a cannon was filmed and broadcast by a television station. The Court recognized the commercial value of Mr. Zacchini's performance had been wrongfully appropriated and protected his commercial stake in his act over the First Amendment claims of the broadcasters.

105. It is not uncommon to defensively obtain URLs for websites that might otherwise be used for critical purposes, such as www.XXXXXSucks.com or www.XXXXXBlows.com. Of course, this could go on forever as well.

106. *Zacchini v. Scripps-Howard Broadcasting Co.*, 435 U.S. 562 (1977).

Since the right of publicity is governed by state law,[107] there are variations in its scope and application. In some states (such as New York), where the right is interpreted as a personal right, the right of publicity terminates upon the death of the individual.[108] In other states (such as California), the right is interpreted as a property right and is descendible.[109] In states where the right is protected by statute, the period of time the right may be protected after death is as long as 100 years.[110] In some states, the laws have been amended to account for a likeness generated by generative artificial intelligence (GAI) and, more particularly, to include an imitation of the subject's voice that is generated by GAI.[111] Since the matter protectable by the right of publicity is distinguishable from the scope of matter protectable by the Copyright Act, state statutory protection of the right of publicity is not

---

107. Notwithstanding that right of publicity is (and historically has been) governed by state law:

On July 31, 2024 and September 12, 2024, respectively, bipartisan groups of U.S. Senators and House Members, respectively, introduced the Nurture Originals, Foster Art, and Keep Entertainment Safe ("NO FAKES") Act intended to protect individuals' voices and likenesses from unauthorized, computer-generated recreations from generative artificial intelligence ("AI") and other technologies. While the NO FAKES Act has not yet become law, in its introduced version it would provide living persons and their heirs (for up to 70 years after death) the exclusive right to produce, publish, reproduce, publicly display, distribute, transmit or otherwise publicly make available such person's voice or visual likeness in a digital replica. It would also preempt all future state laws aimed at the protection of voice and visual likeness rights in an expressive work, but not any pre-2025 state or common law.

Also, on February 15, 2024, the Federal Trade Commission proposed new protections to combat artificial intelligence impersonations of individuals by way of seeking to extend an existing rule banning government and impersonation fraud. While there is as yet no formal extension to the existing rule, the FTC's Supplemental Notice of Proposed Rulemaking (i.e., its formal proposal for the changes) was published in March 2024, and it scheduled a hearing on the proposed rule amendment on January 17, 2025. FTC, "Press Release: FTC to Hold Informal Hearing on Proposed Rule Amendment Banning Impersonation of Individuals," December 19, 2024, https://www.ftc.gov/news-events/news/press-releases/2024/12/ftc-hold-informal-hearing-proposed-rule-amendment-banning-impersonation-individuals.

108. N.Y. Civ. Rights Law § 51 (2000); *Milton H. Greene Archives, Inc. v. Marilyn Monroe LLC*, 692 F.3d 983 (9th Cir. 2012).

109. Cal. Civ. Code § 3344.1 (West 1997).

110. Right of Publicity Act, Ind. Code § 32-36-1-8.

111. The ELVIS Act, Tenn. Code Ann. tit. 39, ch. 14, pt. 1; tit. 47; Illinois Digital Voice and Likeness Protection Act, 815 Ill. Comp. Stat. 550/; Cal. Lab. Code § 907(a); see also pending legislation in states, such as California Assembly Bill 1836 (AB 1836) (Use of likeness: digital replica).

preempted by the Copyright Act.[112] A claim for violation of one's right of publicity may be easier to establish than a trademark claim because proving a likelihood of confusion is not required. Instead, one need only establish that an element of one's identity has been used without consent and that such use was for a commercial purpose.

One of the most important right of publicity cases in the music area involved the performer Bette Midler. On her debut album, Ms. Midler delivered a distinctively seductive performance of what had theretofore been a much-covered up-tempo song called *Do You Want to Dance*. Ms. Midler's version was popular, and she was later approached by the Ford Motor Company to obtain her consent to use her recording in a television commercial for one of its cars. When Ms. Midler declined, Ford instead arranged for the production of a recording of the same song by one of Ms. Midler's former backup singers that mimicked Ms. Midler's performance and used that recording in its commercial. In 1988, Ms. Midler was able to successfully claim that her voice was an element of her identity and that, as such, her identity had been wrongfully appropriated by Ford in its soundalike recording.[113]

Following Ms. Midler's success, Tom Waits sued Frito-Lay in 1992 under similar circumstances. After Waits had declined to authorize the use of his performance for the soundtrack of a Doritos commercial, Frito-Lay used a known impersonator to record a song that was not identical to one Waits had earlier released, but the vocals of which captured Waits's distinctive stylings. Waits was able to successfully assert not only that his identity had been misappropriated, but also that use of an impersonator under such circumstances created a likelihood of confusion as to Waits's sponsorship, approval, or endorsement of the Frito-Lay product in violation of § 43(a) of the Lanham Act.[114] In an interesting twist on this theme, in 2014 a Michael Jackson fan filed an action against Sony Music Entertainment alleging

112. *Toney v. L'Oreal U.S.A., Inc.*, 406 F.3d 905 (7th Cir. 2005).

113. *Midler v. Ford Motor Co.*, 849 F.2d 460 (9th Cir. 1988).

114. *Waits v. Frito-Lay, Inc.*, 978 F.2d 1093 (9th Cir. 1992), cert. denied, 506 U.S. 1080 (1993); see also *Prima v. Darden Restaurants, Inc.*, 78 F. Supp. 2d 337 (D.N.J. 2000) (right of publicity of performer Louis Prima violated by use of soundalike recording in background of television commercial).

that three songs appearing on the 2010 album "Michael" used vocals by someone pretending to be Jackson, violating consumer protection laws and constituting unfair competition and fraud.[115]

While performers with distinctive vocal characteristics have successfully established that those characteristics are features of their identity, they have had less success establishing that a particular recording or song has become so identified with them as to acquire secondary meaning that would grant trademark rights in their identity.[116] For example, Nancy Sinatra, whose biggest hit record was *These Boots Are Made for Walking*, was unsuccessful in asserting a claim against the use of that song in a commercial extolling "wide boots" tires.[117] In like manner, the performing group The Romantics, whose major hit was *What I Like About You*, were unsuccessful in asserting a claim against the developer of the electronic game *Guitar Hero* when it included a version of that song in the game as performed by other people.[118] However, a different result was achieved in a case involving the identity of performer Guy Lombardo, where a recording was one piece of several elements associated with Mr. Lombardo that were imitated in an advertisement.[119]

Identity rights, as with those of trademarks and copyrights, are not absolute rights and must be balanced against the First Amendment rights of those who use a performer's identity noncommercially. For example, a song written by Bob Dylan about Rubin "Hurricane" Carter included the name of a witness involved with the actual trial. The witness sued Dylan, his publisher, and his record company on a variety of grounds, including misappropriation of the witness's identity. While the song and the recording of the song are certainly commercial undertakings, the song did not promote a product or a service, which is a key element of the right of identity

---

115. Jordan Darville, "The Alleged Michael Jackson Impersonator Lawsuit Has Been Settled," *Fader*, August 11, 2022, https://www.thefader.com/2022/08/11/alleged-michael-jackson-impersonator-lawsuit-settled; see also *Serova v. Sony Music Ent.*, Cal. S. Ct. Case No. S260736 (Aug. 18, 2022).

116. See, e.g., *Oliveira a/k/a Gilberto v. Frito-Lay, Inc.*, 251 F.3d 56 (2d Cir. 2001).

117. *Sinatra v. Goodyear Tire & Rubber Co.*, 435 F.2d 711 (9th Cir. 1970), cert. denied, 402 U.S. 906 (1971).

118. *Romantics v. Activision Publ'g, Inc.*, 574 F. Supp. 2d 758 (E.D. Mich. 2008).

119. *Lombardo v. Doyle, Dane & Berbach*, 396 N.Y.S.2d 661 (1977).

claim.[120] On the other hand, a musical featuring performers imitating the Beatles performing Beatles songs was found to appropriate the group's persona. The court found in favor of the Beatles, notwithstanding the argument that the musical work was an expressive commentary on the culture and politics of the 1960s that was entitled to First Amendment protection. The court used by analogy the fair use factors under the Copyright Act to find that the taking of the Beatles' identity overwhelmed the other elements of the musical work, as the performers imitating the Beatles were on stage for 95 percent of the presentation.[121]

Further, the First Amendment may be inapplicable if the use of a performer's identity is wholly unrelated to the material with which it is used. In this situation, the use could be said to be for the purpose of attracting commercial attention to the material. For example, the name of the civil rights icon Rosa Parks was used as the title of a song by the group Outkast. Parks sued for violation of her right of publicity and was able to reverse a summary judgment entered against her on the grounds that a genuine issue of material fact existed as to whether the title of the song was "wholly unrelated" to the content of the song.[122]

As a result of the various claims brought against advertisers based on performers' identity rights, the use of licensed preexisting music for commercials has become more prominent than the use of newly recorded material. Licensed music brings certainty. This circumstance has also created new opportunities for artists to use commercials as a promotional tool, creating more competition among artists for participation in commercials and, in many cases, reducing the amount advertisers have to pay for such recordings as a result of the perception that exposure from being included in a commercial creates value. For some performers, commercials are viewed as a desirable platform, particularly as the playlists of commercial radio stations have become more restrictive and difficult to break through.

120. *Valentine v. CBS, Inc.*, 698 F.2d 430 (11th Cir. 1983).

121. *Apple Corps Ltd. v. Leber et al.*, 229 U.S.P.Q. 1015 (1986). For a discussion concerning identity rights and "tribute" bands, see also Brent Giles Davis, "Identity Theft: Tribute Bands, Grand Rights, and Dramatico-Musical Performances," *Cardozo Arts & Entertainment Law Journal* 24 (2006): 845.

122. *Parks v. LaFace Records*, 329 F.3d 437 (6th Cir. 2003), cert. denied, 540 U.S. 1074 (2003).

Data

Access to market and customer data improves commercial decision making in the music business.[123] Online transactions and other data collection tools enable artists to directly connect with their fans in a variety of ways. Historically, the artist–fan relationship was mediated by record companies and retailers. While information might have been available about how many records featuring a particular artist had been sold, and perhaps generally where in the United States and through what general channel of retailer, no one knew who bought those records so that they could be contacted and persuaded to buy the next one. An artist's fan club was perhaps the only form of direct relationship that existed, and that vehicle, even when available to an artist, was cumbersome and inexpert.

In addition to having a direct link to those likely to support the artist with their purchasing decisions, knowing where an artist's fans are located helps to more precisely route personal appearances and support appeals to promoters making booking decisions. Data also helps measure the effectiveness of promotional efforts and can provide validation to actual and potential sponsors of the ability of the artist to draw an audience and influence buying behavior. Analysis of other data metrics also helps an artist identify trends in their own performances and measure that performance relative to other artists.

Data is also critical with respect to digital marketing and distribution and the tracking of music usage.[124] Before releasing recordings, performers should ensure that correct metadata concerning each of their recordings is properly embedded as part of the mastering process. This metadata should include each master's International Standard Record Code (ISRC),[125] which

123. See, e.g., Derrick Harris, "Data Isn't Just the New Oil, It's the New Money. Ask Zoe Keating," *Gigaom*, November 20, 2012, https://finance.yahoo.com/news/data-isn-t-just-oil-023113330.html?guccounter=2&guce_referrer=aHR0cHM6Ly93d3cuZ29vZ2xlLmNvbS8&guce_referrer_sig=AQAAAK0UhlTyB27etdS0gxEJZHgkDwkj_rrWALRKfOQRCi9bFR-R1aF4P5rwqN50I4eBWQ0qRV14wXEwp6o1wfcDdpFWali5MolxUp8EOPsp-QuQ7qOx2x-CyQq8OrFsQLEGKpmzA_-M9zoNhFaPO6mT3G6CAmnamxQ-01BGwigqIJPU_I.

124. See, e.g., "How Big Data Analytics Is Transforming the Music Industry—The Science of Music," *SG Analytics Blog*, March 2022, https://www.sganalytics.com/blog/the-science-of-music-how-big-data-is-transforming-the-music-industry/; Ed Christman, "Database Dilemma," *Billboard*, June 2, 2012, 8.

125. ISRCs may be obtained online through the Recording Industry Association of America at this website: "International Standard Recording Code," https://isrc.ifpi.org/en/ (last accessed September 2025).

is a unique number assigned to each recording for identification and reporting purposes. The ISRC will assist the detection of usage of the recording and make possible the tracking of proper payments to the correct recipient for the use of the recording.

Online sites that offer music, such as music services or online retailers, obtain album cover artwork, reviews, titles, composers, and other metadata concerning the music they feature so that the music, and information about the music, can be properly presented to their customers. These music sites obtain such metadata from suppliers that create, compile, and sell metadata. These metadata suppliers include www.gracenote.com, https://music-story.com, https://www.tuneregistry.com, and www.allmusic.com. It is important for performers to ensure that such metadata suppliers have correct data concerning the performers and their work within their files so that the performers and their work are correctly presented by the music sites using those metadata suppliers.

Data may be collected by the artist or company itself, by platforms used by the artist or company, or by third parties such as Pandora Amp (formerly Next Big Sound) that, in turn, format and market access to the data. An artist's efforts to collect data that personally identifies an individual fan or consumer will be governed generally by state, federal, and international law.[126] In addition, efforts by an artist to collect data by mining social media platforms will generally require disclosure of the artist's privacy policy concerning how such collected information may be used and may be subject to additional specific restrictions of the social media platform as well.[127]

Ownership of data associated with an artist is not always within the artist's reach. For example, many artist recording agreements provide that the record company will administer the artist's website during the term of the recording agreement. Under such circumstances, data collected by the

126. See, e.g., Children's Online Privacy Protection Rule, 16 C.F.R. pt. 312 (2003); Privacy of Consumer Financial Information, 16 C.F.R. pt. 313 (2003); Standards for Safeguarding Customer Information, 16 C.F.R. pt. 314 (2003); Cal. Civ. Code §§ 1798.29, 1798.82; California Consumer Privacy Act, Cal. Civ. Code §§ 1798.100 et seq.; *Regulation (EU) 2016/679 of the European Parliament and of the Council of 27 April 2016 on the Protection of Natural Persons with Regard to the Processing of Personal Data and on the Free Movement of Such Data (General Data Protection Regulation)*, http://data.europa.eu/eli/reg/2016/679/oj.

127. See, e.g., *Facebook, Statement of Rights and Responsibilities*, Section 5 (January 30, 2015), https://www.facebook.com/legal/terms/previous?_rdr.

record company and associated with the artist may not be made available to the artist. In like manner, ticket sellers collect information concerning the ticket purchaser, and that information is not generally shared with the artist. If an artist engages the services of a third-party payment provider, such as Apple Pay or Google Pay, to facilitate the sale of their products from the artist's website, or third-party product development or fulfillment providers such as CaféPress, certain information concerning purchasers of artist-related merchandise may also not be shared.

When representing an artist, it is important to anticipate how data concerning that artist and the artist's work will be collected. Determine how the artist will be able to control and use that data, and keep in mind that transactions and professional relationships run their course and are superseded by new transactions and relationships. In the event the performing group itself collects personally identifiable information about their fans, the privacy policy under which such information is collected should anticipate all intended uses and how the group members have determined the data will be shared if the group disbands.

Interviews

Musicians view interviews as both the desired result of promotional efforts and a nuisance. Whatever may be the view at the moment the interview occurs, the principal legal issue for the musician being interviewed is "Who owns the results of the interview?" The answer to that question is not clear. An interview is by definition collaborative, which may lead to a conclusion that the interviewer and interview subject are joint owners of the interview, or owners of their respective contributions. Alternatively, each party could claim sole ownership of the entire questions and answers. The issue is further complicated if the interviewer, interviewee, and/or a third party records the interview, because independent rights would be created in the recording(s) produced.[128]

128. Mark Fowler, "Who 'Owns' an Interview?" *Rights of Writers*, January 7, 2011, http://www.rightsofwriters.com/2011/01/who-owns-interview.html; *Trump v. Simon & Schuster, Inc. et al.*, No. 23 Civ. 6883 (PGG) (S.D.N.Y. 2025).

The best way to address the issue of ownership is to agree in writing prior to the event. Although this practice may not be appropriate with respect to quick promotional telephone or virtual interviews in anticipation of an appearance, or interviews conducted to develop material for inclusion in a larger work such as a book, it does apply to extensive interviews to be published as standalone works. In the written agreement, attention should be given to how recordings of the interview may and may not be used, if at all, and how ownership of such recordings will be held.[129]

Contractual Rights

For purposes of this chapter, "contractual rights" are certain provisions that sculpt the market in some manner and help create competitive advantages. Such provisions, often found in entertainment contracts, particularly agreements related to music, include exclusivity, right of first negotiation and refusal, key person, credit, most favored nations, and nondisclosure.

Exclusivity

Grants of rights, whether for copyrights, trademarks, identity rights, or personal services, fall into one of three categories—exclusive, sole, or non-exclusive. If rights are exclusive, that means they are exclusive even as to the grantor. This may seem obvious, but it is an important consideration in any transaction involving a musical property or talent. The broader the scope of exclusivity as to territory, product or service, channel of trade, or duration that is defined in an agreement, the more valuable the right. Exclusivity is particularly applicable to performers. Music industry agreements define, for example, the scope of exclusivity of rights the record company has in the results of the performances of the talent, or of the rights of the publisher in the songs of the songwriter, or of the rights of the promoter in the personal appearances of the performer within a certain period of time or geographic range.

129. *Lennon et al. v. Pulsebeat News*, 143 U.S.P.Q. 309 (N.Y. Sup. 1964) (records of taped interview enjoined from distribution).

If rights are sole, that means they are exclusive *except* as to the grantor. In other words, the grantor retains rights but agrees contractually with the exclusive licensee to not grant any other licenses.

If rights are nonexclusive, the grantor both retains rights themselves and may have multiple licensors. For example, licenses that permit the manufacture and sale of phonorecords of sound recordings, or mechanical licenses, are nonexclusive because music publishers want to have as many performers recording their songs as possible. However, the exclusivity of a mechanical license may be unimportant, as the artist and quality of the specific performance in the recording, which would be exclusive, may create the real market value. Some transactions can be structured so that rights are exclusive for a period of time but become sole or nonexclusive thereafter.

Right of First Negotiation/Refusal

Parties to a music-related transaction often do not know the true value of a property or a talent at the time the agreement is entered. Therefore, the parties may want to leave themselves with some flexibility to adapt their agreement terms as the project unfolds and its success becomes measurable. However, to negotiate all the details and "what-ifs" involving all the possible contingencies of what that success might be, and how the terms of the agreement would be affected and addressed, can derail or smother the progress of an otherwise successful negotiation.[130]

Rights of first negotiation and refusal are methods of preventing a battle about hypotheticals from overcoming negotiations. A right of first negotiation means the artist or property owner is obligated to engage with the producer or distributor first before soliciting interest from any other party. The right gives the producer or distributor the first chance to assess the opportunity available from the artist or property owner and reach terms to continue the relationship. The right also prevents a competitor from initiating negotiations directly with the artist or property owner prior to

---

130. In such circumstances, the talent or property side of the transaction (the seller) may opt to have a shorter agreement to avoid being bound to terms that might later become unfavorable in light of achieved success. However, the production or distribution side of the transaction (the buyer) may want the ability to continue the relationship in some manner if the success occurs.

the expiration of the initial agreement unbeknownst to the producer or distributor.

A right of first refusal, which may either accompany a right of first negotiation or be its own standalone provision, means the artist or property owner may solicit interest from other parties, but then is obligated to offer to the producer or distributor the ability to continue the relationship by meeting the offer made by another party.

When the right of first negotiation and right of first refusal are combined, the producer or distributor in effect gets two shots at continuing the relationship, which can be powerful.

Key Person

A key person provision in an agreement generally means that in the event a particular person is no longer affiliated with a company, or is otherwise not available to manage the relationship of the talent with an organization, then the talent has the right to terminate the agreement. This may be significant in a management or agency agreement, where the personal relationship of the talent with an individual may be the principal reason the talent is signed to the organization. One of the authors also had the experience of representing a musical performer who insisted on what might be called a "reverse" key person provision in his agreement with a recording company. In that case, in the event a certain named individual ever became associated with the record company, the artist would have the right to terminate the agreement. The label was small enough that it felt the artist's *bête noir* would never be affiliated with it, so it conceded the point.

Credit

Credit for a performer, producer, songwriter, or company is a key component of the consideration they will receive in a transaction. What credit is given, and how and where that credit is accorded in a project and the packaging and advertising for products embodying the project, is usually heavily negotiated. Credit influences industry and public perceptions of an artist or company, enables participation in further and better projects, and can drive financial compensation arrangements. However, credit obligations will be enforced only by means of contractual provisions, whether through direct agreements between talent or licensors and producers or indirectly through the provisions of certain union or guild agreements covering talent to which a producer becomes a signatory.

There is no general statutory right to receive a credit for one's contribution to a work. Efforts to bring a cause of action under the federal trademark laws against a work that fails to accord credit on the grounds that such work is mislabeled have failed. In the case of *Dastar v. Twentieth Century Fox Film Corp.*,[131] the Supreme Court held that § 43(a) of the Lanham Act[132] did not address the misappropriation of authorship, which in that case involved an alleged "reverse passing off" claim concerning repackaged public domain content that did not accord credit to those originally involved with the content. The Court ruled that the word "origin" in § 43(a) did not include the intellectual contribution made to a good or service, but rather, only the producer of the good or service. Since that decision, courts have invalidated claims concerning misattribution of credits brought under the Lanham Act and have pointed out that one desiring credit has the right to obtain such credit by contract or union collective bargaining agreements.[133] Further, failure to properly accord credit is not a violation under the Copyright Act.[134]

The takeaway from this circumstance is that the credit provisions of an agreement—whether for an artist or a production company licensing rights to its works—and the remedies available to the artist or production company if credit is not properly accorded are to be given very careful attention in any transaction, as valuable consideration may be lost if not found within the terms of the agreement.

Most Favored Nations

A most favored nations clause essentially says that in the event one party to an agreement enters a third-party transaction involving the subject matter

---

131. *Dastar v. Twentieth Century Fox Film Corp.*, 539 U.S. 23 (2003).

132. 15 U.S.C. § 1125(a) (2012).

133. See, e.g., *Dutch Jackson IATG, LLC v. Basketball Mktg. Co.*, 846 F. Supp. 2d 1044 (E.D. Mo. 2012); *Williams v. UMG Recordings, Inc.*, 281 F. Supp. 2d 1177 (C.D. Cal. 2003); see also *King v. Ames*, 179 F.3d 370 (5th Cir. 1999) (claim that individual falsely accorded himself credit on packaging of CDs to be producer of live recordings rejected).

134. *UMG Recordings, Inc. v. Disco Azteca Distribs.*, 446 F. Supp. 2d 1164, 1178 (E.D. Cal. 2006).

of the initial agreement, and the terms or conditions of that third-party transaction are more favorable to the third party than are the terms and conditions in the initial agreement, then the more favorable terms and conditions of the third-party agreement will be deemed incorporated into the initial agreement and applicable. Most favored nations provisions appear in a number of circumstances. For example, when a sound recording is licensed for use in an audiovisual work, the financial terms for use of the recording and the underlying composition performed in the recording are often negotiated on a most favored nations basis, through which the master rights holder and the composition publisher receive the same payment. Also, when multiple works are being assembled for a compiled work, the terms applicable to each of the individual works are often offered on a most favored nations basis. All terms are equal, with no individual owner receiving more favorable terms than any other. Credit provisions are also often established on a most favored nations basis, with each credit recipient receiving credit in the same manner as everyone else.

A most favored nations approach to a negotiation can expedite a transaction because the party receiving the benefit of the most favored nations treatment knows that they will not receive less than any other party and that they will be the beneficiary of any improved terms that might be obtained by a stronger party.

Nondisclosure

Nondisclosure provisions prohibit the recipient of certain information, such as a contractual party, from disclosing that information to others. In music transactions, nondisclosure of the terms of an agreement, particularly the financial terms, protects the business model of a record label or producer and prevents terms from being known to other artists that could be used to the detriment of the label or producer in other negotiations. Nondisclosure of material transactional terms may also be beneficial to artists, who may wish to shield such sensitive information from public scrutiny to avoid possible resulting negative reactions. Maintaining privacy of terms is also wise when the musician may not want to inform other possible transactional partners of the terms under which they are prepared to work.

Chapter 3
Music Publishing

Music publishing is the engine that drives the music industry. There is not a transaction involving music that does not implicate publishing in some manner. While some of the practices of the industry are arcane, or may seem so, the industry also relies upon sophisticated systems to track music uses, collect payments, and disburse proceeds throughout the world. The music publishing industry can be characterized as centralized in the context of the large international companies affiliated with the few major international record companies. However, the industry beyond the few majors is quite Balkanized, with low organizational and financial barriers to launch and operation. Since the business of music publishing today is principally the administration of the rights that are derived from the copyright interest in a composition, without the need to physically distribute products, there are many tens of thousands of music publishing companies operating within a wide range of size. And it all starts with a song.

As explained in the section about copyright, copyright rights in a musical composition arise automatically upon the fixation of that composition in some tangible medium—the song is written down in some form of transcription or is recorded. Music publishing involves the question of who owns the composition's copyright at that moment of fixation and the terms under which the various rights in that composition are exploited.[1]

Most musical compositions will begin their lives owned by the composer. It is possible, however, for someone other than the composer to own the copyright when created. For example, if music is being composed by an employee within the scope of their employment, such as for a commercial jingle production company, the composer's employer is deemed to be the creator (i.e., the author) of those works as works made for hire. Another common circumstance involving a composition being deemed a work made for hire would include a composer hired as an independent contractor to create music for an audiovisual work, such as a film or television program. Remember, to constitute a work made for hire, there must be a written agreement that defines the work as one made for hire *and* the work(s) created must fall within one of the categories specified by § 101 of the Copyright Act (one of which is a contribution to a collective work, as a part of a motion picture or other audiovisual work).

To illustrate and explain how music publishing works, we will organize this chapter around the fictitious circumstances of a new songwriter who is not working in a work-for-hire relationship and has composed a group of songs they now want to exploit. What should the composer do? Assuming the songwriter is not already affiliated with a music company (which we will discuss later), the songwriter should first become affiliated with one of the performing rights organizations.

Performing Rights Organizations

Copyright owners were first granted the exclusive right to publicly perform their musical compositions for profit in 1897. The American Society of Composers, Authors and Publishers (ASCAP) was formed in 1914 to enforce this right for composers, and the Society of European Stage Authors & Composers (SESAC) and Broadcast Music, Inc. (BMI) were formed in 1930 and 1939, respectively, for the same purpose.[2] Since 1941, ASCAP and

1. See generally Darren M. Richard, "Music Licensing 101," *Entertainment and Sports Lawyer* 29, no. 4 (2012): 12.

2. The early history of ASCAP, and the circumstances of the formation of BMI as an alternative to ASCAP, are recounted in the following titles: John Ryan, *The Production of Culture in the Music Industry: The ASCAP-BMI Controversy* (Lanham, MD: University Press

BMI have operated under consent decrees resulting from antitrust actions brought by the government that, among other things, limit their authority to the nonexclusive licensing of nondramatic performances and establish procedures for setting license rates and conditions.[3] These three performing rights organizations (PROs) now license for composers, on a nonexclusive basis, the nondramatic performance rights in almost all domestic compositions to entities publicly performing music, such as commercial radio and television stations, restaurants, clubs, online music services, and other such establishments. In recent years, both private equity interest in the performing rights business and technology advances have given rise to competitors to the "big three" PROs, from new, competing entities such as GMR and AllTrack.[4]

Most arrangements are through blanket licenses of each organization's entire repertoire.[5] While the blanket licensing practices of ASCAP and BMI

---

of America, 1985); Russell Sanjek and David Sanjek, *American Popular Music Business in the 20th Century* (New York: Oxford University Press, 1991).

3. *United States v. Broadcast Music, Inc.*, 1996–1 Trade Cas. ¶ 71,378 (S.D.N.Y. 1994); *United States v. BMI*, 1966 Trade Cas. ¶ 71,941 (S.D.N.Y. 1966); *United States v. ASCAP*, 1950–1951 Trade Cas. ¶ 62,595 (S.D.N.Y. 1950); *United States v. ASCAP*, 1940–1943 Trade Cas. ¶ 56,104 (S.D.N.Y. 1941); *United States v. BMI*, 1940–1943 Trade Cas. ¶ 56,096 (E.D. Wis. 1941).

4. Chris Cooke, "Does the U.S. Really Need So Many Performing Rights Organisations and Are They Doing a Good Enough Job, Asks U.S. Copyright Office," *Complete Music Update*, February 10, 2025, https://completemusicupdate.com/does-the-us-really-need-so-many-performing-rights-organisations-and-are-they-doing-a-good-enough-job-asks-us-copyright-of/.

5. However, DMX, a background and foreground music service provider, was able to successfully establish a rate for its service through ASCAP that allowed it to offset the costs of direct licenses with ASCAP members; see *Broadcast Music, Inc. v. DMX Inc.*, 683 F.3d 32 (2d Cir. 2012). Also in 2011, one of the largest music publishers, EMI Music Publishing, withdrew the right to license digital services from ASCAP in favor of direct licenses; see Ed Christman, "EMI Music Publishing Taking Over Licensing Digital Rights from ASCAP," *Hollywood Reporter*, May 4, 2011, http://www.hollywoodreporter.com/news/emi-music-publishing-taking-licensing-184688. This move was then followed by Sony/ATV, which acquired EMI Music Publishing in 2012. See "Op-Ed: Cutting But Not Running," *Billboard*, October 15, 2012, https://www.billboard.com/music/music-news/op-ed-cutting-but-not-running-1083408/. The subsequent direct negotiation by Sony/ATV of digital performance rights with Pandora resulted in a 25 percent increase in the license rate paid to Sony/ATV. See Ed Christman, "The Deal: Sony/ATV's Pandora Pact," *Billboard*, January 14, 2013, https://www.billboard.com/music/music-news/the-deal-sonyatvs-pandora-pact-1526304/#:~:text=WHAT?,5%25%20of%20revenue%E2%80%9D%20pool. Pandora then initiated a rate proceeding concerning whether the consent decree governing the licensing activities of ASCAP unambiguously precludes partial withdrawals of public performance licensing rights and seeking a rate setting for the Pandora-ASCAP license, wherein it was held that partial withdrawals do not affect the scope of Pandora's license and affirmed the rate set by the district court at 1.85 percent of revenue; see *Pandora Media v. American Society of Composers, Authors & Publishers*, No. 14–1158 (2d Cir. 2015).

have been challenged on antitrust and copyright misuse grounds in several private actions, they have been upheld as to broadcast television networks;[6] local television broadcasters;[7] and small establishments offering music, such as bars, nightclubs, and restaurants.[8] The blanket licensing practices of a single publisher of religious music granting performance and reprint rights to Catholic parishes has also been upheld.[9] SESAC, too, has faced antitrust allegations, for example in private antitrust actions filed against it by commercial television and radio broadcast stations seeking to establish a rate-setting process, though that action ultimately settled out of court for an agreement that lasts until 2037 to arbitrate in the event of a failure to agree on periodic rate increases.[10] ASCAP and BMI settled *their* disputes with the radio industry on this issue in mid-2025, with an agreement that lasts until 2039.[11] Also recently, in early 2025, the U.S. Copyright Office began an inquiry, at the behest of Congress, regarding issues related to an increase in the number of PROs and the licensing revenue distribution practices of PROs.[12]

Until 1948, ASCAP also licensed to theater operators and exhibitors the right to publicly perform music in motion pictures. That practice was ended by court order in the case of *Alden-Rochelle, Inc. v. ASCAP*.[13] The

---

6. *Broadcast Music, Inc. v. Columbia Broad. Sys., Inc.*, 441 U.S. 1 (1979), aff'd on remand, 620 F.2d 930 (2d Cir. 1980), cert. denied, 450 U.S. 970 (1981); *Columbia Broad. Sys., Inc. v. American Soc'y of Composers, Authors & Publishers*, 400 F. Supp. 737 (S.D.N.Y. 1975), rev'd, 562 F.2d 130 (2d Cir. 1977), rev'd sub nom.

7. *Buffalo Broad. Co. v. American Soc'y of Composers, Authors & Publishers*, 744 F.2d 917 (2d Cir. 1984), cert. denied, 469 U.S. 1211 (1985).

8. *Broadcast Music, Inc. v. Moor-Law, Inc.*, 527 F. Supp. 758 (D. Del. 1981), aff'd, 691 F.2d 490 (3d Cir. 1982).

9. *F.E.L. Publ'ns, Ltd. v. Catholic Bishop of Chicago*, 214 U.S.P.Q. 409 (7th Cir. 1982).

10. For a discussion of the general history of this dispute, see *Meredith Corp. v. SESAC, LLC*, 2011 WL 856266 (S.D.N.Y. 2011); *Radio Music License Comm., Inc. v. SESAC, LLC, et al.*, Civil Action No. 12 5807 (E.D. Pa. 2012); Ed Christman, "SESAC Settles Antitrust Suit Brought by Commercial Radio Group," *Billboard*, July 24, 2015, https://www.billboard.com/pro/sesac-settles-antitrust-suit-rmlc-commercial-radio-group/; "Arbitration Will Once Again Decide How Much Radio's New Deal with SESAC Costs Stations," *Inside Radio*, September 20, 2023, https://www.insideradio.com/free/arbitration-will-once-again-decide-how-much-radio-s-new-deal-with-sesac-costs-stations/article_3d3602d2-5784-11ee-a8ed-ff7407aea4f8.html.

11. Dylan Smith, "RMLC Settles BMI and ASCAP Rate Disputes—BMI Agreement to Run Through 2029," *Digital Music News*, August 19, 2025, https://www.digitalmusicnews.com/2025/08/19/rmlc-ascap-bmi-settlements/.

12. U.S. Copyright Office, *Issues Related to Performing Rights Organizations*, February 10, 2025, https://www.federalregister.gov/documents/2025/02/10/2025-02418/issues-related-to-performing-rights-organizations#footnote-50-p9257.

13. *Alden-Rochelle, Inc. v. ASCAP*, 80 F. Supp. 888 (S.D.N.Y. 1948).

right to perform music in motion pictures by way of theatrical exhibition is now acquired directly by motion picture producers. The performance rights to the same music when the motion picture is transmitted by other means, such as by broadcast or satellite, are still controlled by the performing rights organizations.

Registering with one of the PROs is relatively easy. One may apply to ASCAP (www.ascap.com) and BMI (www.bmi.com) online, as either a songwriter, a publisher, or both. Affiliation with SESAC requires submission of one's work and an invitation from SESAC to become a member. Since our fictitious songwriter is not already affiliated with an existing music publishing company, they may wish to affiliate as both a songwriter and as a publisher by way of establishing their own self-owned publishing company.

The financial considerations impacting our fictitious songwriter's selection of which PRO to join are beyond the scope of this book but are comprehensively reviewed in the book *Music, Money, and Success* by Jeffrey Brabec and Todd Brabec,[14] wherein ASCAP, BMI, and SESAC are profiled in detail. The authors write:

> The primary areas that need to be considered include the length of a writer's or publisher's contract and the procedures to terminate that contract if one wants to leave, the actual dollar amounts paid for every type of use (scores, themes, visual vocals, etc.), recognition of the value of all of a writer's and publisher's copyrights whether they be new or old works, procedures whereby each organization changes its payment rules, dispute resolution procedures, the bonus systems in place, relationships with foreign performing right organizations, maximum and accurate collection of foreign income, among others.[15]

Sometimes the selection of a PRO is made on other grounds. Some people select on the basis of affinity with the historical background of the organization. ASCAP began its life in New York and has a legacy strong in the Tin Pan Alley and show tune tradition that existed there. BMI gathered its initial repertoire among certain genres of music that had been overlooked

14. Jeffrey Brabec and Todd Brabec, *Music, Money, and Success* (New York: Schirmer Trade Books, 2022), 353–409.

15. Ibid., 366.

by ASCAP, such as country, jazz, and R&B. This factor is of much less importance today, as both organizations are now strong in each genre, but some songwriters may feel a stronger connection with one over the other because of the songwriters and catalogs they and their songs may be joining.

Another factor may be how the songwriter feels about the ownership of the PRO. ASCAP is an unincorporated membership association that reported $1.835 in revenue for 2024. BMI and SESAC are each owned by private equity firms. BMI was purchased in 2024 by New Mountain Capital for a reported $1.7 billion, and SESAC was purchased in 2017 by Blackstone, Inc. for a reported approximate $1 billion.[16]

Another factor may be the methodology and technology by which a PRO detects and collects performances. Each of the PROs—ASCAP, BMI, and SESAC—uses digital technology to detect and track performances. This enables each PRO to obtain more comprehensive and accurate data concerning such performances and more correctly allocate their license proceeds among their members.

Finally, another way to help the selection process is to compare actual results between the organizations. The only apples-to-apples comparison that would yield helpful results is the respective payouts for a song co-written by, for example, an ASCAP member and a BMI member. Unfortunately, that information is not generally available or, if so, is merely anecdotal.

Once the songwriter has selected a PRO with which to affiliate, the next most significant issue is the name of their proposed publishing company. ASCAP and BMI will ask the songwriter for three name choices of their proposed publishing company, in order of preference. Creative name selections are encouraged, as there are tens of thousands of music publishing companies and each organization will check for confusingly similar names not only within their own membership but also within the membership of one another and their respective foreign affiliates. Once affiliation is completed, the songwriter will submit their compositions to the PRO they have joined so that any performances of such songs that are logged by the PRO can be tied to the composer.

---

16. Murray Stassen, "New Mountain Capital-Led Group Closes Acquisition of BMI" (February 8, 2024), *Music Business Worldwide*, https://www.musicbusinessworldwide.com/new-mountain-capital-closes-acquisition-of-bmi1/; "Leading Music Rights Organization SESAC to Be Acquired by Blackstone" (January 4, 2017), *Blackstone*, https://www.musicbusinessworldwide.com/companies/sesac/#:~:text=Blackstone%20Group%20takeover%20of%20SESAC,be%20close%20to%20%241%20billion.

The PROs are indifferent to the form of business entity that the songwriter takes for their publishing company—sole proprietorship, corporation, or limited liability company—and the songwriter's choice of business-entity type will of course depend upon their individual circumstances. However, affiliation with a PRO is suggested as a first step, as clearance of the proposed name of the publishing company through the PRO will be the most important consideration in name selection.

There are many alternative next steps our fictitious songwriter might take after the organization of their own publishing company. For our purposes, let us assume the songwriter initially elects to operate on their own as a self-publisher. The principal business of the company will be to administer the granting of rights in the compositions controlled by the company, the most important of which are mechanical rights and synchronization rights.

Mechanical Licenses

Observation tells us that, as people, we tend to integrate change through the use of analogy. For example, the first automobiles looked like wagons, many of man's first efforts to fly mimicked the flapping of birds' wings, and the first on-screen digital music players looked like CD players. That is the only way one can explain why, after over one hundred years, the music industry still uses the term "mechanical" to describe a circumstance that has long lost any association with a mechanical process.

Piano rolls were an early form of musical exploitation. The mechanical process involved scrolling paper in which holes had been punched through a specially equipped piano, which caused the piano to perform a composition. The Copyright Act of 1909 recognized that the scrolling of punched paper constituted a reproduction of the composition that was within the scope of the exclusive rights of the composition's copyright. The license to produce such piano rolls was called a mechanical license, as the composition was considered to be mechanically reproduced in the creation of the piano rolls. This same terminology was later applied to sound recordings on wax cylinders and then to recordings on flat discs or records. As disc records became magnetic tapes, and then discs again in the form of compact discs, the terminology remained. Today, the term "mechanical license" refers to the permission given to fix a recording of a musical composition in any form, whether physical, such as vinyl records (which the Copyright Office calls phonorecords), or digital, such as a download transmission (what the Copyright Office calls a digital phonorecord delivery), or the copy of a recording fixed on a server to facilitate the digital stream of the recording.

Since the Copyright Act of 1909, mechanical licenses have been the subject of a compulsory license recognized under copyright law that essentially permits anyone to market (for private use) a recording of a musical composition that has already been released in recorded form. The caveat is that the second user of the composition must comply with the statutory requirements of the compulsory license.[17] The Music Modernization Act, intended to update and increase fairness and efficiency in copyright law, had multiple effects on mechanical licenses, including extending the blanket license system to qualified digital service providers (DSPs), establishing a "willing buyer/willing seller" rate standard intended to require DSPs to pay fair market value for mechanical licenses, and creating the Mechanical Licensing Collective, a not-for-profit entity that collects mechanical royalties and distributes them to copyright owners.[18] There are a number of requirements for qualifying for the compulsory license, but the most significant requirement is that the second user of the composition must pay the statutory license rate that has been set by the Copyright Office for such use.[19] The statutory royalty rates

17. 17 U.S.C. § 115 (2011).

18. The Music Modernization Act, Pub. L. No. 115–264 (2018); U.S. Copyright Office, *Frequently Asked Questions*, https://www.copyright.gov/music-modernization/faq.html#:~:text=Title%20I%20%E2%80%93%20The%20Musical%20Works,for%20creators%20to%20collect%20royalties (last accessed September 2025). Unfortunately, the Mechanical Licensing Collective is not living up to its potential for at least two reasons. First, an artist's participation in the Mechanical Licensing Collective requires registration, and the organization remains somewhat unknown even years after its formation; see generally Ashley King, "Only 17% of Music Creator College Students Are Familiar with the MLC, Survey Finds," *Digital Music News*, April 27, 2025, https://www.digitalmusicnews.com/2025/04/27/music-creator-college-students-survey-the-mlc/. Second, data inconsistencies within the organization's database are making it difficult to match royalties collected with songwriters to be paid; see generally Paul Resnikoff, "83% of Writers Have Unpaid Royalties in MLC's Database—Muso.AI's New Audit Tool Reveals the Shocking Scale," *Digital Music News*, October 6, 2025, https://www.digitalmusicnews.com/2025/10/06/muso-ai-catalog-audit-mlc-mismatch-solution/.

19. The compulsory license permits the performer to make an arrangement of the composition "to the extent necessary to conform it to the style or manner of interpretation of the performance involved, but the arrangement shall not change the basis melody or fundamental character of the work . . . ," 17 U.S.C. § 115 (2011). For a discussion concerning some of the implications of this "arrangement privilege" for the music business, see also Spender C. Martinez, "The Phonorecord Compulsory License Statute and the Unresolved 'Arrangement Privilege,'" *Entertainment Law & Finance*, February 2009; Eric Lauritsen, "Richard Cheese,

set for mechanical licenses under the compulsory licensing provisions of the Copyright Act of 1909 and the current copyright law eventually became the prevailing standard in most privately negotiated mechanical license agreements. This is because both publishers and users of music knew that if they did not come to terms, the user could elect to pay the statutory rate to the publisher for a recording of the publisher's song once a recording of that song had been released domestically. These rates were 2 cents per recording, per copy, for many years, and were initially raised by the Copyright Act of 1976. They have been adjusted periodically since. The rates for physical phonorecords, on a per-unit basis, are currently set as either 12.4 cents or 2.45 cents per minute of playing time or fraction thereof, whichever amount is larger.[20] In reality, very few marketers of recordings avail themselves of the compulsory licensing provision of the Copyright Act because of the notice and accounting provisions that must be observed to ensure the license's effectiveness, but the rate set by the Copyright Office continues to be the benchmark for private licenses.

There are essentially two methods of issuing or obtaining a mechanical license for a musical composition in the United States. The first is a direct license from the publisher of the composition, which for purposes of this chapter is our hypothetical beginning songwriter/self-publisher. If the songwriter is approached to have their songs recorded by others and released in an audio-only format, the mechanical license is the agreement that would be issued by the songwriter to the proposed user. The terms of the license agreement would address the rate, the format in which the recordings are authorized to be released, the territory in which the recordings would be distributed, the frequency of accountings, and other provisions.

A far more frequent method of issuing and obtaining mechanical licenses in the United States is through mechanical license organizations, the oldest and by far most used of which is Harry Fox Agency. Harry Fox Agency was formed in 1927 by the Music Publishers Association as a central clearing house for the issuance of mechanical licenses on behalf of its members. Today, Harry Fox Agency is owned by SESAC and issues licenses for the production and distribution of digital downloads, CDs, tapes, vinyl, and

Seu Jorge and the Scope of Permissible Changes Under Section 115 Licenses," *Entertainment & Sports Lawyer* 31, no. 2 (Summer 2014).

20. Royalty Rates for Making and Distributing Phonorecords, 37 C.F.R. § 385.11(a)(1) (2024).

other audio-only configurations for the great majority of music publishers in the United States; monitors the payments of fees due under such agreements; and acts as a source of information about music licensing on behalf of the music publishing industry. As already mentioned, the Mechanical Licensing Collective is a not-for-profit organization designated by the Copyright Office under the Music Modernization Act of 2018 for the purpose of issuing blanket mechanical licenses to DSPs for streaming. Our hypothetical beginning songwriter should register with the Mechanical Licensing Collective for that purpose, and might also consider affiliating with Harry Fox Agency as a self-publisher to handle mechanical licensing for non-streaming for a number of reasons. Harry Fox Agency is generally the first place the music industry checks for licensing information about a composition, contact information for the writer and publisher is made easily available, Harry Fox Agency has a convenient online system for the issuance of licenses under publisher-favorable terms without the writer/publisher involvement, and Harry Fox Agency has the collective power to enforce payment of license fees that can be more effective than the individual action of a single writer/publisher. Affiliation as a writer/publisher requires that at least one composition controlled by the publisher has been recorded and commercially released by a third party. The current commission charged by Harry Fox Agency for its services is 8.5 percent of collected license proceeds.[21]

Synchronization Rights

The so-called synchronization right is the right of musical composition owners to control the right to have their compositions reproduced in timed sequence in an audiovisual work. The synchronization right is implicated whenever the recorded performance of a musical composition is used in a motion picture, television program, music video, commercial, or other form of audiovisual work. Even if the audiovisual work itself is in the public

---

21. Harry Fox Agency, *Frequently Asked Questions*, http://ec2b-www-harryfox-com-2470-780317655.us-east-1.elb.amazonaws.com/find_out/faq.php (last accessed September 2025); for a discussion concerning some of the intricacies of mechanical licenses and royalties, see *Mechanical Royalties Guide | 2021*, The Royalty Exchange, February 2, 2021.

domain, one who commercially reproduces the public domain work can be subject to an obligation to license the music incorporated in the work.[22]

The synchronization right is derived from the owner's exclusive right of reproduction.[23] The synchronization right first appeared when sound became a feature of motion pictures, which involved the reproduction of a recording of the composition on a separate track appearing on the film stock of the sequential images comprising the motion picture. The reproduction of a composition's recording may be sequenced differently today, but the right remains.

Unlike a mechanical license, there is no compulsory license or statutory rate for a synchronization license for a musical composition that might provide a backup alternative to a user of a composition in the event negotiations are unsuccessful. Instead, the terms for each synchronization license are individually negotiated. Compensation for a synchronization license can range from no charge (if the owner of the composition believes there is promotional benefit from a proposed use) to seven figures, depending on the status of the composition, the type of use being made (commercial, opening credits for movie, background for scene in television program, etc.), territory, length of use, and format. A strong interest in diversifying revenue streams for artists of all levels has created a cottage industry of licensing companies like Musicbed, Artist.io, and Soundstripe, which aggregate music for licensing at relatively low prices under click-to-accept contracts for wedding photographers, independent filmmakers, and the like.

If a preexisting sound recording is licensed for synchronization use in an audiovisual work, it is not uncommon for the fee paid for use of the master recording and the underlying composition to be determined on a most favored nations basis, meaning each rights holder receives the same compensation for the use of their respective property—the master and the composition. While the consideration under some synchronization licenses may be determined on a royalty basis, which would take into account contingent sales volume or other factors, many synchronization licenses today are issued on a flat fee basis. This enables the producer of the audiovisual

22. *Maljack Prods., Inc. v. Good Times Home Video Corp.*, 81 F.3d 881 (9th Cir. 1996).
23. 17 U.S.C. § 106(1) (2011).

work both budgetary certainty and the flexibility to exploit the work across all platforms without having to obtain additional rights or anticipate new royalty models.

Dramatic Rights

Whenever a musical composition is incorporated into a theatrical work, such as a musical play or revue, the rights that must be obtained are referred to as either dramatic rights or grand rights. The two terms are often used interchangeably, but generally dramatic rights refer to the right to incorporate a composition in a staged work, and grand rights refer to the right to use a portion of a staged work in a second staged work, or to reproduce the staged work in a different medium. In any event, like synchronization licenses, there are no compulsory licenses or statutory rates applicable to dramatic or grand rights licenses. Each such license is negotiated individually, and the rights holder, the publisher, is free to withhold consent to the use of the composition without fear of a statutory license as a backup alternative for the producer.

One significant issue that arises in connection with dramatic and grand rights licenses is determining where the nondramatic performance rights for compositions licensed by ASCAP, BMI, and SESAC end and the need to obtain a separate dramatic rights or grand rights license from the publisher for a work begins. A series of cases involving the work *Jesus Christ Superstar* several years ago provides some guidance in helping draw that line.

When *Jesus Christ Superstar* was first released, it existed only as a double-disc vinyl LP. While the songs from the work were sequenced on the LP to provide a narrative and the performers of the songs on the album assumed certain character voices, the work did not exist as a dramatic presentation. When the album became successful, certain producers conceived the idea of presenting choral performances of the songs from the album in the same sequence as they appeared on the album. For the right to present the performances, the producers relied upon the nondramatic performance licenses from ASCAP and BMI already in place with the performance venues. This practice was successfully challenged in several lawsuits, the opinions to which set out some of the features of a stage presentation that distinguish a nondramatic performance—a singer or group performing a series of songs—from a dramatic performance.[24] A key element is whether the performance features a narrative—meaning, does it tell a story? Are there characters? Is there character costuming? Is scenery tied to a story being told?[25] To the extent such elements exist, the presentation takes the form of a dramatic work, for which the nondramatic rights controlled by ASCAP, BMI, and SESAC do not suffice.

The phenomenon of so-called tribute bands raises issues in a number of areas, including whether the staging of a tribute performance incorporating the "characters," iconography, and other elements of a performing group, implicates any dramatic rights in the compositions being performed.[26] The issue has generally been more theoretical than real. While some artists have sought to bar the performance of tribute bands (e.g., the Beatles, Blues Brothers, Bon Jovi), such actions generally have been grounded on trademark or right of publicity rights rather than music copyright rights.

In the case of a composer or lyricist preparing work for a musical stage play, the composer, lyricist, and playwright generally receive an equal portion of the advance and royalty pool made available for the play's creators. There are a number of ways in which such pools may be determined,[27] but the contributions of each generally are considered of equal value in the

24. *Robert Stigwood Group Limited v. Sperber*, 457 F.2d 50 (2d Cir. 1972); *Rice v. American Program Bureau*, 446 F.2d 685 (2d Cir. 1971); John R. Allison, "Protection of Performance Rights to 'Jesus Christ Superstar': The Dramatic-Nondramatic Dilemma," *Performing Artist Review* 4 (1973): 13.

25. See *Gershwin v. The Whole Thing Co.*, 208 U.S.P.Q. 557 (C.D. Cal. 1980); *April Prods. v. Strand Enters.*, 221 F.2d 292 (2d Cir. 1955).

26. Brent Giles Davis, "Identity Theft: Tribute Bands, Grand Rights, and Dramatico-Musical Performances," *Cardozo Arts & Entertainment Law Journal* 24 (2006): 845; Philip Auslander, *Liveness: Performance in a Mediatized Culture*, 3d ed. (2023); Samuel Cameron, *Music in the Marketplace: A Social Economics Approach* (2015); Tristan Griffin, "Mark My Word: Trademark Your Band Name," *Texas Review of Entertainment & Sports Law* 15 (2013): 177, https://heinonline.org/HOL/Page?handle=hein.journals/tresl15&id=197&div=&collection; Shane Homan, "'Knowledge of Beatles Songs and McCartney Parts Essential': Tribute Acts, the Music Industries and the Value of Heritage," in *The Routledge Companion to Popular Music History and Heritage* (Abingdon, U.K.: Routledge, 2018); Shane Homan, "Fake Histories? Original Bands, Contemporary Formations and Little River Band," *Continuum* 36 (2022), https://www.tandfonline.com/doi/full/10.1080/10304312.2021.2000587; Amnon Lehavi, "The Law of Trusts and Collective Action: A New Approach to Property Deadlocks," *SSRN Journal* (2020), https://www.ssrn.com/abstract=3643755.

27. See generally Donald C. Farber, *Producing Theater*, 3d ed. (New York: Limelight Editions, 2006), chap. 4.

allocation. With respect to preexisting compositions that are incorporated in a musical stage play, the compensation will depend on how the song is used in the play, the capacity of the theater in which the work is presented, ticket prices, number of performances per week, and whether the production is commercial or not-for-profit. Payment may take the form of a set per-performance fee, a percentage of the gross box office receipts, or a combination of the two.

Publisher Agreements

While our hypothetical songwriter/self-publisher may elect to continue as an independent, self-administrating entity through all levels of success, success alternatively may bring the need to affiliate with another publishing company in one form or another. These various arrangements can be generally categorized as a single song agreement, an exclusive songwriter agreement, a copublishing agreement, or an administration agreement. The features of each of these arrangements are described next.

Single Song Agreements

The structure of a single song publishing agreement is essentially this: The songwriter assigns full ownership of the song—the copyright—to the publisher in return for the services of the publisher to promote the song, administer rights in the song when used by others, collect proceeds from uses of the song, and account for those proceeds to the songwriter. Although referred to as a single song agreement, the agreement could apply to a group of songs assigned to the publisher in a single document and transaction, each of which songs would be treated in the same manner as described herein.

The compensation payable to the songwriter will generally fall into two categories: compensation for uses of the song that are made by the publisher and compensation for uses of the song that are made by others under license from the publisher. Today, almost all publishing income under song publishing agreements falls in the second category, as very few music publishing companies actually themselves exploit rights in compositions. Nevertheless, music publishing agreements almost universally contain provisions describing the royalties due the songwriter from the sale of print or piano roll copies of the composition. Why do agreements include provisions for such marginal forms of music use? First, remember that the music publishing industry is generally very tradition-bound, and changes in the form agreements used by publishers have been and remain slow to occur. Second, music publishing companies are frequently bought and sold. In the lifetime of the copyright in a composition, it may be owned by a music publishing company that actually exploits that composition in print or as a piano roll, in which case the royalty to be paid has been determined. Rates for sheet music and piano rolls are generally stated in a certain number of cents per copy sold, which generally ranges from 8 to 12 cents.

Tradition has determined that when a songwriter assigns rights in a composition to a publishing company, most of the compensation received by a music publishing company from the licensing of rights in that composition is divided equally between the publishing company and the songwriter (or songwriters as a group). The 50 percent songwriter portion is paid to the songwriter(s) as a royalty. This arrangement applies to mechanical licenses, synchronization licenses, print licenses, and other, more specialized categories of licenses for such products as apparel, greeting cards, or the use of a song's title, characters, or narrative as the basis for adapted works in other media, such as audiovisual works or books. The 50 percent portion of the proceeds retained by the publisher is generally referred to as the "publisher's share," and the other 50 percent portion that is paid by the publisher to the writer is generally referred to as the "writer's share." If there is more than one writer, the writers share the writer's share and the publisher's share remains at 50 percent. While this math is about as simple as one might encounter, it nevertheless leads to confusion. This generally occurs when negotiation depends upon how the respective shares of the writer and the publisher might be allocated.

One source of income from music publishing that is treated differently when a publisher is not a self-publishing extension of the songwriter but is an independent, separately owned entity is performance income. The performing rights organizations—ASCAP, BMI, and SESAC—have elected to directly pay music publishers and songwriters their respective shares of performance income. The payment by the PROs of the writer's share to the writer(s) and the publisher's share to the publisher is in the same allocation as the payments made by music publishers of other proceeds. Each receives 50 percent of performance income directly from the respective performance right organizations. Because the songwriter is already receiving their portion of performance income directly from the PROs, the publishing company does not account to the songwriter for any of that income, which is generally recognized in the single song agreement.

The following are some additional issues that are typically included in a single song agreement.

Initial Payment

Generally, a songwriter receives a payment from the publisher when the publisher obtains ownership of the song or songs from the writer. This payment can be categorized either as an advance paid by the publisher against royalties to be paid under the publishing agreement or the purchase price of the copyright being assigned. The latter would not necessarily be recoupable from future royalties. The difference is clearly material. If the payment is characterized as an advance, then the songwriter has in effect received the benefit of a guaranteed payment for the future use of their song, but will not receive any further payments until that advance is recouped from actual credits to the songwriter's account. In effect, while the publishing company is taking the risk whether future proceeds will be enough to earn back the advance, the publishing company is paying for the composition with the songwriter's money (or, to be fair, with the songwriter's potential money). If the initial payment is characterized as a purchase price in exchange for the assignment of the copyright interests in the songs, then the publishing company will obtain the songs subject to an obligation to pay royalties to the songwriter from the first proceeds received by the publisher.

Whether an initial payment is characterized as an advance or as a purchase price may turn on the status of the compositions being acquired. The payment for the acquisition of an established composition, with a history of revenue over a period of time (or a clear projection based on success achieved at that time), is more likely to be treated as a purchase price, particularly if the seller is not the songwriter but, rather, a downstream owner of the copyright(s). Payment for the acquisition of an unproven composition directly from the songwriter is more likely to be treated as an advance.

Approvals

Songwriters, particularly emerging songwriters, generally are not granted the right to approve how the publisher uses their compositions. However, there is one area in which even emerging songwriters should seek approval rights, and that is for the issuance of synchronization licenses. Using a composition in connection with a visual image contextualizes the composition—it creates an association that is very powerful and that might change the way audiences relate to the composition. Use of a tender ballad to ironically underscore a violent scene, for example, could materially impair performance of that ballad in the future if it conjures up the violent association in audience members. Writers may also not want their compositions used in connection with certain audiovisual works generally, such as movies of a certain genre, commercials generally, or commercials specifically in support of such things as politics, religion, alcohol, tobacco, firearms, personal care products, or certain foods. Because of this sensitivity, many music publishing companies will seek input from writers before authorizing a license. However, songwriters are always on firmer ground if their songwriter agreement specifically requires approval for such licenses.

Another area of possible approval for the songwriter is to authorize the first artist to record one of the writer's compositions. An initial recording of a composition often defines the composition, although there are many examples of subsequent recordings of compositions creating new or more popular perceptions or values.[28] Writers often write with specific performers in mind and wish to see the initial commercial release of a recording of that composition feature that performer, or at least a performer of enough perceived stature to boost the likely success of the composition.

Finally, another general topic area in which writer approval is considered has to do with the integrity of the song itself and how the song might be

28. For a comprehensive collection of information about the initial recordings of well-known songs, see Dick Rosemont, *The Originals Project* (May 10, 2023), http://www.originalsproject.us.

adapted. For example, at what point is the song considered "complete"? May the publisher add new words or new musical material, or authorize the inclusion of the song in a medley or as a portion of a different song? Will the writer be able to approve translations of the song, or parody versions? Unless addressed, general rights language in a single song agreement might permit adaptations along these lines (although the right of a publisher to do something does not always mean that right is exercised without seeking consultation and approval from the writer).

Obligation to Promote

The exclusive nature of the relationship between the composer and the publisher creates an implied general obligation to use commercially reasonable efforts to promote the composition.[29] It is also possible to contractually require the publisher to use its "best" efforts, but since it is not clear what that standard actually implicates, any specific efforts meant to be undertaken should be described in the agreement. The relationship between the composer and the publisher, in and of itself, is generally not considered one of a fiduciary nature that creates any special form of trust or obligation.[30] Indeed, the holder of exclusive rights in a property has the right to reject opportunities as long as the intent is not to harm the royalty participant.[31] However, a breach of the implied obligation to exploit a composer's work with no motive other than to harm the composer would constitute a tort.[32]

Demo Costs

A key method of promoting compositions is to create demonstration recordings, or demos, that can be circulated to record companies, producers, managers, and artists. Demos can bring a song alive and present arrangement details that might otherwise be lost to the person to whom the song is being presented. Demos may be produced independently by the songwriter or under the auspices, and at the expense, of the publishing company. Demo costs may be recoupable either in full or up to 50 percent and may be recouped from either the songwriter's share of income or from first receipts generally. The publishing agreement could provide limits on the

---

29. *Wood v. Lucy, Lady Duff-Gordon*, 118 N.E. 214 (N.Y. 1917).
30. *Mellencamp v. Riva Music, Ltd.*, 698 F. Supp. 1154, 1159 (S.D.N.Y. 1988).
31. *Third Story Music, Inc. v. Waits*, 41 Cal. App. 4th 798 (Ct. App. 1996).
32. *Mellencamp v. Riva Music*, 698 F. Supp. at 1159.

amount a publisher might spend on each demo and should address how the songwriter might be reimbursed for costs incurred in producing demos on their own. The agreement should also address ownership of the demos and acknowledge that they will not be commercially released.

Warranties and Indemnifications

Similar to all agreements granting rights in copyrighted works, music publishers will want to receive warranties and representations from the songwriter that the works being conveyed are innocent and freely obtainable by the music publisher. These are some typical warranties:

- The song is original with the songwriter, and the songwriter is the sole writer/composer (or all cowriters are identified).
- The song has not already been published.
- There are no prior agreements pertaining to the song.
- The song does not infringe the rights of any third party.
- No claims have ever been asserted against the song, and the writer knows of no unasserted claims.
- The songwriter is free to enter the transaction with the music publisher.
- There are no existing agreements that would impair the ability of the publisher to fully exploit the song and all rights in and to the song.

Coupled with the warranties and representations will be the songwriter's indemnification of the music publisher, which is subject to the same considerations as indemnification provisions generally. Two additional key points should be addressed. First, because of the continued obligation of the publisher to pay royalties to the songwriter, the single song agreement will often permit the music publisher to withhold payments that might otherwise be due to the songwriter in the event a claim that implicates the indemnification terms is made against the publisher. The terms under which such funds can be held, including when the withholding may be triggered and how long thereafter the funds may be held, should be negotiated. Second, the agreement may state that the indemnification may be asserted against any funds otherwise due under the music publishing agreement, or "any other agreement between Music Publisher and Writer." The language in quotations permits cross-collateralization between agreements, the implications of which need to be fully considered.

Accountings and Audits

Accountings under music publishing agreements are generally provided quarterly, generally within forty-five to ninety days following the end of each calendar quarter. It is not uncommon for music publishing agreements to feature a contractual limitation on the period of time within which the recipient may challenge the accuracy of the statements rendered, after which the recipient will be barred from pursuing any claim for unpaid royalties. Such provisions are enforceable,[33] so the period of time—generally between two and three years after submission of the statement—should be carefully considered. As with any circumstance involving periodic contingent payments, the royalty recipient should have the right to audit the publishing company in order to know if a claim for unpaid funds exists.

The terms considered in an audit clause in a publishing agreement include: when and where the audit may take place, how long it may take place, the frequency of audits, the length of time after the end of an accounting period during which that accounting period remains open for audit, how many times a single accounting period may be audited, what materials may be reviewed, any cost shifting in the event a discrepancy is discovered, confidentiality of disclosures, and whether any audit report will be shared. How the audit provisions tie to the contractual limitations on when claims for unpaid royalties may be initiated should be carefully reviewed.

The relationship between a songwriter and music publisher will generally not rise to one of fiduciary, so the writer's right to receive accountings and royalties will not create a special publisher obligation. Efforts have been made to impose a higher obligation to pay royalties on the part of the publisher by contractual language that defines license proceeds as funds held in trust by the publisher on behalf of the songwriter,[34] but acceptance of such language by a publisher is rare, if nonexistent. While failure to pay royalties will result in a claim for the unpaid amount, such failure will generally not give rise to an action for recession of the publishing agreement and reassignment of the copyright to the author unless the failure to pay

33. *Clinton v. Universal Music Group*, 2011 WL 3501818 (C.D. Cal. 2011); *Allman v. UMG Recordings*, 530 F. Supp. 2d 602 (S.D.N.Y. 2008).

34. See, e.g., The Songwriters Guild of America, *The Songwriters Guild of America Popular Songwriters Contract* ¶ 4(l) (1978), https://www.songwritersguild.com/sga-contract.

was both intentional and at least nearly total.[35] Agreements can provide, however, that in the event a commercial recording of a composition is not secured by the publisher within a certain period or royalties are not paid, all rights shall be reassigned to the composer.[36]

Credit and Identity

The music publisher will generally want to have the right to use the name, likeness, and other elements of the songwriter's identity in connection with the exploitation of the compositions. This is particularly true with respect to popular singer/songwriters. How this right extends to the publisher's licensees must be addressed, particularly with respect to the licensing of nontraditional uses of compositions, such as on apparel or posters, where use of the writer's identity might add value. The writer might also have particular interests in how their identity is credited. If the songwriter wants their name presented in a particular fashion, or if cowriters have agreed on the order in which their names should appear in connection with their compositions, then the music publisher should be instructed on these decisions.

International

A songwriter is presented with several choices in how to deal with exploitation of their compositions outside of the United States. For example, many large music publishing companies have an international presence, so their agreements would generally extend to all territories (although more limited rights could be granted, if the publisher were to agree). Even if the publishing company is not a multinational entity, it may nevertheless have established relationships with local sub publishers throughout the world, effectively creating a network administered by the domestic publisher. Finally, the songwriter has the option of entering agreements directly with publishers on a territory-by-territory basis outside the United States.

Each option has advantages and disadvantages. A territory-by-territory approach has the advantage of a potentially larger aggregate advance than one may receive from a single publisher. Having separate agreements also

35. See, e.g., *Nolan v. Williamson Music, Inc.*, 300 F. Supp. 1311 (S.D.N.Y. 1969); see also *Peterson v. Highland Music, Inc.*, 140 F.3d 1313 (9th Cir.), cert. denied, 525 U.S. 983 (1998) (rescission granted for failure to pay sound recording royalties).

36. See, e.g., The Songwriters Guild of America, *The Songwriters Guild of America Popular Songwriters Contract* ¶¶ 6(a), 8, 12 (1978), https://www.songwritersguild.com/sga-contract.

prevents cross-collateralization between the activities of the separate territories and reduces the risk of loss or withheld payments if a particular publisher experiences financial difficulty or has a dispute with the writer. On the other hand, entering and administering multiple publisher relationships in foreign territories requires greater dedicated resources, and unless a foreign entity has a presence in the United States making it subject to the jurisdiction of the courts in the United States, dispute resolution and enforcement may be difficult, expensive, or impossible.

Whichever option a songwriter selects, there are several key issues that should be addressed in the publishing agreement. First, if the publishing agreement permits the publisher to enter agreements with sub-publishers in territories other than the United States, the payments made to the songwriter for such foreign territories should be calculated by the music publisher on the basis of the payments made "from the source." Being paid "from the source" means that the songwriter's royalties are calculated on the basis of reported revenue from uses of the songwriter's compositions within the territory in which the revenue was earned—the source of the revenue. This language is necessary to prevent an unfortunately common situation where sales are earned in one territory, then reported to a publisher in another territory (which takes its cut), then reported to a publisher in another territory (which takes its cut), then reported to the entity reporting to the songwriter, by which time the royalty amount has been significantly diminished due to all the intermediary publishers' cuts. Such sequential arrangements are usually with related companies, which results in an overall benefit to the publisher at the artificially inflated expense of the songwriter.

Sub-publishers generally charge a fee of between 10 percent to 25 percent of collected funds for their services in their designated territory. This fee may increase with respect to revenue derived from local recordings of the composition the sub-publisher may arrange. Requiring the domestic publisher to calculate the songwriter's portion of payments from the sub-publisher "from the source" means the songwriter will receive their payment based on what the sub-publisher collects, less the sub-publisher's direct fee, not on any lesser amount that might result if such sub-publisher payments were to be channeled through a series of intermediate parties (perhaps affiliated with the U.S. publisher), each of which extracts its own fee and thereby creates a greatly diminished sum delivered to the domestic publisher from which it then might calculate the songwriter's portion.

Performance income generated in a foreign territory is treated the same way as in the United States: The amounts due to the songwriter and the publisher are allocated by the performing rights organization (PRO). The songwriter portion is remitted by the foreign PRO directly to its U.S. counterpart and then paid to the songwriter. The publisher portion can be either remitted to the local representative of the U.S.-based publishing company or paid to the U.S. counterpart PRO, which will then pay the publisher. Whether one elects to have performance income paid to a local sub-publisher or processed through interorganizational means may turn on whichever method results in quicker payment.

Another international consideration for publishers and songwriters is to ensure that any translations or other adaptations of compositions will be undertaken only with the consent of the songwriter. Consent protects the integrity of the composition, ensures that there is not a dilution of interest in the composition by those who may claim rights for the translation, and ensures that any new title to the translation is properly tied to the original composition for purposes of logging performances that result in revenue.

The songwriter will also want to ensure that approval must be obtained for any synchronization licenses or grant of rights for any grand or dramatic uses. Since the distribution of works using such rights (movies, plays, television shows) often extends across multiple countries, a publisher/songwriter will want to license such uses directly to protect the integrity of the composition and avoid paying sub-publisher fees for revenue generated by such works beyond the territory controlled by the sub-publisher. The publisher/songwriter will also be in the best position to understand how a use licensed in a foreign territory might impact the broader market for the composition or other anticipated or developing projects.

Exclusive Songwriter Agreements

The most common form of agreement between a music publishing company and a songwriter is the exclusive songwriter agreement. In essence, the exclusive songwriter agreement provides that all compositions created by the songwriter during the term of the songwriter agreement will be assigned to the publishing company. The agreement may also address compositions already in existence at the time the agreement is entered by assigning such compositions to the publishing company in the same way that a single song agreement might operate. The key difference with an exclusive songwriter agreement from a single song agreement is that the publishing company knows it will receive the full creative output of the writer for the term of the agreement.

Exclusive songwriter agreements are generally structured with an initial defined term, which can be renewed at the option of the publisher for a certain number of renewal periods of like duration. If the songwriter agreement is with a recording artist signed to a record company that is affiliated with the music publishing company, the term of the music publishing agreement, and perhaps other contractual terms, might be aligned with the term and other contractual terms of the recording agreement.

The exclusive songwriter agreement will generally describe the delivery requirements of the songwriter during each contract period, which is usually stated in terms of a minimum number of acceptable compositions. This number will be described with respect to songs written 100 percent by the songwriter, so if the songwriter delivers cowritten material, such material would satisfy the delivery obligation only to the extent of the songwriter's proportionate share of such collaborations. To be acceptable, the material must also be deemed reasonably satisfactory to the publisher.[37] In the event the required number of acceptable compositions is not delivered during the defined contractual period, the songwriter agreement generally will permit the publisher to extend the term of the agreement until such minimum number of compositions is delivered. If the songwriter is also a recording artist, the minimum composition delivery commitment might further require the commercial release (by either the songwriter or their record company) of the songwriter's own recordings of that songwriter's compositions.

The royalty compensation payable to a songwriter under an exclusive songwriter agreement will be the same as described for the single song agreement. The key additional compensation issue is advances. The exclusive nature of the songwriter agreement typically requires some form of guaranteed advance payment to the songwriter in consideration for the exclusive commitment the songwriter is giving to the publisher. The advance may take the form of an initial portion upon signing and additional portions as the songwriter's

37. For a discussion concerning the acceptability of compositions delivered by a songwriter under an exclusive songwriter agreement, see Richard Schulenberg, *Legal Aspects of the Music Industry* (New York: Billboard Books, 2005), 277–80.

delivery requirement is satisfied. Some exclusive songwriter agreements schedule regular periodic payments on a monthly or even bimonthly basis, akin to a paycheck. Merit advances for the commercial release of a recording, the achievement of a certain level of success of such recording (sales or chart position), or the receipt of certain awards might also be negotiated.

Additional terms of the exclusive songwriter agreement might address the fact that the agreement involves compositions not in being at the time the contract is entered. Managing the creative process between the publishing company and the songwriter for the creation of songs might involve a key person from the songwriter's perspective, the loss of whose relationship might cause the songwriter to want to avoid contract extensions. Also, because the scope of an exclusive songwriter agreement embraces all compositions created by the songwriter during the term of the agreement, irrespective of the commercial prospects of such songs, the songwriter might wish to have rights in compositions that remain unrecorded after a period of time revert to him or her. If such a reversion right were to be agreed to by the publisher, it would generally be subject to the reimbursement of any advances associated with such compositions.

The issues discussed earlier with respect to the single songwriter agreement concerning approvals, warranties and indemnifications, accounting, sub-publishing, and credit will also be present in the exclusive songwriter agreement.

Copublishing Agreements

Copublishing agreements generally arise under two circumstances. First, whenever two or more writers collaborate in the creation of a composition, a copublishing agreement can address their respective interests in the composition (unless they are both published by the same publishing company). The second copublishing circumstance occurs when a second publishing company—usually one with greater administrative resources than the first—obtains a co-ownership interest in the composition through an assignment of a partial interest from the original publisher. Why would either party enter such an agreement? From the perspective of the original publisher, such an agreement might involve a substantial advance payment from the second copublisher to the original publisher, or periodic guarantees, or both, that might not be available under an administration agreement. From the perspective of the acquiring publisher, such an agreement might be the best compromise the acquiring publisher can achieve with an original publisher unwilling to give up all its interests in the compositions.

Decision making concerning the use of a composition between co-owners begins with one of the principles of copyright law, which is that a co-owner of a copyright is permitted, absent a contractual obligation not to do so, to authorize nonexclusive uses of the rights in the co-owned copyright without the consent of the other co-owner(s). All the authorizing party must do is account to the other co-owners for their share of the proceeds from such nonexclusive uses. Many valuable rights in a composition, such as mechanical, synchronization, and dramatic rights licenses, can be issued on a nonexclusive basis. Therefore, it is important for co-owners to have an understanding between themselves concerning which rights, if any, an individual co-owner could exercise with a third party on a nonexclusive basis. Without such an arrangement, each co-owner could enter into agreements that conflict with agreements entered by the other co-owner, or cause the other co-owner to go into breach of certain warranties and representations the other co-owner has made in their nonexclusive agreements concerning the same composition(s). This issue does not arise with respect to the granting of exclusive rights, since such grants require the consent of all owners in order to be effective.

In the case of copublishing agreements between collaborators, the respective interests of the publishing companies generally reflect the allocation of interests agreed to by the collaborators. This may be fifty-fifty, or it may be some other allocation. Whatever the proportion, it applies to the full ownership of the song—both publisher and songwriter. The key issue to be determined in such an agreement (apart from the respective shares of the publishing proceeds each collaborator will receive) is administrative control—in other words, which of the co-owners will have the responsibility of issuing licenses and collecting proceeds. Each of the publishing companies could receive proceeds directly from their respective performing rights organizations, such as ASCAP or BMI, and could also receive their respective shares of mechanical license proceeds issued by Harry Fox Agency. However, the process by which other rights and licenses are administered should be resolved in the copublishing agreement.

In the event one of the co-owners does perform administrative functions, it normally would be entitled to receive an administration fee, perhaps 10 percent, in consideration for the services. Like a shareholder agreement in a closely held corporation, or an operating agreement in a limited liability company, a copublishing agreement could also address issues relating to the transfer of the interests in a composition held by either of the companies.

Assuming the parties to a copublishing agreement between co-composers reach terms concerning control and administration, it is important to understand structurally how the proceeds from the exploitation of the copublished compositions will flow. Conceptually, each publishing company will have some form of agreement with the co-composer of the composition from whom the publishing company derives its rights. In reality, there may not be a distinction between the songwriter and their sole proprietorship publisher, but in concept each publishing company is bound to an obligation to account to the songwriter from whom it derives its rights for the proceeds. Publisher A accounts to its songwriter and Publisher B accounts to its songwriter. The structure of this arrangement can be Illustrated like this:

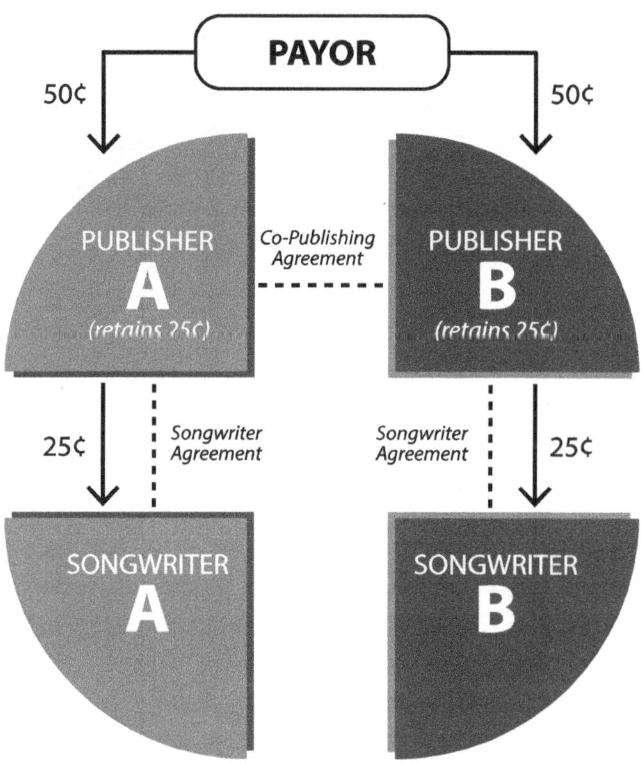

If one of the copublishers exclusively administers the composition for a fee (let us use a 10 percent administration fee as an example), the structure would be along these lines:

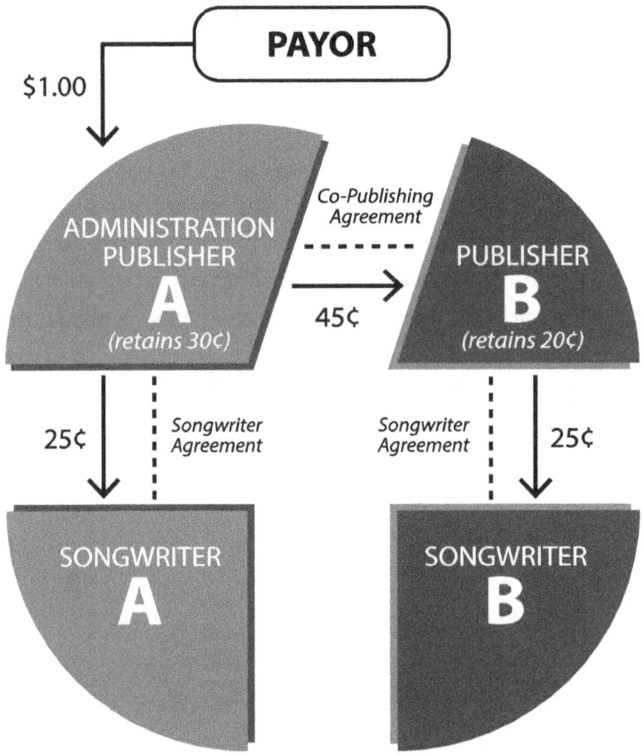

When the co-owner of a composition is not a collaborator, but a purchaser instead, the issues just discussed still pertain. However, unlike the copublishing arrangement between co-composers, which deals with 100 percent of the interests in the composition, the copublishing arrangement involving a purchaser is with respect to the publisher's interest in the composition only. Also, in most such circumstances, the purchaser will require that it exclusively administer all rights in the co-owned compositions and be compensated with the payment of an administration fee (generally 10 percent) in addition to the co-ownership share of the composition that it holds. Co-ownership allocations of the publisher's interests under these circumstances are generally fifty-fifty. This is the structure of the arrangement, assuming a 10 percent administration fee:

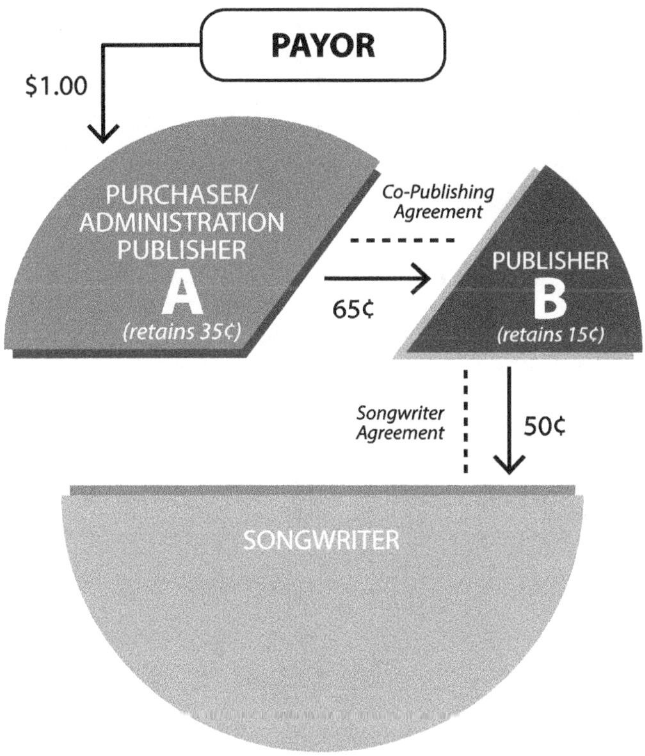

Note in this case that the publisher with the direct relationship with the composer remains obligated to account to and pay the composer, while the administrating copublisher is only required to account to and pay the other copublisher. The parties can agree to direct the administrating copublisher to pay the other copublisher and the composer for their respective portions of the proceeds derived from the song, which would look like this:

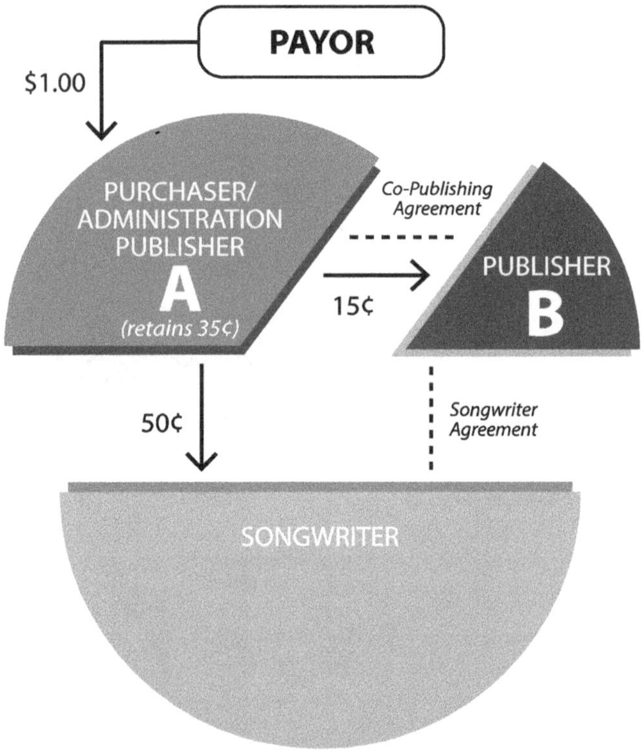

A copublishing agreement will also contain customary warranty and indemnification provisions from each party to the other and accounting and auditing provisions for the party providing administrative services. The agreement should also address decision making with respect to the selection of sub-publishers and the terms under which they may be engaged, whether adaptations of a composition may be made, and how litigation to enforce rights in the composition against infringers will be handled.

Administration Agreements

Administration agreements for music publishers are as they sound. The publishing administration company agrees, for a specific period of time, to provide publishing administration services such as the issuance of licenses, the collection of license proceeds, and the accounting of the resulting activity. Companies such as BMG Rights Management, Kobalt Music, Songtrust, and Sentric Music provide such services, generally to artist-owned publishing entities that do not require the promotional and placement services that a regular publishing company might undertake. The most likely candidate for an administration agreement is a singer/songwriter who performs and records their own material and, through the release and promotion of their recordings through a record company, is creating recognition, market demand, and revenue for their compositions. A catalog of well-known songs, or "standards," featured on recurrent recordings or often rerecorded without the need for promotional effort would also be a good candidate for an administration agreement. Even a music publishing company with a small administrative staff might avail itself of the services of an administrator, particularly with respect to the collection of publishing income generated in foreign territories where the publishing company may not have a presence.

Under the terms of an administration agreement, the administration company does not take ownership or co-ownership of the compositions. The company is simply engaged for a defined period of time to act on behalf of the publisher in providing the defined services. A typical fee arrangement may be 15 percent of the proceeds collected by the administrator. This is the structure of such an arrangement, assuming a 15 percent administration fee:

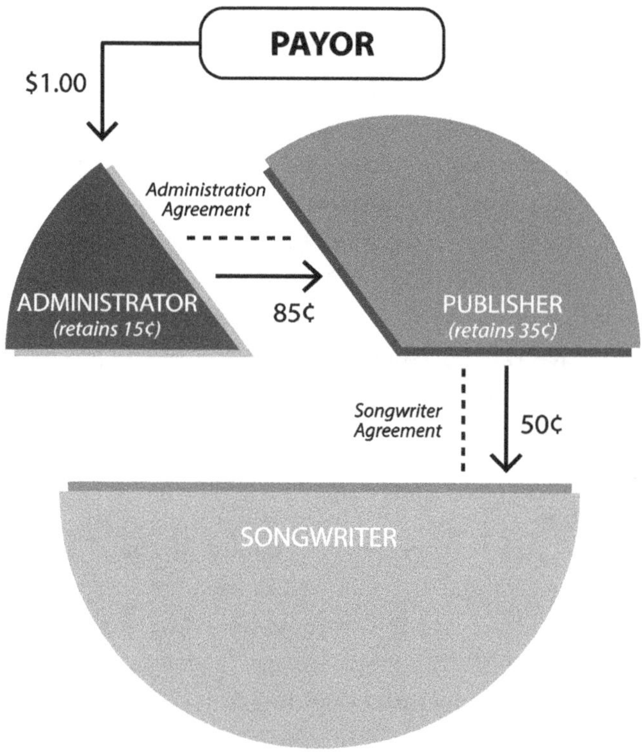

Some administration agreements further provide that, in the event the administrator is able to achieve a recording of one of the songs in the publisher's catalog, the fee arrangement for the proceeds of that recording might be higher. A typical period of time for an administration agreement to be in place is between three and five years. An important feature for any administration agreement is the scope of authority given the administrator to grant licenses for the use of the songs subject to the agreement. At a minimum, a publisher will want to approve any synchronization licenses, for the same reasons stated earlier with respect to songwriter and sub-publishing agreements.

Chapter 4

How Bands Are Organized and Financed, and Planning for the Eventual Breakup

Assembling a band may be fun, but maintaining a musical performing group over a period of time is tough business. First, there are the pressures that can doom any kind of business collaboration—different visions for the direction of the business; disputes concerning control or compensation; unequal contributions of commitment, effort, financing, or other resources; or incompatible temperaments. When one adds differing levels of musical ability, differing views on creative direction, the sacrifices necessary to succeed against extraordinary odds, the short windows of commercial opportunity that can open and close without regard to the personal feelings of the individuals involved, the corrupting influence of outsiders to the group, and the demands imposed on those who do succeed, it is little wonder that the makeup of musical groups is fluid.

Most musicians recognize these circumstances. Further, many musicians are required, as a condition of surviving as a performer, to play in more than one performing group, the members of each of which may change for reasons that may involve no more than availability. This is neither good nor bad, just the reality of the industry. For this reason, most musical groups are organized informally. The exact form of organization under such circumstances may not be declared, in which case a form of organization often results by default as a matter of law. A group may be the enterprise of a single individual who owns the identity associated with the group either as a sole proprietor or through an organized business entity. This person may be one of the performers in the group or may be a manager or agent. The group could also be simply an assembly of backup performers, engaged by the lead performer on a fee basis to rehearse, perform, and record with the lead performer. The group could also be an undeclared partnership, with revenue, expenses, and properties shared between the group members but without a more formal documentation of the arrangement.

At a certain point, a group may cohere and reach an understanding that a more formal form of business entity is desirable to establish grounds for moving ahead with shared commitment. Recommendations for the selection of one form of entity over another are beyond the scope of this book, given the great range of individual considerations that impact the selection of a form of organization and the differences between the laws of the various states concerning business entities. Whichever form of business entity is selected, though, the band-member owners will need an organizational document—a partnership agreement, a shareholder agreement, or an operating agreement. These documents will assist the band with issues surrounding the business of the band and are the subject of this chapter.

Treatment of Assets

The first key issue is the scope of the rights that will be handled by the entity. Is the entity intended to be the owner of the sound recordings produced by the group and/or the publisher of the musical compositions written by the members? Will the entity be the owner of the identity of the group for purposes of establishing and protecting trademark rights or authorizing the use of such trademark rights? How will personal appearance revenue be handled? And very importantly, what is the scope of the exclusive and nonexclusive rights that the entity has in the entertainment careers of the individual owners? Is the entity the means by which all activities of the group are facilitated and the payee of all earnings from such activities? May any of the members of the group make personal appearances apart from the group, or otherwise contract for their talent services in any way?[1] Or are there certain areas that are left within the control of the individual members, who may personally retain any compensation resulting from such activities? For example, may individual members perform, write, or record with other performers and retain whatever earnings that might result, or engage in other expressive activities unrelated to music, such as book publishing or acting, and retain compensation for that?

These questions are critical for several reasons. First, reaching an agreement on terms helps establish shared expectations among band members that can reduce disagreements in the future. But even more important is the fact that written agreements are necessary if the entity is to be the owner of certain works for which copyright, trademark, and identity rights may exist. Those written agreements may include employment agreements, work-for-hire arrangements, or assignments. If such agreements are not in place, the entity may not have the ownership interest the band-member owners may believe exist and rely upon. Further, if the group is going to expend resources for purposes of preparing to present personal appearances, and commit to such personal appearances, the group members should be committed to performing at such personal appearances by means of an employment agreement. Finally, defining the scope of rights held by the entity, and specifically carving out certain areas that are retained by the individual owners, will assist those owners in securing individual arrangements for the retained rights and properties.

The likelihood of a band breakup needs to be taken into account when deciding which rights and properties are to be lodged with the entity. In that respect, the agreement acts as a form of prenuptial agreement. For example, if the entity is intended to hold all rights in the group name and

1. For descriptions of the fallout affecting personal appearances caused by a leaving member, see Billy Shields, "*Pretty Ricky Leaving Member Spurs Litigation*," *Entertainment Law & Finance*, February 2008; Jordan M. Whitford, "A 'Journey' Through Band Agreements," *43 Hastings Communications and Entertainment Law Journal* 189 (2021), https://repository.uchastings.edu/hastings_comm_ent_law_journal/vol43/iss2/4.

identity, then the rights of the then-current members of the band to use the name and identity of the band following a breakup should be addressed. If a band member leaves or is expelled, may the remaining members continue using the name, and does the answer differ depending on whether the band member left or was expelled? If the remaining members may continue using the name, how many original members of the group need to remain before the name has to be abandoned? Is there any key member who must be an active member of the group in order for the group to use the name, or who could use the name without any of the other band members? May leaving or expelled members of the group regroup at some point and begin using the name again? Or is the name simply something that belongs to the entity and, consequently, whoever ends up owning the entity?[2] If any registrations of a trademark or service mark have been undertaken, who will be the successor to the ownership of the registrations? What about URLs and social media site addresses—in whose name will such properties be acquired, and is there any understanding about the ownership and maintenance of such properties in the event of a dissolution? History is replete with disputes between former bandmates who organized their business structure either poorly or not formally at all.[3]

---

2. Through the passage of time, some groups eventually end up with no original members, or no members who performed in the recordings that are famously associated with the group. Efforts have been undertaken on the state level in more than thirty states to protect consumer interests by prohibiting misrepresentations concerning the authenticity of live performers appearing under the names of famous group recording artists. See, e.g., New Jersey Truth in Music Act, N.J. STAT. ANN. § 2A:32B–2 (2007); False, Deceptive, or Misleading Advertisement of Live Musical Performances, FLA. STAT. § 817.4115 (2007); Unfair Trade Practices, S.C. CODE ANN. § 39–5–38 (2012); Hawaii Truth in Music Advertising Act, HAW. REV. STAT. § 481T-1 (2020); *Singer Mgmt. Consultants, Inc. v. Milgram*, 650 F.3d 223 (3d Cir. 2011).

3. See, e.g., Eriq Gardner, "Third Eye Blind Ordered to Pay $448K to Former Guitarist," *Hollywood Reporter*, October 2, 2013, https://www.hollywoodreporter.com/business/business-news/third-eye-blind-ordered-pay-650001/; RJ Cubarrubia, "Scott Weiland Countersues Stone Temple Pilots," *Rolling Stone*, June 3, 2013, https://www.rollingstone.com/music/music-news/scott-weiland-countersues-stone-temple-pilots-97949/; Eriq Gardner, "Expelling Band Members Isn't Easy: Gogol Bordello and Ariel Pink's Legal Disputes," *Billboard*, July 30, 2013, https://www.billboard.com/music/music-news/expelling-band-members-isnt-easy-gogol-bordello-and-ariel-pinks-5214626/; Kurt Dahl, "Band Name Dispute: Who Can Use the Name?" *Lawyer Drummer*, August 14, 2018, https://lawyerdrummer.com/tag/band-name-dispute/; Matt Friedlander, "Journey's Jonathan Cain and Neal Schon Resolve Legal Dispute over Band's Financial Issues," *American Songwriter*, https://americansongwriter.com/

Whether the band's entity is the owner of music publishing rights to compositions composed by group members must be carefully considered in light of the potential period such rights may be of value. The length of time a composition will be protected by copyright—the lifetime of the composer, plus seventy years—necessarily far surpasses the period any of the band members will be collaborating and/or personally operating their entity. Some groups approach this issue by having each member retain their interests in compositions with their own individual publishing companies. These individual publishing companies may then enter copublishing agreements for collaborative songs. Other groups grant their jointly owned entity the publishing right in songs written by individual members in an effort to recognize the value non-composing members may add to a song by helping arrange compositions, contributing key instrumental flourishes, or performing the compositions in personal appearances. The individual member-composers would retain 100 percent of the songwriter's share of the compositions, and all the group members would share the publisher's share of the compositions in accordance with their interest in the overall entity. If the group agrees to share publishing interests in some manner with non-composing group members, there is a third option, which is to lodge the compositions in a separate company owned by the group and dedicated solely to publishing, with the songwriter retaining their full songwriter share. In that manner, the interests of the group members in the compositions are undisturbed regardless of the makeup of the band entity generally, which may be owned by different people over time for reasons that should not affect the ownership or treatment of publishing revenue as originally established.

Recordings produced by the group using group resources are generally owned by the group's business entity. Post-breakup, if the business entity retains any interest in recordings, there may be issues concerning how such recordings may be used. For example, the group may have produced a number of demonstration recordings that were not meant for commercial release. May such recordings be released by whoever eventually succeeds

---

journeys-jonathan-cain-and-neal-schon-resolve-legal-dispute-over-bands-financial-issues/ (last updated Aug. 29, 2024); Christian Holub, "Lindsey Buckingham Sues Fleetwood Mac After Getting Kicked Out of Band," *Entertainment Weekly*, October 12, 2018, https://ew.com/music/2018/10/12/lindsey-buckingham-fleetwood-mac-lawsuit/.

to the interests of the business entity? If they may be released, who may (and who must) be the credited artist for such recordings? A former group member may not want to be individually identified as the credited artist, particularly if they go on to success in another arrangement. In like manner, certain group members may object to the use of recordings in which they perform in connection with advertising for certain products, services, or causes, or for premiums. There may also be obligations to accord credit for producing or otherwise contributing to the production of such recordings. What will be the status of artwork (drawings, graphics, and photographs) for the packaging of sound recordings that may have been released by the band, which is subject to its own claims of copyright?[4] Who will be the custodian of original multitrack tapes or files of recordings? Finally, may the group's recordings be remixed or otherwise changed in any way without the participation of each group member in the decision-making process for such changes?

Other asset categories that should be addressed include both tangible and intangible properties. For example, will the ownership of instruments be vested in the group's jointly owned company, or will the instruments be individually owned? Does it make any difference if company resources are used to acquire or maintain the instruments? What about other equipment, such as sound, lights, vehicles, or other staging equipment—is there any understanding about how such equipment will be distributed in the event of a dissolution? Will any such equipment be part of the capital contribution of a member, and if so, will that member have the right to reclaim such equipment? Also, the business of the band will develop a significant amount of data that can be valuable, such as email lists and social media followers. Is the collection of such data by the business done so pursuant to policies that permit the data to be shared among band members in the event of a dissolution?

---

4. *Zamoyski v. Fifty-Six Hope Road Music Ltd., Inc.*, 718 F. Supp. 2d 128 (D. Mass. 2010); *Smith v. Trans-Siberian Orchestra*, 689 F. Supp. 2d 1310 (M.D. Fla. 2010).

Other Band Agreement Provisions

Decision making within the band's entity is similar to the decision-making process in any business entity. The organizational agreement should identify the voting percentages that are required for decision making, any category of decisions that might require a greater percentage of votes (or even unanimity), and any possible key person votes that may be required for particular decisions. Voting may be equal or follow the percentage of ownership interests in the entity, which could be equal or disproportionate. The issue of distributions may also be tied to how the voting structure is set up. Compensation may be distributed equally, in amounts equal to disproportionate ownership interests among the members, or in different amounts, depending on the source or type of revenue. Each group will have its own range of competing interests to resolve in a structure that works for them.

A group's organizational agreement should also address issues concerning the makeup of the group. For example, under what circumstances may a member be expelled or added, and what are the consequences of a person quitting the group. Standard shareholder, partnership, and operating agreements generally deal with grounds for expulsion, and, while an agreement for an entity that is a musical group would likely involve those as well, membership in a musical group may present additional, more particular grounds in recognition of the special requirements of artistic collaboration. Under such circumstances, the group members could agree to an expulsion without cause with the affirmative vote of a percentage of the ownership. The risk of expulsion under such circumstances would be one each of the members would take, and the gravity of the risk would depend on the percentage vote required to expel a member and the valuation of each member's interest in the event of such expulsion without cause were to occur.

Valuation of a group member's interest in the event of certain transfers is a key provision in partnership, shareholder, and operating agreements. Standard shareholder, partnership, and LLC operating agreements generally bar any voluntary transfer of an owner's interest without first giving the entity and/or the other owners a right to purchase the interest. The method of valuing the interest under such circumstances would generally be the price offered by a third party. Valuation in the event of an involuntary transfer, however, may vary, depending on the circumstances of the transfer. For example, valuation in connection with a foreclosure action involving the owner may be different than valuation triggered by a divorce action. Valuation in the event of a member's death, disability, or expulsion without cause may be established closer to actual value, which may be agreed to periodically by the members as either a set amount or a certain multiple of a financial feature of the entity, such as net taxable income or gross revenue. Valuation under such circumstances might also be determined by an appraisal process if the parties cannot come to an agreement at the time. Valuation could be established in the form of either (1) a set amount, which takes into account projected future revenue from the assets held by the entity, reduced to present value, (2) contingent compensation based upon a certain percentage of revenue or earning over a defined period, or (3) a combination of both.

Valuation in the event of an expulsion for cause (which would typically be defined in the agreement) may be an entirely different matter, which may relate to an accounting calculation such as book value. Whatever may be the method of valuation, or the amount paid to the selling owner, the payout by the purchasing party could also be scheduled to avoid cash flow issues, which payments from the former group member's perspective should be secured with a security interest in the remaining assets.

Leaving Members and Recording Agreements

Recording agreements generally seek to obtain the exclusive recording services of the members of a group, both as a group and as individual performers apart from the group. Therefore, solo records by individual group members will generally be subject to the claims of the record company. This same circumstance comes into play if a group is signed to a recording agreement at the time one of its members leaves. Group recording agreements frequently contain provisions obligating each individual signatory to remain as a recording artist with the record company even if they are no longer a member of the group. The leaving member provisions of a recording agreement will frequently spell out the terms applicable to the leaving member, such as length of time the original recording agreement will apply to them as an individual artist, the number of recordings they are required to deliver as an individual artist, and their applicable royalty rate as an individual artist (which is often less than the rate payable to the group as a whole).[5] To erase any doubt about the enforceability of the leaving member provisions of a group agreement, and to address the particular circumstances that may exist at the time a group member becomes a leaving member, it is not uncommon for the record company to enter a new agreement with the leaving member, should it wish to retain the leaving member as an artist.

There are several implications for both the leaving member and the group. First, the status of the royalty accounts should be clearly delineated for: (1) the group with the leaving member included, (2) the group without the leaving member included, and (3) the leaving member individually (without the group).[6] The leaving member does not want to have their royalty account cross-collateralized with the royalty account for the group's recordings. Since the leaving member is not in control of any of the costs incurred by or on behalf of the group going forward that might become recoupable under the recording agreement, they will not want royalties otherwise payable to them to be applied to the recoupment of the group's unrecouped account, even if such royalties were only applied to costs associated with recordings in which the leaving artist performed. In like manner, the remaining members of the group may feel the opposite on one or more of the foregoing points, and will not want any costs associated with the leaving member to be associated with their account. Further, the leaving member should arrange for their proportionate share of any royalty income from the group's account to be paid directly to them rather than to any group entity in which they may not have any further ownership interest.

Financing

Financing a group's music business is often a cloudy, ad hoc undertaking, with inexact contributions made to the entity in combinations of cash,

5. See, e.g., *The Gordy Co. v. Mary Jane Girls, Inc.*, 1989 WL 149290 (S.D.N.Y. 1989).

6. For an example of the consequences of not clarifying how royalties will be handled for leaving group members, see *Mitchell v. Faulkner*, 2013 WL 150254 (S.D.N.Y. 2013).

properties, and services. It is a beautiful thing if the band members agree that their contributions are satisfactory for the interests they have obtained in their business. Of course, it doesn't always work out that way, and a lot of resources can be expended unraveling who owes what to whom if the business unravels or fails. Also, the consequences for each of the band members can be different, depending on the nature of their respective contributions.

Group Member Capitalization

If a group is going to be self-financed, it is first important for the members to understand whether their cash contributions are capital contributions in consideration of their ownership interests in the group or are a loan, to be paid back in some manner. Of course, cash can be contributed to the business of the group either in consideration of ownership or as a loan, and financial planning may recommend one form over another. The key point is that the group members should understand, note, and accept the distinction.

In the event services are provided in consideration of an ownership interest in the business, the value of the interest will be considered income to the service provider as compensation for the services provided. From an accounting perspective, the value of an interest in a recently organized band may be insignificant enough that any reportable income to the service provider could be disregarded. However, gaining an interest in an established group in return for services may produce a different result. With respect to equipment and other physical property, the issue will be the same as with cash—is ownership of the equipment being assigned to the business or is it being offered on loan?

If musical compositions or sound recordings are being contributed to the business, it is important to note that ownership or possession of the material object in which a sound recording may be embodied, such as recording tape or a digital file, does not create ownership of the copyright interest in such sound recording,[7] nor does the transfer of any such material object transfer any copyright interest.[8] An assignment of copyright interest in compositions

---

7. *Forward v. Thorogood*, 985 F.2d 604 (1st Cir. 1993).

8. 17 U.S.C. § 202 (2011); *Polygram Records, Inc. v. Legacy Ent. Grp.*, LLC, 205 S.W.3d 439 (Tenn. Ct. App. 2006).

or sound recordings, to be effective, must be in writing and signed by the copyright owner.[9] Further, filing of the assignment in the Copyright Office will be constructive notice to the world of the transfer if the assignment references a registered work. If the work is unregistered, then a filing will not give a priority, as there is no constructive notice. Under those circumstances, the Uniform Commercial Code (UCC) and the particular state law will control.[10] Section 205(d) of the Copyright Act identifies the priority of claims with respect to assignments.[11]

Outside Financing

Outside financing for a musical performing group is generally difficult to obtain, given the significant risks involved with such business. Nevertheless, financial support may be available to a group in the form of patronage, investments, or loans.

Patronage

Patronage is a centuries old form of support for creative endeavors. In its contemporary mode, patronage may simply be a gift in the form of the payment of funds to a group, or providing funds for or access to services such as rehearsal or recording facilities. The primary legal issue that might arise in connection with such support is whether there is clarity concerning the actual status of the payments or the provision of services. It is not unknown for a group to accept what it understands is gratuitous support, only to encounter a demand for repayment, or a claim of ownership, at a later date. Another form of patronage may be a presale of a product, which generally may be a recording in some form. For example, the performer

9. 17 U.S.C. § 204 (2011).

10. *In re World Auxiliary Power Co.*, 305 F.3d 1120 (9th Cir. 2002).

11. 17 U.S.C. § 205(d) (2011), "Priority between Conflicting Transfers.—As between two conflicting transfers, the one executed first prevails if it is recorded, in the manner required to give constructive notice under subsection (c), within one month after its execution in the United States or within two months after its execution outside the United States, or at any time before recordation in such manner of the later transfer. Otherwise the later transfer prevails if recorded first in such manner, and if taken in good faith, for valuable consideration or on the basis of a binding promise to pay royalties, and without notice of the earlier transfer."

Sam Phillips once offered a series of recordings released over a period of time on a subscription basis from her website.[12]

Another form of patronage made possible by online tools that is particularly well suited to musical artists is the crowdfunding ability provided by websites such as Kickstarter, Indiegogo, Patreon, and PledgeMusic.[13] In essence, each of these services permits musical performers to post a description of a project (an album, a tour, an equipment purchase) for which they are seeking funding, the amount of funding they are seeking, and the form of consideration that will be provided to those who make pledges. Akin to a pledge drive by a not-for-profit organization (but without the charitable contribution tax treatment for the contributor), the form of premium given to contributors will vary by level of contribution. A musical group seeking funding for a recording project may, for example, give each contributor a copy of the release when it is completed, and increase the value of the premium all the way up to a live personal appearance for contributors at the top end. The contributions provided by the supporters are not an investment, as the supporters are not obtaining any ownership interest in the group, the project, or any intellectual property resulting from the project, nor are they loans that must be repaid; but they will be deemed prepayments to the group and, for accounting and tax purposes, counted as revenue to the individual or group making the offer. Multiple crowdfunded projects in the music industry have topped the $1 million mark.[14] The commissions charged by current crowdfunding services generally range from 5 percent to 10 percent. Even some performing groups with strong existing

---

12. Randy Lewis, "For Musicians, Economy Is the Mother of Invention," *L.A. Times*, May 9, 2010, https://www.latimes.com/entertainment/la-ca-0509-sam-phillips-20100509-story.html.

13. The federal Jumpstart Our Business Startups (JOBS) Act of 2012 (Pub. L. No. 112–106 (2012)) contains a section permitting "crowdfunding" by means of equity or debt offerings of not more than $1 million. The regulations particularizing the JOBS Act were promulgated in 2016. 17 Fed. Reg. 200–274 (May 16, 2016).

14. See, e.g., *The Voyager Golden Record*, Kickstarter, https://www.kickstarter.com/projects/ozmarecords/voyager-golden-record-40th-anniversary-edition (last accessed September 2025) *Theatre Is Evil: The Album, Art Book and Tour*, Kickstarter, https://www.kickstarter.com/projects/amandapalmer/amanda-palmer-the-new-record-art-book-and-tour (last accessed September 2025).

fan bases (and, therefore, presumably without the need for crowdfunding) have adopted the crowdfunding financing model for offerings made through their own websites and other platforms.[15]

Investors

Certain investors are attracted to the idea of investing in performers, or in certain projects associated with a performer. Terms for such arrangements lie within a broad range and within an environment in which information about the music industry as a whole and the experience of individual performers is often imprecise and anecdotal. Consequently, musicians and producers sell into a market where investor perceptions have been forged to reflect the belief that music investments are risky ventures. Music financing also must be judged on the economic merits of a project, since there are no significant tax incentives to cause an investor to invest, regardless of the likely success of the project. Investors also know success in the music industry is dependent upon not only public taste, which is unpredictable and subject to change without warning or explanation, but also unpredictable intervening events, such as a live event calamity or scandal involving the musical performer or group. Also, since the performer controls the circumstances of how their project is developed and marketed and the investor does not, the investor views the risks of production and financial return as greater than the performer does. Further, whatever business history there may be for a musical performer or group in a traditional form (balance sheet, income statement, management stability and performance, etc.) that an investor might investigate as part of their due diligence, this information is of lesser utility for an investment in a music project. As a result, an investor will generally end up putting their faith not in traditional investment viability indicators but, rather, in the investor's assessment of the creative and personal skills and reliability of the performer and their team to develop and produce the project.

15. See, e.g., Paul Resnikoff, "Indie Band Figures Out How to Raise Money Without Using Kickstarter . . . ," *Digital Music News*, September 14, 2012, https://www.digitalmusicnews.com/2012/09/14/kickstarter-2/.

The following are some key points of negotiation of an investor agreement, which are driven in their development by the foregoing dynamics:

- Amount of investment and how and when it will be contributed
- Any preconditions to payments if made in tranches
- Use of proceeds, for example, to fund a recording or tour, engage in a marketing plan, and so on
- Scope of interest obtained (and exclusions therefrom), for example, co-ownership of property developed with investment or contractual right to receive portion of revenue generated by property (If the latter, the duration of the period payments would be made.)
- Any cap on returns
- Any requirements for the payment of additional funds
- Any creative control given to the investor
- Accounting and auditing provisions
- Any decision-making involvement regarding career direction or transactions for the talent or the results of the talent's services.[16]

Loans

From an investor perspective, if the investment takes the form of a loan rather than an equity or ownership position, the loan should be secured by a security interest in the copyright and trademark interests in the group

16. For an interesting approach to fan investment offered to fans of the band Queensrÿche, which sought to raise $2 million from fans at a minimum of $50,000 per fan investment, see Christa Titus, "Wanna Buy a Piece of Queensrÿche? Now You Can," *Billboard*, November 3, 2014, https://www.billboard.com/pro/queensryche-equity/. To a similar end, online platforms like Royalty Exchange and SongVest, respectively, offer a marketplace for musicians to market investments, in or the outright sale of, the royalty streams of designated songs and/or sound recordings. "About Royalty Exchange," *Royalty Exchange*, https://www.royaltyexchange.com/about-royalty-exchange (last accessed September 2025); "How It Works," *SongVest*, https://www.songvest.com/how-it-works (last accessed September 2025); and Nate Rau, "Investors Betting Big on Music," *The Tennessean* (December 14, 2017), https://www.tennessean.com/story/money/2017/12/14/investors-betting-music/952522001/; Samantha Hissong, "Kings of Leon Will Be the First Band to Release an Album as an NFT," *Rolling Stone* (March 3, 2021), https://www.rollingstone.com/pro/news/kings-of-leon-when-you-see-yourself-album-nft-crypto-1135192/; Dan McCrum, "David Bowie Bonds: The Rise and Fall of the First Music Investment," *Financial Times* (January 11, 2016), https://www.ft.com/content/6b4839dd-0539-34c4-bb1d-0edf95255d72.

or performer. For copyright interests that have been registered, the security interest should be recorded in the Copyright Office to be perfected and should reference the copyright registration(s).[17] For unregistered works of authorship, the UCC and the applicable state law where the debtor is located will control.[18] With respect to federally registered trademarks, there is not a requirement that a security interest be recorded in the United States Patent and Trademark Office (USPTO) to perfect a security interest.[19] Trademarks are considered general intangibles and are controlled by the UCC and the applicable state law where the debtor is located. Nevertheless, it may be advisable to record a notice of security interest with the USPTO as a matter of general notice.

Settlements

In the event a group disbands or one of the members leaves, the best practice is to document the terms under which the group members have settled the outstanding issues between them, to reduce the likelihood of future disputes and litigation.[20] In the event the attorney has represented the group, and not the individual members of the group, the attorney may document the settlement terms as collectively directed by the group. However, individual group members may nevertheless perceive the attorney as bound by a requirement to represent their individual interests as continued band members.[21] This would certainly be the case if the attorney were to participate in strategizing with certain group members about how to expel other

17. 17 U.S.C. § 205(c) (2011).

18. *In re World Auxiliary Power Co.*, 305 F.3d 1120 (9th Cir. 2002).

19. *In re Roman Cleanser*, 225 U.S.P.Q.140, 142 (Bankr. E.D. Mich. 1984), aff'd, 802 F.2d 207 (6th Cir. 1986).

20. See generally R. Robin McDonald, "Sugarland Suit Offers Look at Dynamics of Litigating Intra-Band Disputes," *Entertainment Law & Finance*, December 2010; Conn Kavanaugh, "Backstage Pass: What Lawsuit Pleadings Tell Us About Life in a Rock and Roll Band," *JD Supra*, May 1, 2023, https://www.jdsupra.com/legalnews/backstage-pass-what-lawsuit-pleadings-7099321/.

21. See, e.g., *Adler v. Manatt, Phelps, Phillips & Kantor, L.A.* Supr. Ct. BC O53076 (Apr. 1992) (former member of group Guns N' Roses sued the group's law firm for malpractice in connection with group settlement agreement).

members. Attorneys are best advised, when confronted with contested claims between band members, to refer individual members to other counsel for independent representation.[22]

A settlement agreement will take into account the band assets mentioned earlier: recordings, compositions, equipment, band identity, royalty streams, and data. Additional items of value could include insurance claims or proceeds, existing infringement claims, upcoming performance commitments, inventories of recordings, merchandise, websites, social media addresses, unpublished works, and so-called pipeline income, or income that has been earned but is in the hands of third parties as it moves through various accounting relationships. A non-disparagement provision is also a recommended practice, although its observance may not be respected. Further, provision should be made with respect to decision making about future exploitation of works controlled by the group. If any group members will no longer participate in decision making concerning such exploitation, specific credit obligations should be included in the settlement agreement to ensure proper credit is accorded all group members going forward.

22. For a further discussion around ethical considerations for the attorney representing a band comprised of multiple members, see Chapter 12.

Chapter 5
How Record Companies and Producers Work

Recording agreements for artists are generally the first thing people think about when the topic of the music business is discussed. Achieving the status of a recording artist, sometimes on a particularly prestigious record company, has historically been the goal of many musicians and performers. This vision has been shaped by the promises of financial, artistic, and social success associated with being featured on a sound recording. Yet, stories of artistic and financial loss, ruin, and frustration as a result of dealings between record companies and recording artists are almost as common.[1] There is validity to each of these characterizations.

The functions of a record company generally fall into five areas: (1) discovery (identifying performers, songs, and cultural developments); (2) capital (providing the resources required to engage creative personnel and create sound recordings); (3) production (operating and staffing the recording studios where sound recordings for the company are produced);

1. It has been commonly said that of every twenty major label recording agreement signings, only one results in measurable success. See generally Tim Ingham, "Can Kobalt's AWAL Rewrite the Rules of A&R?" *Music Business Worldwide*, July 9, 2018, https://www.musicbusinessworldwide.com/can-kobalts-awal-rewrite-the-rules-of-ar/.

(4) distribution (providing the means by which recordings can be purchased or otherwise used for value received); and (5) promotion (creating demand for the recordings and the recording artists). While these functions have historically been beyond the resources of most individual musicians, technological developments have created tools that make each of these functions increasingly available outside the traditional record company relationship. In fact, with respect to production, few record companies own and operate their own recording studios today. Nevertheless, record companies continue to play a key role in the development and success of musical artists.

Today, recording agreements are not always with the company that ultimately owns and releases the recordings produced under the agreement. It is common for recordings to be produced by musicians under contract to independent producers and then delivered to the record companies under the terms of producer/record company production agreements. We will address the features of each of these arrangements, but initially we will describe the structure and typical terms found in a direct recording agreement between a performing artist and record company.

Nature of the Relationship

The recording agreement, at its most basic level, will generally be for the services of the musician as a recording artist for the production of sound recordings. The relationship may be exclusive for a defined period, or it could be nonexclusive and related to a specific project only. The most important issue is one of copyright, and whether the relationship between the musician and the company is one that would be characterizable under the Copyright Act as being "for hire."

As discussed earlier, the implications of whether a contribution to a copyrightable work (in this case a sound recording) is made as a work for hire are very important. If the contributions are deemed to be a work made for hire, the copyright in the sound recording will arise automatically with the record company[2] and will not be subject to any right of later termination

2. 17 U.S.C. § 201(b) (2011).

by the musician. The term of copyright protection for a work made for hire is the shorter of 95 years from publication or 120 years from creation.[3] However, if the contributions are deemed to have been assigned to the record company, the copyright in the sound recording will arise automatically with the musician and, in such case, the musician can reclaim their interest in the copyright during a window of time tied to the thirty-five-year anniversary of the assignment.[4] An almost universal provision of recording agreements is a section that describes the contributions of the recording services of the musician subject to the agreement as being works made for hire. Most agreements will also provide some form of failsafe language to the effect that, if the contributions are at any point found to not constitute works made for hire, the musician nevertheless assigns to the record company all interests in the copyright in such contributions. In addition to the contributions of musicians, courts have said that the contribution of a recording engineer, coproducer, and mixer fall within ambit of sound recording authorship.[5] Even the spontaneous contribution of a guest at a recording session has resulted in a claim of rights.[6] Why is work for hire an issue for sound recordings?

Section 101 of the Copyright Act defines two circumstances under which a work may be deemed to be a work made for hire.[7] First, a work produced within the scope of the employment of the creator will be deemed a work made for hire and owned by the employer. Whether one is an "employee" will depend principally on the general common law test of agency and control.[8] A sound recording produced by an in-house employee of a commercial

3. 17 U.S.C. § 302(c) (2011).
4. 17 U.S.C. § 203 (2011).
5. *Diamond v. Gillis*, 357 F. Supp. 2d 1003 (E.D. Mich. 2005); *JCW Invs. Inc. v. Novelty Inc.*, 289 F. Supp. 2d 1023, 1032 (N.D. Ill. 2003) ("A record producer may be an author when he or she is responsible for setting up the session, capturing and electronically processing the sounds, and compiling and editing them to make a final sound recording"); see *Systems XIX, Inc. v. Parker*, 30 F. Supp. 2d 1225, 1228 (N.D. Cal. 1998) (quoting H.R. Rep. No. 94–1476, 94th Cong., 2d Sess. 56 (1976)); see also the dissent in *Brown v. Flowers*, 196 Fed. Appx. 178 (4th Cir. 2006), which discusses the creative role of a recording engineer in the production of sound recordings.
6. *Ulloa v. Universal Music & Video Distrib.*, 303 F. Supp. 2d 409 (S.D.N.Y. 2004).
7. 17 U.S.C. § 101 (2011).
8. *Community for Creative Non-Violence v. Reid*, 490 U.S. 730 (1989).

jingle production company is an example of a sound recording that would fall within the first circumstance of the work-for-hire definition. A person may be an employee even if their payment is in the form of royalties (or an advance on royalties).[9]

Next, a work may be one made for hire if it is specially ordered or commissioned to be created by a nonemployee pursuant to a written agreement with the creator identifying the work as one made for hire. With respect to the second circumstance, the Copyright Act is very specific about which types of works by independent contractors are capable of being deemed works made for hire. Unfortunately, for record companies, the list of specifically identified works that may be specially ordered or commissioned as works made for hire that was originally included in the 1976 Copyright Act did not include sound recordings. In 1999, Congress amended the Copyright Act to specifically include sound recordings within the classes of works that could be created within a work-for-hire arrangement.[10] After a firestorm of dissent from the artistic community, however, this revision was repealed retroactively, without prejudice to either artists or the record companies.[11]

Recordings produced under agreements signed in or after 1978 will be subject to the conflicting interpretations of the work-for-hire provisions contained in those agreements by the record companies and the recording artists who are parties to those agreements. The recording artists may seek termination of the record companies' rights to the recordings on the grounds that such works are not valid works made for hire and the record companies would likely counter that the sound recordings are valid works made for hire and thus the termination right does not apply. However, one court has held that recordings delivered between 1972 (when sound recordings first were protected by copyright in the United States) and 1978 (when the Copyright Act of 1976 became effective) were works made for hire.[12] Given that a termination, if valid, occurs thirty-five years following

9. *Fred Fisher Music Co. v. Leo Feist, Inc.*, 55 F. Supp. 359 (S.D.N.Y. 1944).

10. Intellectual Property and Communications Omnibus Reform Act of 1999, Pub. L. No. 106–113, app. I, § 1011(d), 113 Stat. 1501, 1501A-554 (1999).

11. Work Made for Hire and Copyright Corrections Act of 2000, Pub. L. No. 106–379, 114 Stat. 1444 (2000).

12. *Fifty-Six Hope Road Music Ltd. v. UMG Recordings, Inc.*, 2010 WL 3564258 (S.D.N.Y. 2010).

the granting of rights, the first actual terminations began to occur in 2013 (although the Copyright Act permitted notices of intent to terminate up to ten years prior to actual termination and many notices of termination were served before that year).[13]

Parties

Loan-Out Corporations

The signatory on a recording agreement is not always an individual musician. First, the musician may have formed a business entity through which they provide their personal entertainment services. This entity is typically referred to as a loan-out company. If the loan-out company signs the recording agreement, the individual musician will sign an accompanying "inducement" letter. The inducement letter essentially states that the individual musician agrees to provide all the services required of the loan-out company under the recording agreement and acknowledges that the musician will look to the loan-out company exclusively for all compensation to be received by the musician for their services under the recording agreement.

When a group is the signatory, they may also have organized a loan-out company for the delivery of their collective entertainment services, in which case the same inducement letter would come into play for each of the owners of the loan-out company. If the group has not organized a loan-out company, the recording agreement may be another moment of truth in the life of the group—will all the group members be signatories, or only a subset? From the record company point of view, it will want to contractually obligate every contributor to the production of the sound recordings

13. See generally Jay Rosenthal, "As 2013 Approaches, Artist Termination Right Faces Record Label's Work-for-Hire Argument," *Entertainment Law & Finance*, March 2008. For thorough discussions of practical issues relating to recapture and challenges posed by the law as enacted, see Joe Bogdan, "The Little Law That Could (and Probably Will): Section 203 Copyright Recapture Terminations in America," *American Journal of Arts Management*, November 2015; Dylan Gilbert, Meredith Rose, and Alisa Valentin, *Making Sense of the Termination Right: How the System Fails Artists and How to Fix It*, Public Knowledge, December 2019, https://publicknowledge.org/wp-content/uploads/2021/11/Making-Sense-of-the-Termination-Right-1.pdf.

to be produced under the agreement. However, it may make its offer to fewer than all the current members of the group for any number of reasons. Whether the group goes ahead under such circumstances may depend on the agreements between the group members existing at that time.

There have over time been changes to the tax effects upon artists pertaining to their use of loan-out corporations, most notably in California. In 2019, California enacted its Assembly Bill 5 (AB 5) to codify a 2018 California Supreme Court decision finding that workers are presumed employees unless the hiring entity satisfies a strict, three-pronged, independent contractor test.[14] Despite the years since the enactment of AB 5, because of both some vagueness in the law itself and its silence on certain issues well-settled in related case law pertaining to loan-out corporations in the entertainment industry, it remains somewhat unclear how (or even whether) the three-pronged test applies to music industry loan-out corporations.[15]

Minors

Minors are seen by the law as not having the legal capacity to sign a contract until they have reached the age of majority (i.e., the chronological age at which they are considered adults). That age in all but a handful of states is eighteen.[16] As a result, a minor can generally repudiate, or "disaffirm" (and, therefore, avoid), a contract they signed before they reached the age of majority. While there are some exceptions to the rule (i.e., some cases in which a minor cannot repudiate, such as contracts for "necessities" like housing, food, and water), none of them apply to typical music industry

---

14. Assemb. B. 5, 2019–2020 Leg., Reg. Sess. (Cal. 2019) provides that a worker is classified as an employee unless the employer demonstrates that the worker (1) is free from the control and direction of the hirer in connection with the performance of the work, both factually and under the contract for the work, (2) performs work that is outside the usual course of the hiring entity's business, and (3) is customarily engaged in an independently established trade, occupation, or business of the same nature as the work performed for the hiring entity.

15. Joseph Scudiero and Scott Bishop, "Legal Alert: California's AB 5 Codifies State Supreme Court's Stricter Test for Independent Contractor Status," *Entertainment Partners*, September 30, 2019, https://www.ep.com/legal-and-compliance/California-AB5-Codifies-State-Supreme-Court-Stricter-Test-for-Independent-Contractor-Status/.

16. *Age of Majority by State 2026*, *World Population Review*, 2026, https://worldpopulationreview.com/state-rankings/age-of-majority-by-state.

contracts. This fact raises a significant issue for record companies, since they often cultivate talent below the age of majority.[17]

The states with the strongest entertainment industry business economies have enacted statutory mechanisms for gaining enforceability through court approval of contracts with minors.[18] The California procedure is generally considered to be the most efficient, with the approval determination being made upon only a noticed motion in the family law court.[19]

While the signature of a parent on behalf of a minor will not create an enforceable agreement, the signature of a parent in their own capacity (e.g., the parent signing their own contract with the record company that includes a representation and warranty that the minor will not repudiate) can enable the record company to recover from the parent whatever damages the record company suffers as a result of a disaffirmance by the parent's minor child. Further, even though an entertainment contract with a minor may be disaffirmed, the termination of the agreement may not foreclose the enforcement of the agreement for purposes of collecting fees due under the agreement from when it was in place.[20]

Some artists who signed their recording agreements without the record company having undertaken the precautionary procedures discussed earlier have successfully avoided their recording agreements.[21]

---

17. See generally Joe Lynch, "These 11 Solo Artists Scored a No. 1 Album Before Turning 18," *Billboard*, April 29, 2015, https://www.billboard.com/music/pop/youngest-solo-artists-no-1-album-6539008/.

18. See, e.g., CALIFORNIA FAMILY CODE § 6751, Stats. 2019, ch. 115, § 74 (AB 1817) (effective Jan. 1, 2020); 820 ILL. COMP. STAT. 20/1 et seq. (2023); N.Y. Arts & Cultural Affairs Law § 35.03 (McKinney 2023).

19. Tabetha Bennett, "Child Entertainers and Their Limited Protections: A Call for an Interstate Compact," *Child and Family Law Journal* 9, no. 1 (2021): art. 6, https://lawpublications.barry.edu/cflj/vol9/iss1/6; Alyssa Rodriguez, "Children in the Entertainment Industry: The Right to Childhood. An Analysis of Federal Laws Regarding Mental Health & Minors in the Entertainment Industry," *Florida Entertainment and Sports Law Review* 2, no. 1 (2022): art. 7, https://scholarship.law.ufl.edu/feslr/vol2/iss1/7; S. Star and D. Dhankar, "Major Differences in Minors' Contracts: A Comparative Analysis into the Validity of Contracts with Minors in the Sport and Entertainment Industry," *Liverpool Law Review* 43, no. 2 (2022): 203–35, https://doi.org/10.1007/s10991-022-09308-4.

20. *Scott Eden Mgmt. v. Kavovik*, 563 N.Y.S. 2d 1001 (N.Y. Sup. Ct. 1990), aff'd, 197 A.D.2d 569 (1993).

21. See, e.g., Paul Resnikoff, "Malu Trevejo Wins a Federal Court Injunction Against Universal Music Group," *Digital Music News*, August 1, 2018, https://www.digitalmusicnews.com/2018/08/01/malu-trevejo-injunction-universal-music/.

Scope

Over the decades the scope of rights in recording agreements has changed as new forms of expression and distribution, and new markets, have developed. Early recording agreements applied only to the recordings produced during a particular recording session, for which an artist may or may not have been promised royalties in addition to whatever set amounts they received at the time. Then agreements became exclusive and engaged artists over a defined period for the purposes of producing recordings for use in the production of phonograph records.[22] At a certain point, as the means for producing sound recordings became more widely distributed, and the use of sound recordings more varied than just for purposes of the production of phonograph records, the scope of recording agreements began to apply to *any* sound recordings produced during the term of the agreement, whether produced by the record company or not, and to any use of such sound recordings. For example, recording agreements began to apply to live recordings produced by others than the record company or recordings produced for inclusion in motion pictures or television programs. In like manner, recording agreements grew to embrace interests other than sound recordings—first music publishing for compositions created by the recording artist, then such things as music videos, merchandising, fan clubs, and touring.

Today, it is not uncommon for a record company, particularly one of the major three companies (Sony Music Entertainment, Universal Music Group, and Warner Music Group), to insist on a broad range of rights in a musical performer's creative output under what are characterized as "360" deals for the breadth of their application. We will review specific topic areas further in this chapter, but major recording agreements now typically bring within their scope not only recordings of all types and methods of exploitation but also merchandising, touring (including tour-ancillary activities, such as VIP fan experiences), artist vanity label activities, biopics, fan clubs, websites,

22. See, e.g., *Polygram Records, Inc. v. Legacy Ent. Grp., LLC*, 205 S.W.3d 439 (Tenn. Ct. App. 2006) (recordings produced for syndication as radio programs were distinguished from recording produced for purposes of sale as records).

social media platforms, management, and other aspects of the entertainment career of the artist. Whether this expanded scope of rights makes sense to the artist will depend on the capabilities of the company requesting the rights and the consideration being given in return for the grant.

Term

Recording agreements generally have an initial period during which a certain minimum number of recordings will be produced and delivered to the record company. While this period is sometimes defined by a certain number of months, it will quite often be tied to the delivery and/or release of a certain minimum number of recordings satisfactory to the record company. For example, the initial period might commence at the execution of the agreement and end six to eighteen months following the initial commercial release of the recordings required to be delivered by the artist during the initial period. This method of determining the duration of the agreement has the benefit to the record company of extending its exclusive rights to the artist's work for however long it actually takes the musician to complete their creative recording process. It also provides the record company with the time to measure the commercial prospects of the artist following the release of the recordings. Of course, the artist may find their interests are best served by a shorter period, particularly if success is not occurring at the rate they had envisioned. If the initial album to be delivered under the recording agreement was already independently produced by the artist prior to the agreement, then the risk attendant to the production of new recordings does not exist for either party and the initial period should be correspondingly reduced.

Following the initial period, the recording agreement will generally have a certain number of options for the record company to extend the agreement. The options generally vary between three and five, and the duration of these option periods generally mirror the duration of the initial period. The options might be exclusively exercisable by the record company, but it may be possible for the artist to negotiate certain contingencies that must be satisfied in the prior period in order for the exercise to be valid, such as the commercial release of a certain number of recordings, the obtainment of a certain method of distribution, or the achievement of a certain level of sales. In contrast, the record company will want its exclusive rights to extend for a period of time following the delivery of the final recorded works required under the agreement in order to give it sufficient time to market such recordings as the musician's newest release without competition with recordings released by the artist's new record company.

Production and Release Commitment

The delivery requirement of the artist under the recording agreement is generally described in terms of a minimum number of individual masters that are satisfactory to the record company. The required number of masters generally will be enough to comprise a traditional long-play album (LP) featuring a certain minimum number of recordings. The record company may want a certain number of additional recordings uses such as so-called B sides, inclusion in albums released in foreign territories or through exclusive retailer arrangements in order to distinguish such albums from the regularly available editions, or seasonal, tribute, or other thematic collections.

The nature of the masters to be delivered is often described in detail, such as whether they will be of studio recordings rather than live, what their minimum and maximum length may be, that the songs were not previously recorded by the artist, and so on. The level of record company satisfaction that must be obtained is sometimes a negotiated point. Must the master be commercially satisfactory to the record company (and, if so, satisfactory in the record company's sole discretion or its reasonable discretion), or must the artist only deliver masters that are technically satisfactory for the production of phonorecords?

Delivery may also be described in actual physical terms, as the record company will want to possess the actual multitrack master tapes, digital files, or other physical media embodying the recordings featuring the artist. This is important not only because the record company will want to ensure safekeeping of such physical media, but also because future playback formats or uses such as multichannel surround-sound formats may require access to such original multitrack media rather than second generation media prepared for reproduction in a specific earlier format.

While the artist is generally required to deliver a certain number of recordings to the record company, the record company is generally not required to release any particular number of such recordings, or to do so in any particular format or sequence. A release commitment is therefore often negotiated on behalf of the artist. The release commitment would often include the dates by which the release would be achieved and the configuration(s) in which the recordings would appear (digital only, compact disc, vinyl, etc.). If negotiated correctly, the failure to release could trigger the right of the artist to terminate the agreement, terminate an option for the label to extend the agreement, or give rise to an artist right to obtain the return of masters delivered under the agreement.

Obligation to Promote

The relationship between a recording artist and a record company is generally considered a conventional business relationship that does not rise to the status of a fiduciary relationship. Because of the exclusivity of the arrangement, the record company will have a general obligation to use its reasonable efforts to promote the recordings subject to the agreement.[23] This general obligation may be supported by express provisions in the agreement concerning budgets and specific promotional efforts to be undertaken by the record company. But, even compliance with such specific requirements does not immunize record companies against claims that their promotional efforts have been inadequate.[24] Nevertheless, an implied covenant of good faith and fair dealing can be overcome with express language granting discretionary authority about how rights might be exercised, particularly when

23. *Wood v. Lucy, Lady Duff-Gordon*, 118 N.E. 214 (1917).

24. See, e.g., *Contemporary Mission, Inc. v. Famous Music Corp.*, 557 F.2d 918 (2d Cir. 1977); *Simon v. Starbucks Corp.*, No. 09–09074 (C.D. Cal. Jan. 17, 2012) (order granting motion to dismiss the appeal).

that discretionary authority is supported by actual consideration, such as guaranteed payments.[25]

Recording Budgets and Advances

Record companies generally fund the costs of producing the recordings they obtain. For recordings produced on speculation prior to the entry of a recording agreement that are acquired under the terms of the agreement, an advance payment is generally made to the artist to compensate them for the cost they incurred in producing the recordings. This payment is characterized as an advance against potential future royalties. For recordings produced during the course of the recording agreement, the record company generally approves a budget for the production of the recordings that it funds and that either it or the artist administers. In either event, the amounts paid by the record company will be recouped by the record company, from royalties that might otherwise be payable to the artist, before the artist receives any further payments.

The amount of the production budget for recordings under the recording agreement may be a set figure or may be determined according to a formula that takes into account earnings from the immediately prior recording(s) from the artist that the company released. This variable amount is generally collared with a minimum and a maximum figure. The budget may or may not include amounts meant to be retained by the artist in the form of personal advances if the full amount of the budget is not expended.

It is important to recognize that amounts paid by the record company in the form of advances and recording costs are not obligations to be repaid by the artist to the record company in the event they are not recouped from exploitation of the recordings. While it is possible for the record company and the artist to enter loan agreements, advances and amounts paid for recording costs will not create indebtedness by the artist to the record company. It is also important to note how recording costs are defined in a recording agreement. Costs other than as anticipated may be embraced in

25. See, e.g., *Third Story Music, Inc. v. Waits*, 41 Cal. App. 4th 798 (Ct. App. 1996).

such a definition, thereby increasing the recoupable amount faced by the artist. For example, the definition of recording costs could include hospitality or travel expenses the recording artist may anticipate are the responsibility of the record company.

Royalties

Royalties have historically been the subject of Byzantine provisions of recording agreements. It is not enough to understand a quoted royalty rate for an artist—one must carefully examine the way such a rate is adjusted, modified, and qualified to reasonably determine an anticipated payment for the use of a recording. Some of the royalty provisions discussed next are becoming anachronistic as digital transmissions have replaced physical products. However, it is not uncommon for an attorney to be asked to provide advice concerning the terms of old agreements, which include the provisions discussed next; and the music industry is somewhat notorious for its utilization of template contracts that lag behind the times (sometimes intentionally).[26]

Royalty Basis

The first royalty provision to be determined is for products that have existed in the music industry for decades, although their form of distribution may have changed (e.g., what used to be vinyl is now a digital file). For that first royalty provision, the first order of business is what the royalty rate will be based on. Historically (and, therefore, in a legacy agreement), the primary

26. Two examples of provisions that likely present in a legacy recording agreement, but likely *not* present in a modern recording agreement, are those concerning "digital royalties" and so-called container charges. The digital royalties provision remains in concept, but has matured into its own section of several provisions (perhaps several pages) in a modern recording agreement, though in a legacy agreement it would have been short and simple, and merely provided for payment to the recording artist, for so-called digital transmissions, a percentage of net revenue (and, again, that deducted from gross to reach net would be crucial). The container charges provision historically reduced the base for the calculation of royalties by a percentage that varied according to the physical configuration in which the recording was sold (e.g., royalty base reduced by 12.5 percent for vinyl albums, 20 percent for cassette tapes, and 25 percent for compact discs).

cornerstone of the royalty rate has been the suggested retail selling price or wholesale price of the physical product, and only rarely based upon actual net revenue to the record company. In modern recording agreements, the actual net revenue to the record company is likely to be the cornerstone; and in such cases, as well as in cases in which a legacy agreement refers to net revenue, that which gets deducted from gross to reach net is crucial to the economic effect of the contract.

In a legacy recording agreement, since wholesale price may be a significant discount from a suggested retail price, the artist typically would have negotiated for the royalty rate to correspondingly adjust upward to account for the lower price. For example, if the wholesale price is one-half the suggested retail selling price, the royalty rate as applied to the suggested retail selling price would have to be doubled if based on the wholesale price in order to yield the same result.

It is also important to understand the percentage of sales upon which royalties will be calculated. One historical practice in recording agreements was to base royalties on 90 percent of record sales, which was justified by the claim that many records broke in shipment. While that justification no longer exists, the practice became baked into many royalty systems and may appear, almost zombie-like, in current agreements (see preceding, regarding the music industry's utilization of template contracts that sometimes lag behind the times). If the provision cannot be negotiated out, then the rate should simply be adjusted upward.

Royalty Rates

Basic royalty rates for recording agreements vary across a wide range, depending on the success level of the artist, projected sales for the music genre involved, or the policies of the particular record company. Generally, a base rate applicable to so-called top-line recordings will be determined under the agreement, and that rate will serve as the reference point for rate adjustments applicable to products other than top-line recordings.[27] Royalty

27. "Top line" means the record company's highest price for records sold, and the "top-line price" is typically defined in a recording agreement as a percentage of that highest price. A sample recording agreement definition of Top-Line Price might read: "Label's top-line price

rates are also deemed to be "all in," meaning that all royalty participants involved with a particular recording are meant to be included within the single rate. Thus, if a royalty rate for an artist is 12 percent, and the producer of a recording featuring that artist is entitled to receive a 3 percent royalty rate, the artist's effective royalty rate for such recording is reduced to 9 percent.

Royalty rates do not have to remain static during the term of an agreement. Rates could escalate during option extension periods, for recordings that achieve certain sales levels, or for recordings appearing on certain configurations, such as a "best-of" release.

Licensing and Other Income

The royalty rates just described are applicable to products sold by the record company. Of course, the record company can also authorize others to exercise any of the rights held by the record company by entering license agreements that result in licensing income to the record company; and a modern recording agreement will also authorize the record company to exercise other means of exploiting (i.e., generating revenue from) the artist's creative output. Historically, licensed uses of recordings for such things as compilation albums or soundtracks generally occurred after the record company realized more profitable proceeds from the sale of their own products. Licenses would be permitted if the licensed uses did not cannibalize the company's own sales. Licensing revenue was a secondary source of income, and most recording agreements provided that 50 percent of such licensing income would be paid to the recording artist.[28]

With the growth in maturity of digital music services and retailers, streaming services, and synchronization and promotional purposes, the once-secondary source of income became primary, which has caused much

---

means a price greater than 80% of the record company's then-current highest wholesale price for records in a particular configuration in the territory concerned."

28. Not all earlier recording agreements addressed the issue of licensing, which has led to litigation concerning the record company's right to do so under the language of the applicable agreements. See, e.g., *Thomas v. Gusto Records, Inc.*, 939 F.2d 395 (6th Cir. 1991), cert. denied, 502 U.S. 984 (1991); *Greenfield v. Philles Records, Inc.*, 780 N.E.2d 166 (N.Y.S. 2002).

disagreement.[29] The issue is this, for example: Is the relationship between a record company and a digital music retailer such as iTunes or Amazon (or Bandcamp for independent artists' music), which stores a digital music file on its own server and creates and transmits a copy of that file to its customers when purchased, one of a wholesaler and retailer or of licensor and licensee? If the relationship is one of wholesaler and retailer, then the royalty provisions based on the wholesale or retail price of the music will apply. If the relationship is one of licensor and licensee, then the percentage of licensing proceeds provisions will apply. These hypotheticals illustrate the material difference. Assume that the royalty rate under an artist's agreement is 20 percent of the wholesale price, which we will also assume, for simplicity purposes, is not adjusted for any of the reasons to be later discussed. The typical "wholesale" price of a single recording sold as a digital download is 70 cents. Therefore, the royalty payable to the artist under the wholesaler–retailer arrangement would be 14 cents. If that same transaction is characterized as one between a licensor and a licensee, the royalty would be 50 percent of 70 cents, or 35 cents, which is greater than two-and-one-half times more than if the arrangement is characterized as a sale to a wholesaler.

Multiple lawsuits have been brought by artists whose recordings were produced under contracts that did not anticipate digital sales by others as becoming the principal source of income for the record companies owning those recordings. The results of those lawsuits have been mixed.[30]

---

29. Michael McCubbin, "The Aftermath of Aftermath: The Impact of Digital Music Distribution on the Recording Industry," *University of New Hampshire Law Review* 10, no. 2 (2012): 323, https://scholars.unh.edu/unh_lr/vol10/iss2/6; Joseph Dimont, "Royalty Inequity: Why Music Streaming Services Should Switch to a Per-Subscriber Model," *Hastings Law Journal* 69, no. 2 (2018): 675, https://repository.uclawsf.edu/hastings_law_journal/vol69/iss2/5; Oisin Lunny, "Record Breaking Revenues in the Music Business, but Are Musicians Getting a Raw Deal?" *Forbes*, May 12, 2019, https://www.forbes.com/sites/oisinlunny/2019/05/15/record-breaking-revenues-in-the-music-business-but-are-musicians-getting-a-raw-deal/; Paul Sweeting, "The Revenue Stream for Music and TV Royalties Is Changing," *Variety*, September 22, 2021, https://variety.com/2021/biz/news/music-royalties-changing-rights-streaming-1235054953/.

30. See *Allman v. Sony BMG Music Ent.*, 2008 WL 2477465 (S.D.N.Y. 2008) (the court found that the transaction between the record company and the online sellers of downloads was one of sale and resale, and royalty formulas applicable to sales rather than licenses applied); see also *F.B.T. Prods., LLC v. Aftermath Records*, 621 F.3d 958 (9th Cir. 2010), cert. denied,

Current recording agreements generally seek to characterize sales through digital transmission under the authority of the record company as sales subject to the regular royalty scheme set up for the sale of physical products, and to distinguish such sales from more traditional licenses such as for soundtracks or compilations. The issue with respect to legacy agreements, however, continues to give rise to litigated disputes, given the large financial amount at stake.

Record Company Income from Enterprise-Level Label Activity

As the music industry has changed, so have record companies. Record companies no longer use their assets solely to generate record royalties. Over time, record companies have leveraged the value of the intellectual property portfolios to take ownership interests in companies in industries adjacent to record sales, such as streaming.[31] Record companies have also licensed to streaming services, on a blanket basis, large portions of their available catalogs of sound recordings.[32] As a result of persistent artist pushback concerning revenue to the record companies from such enterprise-level activity, modern recording agreements typically now include provisions recognizing the value of equity ownership by the record companies in third parties (such as Spotify) and blanket licenses. The financial terms around these provisions, like those included in 360 deals regarding ancillary revenue streams, usually focus on either a specific percentage to the artist of net receipts of

131 S. Ct. 1677 (2011) (recording agreement unambiguously provided that the sale of downloads and ringtones resulted in licensing income subject to the higher royalty provisions of the agreement); see also *James v. UMG Recordings, Inc.*, 2012 WL 1376977 (N.D. Cal. 2012); *Clifford v. Concord Music Group, Inc.*, 2012 WL 380744 (N.D. Cal. 2012).

31. See, e.g., Tim Ingham, "Who Really Owns Spotify?" *Rolling Stone*, February 23, 2020, https://www.rollingstone.com/pro/news/who-really-owns-spotify-955388/; *Music Business Worldwide*, "Who Owns Spotify Today?" May 10, 2023, https://www.musicbusinessworldwide.com/who-owns-spotify-today/.

32. See, e.g., Joan E. Solsman, "Spotify Reaches Deal with Universal Music, World's Biggest Record Company," *CNET*, July 22, 2020, https://www.cnet.com/culture/entertainment/spotify-reaches-deal-with-universal-music-worlds-biggest-record-label-umg/; Kaitlin Tiffany, "Spotify Just Struck a Crucial Deal with Sony Music," *The Verge*, July 11, 2017, https://www.theverge.com/2017/7/11/15953006/sony-music-spotify-agreement-licensing-public-offering.

the record company, or a good faith allocation of a certain percentage of net receipts as among all recording artists signed to the record company.

Format, Territory, Channel of Trade, and Other Adjustments

Recordings have been and are sold in a variety of formats and circumstances that produce differing margins for the record companies and, thus, in certain royalty-rate adjustments. For example, record companies often reduce the price of certain recordings after the initial demand for such recordings has been satisfied and price becomes a material purchase incentive for the consumer. These reduced-price line categories are generally referred to as "mid-price" and "budget," and the royalty rate applicable to such releases may be reduced by between 25 percent and 50 percent, respectively, from the rate originally paid. Royalties are also sometimes reduced for new product formats characterized as "new configurations," on the grounds that the development, manufacturing, and marketing costs of such new configurations produce lower margins commanding lesser royalty payouts. The same argument sometimes applies to high-end, so-called audiophile recordings having a specialized market, bundles, compilations. New configuration provisions appear less frequently in contemporary contracts and should be narrowly defined to prevent their application to a new format that becomes prevalent.

Sales of products in foreign territories and through channels of trade other than regular retail, such as direct-to-consumer and travel/hospitality, carry additional costs that affect royalty rates. Accordingly, the rate for foreign territories will generally be reduced from between 10 percent and 50 percent, depending on the territory, and rates for nontraditional channels of trade may be reduced between 25 percent and 50 percent. As digital transmissions, which do not bear the same incremental territory or channel of trade costs, surpassed physical products in sales volume, the applicability of such provisions faded, though it still exists in legacy agreements and does persist even in some modern agreements.

Free Goods

Promotion of a recording is generally an organized and coordinated effort to build commercial demand during a certain period. Record companies want to know that the promoted recording will be available for purchase when that demand is being created, since records are often an impulse purchase, or a purchase based upon an interest that can quickly diminish or disappear. Record companies, therefore, historically wanted to have a sufficient inventory of physical configurations of their recordings available to meet anticipated demand. As a result, the practice grew in the industry of incenting retailers to purchase physical units of recordings by giving the retailers a certain number of records free for every amount that they purchased, rather than a discount on the purchase price. Records distributed for free also had the advantage of generally being non-royalty bearing. This practice became fairly standardized, with the percentage of album products purchased generally being 15 percent. Therefore, the royalty payments made to artists historically had been reduced by this 15 percent to reflect the free nature of this distribution. Records distributed as so-called free goods are not the same as records distributed for promotional purposes for free, to such persons as reviewers or broadcasters, although royalties are not payable on promotional records either.

In today's digital world, the concept of free goods does not have the same importance as it had historically. However, the provision remains in modern recording agreements, as applying to publishers, employees, and affiliates of the record company, and so-called server copies provided, for example, to a digital retailer.

Payment Timing

It is important to note that there is a significant lag time prior to payment to the artist after the exploitation of a sound recording (or other generation of revenue through a recording agreement for which payment is due the artist). A recording agreement will typically provide that the record company has no obligation to pay the artist unless and until the record company receives payment, that the record company will issue semiannual (i.e., twice yearly) accountings and payments to the artist, will deliver royalty statements specifying amounts due to the artist within ninety days of the end of the semiannual accounting period, and will pay the artist within ninety days of delivery to the artist of the royalty statement. Further, analogous provisions would be contained in all the contracts the record company signs with downstream sellers of the sound recording. This could mean, for example, if a digital retailer, like Amazon, sells a copy of a sound recording to a consumer on January 1, its payment to the record company might not be made until ninety days after the end of its next subsequent, semiannual accounting period to the record company, or September 30; in turn, the record company's accounting to the artist would not be due until the succeeding March 31, and the record company's payment to the artist might not be until the succeeding June 30, so a full fifteen months after payment by the consumer for the sound recording.

The recording agreement will also typically allow the record company to retain, from otherwise payable royalties and other sums due the artist, a reserve to be reconciled based upon future charges, credits, bad debts, and returns experienced by the record company. A typical reserve amount would be in the range of 15 percent to 25 percent, and such amount would typically be liquidated and reconciled, on a rolling basis with later reserves, within two years of its first having been withheld as a reserve. Thus, considering both the lag time discussed in the previous paragraph, and reserves, the artist would not be paid some of their money until thirty-nine months after the consumer has paid.

Royalty Calculation Example

When advising an artist as to the royalty provisions of a proposed recording agreement, it is a good idea to apply the royalty scheme set out in the agreement to some hypothetical situations to see the actual output in dollars and cents. Doing so not only establishes correct expectations for the return to the artist but may also reveal inconsistencies or ambiguities in the agreement to be corrected. It also provides grounds for further negotiation with the record company if the output is unreasonably low.

For example, assume a base rate for top-line recordings of 20 percent applied to a digital download with a wholesale price of $7. A typical royalty scheme, taking into account the factors identified earlier, would be as follows: $7.00 × .20 (the royalty rate) × .90 (the amount of sales the royalties are paid on due to the outdated, but often still present, "breakage" deduction), resulting in a royalty of $1.26 per download. If royalties of

5 percent are due to the producer of the hypothetical recordings, the artist's portion of royalties would be reduced by an additional 25 percent, or to approximately 95 cents per download.[33]

Several years ago, when one of the authors was with a television production company that was negotiating royalty agreements with participating artists for the release of products featuring the programs his company was producing, that company elected to make its recording agreements more transparent by eliminating the container charges, new configuration reductions, producer royalties, and other adjustments that customarily appeared at the time. The royalty rate of course was lower, since it was not being reduced by all the historically customary factors. Expecting to receive compliments for their efforts from the attorneys representing the artists, the author and his company instead received an almost universal condemnation of the rate as being too low. Instead of creating goodwill by simplifying the negotiation, they had to overcome negative initial impressions created by an analysis of the agreement that went no further than the review of a single number. In the end, after lengthy explanation, the rate was accepted, but not having received any "love" for the effort at transparency was yet another example of the entrenched effect of legacy recording agreements. And a good illustration of why it is important to actually test the royalty formula with hypotheticals to determine their merit.[34]

---

33. Note that under a legacy recording agreement, even for a digital download thereunder, the container charge and free goods discussed earlier in this chapter would also be deducted.

34. Many have similarly tried to simplify the arcane contracting process in the music industry with about as much success. For discussion of a current effort in this regard—a contract-lifecycle-management platform intended to replace disconnected applications and sharing protocols like Gmail/Google Docs and Dropbox by using automated contract drafting with templates and forms, sending/signing/storing contracts, and integrating with third-party management and royalty systems—see Paul Resnikoff, "Earlier This Year, an Upstart Company Named Flou Vowed to Simplify Music Contracts Forever. Now, They've Got Indie Labels and Publishers Using Their Platform," *Digital Music News* (September 6, 2024); Paul Resnikoff, "Flou's on a Mission to Revolutionize Music Agreement: Here's a Detailed Breakdown of 'Music Contracts 2.0,'" *Digital Music News*, April 9, 2025, https://www.digitalmusicnews.com/2025/04/09/flou-mission-revolutionize-music-agreements-contracts-white-paper/.

Accountings and Audits

Royalty accountings under recording agreements are generally rendered on a semiannual basis, usually between sixty and ninety days after the close of each half calendar year. Because recordings in physical formats are sold to retailers on a full returns basis (meaning the retailer may unconditionally return unsold units), the record company will establish a reserve against anticipated future returns before remitting payments to the artist. Reserves are generally in the value range of 20 percent to 25 percent of units shipped to retailers and liquidated within a reasonable period, perhaps eighteen months. The accounting provisions also might state that the accuracy of each statement will be deemed accepted if specific objection is not given within a certain period of time after the statement is rendered, perhaps two to three years. As a matter of contract law, this becomes an enforceable reduction of the otherwise applicable statute of limitations to litigate claims, so is very important to note and observe in practice.[35]

The record company will generally treat all recordings produced pursuant to the terms of the agreement under a single account, meaning that the costs of all records produced under the agreement are cross-collateralized against each other. This means that the earnings from a successful recording will not be paid out until the costs from all recording are recouped. Language may appear in the recording agreement also permitting the record company to recoup costs "from this *or any other* agreement" between the artist and the record company. This language would permit, for example, recoupment of recording costs from earnings derived from a music publishing agreement between the artist and the record company. Such cross-collateralization language between agreements is objectionable and should be struck.

As with the music publishing agreements, the recording artist should have the right to audit the books and records of the record company to ensure the accountings are proper. The considerations raised earlier in Chapter 3

35. *Allman v. UMG Recordings*, 530 F. Supp. 2d 602 (S.D.N.Y. 2008); *Am. Steamship Owners Mut. Protection & Indemn. Ass'n v. Dann Ocean Towing, Inc.*, D. Md. No. CCB-08–2195 (2013) U.S. Dist. LEXIS 40218 (Mar. 22, 2013) ("Failure to comply with a contractual limitations period will subject the action to dismissal, absent proof that the limitations provision was obtained through fraud, duress, or other wrongdoing.").

applicable to audit provisions in music publishing agreements—when and where the audit may take place, how long it may take place, the frequency of audits, the length of time after the end of an accounting period during which that accounting period remains open for audit, how many times a single accounting period may be audited, what materials may be reviewed, any cost shifting in the event a discrepancy is discovered, confidentiality of the material and information disclosed, and whether any audit report must be shared with the musician—apply to recording agreements as well. As also mentioned in the discussion concerning music publishing agreements, failure to make required royalty payments may not give rise to an action for rescission unless the failure to pay is both willful and near total.[36]

Approvals

Creative endeavors require myriad important decisions, many of which may create tensions between the interests of the artist and those of the record company as they each seek to control the creation and marketing of the artist's recordings. These areas may include the selection of compositions, the producer, the studio, the participating musicians, the budget, when the recordings are considered complete and accepted, the remixes or edits of recordings, the artwork, the label on which the artist will be released (assuming the record company has more than one label), how the artist is depicted in advertising and promotional material, the directors and storylines for music videos, and the use of recordings for certain purposes by third parties under license or in connection with premiums. At a minimum, the artist should be consulted concerning major decisions concerning the production and exploitation of recordings. As a practical matter, the artist is very much in control of the creative process involving the recording of the masters, as the forced performance by an artist is unlikely to be commercially viable, if the recording takes place at all. However, a record

36. *Peterson v. Highland Music, Inc.*, 140 F.3d 1313 (9th Cir. 1998), cert. denied, 525 U.S. 983 (1998); *Robinson v. Sanctuary Record Groups, Ltd.*, 826 F. Supp. 2d 570 (S.D.N.Y. 2011); *Walker v. Blackground Records, LLC*, 2017 U.S. Dist. LEXIS 222130, 2:16-cv-04833 (C.D. Cal. Sep. 19, 2017).

company may change recordings after delivery without the artist's approval unless it is contractually denied that opportunity. While the record company will want to exploit recordings to their full commercial potential, the artist may not wish their recordings to be used in association with certain areas previously mentioned with respect to composers: alcohol, tobacco, firearms; certain food products; religious, political, or other issue-oriented messages; or audiovisual works of a certain genre.

Controlled Compositions

A controlled composition is generally defined as a musical composition that is written, owned, or otherwise controlled by the recording artist or the recording artist's publishing company. The controlled composition provisions of the recording agreement include a license from the recording artist to the record company permitting the record company to exploit recordings of each controlled composition. This is critical from the record company's perspective, as the company does not want to expend resources for the production of recordings, only to have their ability to exploit such recordings frustrated by a refusal by the recording artist, in their capacity as the songwriter, to issue a first-time mechanical license or synchronization licenses, for which compulsory licenses are not available. The controlled composition clause insures that, if the recording artist records their own composition, the company's ability to exploit that recording will be unimpaired, both with respect to the initial release of the recording and other uses.

The more critical function of a controlled composition clause is to reduce the record company's license costs, which can be achieved in a number of different ways. First, the record company may seek a discount from the statutory rate for compulsory mechanical licenses. A discount to 75 percent of the statutory rate is common, and deeper discounts for mid-line and budget releases may also be sought. Also, since the statutory rate increases for recordings that are longer than five minutes, the controlled composition clause may seek to apply the minimum rate (or the discounted rate), no matter the length of the recording. The clause may also provide that multiple versions of a particular recording appearing on the same product would be paid as one. The language may also seek to establish as the rate going forward for all time the statutory rate in existence at the time the agreement was entered. Since the statutory rate is periodically adjusted through Copyright Office proceedings, such language should be resisted. Finally, the clause will sometimes seek to set an even lower percentage of the statutory rate (sometimes as low as 2 percent) for compositions that are in the public domain, but for which the recording artist claims some right of ownership for arranging or adding to the original composition in the recording process.[37]

The controlled composition provisions may further seek to establish a cap on the aggregate amount the record company will pay for publishing on albums or other configurations. This cap is generally calculated as a multiple of a certain rate otherwise applicable to an individual recording. For example, the cap for an album might be established by multiplying the then-applicable statutory rate by a number meant to approximate the expected number of tracks on an album. This number is negotiable but generally falls in the range of ten to thirteen. Efforts to use any discounted statutory rate as the basis for determining the cap should be resisted, as the effect of such a low cap can be material. This is particularly so when non-controlled compositions are included on a release, since non-controlled compositions are likely to be available only on the basis of a full statutory rate and their inclusion at that rate as a portion of an aggregate amount determined on the basis of a discounted rate may drive the effective rate for a controlled composition to little, if anything.

The problems with controlled composition clauses for artists have been somewhat mitigated by Congress. In 1995, the Digital Performance Right in Sound Recording Act declared that a controlled composition clause shall not be enforceable for digital downloads of recordings released pursuant to a contract entered after 1995.[38] As digital downloads ascended to

37. Todd Brabec and Jeffrey Brabec, "How Royalties Are Determined for New Material Written for Public Domain Compositions," *Entertainment Law & Finance* 29, no. 5 (August 2013).

38. 17 U.S.C. § 115(c)(3)(E) (2011). See generally Jay Rosenthal, *The Recording Artist/Songwriter Dilemma: The Controlled Composition Clause—Enough Already!*, *Landslide: A Publication of the ABA Section of Intellectual Property Law*, March/April 2011; Brian S. Mencher and Vidal C. Maurrasse, "Revisiting the Convergence of Technology, Legislation,

dominance over physical products, the impact of controlled composition clauses diminished.

Samples

Historically, recording agreements contained only generic representations and warranties around ownership and non-infringement of the intellectual property embodied in the recordings created by the artist, and the artist's obligation to procure rights to third-party performances. Those generic provisions remain in modern recording agreements, but in addition there are now also typically included specific (and much longer) provisions around sampling.[39] This is both because the interest in policing unauthorized sampling has increased as the economics of the music industry have changed and because the ability to police unauthorized sampling has increased as technology has advanced.[40]

As a result, the sampling provision found in a modern recording agreement typically requires the artist to provide the record company with prior

---

and Industry: The Effect of 17 U.S.C. § 115(c)(3)(E) of the Copyright Act on Mechanical Royalties and the Controlled Composition Clause," *Ohio Northern University Law Review* 39, no. 3 (2023), Article 3, https://digitalcommons.onu.edu/onu_law_review/vol39/iss3/3.

39. Sampling is an electronic process used by musicians to digitally copy exact sound fragments of music previously recorded and owned by third parties in order to manipulate those previously recorded fragments and aesthetically integrate them in new recordings. See Tracy L. Reilly, "Debunking the Top Three Myths of Digital Sampling: An Endorsement of the Bridgeport Music Court's Attempt to Afford 'Sound' Copyright Protection to Sound Recordings," 31 *Columbia Journal of Law & Arts* 355, 359 (2008); Benjamin Franzen (Director), *Copyright Criminals* (September 19, 2009).

40. The creation and rapid development of digital sampling technology in the 1980s, and rampantly utilized by musicians without prior authorization from the sampled artists or their record companies, led to an increase of sample-related copyright infringement lawsuits filed in the 1990s, and remains a contested issue today. See Tracy Reilly, "Good Fences Make Good Neighboring Rights: The German Federal Supreme Court Rules on the Digital Sampling of Sound Recordings in 'Metall auf Metall,'" 13 *Minnesota Journal of Law, Science & Technology* 153, 159 (2012). Early legal rulings on sampling such as *Grand Upright Music Ltd. v. Warner Bros. Records, Inc.*, 780 F. Supp. 182 (S.D.N.Y. 1991) and *Bridgeport Music, Inc. v. Dimension Films*, 410 F.3d 792 (6th Cir. 2005) clearly held that unauthorized sampling violates the exclusive copyright rights of the musicians who are sampled. In more recent cases, though, courts are trending toward exonerating sampling musicians when their unlicensed takings are considered either *de minimis* or unrecognizable, thus creating an ongoing split in the circuit courts on the issue. See, e.g., *VMG Salsoul, LLC v. Madonna Louise Ciccone, et al.*, 824 F.3d 871 (9th Cir. 2016).

written notice of all samples the artist intends to use, gives the record company a right to approve (or not) such samples, and provides that the cost of clearing such samples be included in the recording budget for a release. The inclusion of the cost in the recording budget has the effect of both reducing the available budget for the non-sample aspects of recording and potentially extending the time to recoupment of the royalty account of the artist.

Re-recording Restrictions

Re-recording by an artist of songs previously recorded and commercially released is of interest to many artists for a variety of reasons, including the artist's changed artistic vision for the song(s), dissatisfaction with the production of the original commercially released version(s) of the songs, a desire to change the economic impact of exploitation of the song, or just plain spite.

Re-recording restrictions in recording agreements generally prevent the artist from recording apart from the record company any new version of the songs they recorded for the record company under their recording agreement with the record company. Traditionally, the artist was required to wait until the later of five to seven years after the initial release or two years after expiration of their recording agreement to re-record their music, and the restriction applied to any sound recording, even if the original master thereof was never commercially released.

Notwithstanding that historically long tail on re-recording restrictions, some well known recording artists have still achieved success re-recording songs long after their initial release.[41]

In response, record companies have steadily increased the length of the re-recording restriction, with some reports indicating a re-recording restriction

41. See, e.g., Michael Hann, "*Remake, Remodel: What Makes Musicians Rerecord Old Albums?*" *The Guardian*, January 18, 2018, https://www.theguardian.com/music/2018/jan/18/what-makes-musicians-rerecord-old-albums-shins-car-seat-headrest; Tyler Golson, "Why Ozzy Osbourne Re-recorded Two of His Biggest Albums," *Far Out*, October 3, 2023, https://faroutmagazine.co.uk/ozzy-osbourne-re-recorded-two-biggest-albums/; and Raisa Bruner, "Here's Why Taylor Swift Is Re-Releasing Her Old Albums," *Time*, August 2, 2024, https://time.com/5949979/why-taylor-swift-is-rerecording-old-albums/.

of even thirty years after the end of the term of the recording agreement (and even with respect to compositions that might have been originally recorded at the beginning of that relationship).[42]

While the record companies have become more aggressive with respect to the length of the re-recording restriction, that length should be included in the negotiation process, as should certain exceptions to it (e.g., performances intended for later broadcast by radio, television, or web streaming).

Merchandising

Merchandising generally refers to taking a product or service from a company and selling it to a consumer. For our purposes, however, it refers to a more specific activity, which is the marketing of products or services that have been branded or otherwise associated with a musical individual or entity, usually under license from the individual or entity. Merchandising implicates a number of different rights, depending upon what is used to create the desired association. For example, a T-shirt might simply display the name of an individual performer, in which case the performer's right of publicity is implicated. Use of the name, especially in a distinctive logotype or design, would implicate trademark rights for either an individual performer using their own name or a collective name used by a group. If a photo of a performer is used, or a graphic image, the copyright in such photograph or graphic would be implicated. It is not uncommon for all three interests to be combined in a single property (e.g., a photograph of a performer that is used on an album cover that is then silk-screened onto a T-shirt to be sold on the performer's tour) and, in those ways, used as a service mark by the performer for their musical performance or recording services. Merchandising can be a very lucrative part of an individual performer's income. The group Kiss, perhaps the most aggressive and successful

42. Steve Knopper, "Labels Want to Prevent 'Taylor's Version'-Like Re-Recordings from Ever Happening Again," *Billboard*, October 30, 2023, https://www.billboard.com/pro/taylor-swift-re-recordings-labels-change-contracts/.

of all merchandising performers, has reportedly issued over 5,000 licenses for products ranging from condoms to caskets.[43]

The merchandising provisions of recording agreements have grown from initial modest terms that permitted the record company to use album cover artwork on selected apparel items and posters to the granting of all rights to use a performer's identity and trademarks across all product categories. The expansion of such rights has followed the growth of merchandising capabilities by record companies, particularly major labels that have either launched their own merchandising divisions or purchased merchandising companies. In turn, the expansion of rights and the growth of merchandising capabilities of record companies, and the supplemental revenue stream those events provided for record companies, made merchandising provisions a catalyst to what has come to be known as the "360 deal," discussed later in this chapter. Whether a recording artist grants merchandising rights to a record company and the scope of such rights, if any, should depend on the ability of the record company to actually implement such rights. Granting a record company rights beyond its unaided ability to exercise simply interposes the company between the artist and the actual party producing the product, generally without delivery of value by the record company or real benefit to the artist.

The more critical terms of the merchandising provisions of a recording agreement are control and royalties. Who controls what words and/or images will be applied to products or services, and what products or services might be marketed? Who chooses the licensees of the words and/or images, if the record company does not produce and sell the product itself, and what will be the terms and conditions of such licenses? What personal services might be required of an artist in connection with the promotion

43. "Kiss and Sell," *Billboard*, October 3, 2009, 24; Andy Gensler, "Paul Stanley Talks Kiss Merch Milestone: From Waffle Irons to Moisturizing Face Masks," *Billboard*, April 2019, https://www.billboard.com/music/music-news/paul-stanley-talks-kiss-merch-milestone-from-waffle-irons-to-moisturizing-7694042/; Maria Sherman, "Kiss Sells Catalog, Brand Name and IP. Gene Simmons Assures Fans It Is a 'Collaboration,'" *Associated Press*, April 4, 2024, https://apnews.com/article/kiss-sells-catalog-brand-name-ip-pophouse-061d34ce4e92efffc25f-35c62670a4f2. For an interesting discussion of one academic's hypothesis around exactly why it is that Kiss' merchandise machine became so successful, see also Rob Ahlers, "Benjamin's KISS: A Perspective on Music, Spectacle and Aura," *International Association for the Study of Popular Music (IASPM) Journal* 6, no. 1 (2016).

of a licensed merchandising product? Does the recording artist retain any rights to produce their own merchandise, perhaps for sale in connection with personal appearances? What flexibility will the artist have to participate in sponsorships or endorsements within the context of the merchandising rights held by the record company?

Since the function of trademarks is to identify source, sponsorship, or approval, quality control is the key term to any trademark license agreement. Unsupervised uses by third parties do not serve to identify the trademark owner and create the risk that a trademark owner will no longer be able to retain rights in their mark.[44] Therefore, to the extent that a merchandising agreement implicates a trademark right (and most music-related products will), the agreement must establish a standard for quality. The agreement must also identify procedures to ensure that the standards will be met, such as the submission of prototypes for approval and periodic inspections. The agreement also should contain language acknowledging that all the goodwill created by the promotion and sale of the licensed product inures to the benefit of the artist as owner of the mark. This may be critical in supporting applications to register artist-owned trademarks, or to maintain such registrations, that are based on licensed uses rather than uses produced directly by the artist.

The financial terms of the merchandising provisions generally provide payment to the artist of 50 percent of proceeds received by the record company from the exploitation of merchandising rights, net of manufacturing costs, sales agents, and perhaps a percentage of sales revenue to represent the recapture of overhead costs. The artist will want the agreement to provide that the revenue earned through merchandising is not cross-collateralized with the recoupable costs that might be due from the recording, publishing, or other activities under the agreement. Care should also be taken to limit the merchandising rights to the term of the recording agreement. The record company of course will require the ability to use the artist's identity to promote recordings produced under the agreement after the artist is no longer an exclusive recording artist with the label, but there should be no companion requirement that the record company be either allowed or

44. See, e.g., *Barcamerica Int'l U.S.A. Tr. v. Tyfield Imp., Inc.*, 289 F.3d 589 (9th Cir. 2002).

required to produce new merchandising products. Further, the artist may be required by their successor record company to grant exclusive merchandising rights to the successor record company, which the artist cannot do if the prior record company continues to hold merchandising rights.

Videos

Major label recording agreements have long had tome-like heft. Despite the lengthy agreements, the following is the entire provision that addressed the production of musical audiovisual works in the very first, sixty-page major label recording agreement negotiated by one of the authors:

> You shall, upon our request, appear on dates and at film studios or other locations designated by us upon reasonable notice to you for the filming, taping or other permanent fixation of audiovisual reproductions of your performance.

It wasn't as if music videos were unknown at that time. It also turned out that a music video from the group involved was one of the first twenty videos broadcast on the day MTV launched its service in 1981. The primitive attention given to music videos in the not-so-distant past demonstrates how far the medium advanced in a relatively short time. Perhaps just as quickly, music videos became outdated. Nevertheless, music video language is now a standard feature of recording agreements.

Musical audiovisual works are generally treated in recording agreements in the same manner as sound recordings. They are generally contractually characterized as works made for hire and are subject to the same royalty scheme as sound recordings (with some exceptions). The scope of exclusivity the record company has with the recording artist is generally limited to the production of works featuring musical performances, as opposed to dramatic performances, and to the sale of products reproducing such performances. One-half of the costs of producing music videos are generally treated as recoupable from royalties otherwise payable for the sale of audio-only recordings but fully recoupable from any royalties earned from music video proceeds. While the royalty rates for audiovisual works may not be the same as those provided for audio-only recordings, the royalty adjustments applicable to audio-only recordings, such as container charges, fee goods, and territory and channel of trade reductions, generally apply. License receipts will generally be shared equally between the record company and the artist. However, the allocation may be of a net figure enabling the record company to recover certain required costs it may have incurred to fulfill its delivery obligations under the license, such as transcoding costs. The rates will be all in, meaning all royalty participants will be paid from the single negotiated rate.

Issues of control and commitment also mirror those affecting audio-only recordings. Will the record company commit to the production and release of a music video, and, if so, at what budget? Who will select the director, writer, editor, guests, and recordings used? Will any sponsor support be available or permitted? Since there is no compulsory license for synchronization rights, the record company will generally obtain rights to controlled compositions through the provisions in the agreement otherwise applicable to audio-only recordings.

Over time, market and technology forces created new tensions affecting how audiovisual works are addressed in recording agreements. First, the means by which audiovisual works are produced and distributed became inexpensive and decentralized, giving commercial options and capabilities to many more parties, including the recording artist themselves. Second, distribution platforms for entertainment properties converged. Companies that originally produced works only for broadcast (which the record companies would not control) now routinely seek the right to distribute such programming by means of online and mobile services and devices, when in the past distribution would be the general domain of the record companies. Finally, the growth and acceptance of branded entertainment—music as a sponsored activity—created new opportunities and new requirements for those artists that participate. Sponsors seeking to use music to deliver a commercial message generally will insist upon having exclusive rights for certain periods in custom audio or audiovisual content as a draw to their promotional campaign. Such material may conflict with the exclusivity provisions of the artist's recording agreement.

What does this mean? First, the definition of the scope of exclusive rights in audiovisual works that is held by the record company is critical. What rights might a performer want to hold back? Streaming or downloading of recordings of live performances from the performer's own website or social media platform? Ability by the performer to authorize live performances at events such as festivals to be streamed or archived by the event promoter, or to authorize television broadcast performances by the performer to be distributed as electronic transmissions? Ability to authorize fan recordings to be produced and circulated, or to produce specific audiovisual works for fan club distribution? Ability to fulfill sponsorship commitments for exclusive content to be exploited, if not owned, by the sponsor? If the performer anticipated a certain type and number of outside projects, perhaps the recording agreement could contain a provision preapproving a certain number of outside projects that fell within defined boundaries. If such projects are not carved out, they will be handled on a case-by-case basis.

Second, if audiovisual works are produced and exploited outside the bounds of the exclusivity provisions of the recording agreement, where does the money earned from such works go? Is it paid to the artist, to the record company, or to both? Can a distinction be made as to who receives any advance paid in connection with an outside audiovisual project and who receives royalties that might be generated? Does it make any difference as to who is paid whether the artist's royalty account is recouped or unrecouped? Each of these factors may come into play in sorting out whether the project will be authorized.

360 Deals

Historically, record companies dominated the music industry due to the physical product sales they controlled. As a result of the economic challenges they have faced from the dislocation of physical product sales, their roles and economic models have also changed. Also, the traditional roles record companies controlled of providing artist discovery, capital, promotion, and distribution have become more widely distributed and available from other parties. Selling products (in a variety of physical and digital formats) is still important, but new roles and new revenue streams have evolved. For example, music has increasingly become a means by which a commercial message may be delivered—the means by which an audience is convened, attention obtained, and an impression created. As a supplier of that music, record companies now act in the role of service providers to other industries and marketers. In like manner, record companies understand they have a platform from which commercial messages may issue, which is valuable to brands seeking to affiliate with the values associated with talent and properties owned by the record companies. Finally, record companies have broadened their business capabilities, both in artist management[45] and in ancillary areas that monetize their recording artists, and the results of the talent of those recording artists, to create new revenue streams.[46]

All these new developments have caused record companies to reassess the contractual relationships that they have with their talent. The term "360 deal" is typically used to describe the expanded form of recording agreement that embraces multiple new rights areas.[47] While record companies have long annexed publishing and certain merchandising rights, they now typically seek rights in all merchandising, an artist's management, official website, fan club, social media platforms, touring and other personal appearances (including tour-ancillary activities, such as VIP fan experiences), artist vanity record label activities, biopics, and other areas the company will actively manage and control. Further, record companies now typically seek certain "passive" income, or the right to receive a percentage of the artist's income from entertainment-related activities that are

45. See, e.g., Ray Waddell and Ed Christman, "Giant Steps," *Billboard*, October 1, 2011, 4.

46. See the Merchandising Rights section of this chapter.

47. Ian Brereton, "Beginning of a New Age? The Unconscionability of the '360-Degree' Deal," *Cardozo Arts & Entertainment Law Journal* 27 (2009): 167; Michael Rudell and Neil J. Rosini, "'360' Agreements Reflect Industry's Economic Shift," *Entertainment Law & Finance*, October 2008; Brian Lesser, "Record Labels Shot the Artists, but They Did Not Share the Equity," *Georgetown Journal of Law & Public Policy* 16 (2018): 289; Yngvar Kjus, "Twists and Turns in the 360 Deal: Spinning the Risks and Rewards of Artist–Label Relations in the Streaming Era," *European Journal of Cultural Studies* 25 (2021): 1, https://doi.org/10.1177/13675494211044731; Lee Marshall, "The 360 Deal and the 'New' Music Industry," *European Journal of Cultural Studies* 16 (2013): 77, https://doi.org/10.1177/1367549412457478; Matt Stahl and Leslie M. Meier, "The Firm Foundation of Organizational Flexibility: The 360 Contract in the Digitalizing Music Industry," *Canadian Journal of Communication* 37 (2012): 1, https://doi.org/10.22230/cjc.2012v37n3a2544.

not produced or managed by the record company, both during and after the term of the recording agreement. Some of these rights are given to the record company from the outset, and some of them are provided for in the form of a right of first refusal or right of first negotiation before the artist may sign with a third party therefor. The financial terms around these provisions usually focus on a percentage of net receipts the party receiving the funds (sometimes the record company and sometimes the artist) pays to the other party. The rationale presented to the artist is that if the record company is going to invest significant resources, at great risk, in developing the identity and market value of an artist, the record company should receive a return on that investment from whatever areas the recording artist will receive revenue as a result of that identity and market value.[48] This is not an argument unavailable to record companies in the past, but it is an argument with greater resonance today, when both the costs and the risks of investing in the music industry are much greater.[49]

As the expanded provisions of 360 deals have settled into customary terms or practices, at least where major labels are concerned, some general comments can be made. First, if the recording artist permits the record company to operate the artist's official website, that operation should be in effect only for the term of the exclusivity provisions of the recording agreement. The artist should continue as the owner of the URL for the website, with the record company operating the site with the artist's permission. Further, the record company should be obligated to periodically provide the artist with all data collected in connection with the operation of the

48. The International Federation of the Phonographic Industry (IFPI) estimated that the cost of breaking a new pop artist in a major market was approximately $1 million in 2012, with a more variable, but potentially increased, amount of $0.5 million to $2 million in 2016. See *The Digital Music Report*, IFPI 2012, https://www.musikindustrie.de/fileadmin/bvmi/upload/06_Publikationen/DMR/ifpi_digital-music-report-2012.pdf; *Digital Music Report 2012 Key Facts and Figures*, IFPI, 2012, https://www.fimi.it/wp-content/uploads/2025/06/5098345c35f8f61bbe024add17d3b332.pdf; *Investing in Music: The Value of Record Companies*, IFPI, 2016, https://www.riaa.com/wp-content/uploads/2017/01/ifpi-iim-report-2016.pdf.

49. See Jeff Leeds, "The New Deal: Band as Brand," *New York Times*, November 11, 2007, https://www.nytimes.com/2007/11/11/arts/music/11leed.html?pagewanted=all&_r=0; Tim Ingham, "Warner Music Group's A&R Costs Say a Lot About How Much Labels Need to Spend on Artists in Today's Music Industry," *Rolling Stone*, February 16, 2020, https://www.rollingstone.com/pro/features/warner-music-group-ipo-ar-costs-952821/.

website, such as email and postal mail addresses, purchasing history, and other fan/customer activity. This is achieved by sharing that information with the artist during the term of the agreement. Finally, use of the artist's identity and trademarks should be under proper licenses to the record company to ensure that the goodwill created through the operation of the website inures to the benefit of the artist. The same comments would hold true for the operation of an artist's fan club, social media platforms, and similar accounts.

Second, artists' revenue sources have been turned on their head from traditional models, with the sale or other exploitation of sound recordings no longer being an artist's principal source of revenue. It may seem anomalous that an agreement nominally dedicated to the production of sound recordings would control other areas of a performer's career that are likely to be more revenue producing than sound recordings, but that is the value proposition offered by a 360 deal. As long ago as 2013, data showed that, for musicians who perform, live performance income was their primary and essential revenue stream.[50] Further, live performances provide leverage for other sources of income from the on-site sale of music and merchandise and VIP packages (e.g., meet and greet).[51] According to Billboard, as production costs for major festivals have grown (often exceeding $10 million), premium concertgoer experiences have become a popular means of fattening the thin margins of live entertainment while keeping the bulk of ticket prices lower. They can add 3 percent to 5 percent to the gross of a tour or event. For a concert tour, that amounts to the total revenue

50. *Rethinking Music: A Briefing Book*, p. 85, compiled and presented by The Berkman Center for Internet & Society at Harvard University (April 25–27, 2011), https://cyber.harvard.edu/sites/cyber.law.harvard.edu/files/Rethinking_Music_April-25-2011_hi-res.pdf; Paul Sergent, "Revenue Streams in the Modern Music Industry," *Medium*, October 15, 2022, https://medium.com/@paul.m.sergent/revenue-streams-in-the-modern-music-industry-307cf96155cc.

51. Emmanuel Olusegun Stober, "The Rise of the Concert Economy: A Modern Phenomenon with Afrobeats at the Forefront," *TheMarketForIdeas*, https://www.themarketforideas.com/the-rise-of-the-concert-economy-a-modern-phenomenon-with-afrobeats-at-the-forefront-a942/; *New Trends Impacting Festival and Consumer Events 2013*, Eventbrite, https://eventbrite-s3.s3.amazonaws.com/marketing/britepapers/Britepaper_6newtrends_webVersion.pdf; Katie Sawyer, Eventbrite U.S. Blog, "How to Meet the Growing Demand for VIP Experiences," *Eventbrite*, September 21, 2017, https://www.eventbrite.com/blog/growing-demand-for-vip-experiences-ds00/.

generated by a single show; and for a festival that grosses $20 million, that can add $1 million to the bottom line.[52]

The point of these observations is that how one approaches the negotiation of the expanded rights of a 360 deal will depend on the anticipated relative revenue from the various rights being granted to the record company. There is little point in obtaining a greater royalty rate for sound recordings in consideration of granting a percentage of personal appearance income when the revenue from such sound recordings will be relatively less important to the artist. It would be better to retain more of the personal appearance income and accept the lesser royalty rate.

Third, a record company should be granted only enhanced active or passive rights in an artist's talent under a 360 deal when the company has both corresponding operational capabilities to directly manage such rights and makes commitments ensuring value will be created for the artist through the expenditure of record company resources. There is little point in granting a right to a record company that has no means to directly exercise it. To do so only means that the record company will be interposed between the artist and a third party the artist could have contracted with directly, with perhaps both loss of control to the record company and little value added by the record company for the value extracted.

The record company commitments for expanded rights under a 360 deal could take the form of confirmed budgets, payments, or release or promotional commitments. The agreement could also establish defined triggers, such as the commercial release of a certain number of albums or the achievement of certain sales or chart positions, which must be achieved before passive income rights vest. The point is that rights should not be granted without assurances that there is an exchange of value and not just a shift in the revenue payee to offset the record company's risk.

Finally, there are multiple points of negotiation with respect to the expanded rights of a 360 deal. In addition to the scope of the actively

52. Ray Waddell, "The Business of VIP Packages," *Billboard*, September 26, 2014, https://www.billboard.com/music/music-news/the-business-of-vip-packages-6266429/; Glenn Peoples, "From VIP Tickets to Premium Streaming Plans, the Music Business Is Entering a New Era of Upselling," *Billboard*, November 15, 2024, https://www.billboard.com/pro/concert-business-vip-strategy-expanding-streaming-vinyl/.

exercised rights granted to the company, the scope of noncontract revenue subject to a passive percentage interest by the record company needs to be carefully considered, together with the issue of what that percentage might be, what the rate is based on, how long it is paid, and whether it varies over time or with respect to certain revenue sources. Are there separate advances paid for specific rights, and are any rights categories cross-collateralized with other accounts under the agreement? What approvals are required with respect to actively managed rights? With respect to the record company's passive percentage interest, does it have the right to audit the books and records of the artist in the same way that the artist has the right to audit the books and records of the record company? All these questions should be weighed in the balance with the capabilities and commitments of the record company to determine whether a 360 deal is appropriate for the artist.

Alternative Recording Agreements

At the same time that major record companies were increasing the scope of their capabilities and obtaining a broader range of rights to exploit, the decentralization away from the record companies of the means by which recordings may be produced, distributed, and sold has had broad implications for artists looking for alternatives. Tools are available for artists to control many more of the functions previously controlled by the record companies. But just as there is the potential for greater direct reward, there is greater responsibility and risk. Opportunities for arrangements alternative to those generally followed by the major labels exist for artists preferring the independent route.

One nontraditional arrangement is a license agreement between the artist and the record company. Under this scenario, the artist finances the production of the recording and delivers the finished recording to the record company. The record company exploits the rights in the recording that are defined in the license agreement for the period of time and in the territory that are also defined. The record company will generally pay an advance for such rights (which would generally be less than the recording costs incurred by the artist to produce the recording) and a royalty on exploitation revenue.

The royalty could be calculated in the same manner as described earlier for a recording artist agreement, or it could be arranged on an alternative basis. Alternatives include a set fee if the rights to be exercised by the record company are narrowly restricted. At the end of the license term, all rights to the recording revert to the artist. The artist is also in a position to license the recording to multiple licensees on a territory-by-territory basis if that is a more favorable arrangement. A license arrangement also does not commit the artist to an exclusive recording arrangement with the record company, although some companies will, as a condition to licensing and promoting a recording, request one or more options to obtain further recordings if the initial licensed recording is successful. Royalty rates are generally higher for licensed recordings than recordings produced under artist agreements, as the risk to the record company is much lower. The record company does not have to advance as much cost, and it is able to assess the commercial prospects of a completed recording as opposed to advancing funds for the production of recordings not in being, with all the attendant risks of unfavorable or untimely results.

Another alternative arrangement offered by some record companies is a profit-sharing deal. The arrangement could be in the form of a license of master recordings, co-ownership of the master recordings between the artist and the record company, or a more traditional artist agreement. The principal distinguishing feature of such agreements is that instead of royalties, the artist and the record company share profits derived from the exploitation of the recordings on some defined basis. The key term to be negotiated in such an agreement is of course the definition of the "profits" to be shared; in other words, what gets netted against gross revenue to reach net (a/k/a profit). Usually, the recording costs incurred in producing the record, the manufacturing costs of products (including artwork), advertising and promotional costs (perhaps pursuant to a mutually approved budget), and distribution fees are netted against gross revenue received by the record company. A company overhead charge calculated as a percentage of gross revenue might also be netted against gross revenue. As net profits are realized, they are distributed to the artist in the negotiated portion allocated to the artist, which could remain constant or vary as certain milestones are achieved (or not).

Another alternative arrangement offered by some record companies is a service provider agreement. Under this agreement, the recording is produced by the artist at the artist's expense (and, therefore, owned 100 percent by the artist) and delivered to the record company for manufacture, distribution, promotion, sale, and data analytics. However, instead of receiving a royalty or a share of the profits, the record company simply is allowed to deduct from the sums paid over to the artist an amount equal to either a set percentage of sales revenue or the cost to the record company of the service provided plus a service fee to the record company for managing the release of the recording. In the latter situation, this fee could be a set amount for certain defined responsibilities over a period of time, an actual cost figure uplifted by a certain percentage, a certain percentage of gross revenue, or a blend of any of these factors. The artist realizes their return on the profit represented by the remaining sales proceeds. While the record company has a lesser potential return with such an arrangement, its risk is significantly reduced as it has little outlay. The company also recovers its fee and costs from the revenue from the sale of the recording, after which it remits any funds to the artist.

Producer Agreements

The role of a producer of sound recordings has changed over time as recording technology has advanced. The initial functions of record producers were more along the lines of what is generally performed today by A&R personnel—they identified artists to be recorded by the record company, they helped select compositions to be recorded, and they supervised the recording sessions, which included aligning the performers in front of the primitive sound horns and recording equipment to capture the best sound. As recording technology advanced, the process became more technical. Lab coats were not an infrequent apparel item for sound engineers pictured in photographs of early recording sessions,[53] but the role of the producer

53. See, e.g., Peter Martland, *Since Records Began: EMI the First 100 Years* (London: Batsford, 1997), 138.

mostly remained that of a talent spotter and wrangler. It was their responsibility to capture what a performer sounded like, and make it technically satisfactory for the production of records that could be manufactured and played back. It was with the advent of tape recording, however, that the role of producer as a creative force really came into being.[54]

Prior to the development of tape as a recording medium, recordings captured actual linear performances in a singular process. Nothing could be added to or taken from the recordings, and they were of performances occurring in real life.[55] Tape changed everything. Tape permitted editing and multitracking of sound over sound, or, more accurately, sound side-by-side with sound. Tape also permitted manipulation of the recording and playback process to create special effects. In short, tape opened the door for innovation and creative contributions by producers. Today, very little of what we hear in recordings is an accurate capture of the actual sound of a performance. Most popular recordings today are built up through multiple inputs over a period of time that in their final result in no way reflect the capture of anything that actually happened in real life. The creation of such recordings is the role of a producer today, and it has become a very important role, in some cases even more important than the role of the credited performer. At the same time, an increasing number of artists have themselves become able, aided by ever-easily-used technology, to perform producer duties.

Producers may be engaged either directly by the artist, if the artist is in charge of creating the recording, or by the record company. In either case, it is critical that the agreement with the producer treat the contributions of the producer in the same manner as the contributions of a recording artist are treated in a recording agreement. The contributions should be

54. See Greg Milner, *Perfecting Sound Forever: An Aural History of Recorded Music* (London: Faber & Faber, 2009) (background on the introduction of recording tape technology in the United States).

55. Notwithstanding this statement, experiments were conducted as early as 1930 to produce multitrack recordings through the mechanical means of recording individual parts and then recording the simultaneous playback of such recordings, e.g., Paul Hindemith, *Originalwerk für Schallplatte: Instrumental Trickaufnahme* (1930), excerpt included in *Capturing Sound: How Technology Has Changed Music*, ed. Mark Katz (Berkeley: University of California Press, 2004).

defined as works made for hire, or, alternatively, assigned to the artist or the record company, respectively. The producer's role in the production of the sound recording will be recognized as subject to copyright protection, and the producer will be considered at least a co-owner of the copyright in the sound recording if a written agreement is not in place addressing that ownership.[56]

The fee producers are paid for their production services generally acts as an advance against royalties, or "points," payable to the producer when the recording is exploited. If the producer is engaged by the artist, the royalty arrangement can be on any terms the parties agree. If the producer is engaged by the record company, however, their royalties are generally calculated and paid in the same manner as the royalties for the recordings produced by the producer are calculated and paid for the artist. The principal difference with respect to producer royalties, however, is that producers start to accrue royalties from the sale of the first record—they are typically not subject to the recoupment of recording costs as the recording artist is. However, the key word is "accrue." While royalties may start to accrue for the producer upon the sale of the first record, those royalties are held by the record company and not paid to the producer until the recording costs attributed to the recording produced by the producer are recouped. At the point of recoupment, all accrued royalties are paid, net of any advance that may have been paid to the producer for such recordings, which, of course, works against the interests of the artist, whose own recoupment is not complete until the producer is paid. The key negotiating point to watch for is the rate at which the recording costs will be deemed "recouped." Will it be the full artist royalty rate, which favors the producer, or the artist's royalty rate, net of the royalty payable to the producer, which favors the record company, since application of a lesser rate will require greater revenue before recoupment occurs.

Another key provision of producer agreements is credit. Credit for the production of recordings is critical to the success of a producer's career, as their standing within the industry and ability to command prestigious assignments and fees may turn on their association with successful projects. As

56. *Diamond v. Gillis*, 357 F. Supp. 2d 1003 (E.D. Mich. 2005).

discussed earlier, credit will only be enforceable to the extent it is contractually obligated.[57] Therefore, the credit provisions of a producer's agreement should identify the wording of the credit that will be accorded the producer for both original recordings and remixes, the relative size of the credit, and when and where the credit will be accorded. In addition to the producer's name, the producer may want credit to be accorded to the producer's production company, either by name, logo, or both. Failure to accord credit as agreed to may result in significant damages for the record company or artist (depending on which of them signed the agreement with the producer).[58]

Production Company Agreements

The importance of the role producers currently play in the creation of sound recordings is reflected in the variety of ways record companies arrange their relationships with producers. With the exception of an independent label that might be headed by a producer or organized around the output of a particular recording studio, most producers today operate independently from record companies. Few record companies engage staff producers anymore, particularly in large numbers and for solely the producing function. Producers in that discreet role often work on a project-by-project basis, as described earlier, but their work can also involve entering into agreements with undeveloped recording artists to produce and shop recordings to record companies or even more complex and exclusive joint venture arrangements with record companies.

---

57. Interestingly, this issue is treated differently in most of the world outside the United States, where so-called moral rights typically provide the author with an inalienable right of attribution. *Understanding the International Copyright Law Moral Rights*, LAWS.COM, October 15, 2023, https://copyright.laws.com/international-copyright/international-copyright-law-moral-rights.

58. *Popovich v. Sony Music Ent. Inc.*, 508 F.3d 348 (6th Cir. 2007) ($5.6 million judgment for failure to affix producer logo affirmed); "*Composer Is Awarded $241,000 in Damages Due to Omission of Their Artist Credit on Single Record*," *Entertainment Law Review* 5, no. 6 (1983) (discussing Barry De Vorzon's claim regarding the song *Nadia's Theme*); Stan Soocher, "Lack of Logo Placement at Center of Ruling over Meat Loaf Album Packaging," *Entertainment Law & Finance*, January 2008.

It is not uncommon for an artist's first recording agreement to arrive in the form of an offer from a production company rather than a record company. The key difference between a production company and a record company is that the principal role of the production company is the production of recordings. The production company does not have the structure or resources to actually market and sell the recordings—those roles are undertaken by a record company to which the recordings produced by the production company are ultimately delivered. An independent production company may consist of an individual producer with a recording studio or access to studio facilities, or may be the co-venture partner of a major label with a significant staff and other resources. What is common within this range of capabilities is the fact that the production company does not actually release the recordings it produces but relies upon its relationships with record companies to do so.

An offer to an artist from a production company may feature many of the provisions that are otherwise found in an offer from a record company, particularly with respect to the scope of rights acquired and how royalties are calculated. This is because the production company is either modeling its business arrangements after those customary arrangements adopted by record companies or anticipating becoming a record company itself at some time in the future. The production company may also anticipate assigning the production agreement with an artist to a record company, which the production company anticipates will want to succeed to terms they would have obtained if they had originally signed the artist directly. But because the production company, at least initially, will be relying upon others to actually release and market the recordings, the offer presented by the production company may reference either existing or anticipated record company agreements in several key provisions.

Development Agreements

Production companies without a distribution or other form of agreement with a record company or the resources or interest in releasing and marketing the recordings itself will generally have interest in developing an artist as a recording artist and shopping the recordings and/or the artist to a record company. The agreements such a production company may offer are speculative. Whether the recordings produced under the agreement are ever commercially exploited depends upon the production company's success in interesting others to acquire the recordings. Under such circumstances, the royalty provisions of the production company offer to the artist are likely to be structured as a percentage of the revenue received by the production company from the buyer or licensee of the recordings. Further, the scope of rights obtained by the production company—merchandising, publishing, and so on—are likely to be defined as those necessary to conform the agreement to the requirements of the buyer or licensee of the recordings.

If the development offer from a production company is speculative, what are the issues the artist should be concerned with? First, the period of time the producer is allowed for the actual production and shopping of the recordings should be carefully defined. This period is likely to be exclusive, as the producer does not want to devote resources to the production and marketing of the recordings and be vulnerable to circumvention. In like manner, the artist does not want to be tied to an agreement that bars the artist from other offers if the development work of the production company is not rewarding. A development and shopping period of nine to twelve months is not unreasonable. The agreement should also address how ancillary rights might be handled during the period of the production agreement. Although the producer may not be in a position to exploit any ancillary rights, they may need the ability to convey such rights to a buyer that does have exploitation ability. One solution would be to permit the artist to continue to exploit such rights but to not grant rights to any third party that might restrict or impair the production company's ability to grant such rights to a buyer or licensee.

The development agreement should also address issues related to the production of recordings. For example, how many recordings are to be produced, who is responsible for the payment of the costs of producing the recordings, and what is the status of the recordings if the development agreement ends without a buyer or licensee being found? In the development of an artist, many possible paths may be explored, which may be affected by the responses received by the production company to the initial recording efforts from prospective buyers. From the artist's perspective, such early recordings, if they become available, may reflect unfavorably or cause confusion with their later efforts.

The extent to which the artist will be involved in the transaction with a buyer or licensee of the recordings produced under the production agreement is very important. Will the artist have the ability to approve the buyer or licensee, or any terms of the transaction? Will the production company continue as an intermediary between the artist and the record company buyer/licensee, or will the artist be obligated directly to the buyer/licensee? If the intention of the buyer/licensee is to enter a long-term agreement with the artist, then the artist will have significant control, as the transaction is not likely to be completed under such circumstances without the assent of the artist.

The financial implications to the artist of a production company continuing as an intermediary between the artist and the record company are significant. First, the recording cost recoupment arrangement between the artist and the production company may be broader and more inclusive than the arrangement between the production company and the buyer/licensee. This could delay or otherwise unfavorably impact payments to the artist from the production company. There may also be a cash flow issue that could affect the production company's ability or willingness to pay royalties. For example, the artist's account with the production company may be recouped, but the production company's account with the buyer/licensee might not be. This may be caused by any number of circumstances, including the possibility that the production company's account with the buyer/licensee is cross-collateralized with the account of other artists delivered by the production company. A cash flow issue could also occur if the production company gets into a dispute with the buyer/licensee for reasons unrelated to the artist and, as a result, the buyer/licensee withholds payments to the production company or stops promoting or selling the artist's recordings.[59]

Retaining the production company as an intermediary between the artist and the buyer/licensee also has financial impact if the production company experiences financial distress. The party marketing the artist's recordings

59. See *TVT Records v. The Island Def Jam Music Group*, 412 F.3d 82 (2d Cir. 2005).

may be financially healthy, but the amounts otherwise payable to the production company for remittance to the artist could be attached by the creditors of the production company and never see their way to the artist. Further, to the extent to which funds might be available to the production company, they may be exhausted by payments made to creditors or other artists, which in effect would create a form of unintended cross-collateralization. Finally, the artist's recordings could be embroiled in a bankruptcy or other insolvency proceeding or conflict involving the production company, notwithstanding success that might be achieved by the buyer/licensee with such recordings. Bankruptcy proceedings may even extinguish the obligation to pay royalties on a go-forward basis by the successor in interest to the recording and publishing assets of the production company.[60]

Other nonfinancial implications occur when the production company continues as an intermediary between the artist and the buyer/licensee. Artistically, the artist may wish to work with producers who are not affiliated with the production company. This may be difficult or impossible if the artist remains signed to the production company as opposed to directly with the buyer/licensee. Also, even if the production company has a distribution/marketing agreement with a record company, the production company could lose that arrangement or change to a different record company in a manner disadvantageous to the artist. Finally, a producer may claim rights to aspects of the artist's career in addition to those connected with sound recordings alone, particularly if the producer was instrumental in developing the overall artistic presentation of the artist.[61]

Established Production Company

At a certain point in the successful career of a producer, a record company may want to have an exclusive arrangement with the producer in the same way they have exclusive arrangements with artists. This arrangement could take the form of delivery/output for a specific number of recordings during a certain period of time or even a form of joint venture with the record

60. *Thompkins v. Lil' Joe Records, Inc.*, 476 F.3d 1294 (11th Cir. 2007).

61. See, e.g., *Rob Fusari Prods. LLC v. Team Love Child LLC*, No. 650179 (N.Y. Sup. Ct. 2010); see also Christopher John Farley, "Rob Fusari Vs. Lady Gaga: Inside the Lawsuit," *Wall Street Journal*, March 19, 2010, https://www.wsj.com/articles/BL-SEB-28067.

company. In a joint venture, the record company becomes a co-owner of the production company and its recordings.

An agreement between a production company and an established outlet for the distribution and marketing of its recordings is clearly a different prospect than the development arrangements discussed earlier. Yet, these arrangements still present some of the same issues, particularly with respect to the payment of royalties. If a production company has an established distribution arrangement, it will remain an intermediary between the artist and the record company. The artist is being brought into the transaction as part of the agreement between the production company and the record company. The production company also has certainty it can offer concerning key contractual issues, such as the ownership of recordings produced by the production company, the rights the production company is required to obtain from any artist signed to the production company, and the existence of a royalty structure. Because the established production company is not in a position to be dislodged as an intermediary, the provisions of the production agreement with the artist should be carefully assessed to determine the outcome of the occurrence of any of the adverse financial circumstances mentioned earlier with respect to a development agreement. This may require inquiry into the terms of the production company/record company agreement or specific undertakings by the record company on behalf of the artist.

Chapter 6
Personal Representatives

The music industry, like the entertainment industry generally, is characterized by the presence of intermediaries. These representative intermediaries include agents, managers, attorneys, business managers, and others. There are several reasons for this.

First, musicians quite often are away from home for great periods of time, traveling from performance to performance or otherwise engaged in activities demanded by their careers. This disrupts the ability to conveniently confer with them about matters that require attention, or to obtain from them execution of agreements. Also, artists may not want to give attention to certain business matters for a variety of reasons, including the distraction such matters can give to creative activity. As a result, intermediaries are engaged to handle such matters to relieve the artist of that burden. Artists may also believe the intermediary will be able to relate more knowledgably with business matters to a better result.

Second, performers generally are engaged on a project-by-project basis. They are not employed as regular employees on the payroll of a company over a length of time. This means that the conditions of their work, and their compensation, must be repeatedly negotiated many more times than the employment conditions and compensation applicable to a regular employee. Representatives are specialized in understanding the terms of engaging talent and assume a time-consuming responsibility that would otherwise distract talent from what talent does best.

Third, at their most successful level, the results of a performer's talent create a large and complicated business requiring expertise in many subject matters and, consequently, the contributions of many advisors and assistants. One would assume that a business that grossed, as an example, $1 million or even $500,000, would have a staff of employees to handle the myriad administrative and operational details that the business created. With a performer, the business may consist solely of the individual performer and the results of their talent, such as personal appearances, recordings, songwriting, and other activities. Talent representatives and assistants for a performer are all part of the team that any executive running a generic business would have to carry out the business of the company. In the talent's case, the business is the talent's career.[1]

Fourth, since talent is engaged on a project-by-project basis, representatives play the dual role of being a scout for opportunities and a filter of proposals. To sustain a career, talent needs a consistent deal flow of financial and career-enhancing opportunities. These opportunities may include a local club performance, the opening performance with a popular artist, or a key merchandising deal. Agents and managers (and often attorneys) make it their job to identify and promote such opportunities. Conversely, representatives are in a position to deflect or vet proposals that are made to talent that might otherwise be distracting or difficult to avoid. This can also take the form of being the "bad cop," whereby the representative is the person delivering bad news or expressing difficult views, from which the talent may disassociate themselves in an effort to create goodwill, avoid friction, and allow professional relationships to exist in a creative environment.

---

1. An interesting statement of this perspective of the performer-as-business mindset is made by Jon Bon Jovi in the documentary *When We Were Beautiful*, wherein Jon repeatedly refers to himself as the "CEO of a major corporation." Phil Griffin, *Bon Jovi: When We Were Beautiful*, directed by Phil Griffin (New York: RadicalMedia, 2009), film.

Agents

The relationship between agents and talent is generally thought to arise under circumstances of good faith and goodwill. Yet, many collapse under circumstances that cause some people to liken it to the relationship between Faust and Mephistopheles:

> I will bend myself to your service in this world, to be at your beck and never rest nor slack. When we meet again on the other side, in the same coin you shall pay me back.[2]

While the relationship between an artist and an agent may be just as exclusive and, perhaps, just as stubborn to terminate, the requested commission seldom equals the consuming tribute exacted of Faust, nor does the relationship share that bond's term, impliability, and scope.[3]

The principal role of an agent is to find work for their clients. This activity is generally something that is controlled by state or local statute, as agency work has historically been characterized by many abusive practices. In Illinois, for example, employment agencies are required to obtain a license from the Illinois Department of Labor, which involves an application, the posting of a bond, the use of forms that have been approved by the state, and an annual fee; and a license is also required in California, which requires submitting an application supplemented by business registration documents, affidavits of character, sample contracts, a fee schedule, fingerprints, a premise certification, and a $50,000 surety bond.[4] Securing or attempting to secure employment for persons seeking employment without a license is a misdemeanor in Illinois, and in California it can give rise to both suspension or cancellation of license and civil penalties. More importantly, failure to be properly licensed when engaged in agency activities can be a bar to

2. Johann Wolfgang von Goethe, *Faust*, trans. Louis MacNeice (New York: Oxford University Press, 1951).

3. "The agreement between Mephistopheles and Faust is against public policy." *United Aircraft Corp. v. Boreen*, 284 F. Supp. 428, 447–48 (E.D. Pa. 1968).

4. See generally Private Employment Agency Act, 225 ILCS 515; CALIFORNIA LABOR CODE §§ 1700–1700.47 (2017).

recovery of fees that might otherwise be payable to the agent for their successful efforts, or grounds for a disgorgement of fees already received. We will address this more fully in the section about personal managers.

Agency relationships with talent are usually unilaterally exclusive, meaning that the agent may have many clients, but each client may have but one agent. This is not only because agents want to be the exclusive beneficiary of any promotional efforts that they may make on behalf of the talent they represent, but also because clients with multiple agents could be put at risk of becoming subject to conflicting work obligations. Notwithstanding the foregoing, some agencies work on a nonexclusive basis, particularly those who sell into a market where the identity of the performers may not be critical, such as weddings, private parties, or corporate events. In such cases, a performer may be affiliated with more than one such agency, which will reach out to performers as appropriate to meet client requests.

Agencies generally work on a contingency basis, generally receiving between 10 percent and 15 percent of the compensation payable to the talent for the engagements arranged by the agent. Compensation for the talent, including deposits for performances, is generally paid to the agent, which then deducts its fees and remits the balance to the talent. The scope of an agent's responsibility may be a negotiated term. This is particularly important for performers with career opportunities in entertainment areas other than music, such as book publishing or television or film appearances, where more specialized agents in each industry may offer better representation.

The time period of an agent's representation is a negotiated term that has greatest importance when the relationship is exclusive. Because of the personal nature of the relationship between talent and an agent, some talent may want to negotiate a provision that allows the talent to terminate the agreement upon their election after a certain notice period. If that provision is not obtainable, then the talent's right to terminate could be tied to a certain performance achievement by the agent, such as a minimum dollar amount of compensation earned during a defined period. If the talent is drawn to the agency because of the presence of a certain individual with whom the talent prefers to work, the talent might obtain a key-man provision, permitting the talent to terminate the agency agreement if the key individual became unavailable or unwilling to work with the talent.

The legal relationship between an agent and talent will depend on the express provisions of the agency agreement and upon their respective circumstances in the relationship. Agency agreements typically contain a power of attorney provision permitting the agent to execute agreements on behalf of the talent and to negotiate certain instruments, such as checks. Since the agent is the business office of the talent for purposes of finalizing agreements and collecting payments, permitting the agent to sign contracts for the talent's performances and deposit payments is generally necessary and desirable. Granting a power of attorney beyond these functions is generally not advisable.

Whether the relationship between the agent and the talent is one of a fiduciary is determined on the basis of the respective circumstances of the parties at the time. The fact that the agent is a representative of the talent does not in and of itself create a fiduciary relationship. There must be the repose of trust and confidence by the talent in the agent beyond a conventional business relationship.[5] One approach to this point is to address it in the agreement between the agent and the talent. Some suggested language concerning the remittance of payments to the talent is the following:

> Any portion of the compensation for Artist's services which may become due to Artist shall, if not paid immediately on the receipt thereof by Agent, belong to Artist and shall be held by Agent in trust for Artist until payment is made; Agent shall not question Artist's ownership of such trust fund regardless of whether the monies are segregated.

The efforts the agent must expend on behalf of the talent when the relationship is exclusive are generally the agent's commercially reasonable efforts. Since such efforts are difficult to assess in retrospect and will of course differ from the subjective perspectives of the parties, the agreement between the agent and talent could establish specific initiatives or goals to

---

5. *Staudinger+Franke GmbH v. Casey*, 2015 U.S. Dist. LEXIS 73912 (S.D.N.Y. June 6, 2015); *Newton v. Meyer*, 2023 U.S. Dist. LEXIS 45576 (S.D.N.Y. Mar. 17, 2023) ("[The plaintiff] does not cite any authority suggesting that a fiduciary relationship automatically arises between a talent agent and his or her client. Indeed, Courts have suggested the opposite.").

help quantify this effort. From the talent's perspective, the responsibility could also be elevated to require the agent's "best" efforts to obtain engagements under the best possible terms and conditions. Following is suggested language along these lines to include in the agency agreement:

> Agent shall conduct all transactions with respect to Artist diligently and in good faith and at all times give Artist full and accurate information and truthful explanation of all matters relative to Agent's activities under this agreement, including to the persons with whom Agent is in contact during the Term in connection with Artist. Agent shall report to Artist immediately of any offers that Agent obtains.

One development that arose after public availability of the internet and has grown consistently since is the availability of online services to help musicians obtain paid performance opportunities. Companies such as The Bash (formerly GigMasters), Gig Salad, ReverbNation, and Sonicbids offer the ability for musicians to identify opportunities appropriate for their music and promote themselves to potential buyers. The online services are not active agents soliciting and promoting talent but instead are creating a more efficient market by providing the means by which buyers and talent may communicate and connect among themselves. These services generally operate on a subscription basis with various tiers of service available, and may charge an additional fee for engagements they have successfully facilitated.

Another online form of agency that has recently arisen is the music licensing services offered by websites such as Deep Sounds, Taxi, Soundstripe, Audio Jungle, Artist.io, Jingle Punks, and UnitedMasters. These services generally represent the recordings of their clients to music users on a nonexclusive basis under business models that vary from site to site. The services are often referred to as "retitling" libraries for the reason that in order to distinguish and track the usage of recordings they have licensed apart from licensed uses of the same recording that may have been arranged by others, the agency will retitle the recordings they represent with titles that are unique to their service. As a result, one's work may appear in the market under various titles, with usage calculated on an individual project basis as opposed to what may be a more favorable aggregate basis.[6] Of course, this may be a happy problem for the owner of a recording, who may be very pleased that their recordings are being used multiple times.

Personal Managers

The principal role of a personal manager is to guide the careers of the talent they manage.[7] The responsibility is broader than that of an agent. The following is typical language from a music manager agreement published by the National Conference of Personal Managers:

> As and when requested by me during and throughout the term hereof, you agree to perform for me one or more of the services as follows: advise and counsel in the selection of literary, artistic, and musical material; advise and counsel in any and all matters pertaining to publicity, public relations and advertising; advise and counsel with relation to the adoption of proper format for presentation of our artistic talents and in the determination of proper style, mood, setting, business, and characterization in keeping with our talents; advise, counsel, and direct in the selection of artistic talent to assist, accompany, or embellish our artistic presentation; advise and counsel with regard to general practices in the entertainment and amusement industries and with respect to such matters of which you may have knowledge concerning compensation and privileges extended for similar artistic values; and advise and counsel concerning the selection of theatrical agencies, artists' managers, and persons, firms, and corporations who will counsel, advise, seek, and procure employment and engagements for me.[8]

6. Ron Mendelsohn, "Ron Mendelsohn on Signing with a Non-Exclusive Retitling Library," *Film Music Magazine*, June 18, 2010.

7. For a very helpful review of the provisions of manager contracts for musicians, see Kent Newsome, "Designing Management Contracts for Musicians," *Entertainment and Sports Lawyer* 21 (Summer 2003): 1.

8. *Music Manager Agreement*, National Conference of Personal Managers, Inc., 1 (2009).

You may notice that the preceding description of services does not include soliciting employment for the artist. The manager may in fact counsel a performer to *not* accept proposed engagements when the manager believes such engagements might not be beneficial to the performer. Further, in some cases, as we will see, soliciting employment for an artist client without also being licensed as a talent agency can create serious problems for a manager.

The evolution of the music industry has made the role of personal managers more centric. The traditional functions of record companies that solidified their central role in the development of musical artists—talent discovery, capital, distribution, and marketing—have been challenged by the availability, and relative affordability, of technological tools that more widely distribute such functions more within the means of more artists. Affordably available platforms provide means to create fan followings of artists, make recordings within reasonable budgets, digitally distribute sound recordings, and print and manufacture merchandise on demand through a variety of alternative means. While marketing remains a significant obstacle for artists unaffiliated with a record company, the tools are there for artists to be more self-sufficient and independent. This creates greater opportunity, and responsibility, for managers to manage these tools and relationships. An example at the top end of the industry, the Eagles recorded their own last album and released it through their own distribution setup through Walmart. At the center of all these arrangements was their management company, which managed the central business entity that was the Eagles/the group. Target has also released a number of exclusive albums, with multiple artists like Taylor Swift, Olivia Rodrigo, Harry Styles, Imagine Dragons, Ariana Grande, Gwen Stefani, Shakira, Jason Aldean, and so on.[9]

9. Megan Armstrong, "Here's What We Know About Taylor Swift's 'Reputation,'" *Billboard*, October 16, 2017, https://www.billboard.com/music/pop/taylor-swift-reputation-album-what-we-know-details-7998751/; *Grammy-Award Winning Band Imagine Dragons Announce New Album, Target Exclusive Deluxe Edition*, Target, December 16, 2014, https://corporate.target.com/press/release/2014/12/grammy-award-winning-band-imagine-dragons-announce-new-album,-target-exclusive-deluxe-edition; *Jason Aldean Brings Sixth Studio Album to Target with Exclusive Bonus Tracks*, Target, September 2, 2014, https://corporate.target.com/press/release/2014/09/jason-aldean-brings-sixth-studio-album-to-target-with-exclusive-bonus-tracks; *Target and Gwen Stefani Team Up to Create Live Music Video for New Single "Make Me Like You,"* Target, February 10, 2016, https://corporate.target.com/press/release/2016/02/target-and-gwen-stefani-team-up-to-create-live-music-video-for-new-single-make-me-like-you%E2%80%9D;

The skill set required of managers today has also changed. The availability of tools that permit artists to conduct and operate the business of exploiting rights as the result of their talent, as opposed to turning such rights over to other companies to exploit and remit a royalty payment to them, means that the manager is required to take on different operational functions. The job of operating the business of, for example, merchandising or record distribution instead of managing the relationship between the band and the company that operates such business requires different talents, which should be considered when the selection of management services is being made.

The agreement a manager may have with an artist deals with some of the same issues that are present in an agency agreement. Management agreements are invariably unilaterally exclusive, as the role of the manager is not as easily parsed between entertainment areas, and the efforts of the manager are meant to create value across all entertainment forms. Because the relationship is more personal, the ability to terminate the agreement if the relationship breaks down or a key person becomes unavailable or unwilling takes on greater significance. The measure of a manager's performance may also be quantified in some objective fashion along the lines discussed in connection with agents, such as the undertaking of specific tasks or the achievement of certain financial goals as a condition for continuing the agreement.

Target and Shakira Give Fans More Music with Three Exclusive Tracks on "Shakira," Target, January 27, 2014, https://corporate.target.com/press/release/2014/01/target-and-shakira-give-fans-more-music-with-three-exclusive-tracks-on-shakira%E2%80%9D; *Target Collaborates with Ariana Grande on Exclusive Deluxe Edition of Sophomore Album*, Target, August 25, 2014, https://corporate.target.com/press/release/2014/08/target-collaborates-with-ariana-grande-on-exclusive-deluxe-edition-of-sophomore-album; *Taylor Swift's Exclusive Deluxe Version of "1989," Now Available at Target*, Target, October 27, 2014, https://corporate.target.com/press/release/2014/10/taylor-swift-s-exclusive-deluxe-version-of-1989,%E2%80%9D-now-available-at-target; Jonathan Zavaleta, "The Best Target-Exclusive Vinyl Albums, Including the Deluxe 'Tortured Poets' Anthology," *Rolling Stone*, December 4, 2024, https://www.rollingstone.com/product-recommendations/lifestyle/best-target-exclusive-vinyl-records-albums-1235069251; Ashley King, "Taylor's Target Exclusive Continues: Retailer Selling New Taylor Swift Albums in 500 Stores—Including Exclusive CD Variants—With Dramatic Midnight Openings," *Digital Music News*, September 7, 2025, https://www.digitalmusicnews.com/2025/09/07/taylor-swift-target-midnight-album-release.

Because of the personal aspect of the managerial relationship, managers generally have fewer clients than do agents, though they do usually have more than one. The compensation managers receive is generally a contingent payment based upon the entertainment income of the artist and generally ranges from 20 percent to 25 percent. Of course, there are exceptions, such as Colonel Parker's reported 50 percent commission as the manager for Elvis Presley.[10] The manager's commission is usually higher than an agent's because with fewer clients, the commissionable base for the manager is less than that of an agent. Also, the manager is taking an overall greater risk, as they are responsible for providing management services even when the artist is not engaged in remunerative activities.

The more personal and encompassing responsibilities of a manager often means that the manager will become involved with the overall financial affairs of the talent, with many payments being made by the manager on behalf of the talent. While such arrangements may have the appeal of expediency, the manager should not be given complete control over the talent's financial affairs. Instead, the financial activities of the manager should be subject to periodic review by other members of the talent's team, such as the talent's business manager or attorney. The consequences of reposing complete, unmonitored financial trust and authority in one's manager have often been devastating to performers.[11]

The commission payable to a manager may be negotiated in several ways. The commission may vary depending on the amount of the commissionable base, going either up or down after hitting certain income milestones, or not applying at all until a certain minimum is reached. Funds received by an artist that are dedicated to the production of certain works, such as sound recordings, should be carved out of the commissionable base. Certain investment income that is unrelated to the artist's career should also be exempted. One important issue to resolve is the extent to which the

---

10. Biography.com Editors, "Colonel Tom Parker—Elvis, House & Death," *Biography*, May 19, 2022, https://www.biography.com/business-leaders/colonel-tom-parker; Bryan Rolli, "Was Colonel Tom Parker the Villain *Elvis* Makes Him Out to Be?" *Ultimate Classic Rock*, June 23, 2022, https://ultimateclassicrock.com/colonel-tom-parker-elvis-presley/; Tony Sokol, "*Elvis*: Colonel Tom Parker Really Was That Bad," *Den of Geek*, June 25, 2022, https://www.denofgeek.com/movies/elvis-colonel-tom-parker-really-was-that-bad/.

11. See, e.g., *Natural Wealth Real Estate, Inc. v. Cohen*, 2008 WL 511761 (D. Colo. 2008).

manager will earn a commission on the revenue received by the artist during the term of the manager's agreement that is derived from agreements in existence prior to the commencement of the management agreement. In like manner, the extent to which the manager will continue to receive a commission after the management agreement is over for agreements entered during the term of the management agreement must be resolved. Generally, managers will continue to receive commissions on such agreements, but the post-term commission might be reduced, or "sunsetted," in anticipation of that same revenue being commissionable by a successor manager.

The relationship between a manager and an artist is not per se a fiduciary relationship but may develop into one. One significant case that addressed this issue was *Reznor v. J. Artist Management, Inc.*,[12] which involved claims asserted by Trent Reznor of Nine Inch Nails against a former manager, including a claim for breach of fiduciary duty. In *Reznor*, the court found that, under New York law, a fiduciary relationship exists when one person "is under a duty to act for or to give advice for the benefit of another upon matters within the scope of the relation."[13] In denying cross motions for summary judgment on the issue of fiduciary duty, the court concluded that, at the time Reznor and his former manager entered their management agreement, a jury could find that the relationship was informal enough to be a conventional business arrangement. But the court also concluded that a jury could find that as the relationship progressed, the manager became a trusted advisor such that a fiduciary relationship was created that bound the manager to a standard of fairness, good faith, and loyalty. As with the agency agreement, specific language in the agreement between the manager and the artist could address this issue, although states are split on the question of whether one may disclaim a fiduciary duty by contract.[14]

12. *Reznor v. J. Artist Mgmt., Inc.*, 365 F. Supp. 2d 565 (S.D.N.Y. 2005).

13. Ibid., 574.

14. *BNP Paribas Mortg. Corp. v. Bank of Am., N.A.*, 2012 WL 2026063, 9 (S.D.N.Y. 2012) and *Model Serv., LLC v. MC2 Models Mgt., LLC*, 2015 N.Y. Misc. LEXIS 4766 (2015) (duty may be disclaimed); *Hands on Video Relay Servs., Inc. v. American Sign Language Servs. Corp.*, 2009 WL 8691614 (E.D. Cal. 2009) and *Hands on Video Relay Servs. v. Am. Sign Language Servs. Corp.*, No. 09–996, 2009 U.S. Dist. LEXIS 124899, 2009 WL 8691614, at *6 (E.D. Cal. Aug. 12, 2009) (duty exists apart from contract); *Margaritis v. Vast Mt. Dev. Inc. Margaritis v. Vast Mt. Dev. Inc.*, 2022 U.S. Dist. LEXIS 8705 (2022) (contractual disclaimers of fiduciary duties not necessarily dispositive).

Another interesting case that addresses the responsibility of an artist's manager after the end of the management relationship is *ABKCO Music, Inc. v. Harrisongs Music, Ltd.*,[15] which involved a dispute between George Harrison of the Beatles and his prior manager, Alan Klein. During Klein's tenure as Harrison's manager, he handled matters relating to a copyright infringement action brought against Harrison by the publisher of the song *He's So Fine*. The lawsuit resulted in a finding of liability against Harrison. After Klein's management agreement ended, but before damages had been determined in the lawsuit against Harrison, Klein covertly acquired ownership of the song *He's So Fine* and thus a stake adverse to Harrison in the litigation. When all was revealed, Klein was forced to give up his interest in the song based on his violation of his duties to Harrison to not use against Harrison that which what Klein had learned as Harrison's manager. While one certainly hopes one's manager will be a savvy advocate, the case brings to mind Aesop's fable about the snake at the bosom, which repays kindness with a fatal bite: "You knew I was a snake when you took me in."

One area of persistent tension in the manager–artist agreement is the extent to which a manager will seek employment for the artist, and what the consequences are for the manager if they do. As mentioned earlier in connection with agents, the solicitation of employment without a proper license may violate various state laws. The violation of such laws has forced certain managers who sought employment for their artists to return commissions they had previously received for their efforts. In some cases, returning commissions has resulted in restitution of as much as several million dollars.[16] Despite persistently vocal dissatisfaction by some with the breadth of the talent agent licensing requirements (and the potential economic consequence of de facto employment procurement without a license to do so), and the resultant efforts to challenge, modify, or repeal existing law, these licensing requirements remain.[17]

15. *ABKCO Music, Inc. v. Harrisongs Music, Ltd.*, 722 F.2d 990 (2d Cir. 1983).

16. The following cases were decided by the State of California Labor Commission: *Pryor v. Franklin*, No. TAC 17 MP114 (1982); *Gordy v. McLean*, TAC 27195 (2012); *Hall v. X Mgmt.*, No. TAC 19–90 (1991); *Blackstock v. Starstruck Management Group, LLC*, No. 52781 (2023).

17. See generally KCAL News, "Hollywood Managers: Calif. Talent Agencies Act Unconstitutional," *CBS News*, November 13, 2012, https://www.cbsnews.com/losangeles/news/

If managers are aware of the severe consequences for not being licensed as an employment agent, why do more managers not simply obtain a license? California provides some good reasons why not. As already mentioned, to comply with California's licensure requirements for operating as an agent, the agent must submit their contracts with the talent and fee schedules, post and maintain a bond in the amount of $50,000, and maintain records of their efforts for inspection by the state.[18] Most managers do not accept these restraints.

The scope of permissible employment seeking activity in which a manager may be engaged will depend on the state in which the manager is operating. In California, a manager is permitted to seek recording agreements for artist clients without a finding that they are an unlicensed employment agent.[19] In New York, managers may seek employment opportunities for artist clients that are only "incidental" to their management efforts.[20] In Illinois, the licensure provisions of the Department of Labor for employment agents has been interpreted to apply to placement services to the general public, not to managers.[21] The Illinois licensing requirements have also been held to not be applicable to attorneys seeking employment opportunities for their clients.[22]

Over time, the punitive risk managers take when seeking employment for their artist clients has been reduced. In 2008, the California Supreme Court decided in the case of *Marathon v. Blasi*[23] that a near-reflexive policy of disgorgement of all fees by an unlicensed manager that sought employment for their clients was not supportable. Instead, the Court stated that

---

hollywood-managers-calif-talent-agencies-act-unconstitutional/; Eriq Gardner, "Should Agents Still Be Licensed?" *Billboard*, February 13, 2015, 24; David Ng, "The Latest Wrinkle in the Writer-Agent War: A State Law Widely Seen as Outdated," *Los Angeles Times*, April 30, 2019, https://www.latimes.com/business/hollywood/la-fi-ct-talent-agencies-act-20190430-story.html; Michele B. Brown and Saul Bercovitch, "CLA Sponsors Legislation to Remove Unnecessary Restrictions on Your Ability to Practice Law," *California Lawyers Association*, 2024, https://calawyers.org/california-lawyers-association/california-ab-2989/ (last accessed September 2025).

18. See generally *California Labor Code* §§ 1700–1700.47 (1994).
19. *California Labor Code* § 1700.4 (1994).
20. *New York General Business Law* art. 11, § 171(8) (2014).
21. *Zinn v. Parrish*, 644 F.2d 360 (7th Cir. 1981).
22. *Musburger v. Meier*, 394 Ill. App. 3d 781 (1st Dist. 2009).
23. *Marathon v. Blasi*, 42 Cal. 4th 974 (Cal. 2008).

the doctrine of severability could be applied so that the prohibited aspects of the management agreement (procurement) could be severed from the permitted (advice, counseling, and the like). Thus, the court said, "For the personal manager who truly acts as a personal manager, however, an isolated instance of procurement does not automatically bar recovery for services that could lawfully be provided without a license."[24]

After *Marathon* came the opinion in the U.S. Supreme Court case of *Preston v. Ferrer*.[25] In *Preston*, the Court determined whether an arbitration provision in an agreement trumped state regulation of the activity that was the subject of the agreement. The Court found that an arbitration agreement between parties engaged in commercial activity subject to state regulation removed jurisdiction from the state agency empowered to enforce the regulation. By so holding, the Court handed managers a powerful tool to avoid having their disputes with artist clients heard within a framework of unfavorable precedent, which in the case of California was the California Department of Labor. From the perspective of a manager, arbitration provisions are now viewed much more favorably.

As stated in Chapter 5 with respect to record companies and recording agreements, whether the musical artist is a minor at the time of signing the management contract can give rise to risk for the manager that can be mitigated by court approval of the contract or, to a lesser extent, a separate agreement with the parent(s) in which they independently represent and warrant that their minor child will not disaffirm. Where management agreements are concerned, since the monetary consideration flows from the artist to the manager (rather than from record label to artist in the case of a recording agreement), even though a minor may have the ability to disaffirm a management agreement, the termination of the agreement may not foreclose the enforcement of the agreement for purposes of collecting fees due under the agreement from when it was in place.[26]

Conflict resolution is an additional area that bears attention in an agreement between a manager and artist. First, the artist should have strong rights

24. Ibid., 998.

25. *Preston v. Ferrer*, 552 U.S. 346 (2008).

26. *Scott Eden Mgmt. v. Kavovik*, 563 N.Y.S. 2d 1001 (N.Y. Sup. Ct. 1990), aff'd, 197 A.D.2d 569 (1993).

to audit the books and records of the manager to determine the accuracy and completeness of statements and payments made to the artist, both during the term of the management agreement and for a period thereafter. The same general concepts around audits as discussed in Chapter 3 and Chapter 5 with respect to publishing agreements and recording agreements, respectively, apply to manager agreements as well. The applicable law and venue provisions for the law that will apply in interpretations of the management agreement and where dispute resolution will occur are also key. Finally, arbitration should be considered as an alternative to litigation for two reasons. First, the parties could agree to the use of an arbitrator familiar with the entertainment industry, which may expedite the proceeding and perhaps lead to a determination more acceptable to the parties. Second, arbitration maintains the confidentiality of the proceedings, and the parties' financial information.[27] Organizations that offer mediation and arbitration services in the area of music disputes are listed in Appendix A.

Business Managers

A business manager is generally responsible for the financial caretaking of the artist's business matters.[28] The business manager does not provide counsel about the direction of the artist's career, but instead provides accounting services and perhaps ensures that payments are tracked and collected, bills are paid, and the business of the artist runs efficiently and productively. Business managers are quite often certified public accountants and may provide tax planning, return preparation, investment advice, statement review, auditing of royalty accounts, preparation of financial statements and other

27. For an article discussing the benefits of mediation to resolve entertainment disputes, see Richard S. Reisberg, "Why Entertainment Disputes Are Well Suited for Mediation," *Corporate Counsel*, August 2005, A4–5.

28. See generally Glenn Peoples, "Money Never Sleeps," *Billboard*, April 2, 2011, 20–21; Ava Lawrence, "Artists and Their Managers Take Control: The Evolving Role of the Artist in Today's Music Industry," *Journal of the Music and Entertainment Industry Educators Association* 5, no. 1 (2015): 91–101; Elia Pizzolitto, "Music in Business and Management Studies: A Systematic Literature Review and Research Agenda," *Management Review Quarterly* 74 (2023): 1439–472; Arsenli Pushmin, "Music Management: Production System and Promotion in the Music Industry," *Socio-Cultural Management Journal* 6, no. 1 (2023): 140–64.

financial reports, and management of certain vendor relationships such as insurance. Business managers are particularly key in planning and managing personal appearance tours and dealing with settlements with promoters, payroll, and tax obligations in the multiple states where appearances occur.

Business managers' relationships with talent are almost always unilaterally exclusive, meaning that the artist will have but one business manager, but the business manager will have multiple clients. Even a business manager of A-List talent will likely have multiple clients.[29]

The fee arrangements with business managers will depend on the scope of services provided, and can take different forms for different services provided. For example, a business manager may be paid a flat fee for preparation of tax returns, and be paid on an hourly basis for traditional accounting work, and be paid a percentage of the artist's gross income for the more creative aspects of business management such as investment guidance. Where flat and hourly fees are concerned, they are typically in the same range as those that traditional accounting firms of like size and qualification charge for similar work. Where percentages are concerned, it is not uncommon for business managers of established, high-income artists to charge 5 percent of the artist's gross income.[30]

A business management agreement is in many ways what one would expect to find in any engagement letter for accounting and tax services. One material difference, however, is in the broad powers of attorney granted by the artist to the business manager in a typical business manager's engagement letter. For example, a business manager is typically given power of attorney to open and direct the activity of bank accounts, write checks, sign contracts pertaining to financial management, and to open and utilize credit card and other revolving accounts.

Because of the financial aspects of the business manager's responsibilities and the special expertise they typically bring to the role, the business manager relationship will generally be considered a fiduciary relationship.[31]

---

29. See generally Matt Herring, "Where Bieber, Britney and Usher Bring Their Cash," *Billboard*, August 15, 2016, 55.

30. M. S. Mitnick, S. Smith, L. Strauss Jr., and L. Tenner, *Business Management in Counseling Clients in the Entertainment Industry* (Practising Law Institute, 1999), 153–54.

31. *ABKCO Music, Inc. v. Harrisongs Music, Ltd.*, 722 F.2d 990 (2d Cir. 1983).

Chapter 7

Personal Appearances and Live Events

In a world where creative expression is increasingly distributed and consumed in a solitary experience by means of digital transmission, the communal experience of witnessing a live personal performance of a musical performer takes on greater meaning and reward.[1] Witness the surged growth of YouTube Live, Twitch, TikTok Live, and Instagram Live in recent years in evidence.[2] The following are some of the issues relating to a broad range of circumstance involving live performances.

1. Digital distribution also makes it possible for performing musicians to syndicate live personal performances to individual subscribers through platforms such as StageIt, DistroKid, TuneCore, and Ditto Music. Liv Carr, "15 Best Live Streaming Platforms for Creators," *Whop*, October 15, 2024; Arash F., "Best Live Streaming Platforms for Creators in 2025," *Brand Vision*, 2025.

2. Liv Carr, "15 Best Live Streaming Platforms for Creators," *Whop*, October 15, 2024, https://whop.com/blog/live-streaming-platforms/; Arash F, "Best Live Streaming Platforms for Creators in 2025 | Brand Vision," *Brandvm.com*, 2025, https://www.brandvm.com/post/best-live-streaming-platforms-creators-2025.

Busking

Busking, or performing in a public place, usually for the purpose of soliciting compensation, is almost as old as music itself. And regulation of busking has been around almost as long. The Roman Republic, in the Laws of the Twelve Tables, barred the performance of defamatory song upon pain of death.[3] Mayor LaGuardia banned street musicians entirely in New York City in 1935, which lasted until Mayor Lindsey lifted the ban in 1970.[4] Other municipalities have long sought to control public performances for various reasons.

The regulation of busking is generally premised on the need to protect public safety and avoid nuisance. These state interests must be balanced with the First and Fourteenth Amendment rights of the performer. Generally, time, place, and manner regulations affecting expressive conduct may be enforced if they are reasonable, content neutral, narrowly tailored to serve significant government interest, and leave open ample alternative channels of communication.[5] Local regulation of street performers reasonably related to issues of sound volume, access to public ways, building entrances and exits, traffic flow, and the function or management of public places may be enforced.[6] However, unduly burdensome laws, or laws that have as their principal origin the protection of merchants complaining of lost business, have had a difficult time surviving challenges.[7]

---

3. David Cohen and Ben Greenwood, *The Buskers: A History of Street Entertainment* (London: David and Charles, 1981), 14.

4. Robert Hawkins, "'Industry Cannot Go On without the Production of Some Noise': New York City's Street Music Ban and the Sound of Work in the New Deal Era," *Journal of Social History* 46, no. 1 (Fall 2012): 106–23; Heather Jacks, "A History of NYC Busking and Street Performance," *American Noise*, November 9, 2018.

5. See, e.g., *Thomas v. Chicago Park Dist.*, 534 U.S. 316 (2002); *Friedman v. City of Highland Park*, 784 F.3d 406 (7th Cir. 2015); *Ward v. Rock Against Racism*, 491 U.S. 781, 790 (1989); *Friedrich v. Chicago*, 619 F. Supp. 1129, 1142. (N.D. Ill. 1985); *Turley v. Police Department of the City of New York*, 167 F.3d 757 (2d Cir. 1999).

6. See, e.g., *Carew-Reid v. Metropolitan Transp. Auth.* 903 F.2d 914 (2d Cir. 1990); *Berger v. City of Seattle*, 512 F.3d 582 (3d Cir. 2008).

7. See, e.g., *Berger v. City of Seattle*, 569 F.3d 1029 (9th Cir. 2009); *Perry v. Los Angeles Police Dep't*, 121 F.3d 1365 (9th Cir. 1997); *Chase v. Town of Ocean City*, 825 F. Supp. 2d 599 (D. Md. 2011); see also *Horton v. City of St. Augustine, Fla.*, 2000 WL 35918961 (M.D. Fla. 2000).

House and Small Business Concerts

The presentation of musical performances in private homes and at small businesses is not a new idea. Until the emergence of recorded music in the late nineteenth century, of course, the performance of music in the home with and for guests was a common occurrence; and many small businesses attempt to attract potential customers with a variety of entertainment. However, the idea of home concerts has resurrected itself in contemporary form and has become a popular form of social entertaining, although not one without its own set of legal issues.

House concerts implicate local regulation when they begin to take on features of commercial activity. When that occurs, local zoning laws may start to apply. An occasional presentation of musical performances in one's home for one's private guests would not draw regulation. However, the frequency of the events, how they are advertised and promoted (particularly if to a general audience), and whether and how an admission charge is collected may cause the activity to be characterized as commercial. If the activity is characterized as commercial, it may require commercial licensure or presentation at a venue located in a nonresidential area.[8] House concerts can also implicate local regulation when they begin to become hearable beyond the property line boundaries of the property in or on which they are held. When that occurs, local noise ordinances may start to apply.[9] It is also possible that any of the activity described in this paragraph could run afoul of applicable condominium, co-op, or homeowners' association restrictions on the engagement of commercial activities in the homes subject to such restrictions.

Finally, house concerts also raise liability issues for those who host them. Homeowner's insurance policies may or may not cover premises liability for guests, particularly if the guests are deemed to be commercial patrons of a commercial activity. House concerts also may involve staging, lighting, and sound equipment not normally found in the home, which may create

8. *Harris v. Township of O'Hara*, 2008 WL 2265294 (3d Cir. 2008).

9. See generally Jay Stapleton, "Disputes over Noise Levels from Live Performances," *Entertainment Law & Finance*, March 2015.

hazards. Finally, serving alcohol may create liability, particularly if the concerts are deemed commercial and/or the alcoholic beverages are sold.

Public Venues

The range of circumstances under which a musician may publicly perform is broad. The focus of this chapter will be on individual performances, as the issues involved with touring are beyond the scope of this book.

One of the most important aspects of any business is its relationships. Typically, in this context, the word "relationships" includes contracts. Indeed, the word "relationships" can often be used *interchangeably* with the word "contracts." The terms of an agreement engaging the personal services of a musician to perform may be negotiated by the musician's agent or by the musician directly. In so "engaging" a musician, the promoter (sometimes also referred to as the "presenter") will be entering into a contract with the musician, and vice versa. Thus, musician contracts are an important aspect of the live events business.

Many contracts in the entertainment industry as a whole, including those related to live performance, have historically been memorialized by only a mere handshake. This is because, historically, many people in the entertainment community have believed that written contracts are not required for them because the industry self-regulates (e.g., at the simplest level, they believe a musician who does not show up to perform simply will not be booked again, and, conversely, a promoter who does not pay as promised will not find many musicians interested in performing). Many also believe that written contracts "spoil the vibe." While oral contracts can be effective in any industry, it is when things go awry that most parties wish that they had reduced their agreement to writing at the outset, for a better position in the then-current dispute (or even a *clear* position, whether it be better or worse). While not all contracts are in writing, the smart businessperson (including one contemplating a live performance, as either musician or promoter) reduces their agreements to writing for certainty and evidentiary purposes.

Like any contract, a contract for a live performance is adequate for contract purposes only if it is definite and specifies all material points. For example, for a musician's performance at a live event, minimum specificity would include the identity of the musician engaged; the date, time, and place of the performance; and the compensation. From a contracts law perspective, a written agreement that stated just these few things would comprise a valid contract. However, it typically would be wise to include more than that (and many live-performance-related contracts *do* include more than that), such as the time of equipment load-in and sound check, the duration of the performance, and other provisions explained in more detail later.

Where consideration is concerned, keep in mind that consideration is merely *some* benefit conferred by each party to the other. In the live performance context, if a promoter pays a musician $200 to perform, the performance is the musician's consideration for the $200 payment, and the $200 is the promoter's consideration for the performance. Consideration can be anything of value (historically, the courts have said a "peppercorn" is enough), and it is important to note that a contract does not have to be "fair" in order to be enforceable.[10] For example, if an arena-level musician agrees to perform for $10, when their usual fee is $1 million, the $10 is sufficient consideration to make the contract binding, and the fact that the contract is "unfair" is not a defense to the enforcement of the contract. As long as the elements of offer, acceptance, and consideration exist, then the musician and the promoter will each be bound.

Billing

How a musician is billed for a performance may be standardized for certain venues, but any special requirements a musician may have should be addressed in a performance agreement.[11] For example, a musician may wish to be identified in a particular typeface or by a particular logo in advertisements, publicity, tickets, and venue signage. A musician may also have certain sponsor arrangements that require a reference of the relationship

10. While there isn't a definitive U.S. case stating "a peppercorn is enough for consideration," the concept is widely accepted in legal doctrine, often referenced in cases like *Chappell & Co Ltd v. Nestle Co Ltd*, which stated the proposition. *Chappell & Co Ltd v. Nestle Co Ltd* (1960) AC 87.

11. It is also critical that the performer be properly identified when they are being presented to a promoter for consideration of an appearance. See, e.g., *Finley v. River North Records, Inc.*, 148 F.3d 913 (8th Cir. 1998).

between the musician and the sponsor. The relative type, color, size, and position of billing accorded to multiple performers at an event may also be the subject of negotiation.

Promotion

Since the success of drawing an audience to a live performance is typically tied to its promotion, specifying each party's obligations regarding promotional efforts is a good idea. The promotion clause, while not "required" to form a valid contract, provides that one party or each party agrees to promote the show in a specified manner. It can be as simple as "musician will promote the show via all their social media platforms at least once per week in each of the [x] weeks prior to the performance, and promoter will include musician in all venue ads and posters and display the show flyer any place that promoter typically displays flyers for its shows." In this regard, if the promoter is the one doing the promoting, it will need the right to use the musician's name and likeness. A simple, sample clause for that right might read as follows: "Musician hereby grants to promoter the a limited, non-exclusive and non-transferable license to use and publish the use of the musician's name including any professional name, persona, likeness, image, signature and biographical data about musician (all, collectively, the 'Likeness') [solely] in connection with the exercise by promoter of its rights and obligations under this Agreement, along with the right to sublicense such rights [for the same sole purpose]." From the musician's perspective, it would be wise to insert the preceding bracketed words.

Technical Riders

Performances require various levels of technical conformity between the needs of the musician and the capabilities of a venue. On a basic level, a venue will need to know a performer's stage plot—the equipment that will be needed and where it will be placed on the stage. The venue and the musician will also need to communicate in advance concerning the specifics of required lighting, monitors, cabling, microphones, inputs, special effects (e.g., video projections, pyrotechnics), staging, and power. All these things are typically set forth in what is called a "technical rider" to the primary contract. Technical riders may also identify the number and type of personnel required at the venue to accommodate the setup and performance, along with their contact information in order to facilitate necessary advance work.

Compensation

Payment for a personal appearance can take several forms, with multiple variations within each method. Typical forms include flat fee, straight percentage, flat fee against a percentage, flat fee plus a percentage, or guarantee versus a percentage.

A flat fee is a guaranteed set amount, which is not dependent on ticket prices, sales, or any other factor. Payment is generally made by cash or certified check and may be made in installments—a portion paid upon confirmation of the engagement (usually held by the musician's agent if involved) and the balance upon performance.

Percentage compensation is generally based on admission revenue, excluding tax. The percentage can be applied to all admission revenue or to admission revenue in excess of certain delineated costs incurred by the promoter. For example, a performer appearing at a music club may receive 85 percent of all admission revenue in excess of the costs of lighting, sound system, and security.[12] Since the amount the performer will receive is unknown until revenue is calculated on the night of performance, payment is generally made in cash.

The risks of a straight percentage arrangement to a musician are many. If cash is used for admission, all the cash may not be reported to the musician, because of skimming by either the promoter or its employees. Also, the promoter (or its employees) may admit some people for free as a trade-off, or if the promoter believes their portion of the admission revenue is immaterial as compared to the amount the people admitted for free are likely to spend on food or drinks. Because of the potential for abuse, a straight percentage agreement, or "playing for the door," is disfavored by many

12. Note that the four costs itemized in the text would likely exist for any show, but as a venue gets larger and/or a show more complex, the number of types of costs also grows. See generally Eamonn Forde, "Where Concert Ticket Money Goes: Who's Getting Rich Off Live Music's Golden Age?" *The Guardian*, January 30, 2017, https://www.theguardian.com/music/2017/jan/30/where-does-concert-ticket-money-go.

musicians although perhaps inevitable for emerging musicians performing in smaller venues.[13]

An arrangement paying the greater of a flat fee against a percentage guarantees the musician a minimum fee, which can be increased if admission revenue exceeds a certain negotiated amount. For example, an artist might negotiate an agreement to receive $1,000, plus 30 percent of all admission revenue (also known as GBOR, for "gross box office receipts") in excess of 150 tickets sold. The potential percentage fee paid to the musician might also be calculated as a percentage of GBOR in excess of an amount (rather than a number of tickets) permitting the promoter to recover their costs, including the guarantee. That amount is called the break-even point. Whatever the arrangement, the promoter will be required to support their costs at the end of the evening when payment to the musician is settled.

Under a flat fee *plus* a percentage arrangement, a musician is paid a negotiated flat-fee guarantee *plus* a percentage of the GBOR that exceeds the sum of the breakeven mentioned earlier and a certain amount designated as the promoter profit. This sum is called the split point. The promoter profit is frequently calculated as 15 percent of the promoter's break-even point for the presentation of the event, other than the amount paid to the musician as a guarantee. For example, assume the musician negotiates a $50,000 flat-fee guarantee, plus 80 percent of GBOR in excess of the split point. Also assume that GBOR for the contracted event is $250,000, that the promoter's breakeven (without the guarantee) is $100,000, and that the promoter's profit is agreed to be 15 percent. In such case, the split point would be $165,000 ($150,000 [the breakeven plus the flat-fee guarantee] plus 15 percent of $100,000), the amount in excess of the split point would be $85,000 ($250,000, less $165,000), and the amount payable to the

13. As disfavored by musicians as "playing for the door" may be, certain other practices are even more unfavorable to them. For example, some music clubs have as a condition for appearing at the venue the requirement that the performer purchase a certain number of admission tickets, which the performer is then required to resell as their compensation for the appearance; and the appearance of a performer as a supporting act on a tour may be conditioned on the payment of a fee for the privilege of being involved.

musician would be $118,000 ($50,000, plus 80 percent of $85,000). These figures are not representative but are used simply for illustration, as each of the variables in the calculation is negotiable depending on the appeal of the musician and the costs involved in presenting the appearance.

With a guarantee versus a percentage, the musician simply gets paid the larger of the guarantee amount and the percentage of GBOR. For example, assume the musician negotiates $100,000 versus 80 percent, and GBOR for the contracted event is $200,000. In such case, the musician would be entitled to $160,000 (80 percent of the $200,000 GBOR).

Hospitality and Benefits

Compensation can be paid to a musician by means other than dollars. For example, a musician might negotiate for the payment of travel and accommodation expenses by a promoter, who may have sponsor arrangements with hotels or airlines. A musician's agreement may also describe the type of ground transportation provided and the destinations and times involved with such ground transportation. The musician may also negotiate for the promoter to pay the rental costs of instruments or other equipment necessary for the performance, which is referred to as the backline. The musician might also receive a certain number of complimentary tickets or the ability to purchase additional tickets in desirable locations.

While some performers are renowned for the extravagant excesses of their demands, the purpose of the hospitality provisions in a musician's agreement is not vanity. The goal of the performing musician is to deliver a great audience experience. The ability of the musician to do that is enhanced when the musician's comfort and sensibility are supported. Comfortable, private, and well-lit dressing rooms with outlets, towels, mirrors, appropriate food and drink, furniture, and utensils are keys to a musician's ability to deliver a good performance.

Proper security is another way a promoter helps both support a good performance and eliminate liability. This includes securing the backstage area, the route to and from backstage, the equipment, and the access to sound check, as well as proper on-stage protection, audience control, and evacuation instruction.

Cancellations

The consequences of an event cancellation will turn on the terms of the contract and when a binding commitment to perform has been made between the parties.[14] If a promoter paid a deposit to secure the performance of a musician, the promoter will generally forfeit that deposit if they elect to cancel the appearance prior to the performance. A cancellation due to the occurrence of a force majeure will generally excuse the parties from liability, but the issue should be addressed specifically in the engagement agreement. Whether a musician's illness constitutes a force majeure also will depend on the language of the agreement. Generally, the risk of nonperformance due to weather is borne by the promoter. The musician is typically engaged to perform "rain or shine," so if an event is canceled because of bad weather, payment is still due to the musician with it being understood that weather-related risks are insurable by the promoter.[15]

Given the way in which a musician's fortunes may quickly change for the better, some musicians may seek provisions in their engagement agreements permitting them to terminate the agreement upon a certain advance notice if the terms of the engagement are no longer favorable.

Terminations for Immoral Behavior

A promoter may seek to protect itself by insertion into the contract of a so-called morals clause, that allows the promoter to immediately terminate the contract with a musician who, between the time of contract and the time of performance, brings themself into disrepute. The so-called morals clause dates back almost a century. The first morals clause in Hollywood came about when silent film star Roscoe "Fatty" Arbuckle was charged with the rape and manslaughter of Virginia Rappe. Arbuckle was tried three times between 1921 and 1922, with the first two trials ending in mistrials and the third in his acquittal. Due to the media outcry surrounding this case

14. See, e.g., *Allgood Ent., Inc. v. Dileo Ent. & Touring, Inc.*, 2010 WL 3322530 (S.D.N.Y. 2010).

15. Carla Varriale-Barker and Courtney Dunn, "Evaluating Personal Injury Claims and Insurance Policies Covering Live Events," *Law Journal Newsletters*, December 9, 2024; Scott Carroll, "A Changing Live Event Insurance Landscape; Coverage Restrictions in Today's Market Requires Critical Policy Reviews," *Insurance Journal*, May 16, 2022; Chris Cullari, *Understanding Event Insurance with Nichole Jensen*, Wrapbook, June 21, 2024.

and the trials, Universal Studios decided to add a morals clause to all its talent contracts.[16] Additionally, in 1921, Jake Ruppert, owner of the Yankees, attempted to curtail Babe Ruth's notorious drinking and womanizing by adding a contract addendum calling for Ruth to abstain entirely from intoxicating liquors and to not stay up past 1:00 a.m. during the training and regular seasons.[17] Thus, entertainers' morality has been an ongoing concern in the entertainment industry. However, such clauses have taken on increased importance given the ever-increasing number of allegations launched against famous people, including musicians, the ever-increasing media coverage of them, and the ever-increasing negative effects of even unproven allegations.

From a philosophical perspective it is difficult to argue with the promoter's proposition where a morals clause is concerned: "If you do something that brings yourself into disrepute, then I can terminate our contract with no consequence to me because your disreputation might otherwise also have a negative effect upon me." However, the contractual clauses that provide for this proposition come in all shapes and sizes. An example of a morals clause that is broad and vague, and allows the principal wide discretion to determine whether certain behavior is sufficient to give rise to the right to terminate without further obligation to the terminated party, is:

> Promoter will have the right to terminate for cause if you engage in conduct that brings you or promoter into public disrepute, contempt, scandal or ridicule, or which insults or offends the community or any employee, agent or affiliate of promoter or which otherwise injures your reputation in the sole judgment of promoter, or otherwise diminishes the value of the Services to the public or promoter.

On the other hand, an example of a morals clause that has specific, objectively determinable triggers is:

16. Fernando M. Pinguelo and Timothy D. Cedrone, "Morals? Who Cares About Morals? An Examination of Morals Clauses in Talent Contracts and What Talent Needs to Know," *Seton Hall Journal of Sports and Entertainment Law* 19 (2009).
17. Jane Leavy, "Being Babe Ruth's Daughter," *Grantland*, December 19, 2011.

> Promoter will have the right to terminate for cause if: (a) you have committed a dishonest act to the material detriment of promoter or any act of fraud against promoter; (b) you are convicted of or plead guilty or no contest to either a felony or a misdemeanor that involves moral turpitude; (c) you have habitually and unlawfully used (including being under the influence of) or possessed illegal drugs; (d) you lose, for any reason, any license or professional registration necessary to the performance of your duties, which loss continues without reinstatement for a period in excess of 30 days without promoter's written consent; (e) you materially and repeatedly violate promoter's reasonable, lawful and published policies and procedures, which violations continue for a period in excess of 30 days without promoter's written consent; or (f) you flagrantly disregard your duties under this Agreement.

On first review, it might appear that the second of the foregoing sample clauses is more favorable to the promoter, because it is "longer." However, note that the first of the foregoing sample clauses is vague and ambiguous, and gives the promoter far greater discretion as to whether a termination is appropriate. In the second sample clause, while there are more words, and optically a greater number of grounds to terminate, each ground is specific and can be more objectively determined. There is no "right" or "wrong" way to draft these clauses, but it is important that both parties understand the implications and the expectations that are outlined. Note that, while the morals clause for Arbuckle was of the former, vague, pro-employer type, the one for Ruth was, except for its last few words, rather objectively determinable and, as such, pro-employee.[18]

---

18. The form Universal clause catalyzed by Arbuckle read: The actor . . . agrees to conduct himself . . . with due regard to public conventions and morals and agrees that he . . . will not do or commit anything tending to degrade him . . . in society or bring him . . . into public hatred, contempt, scorn or ridicule, or tending to shock, insult or offend the community or outrage public morals or decency, or tending to the prejudice of . . . Universal . . . or the motion picture industry. In the event that the actor . . . violates any term or provision of this paragraph, then . . . Universal . . . has the right to cancel and annul this contract by giving five (5) days' notice to the actor. . . . Ruth's clause read: . . . player shall . . . refrain and abstain entirely from the use of intoxicating liquors and . . . shall not . . . stay up later than 1 o'clock A.M. on any day without the permission and consent of the Club's manager [or] indulge in intoxicating liquors or be

In today's world, reasonable people can disagree as to whether any given relationship should have been terminated for the "immoral" conduct of one of the parties. However, the smart promoter and the smart musician are each wise to pay attention to the morals clause at the outset, to later have a better chance of receiving the benefit of their bargain, should the promoter decide, after the contract is signed, that it does not "like" the musician's behavior.

Exclusivity

Promoters generally want to know that the appearance of a musician for them will be exclusive to them for a period of time within the area from which they draw their audience. The promoter does not want to promote the appearance of a musician, only to find out that the musician is also appearing a few days later (or even worse, a few days earlier) in the same area.

The provision in a musician's agreement that bars them from appearing within a certain geographic location during a certain period of time is called a "radius" clause. The variables affecting a musician's exclusivity commitment will depend on the prominence of the event and the geographic range of attendees. For example, a major music festival may demand that the musician not appear within a 300-mile radius of the festival location 180 days before the event and ninety days after. The radius clause for a smaller club will be correspondingly less in both geography and time, perhaps fifty to one hundred miles within a thirty- or sixty-day period. For musicians who perform only locally, a radius clause would not be practical unless the compensation for an appearance were significant. In any event, any radius clause commitment given by a musician must be carefully considered to avoid impairing the musician's ability to accept other opportunities.

Merchandising

The sale of musician-related merchandise—recordings, apparel, and so on—will be handled differently by different venues. Some musician-friendly venues supply the musician with both facilities and staff at no charge to

guilty of any action or misbehavior which may render him unfit to perform the services to be performed by him hereunder.

help the musician sell merchandise. Other venues may charge a so-called hall fee, ranging from 10 to 25 percent of revenue. Whatever may be the arrangement, it is important to address in the musician's performance agreement the facilities and personnel that will be provided for merchandising sales, if any, and the fees involved. The musician should also be assured that their merchandising arrangements will be exclusive for the event so that the musician's own sales are not in competition with other offerings. A promoter generally does not share in any merchandising revenue unless it owns the venue, in which case it may receive a hall fee.

Representations, Warranties, and Liability Waivers

The promoter may also desire that the musician make certain representations and warranties in the contracting process, such as: (1) no one other than the musician will take the stage; (2) the musician's performance will not infringe any third party's intellectual property or other rights; (3) each person signing the contract for the musician has the legal capacity to contract for the one they purport to bind; and (4) the musician has had the advice of an attorney (or at least the *opportunity* to have the advice of an attorney), in connection with the contract. In addition, and due to the potential liabilities associated with live performances and events, the promoter may also wish to include a liability waiver, basically to the effect that the musician cannot hold the promoter liable for any damage to person or property sustained by the musician or its members as a result of the performance absent the grossly negligent or willfully wrongful act of the promoter. These representations and warranties and liability waiver each concern topics that can cost *somebody* money in connection with a live event, and the contractual provisions are an attempt to shift that potential liability from the promoter to the musician for each of them. As such, the shifting of these potential liabilities can become very important if and when things go wrong.

Indemnity

Hand in hand with the representations and warranties mentioned earlier, the promoter also probably will want to include a basic indemnity provision in the contract, providing that the musician will indemnify the promoter for any damages suffered by the promoter because of either any breach of the contract by, or negligent or willfully wrongful conduct of, the musician. Like the representations and warranties and liability waiver provisions, the indemnity provision is an attempt to shift potential liability from the promoter to the musician for something that goes wrong. As such, it, too, can become very important if and when things *do* go wrong.

Prohibition on Assignment

The promoter will probably also want to include a contractual provision stating that the musician has no right to assign the contract. This is important to the promoter, for at least two reasons. First, the promoter wants certainty that the bargained-for musician will show up to perform, rather than, for example, a friend of the musician looking for a gig—and without the "no assignment" clause, the bargained-for musician could assign the contract, thereby contractually binding the promoter to put the substitute musician on stage, and, more importantly, pay the same amount for the substitute musician. Second, the promoter wants certainty that, in the event there *is* some liability running from musician to promoter (e.g., the musician somehow infringes a third party's copyright in connection with the performance), that liability sticks with the musician, rather than, for example, a homeless man the musician finds on the street—and without the "no assignment" clause, the musician could assign the contract to the homeless man, thereby contractually binding the promoter to look to only the homeless man for the promoter's damages, effectively leaving the promoter without a meaningful remedy.

Specific Performance

In certain cases, the non-breaching party may also sue for "specific performance" (i.e., for a court order requiring the bargained-for performance, rather than the payment of mere money damages).[19]

19. Hanoch Dagan and Michael A. Heller, "Specific Performance: On Freedom and Commitment in Contract Law," *Notre Dame Law Review* 98 (2023): 1323; D. A. Jeremy Telman, "When Specific Performance of Personal Service Contracts Is the Right Remedy," *SSRN*, October 18, 2024; Nathan B. Oman and Kimberly D. Krawiec, "The Case for Specific Performance of Personal Service Contracts," *Iowa Law Review* 110 (2024), Virginia Public

Defenses to Alleged Breaches of Live Performance Contracts

As is the case with all contracts, if one party to a contract claims that the contract has been breached, the party alleged to have breached may try to show that no contract ever existed (and, thus, that no breach occurred). The party alleged to have breached could do so by raising any number of different arguments disputing the formation of the contract. In short, the party alleged to have breached could claim that there was some irregularity in the formation of the contract, and, therefore, that no contract ever existed (and, therefore, there was nothing to breach, and there is nothing to enforce).

One such argument prevalent in the music industry in general, including where live performances are concerned, is lack of capacity (i.e., one party was legally incapable of either making the offer or the acceptance, for example, because they were not of legal age). If successful, this argument (as well as several potential others, such as mental infirmity and involuntary intoxication) can invalidate the contract as having never existed in the first place. See the discussion in Chapter 5 as to how a practitioner might seek to preclude a minor from disaffirming a contract.

Another way a party accused of breach may claim that no contract was ever formed is if the parties did not really reach an agreement on the essential terms of the contract, or both parties were mistaken about a material term of the contract, and, thus, there was no "meeting of the minds." In such a case, no contract was formed in the first place, and, so, no breach can take place. One possible example of a lack of meeting of the minds in the live performance context is a failure to state the currency under which an international contract is to be performed. For example, a U.S. musician agreeing to play in Germany for "100,000" (i.e., without either $ or € having been specified). In this example, if one party actually believed that the agreement spoke to dollars and the other party actually believed it spoke to euros, then the parties did not have a meeting of the minds on a material term of

---

Law and Legal Theory Research Paper No. 2024-41, Virginia Law and Economics Research Paper No. 2024-20.

the contract, and, therefore, no contract was formed (even if each—one thinking dollars and one thinking euros—thought it *had*). Another possible example of a lack of meeting of the minds in the live performance context is a failure to state with particularity the venue at which a performance is to be made in a case in which the promoter owns or controls multiple venues. For example, a musician agreeing with Live Nation to play "House of Blues" (i.e., without specifying which of the more than ten House of Blues locations owned by Live Nation). In this example, if one party actually believed that the agreement spoke to the Orlando House of Blues and the other party actually believed it spoke to the San Diego House of Blues, then the parties did not have a meeting of the minds on a material term of the contract, and, therefore, no contract was formed (even if each—one thinking Orlando and one thinking San Diego—thought it *had*).

A party alleged to have breached may also try to show that, while a contract *did* exist in the first place, the party alleged to have breached has a "defense," and that the defense excuses their failure to perform (i.e., that no breach occurred). One common way in a live performance context that a party accused of breach claims their failure to perform is excused (i.e., that no breach occurred) is by claiming that the purpose of the contract was "frustrated." This defense acknowledges that the contract was valid and enforceable, but that the failure of one party to perform was justified or excusable under circumstances that materially frustrated (or made impossible) performance as bargained for. For example, if a musician dies before the date of a performance for which they are contracted, then their failure to perform would technically be a breach of the contract; but, because the musician no longer exists, performance was made impossible, and therefore is excused. Conversely, if a venue at which a musician is under contract to perform burns down, the promoter's failure (due to that fire) to hold the show, have the musician perform, and pay the musician would technically be a breach of the contract; but, because the venue no longer exists, performance was made impossible, and is therefore excused.

Additional Considerations

One additional consideration particular to music industry contracts in general, if not live performance contracts in particular, is the importance of distinguishing between the legal and performing names of the musician. What is needed from the promoter's perspective is both names, that is, the given name of each individual musician who will sign and the stage name by which the musician or act is commonly known. Having the legal name is important in case the promoter ever needs to find a signatory for some reason, and that importance increases as time passes after the show date. The statute of limitations is many years long for many of the ills that could stem from a live performance. Getting the full, legal name of the musician up front is a good idea for the promoter, so that there is no obstacle of finding a musician who needs to be contacted or sued years after the show. A good practice in this regard is to get a copy of, or at least a look at, the musician's driver's license and copy the name exactly from it.[20]

A second additional consideration to note for a band is that, despite that any number of people may sign the contract (e.g., a manager, an agent, each member of the band, an authorized signatory of an entity through which the band performs), the contract should specify but a single payee. Paying just one payee eases the promoter's administrative burden, and puts the responsibility on the musician(s) for dividing the ultimate payment accordingly. Related to this is having a place in the contract for the single payee's mailing address and tax identification number whether that be a social security number (for an individual payee) or an employer identification number (for an entity payee). Having that information could be crucial for the promoter's tax return preparation and filing, particularly if the musician is paid a large sum. It is beyond the scope of this book and this chapter to discuss the tax implications of a promoter paying a musician to perform at a live event, but suffice it to say that, generally, the promoter is required to report such payments in tax filings (probably on an IRS Form 1099), and to mail a copy of the filing to the payee. Without the payee's address and the tax identification number, the promoter will not be able to fulfill its legal obligation in that regard.

---

20. One of the authors was once a business affairs executive with World Wrestling Entertainment, and one of the ways he made himself valuable was knowing (by his earlier reference to a driver's license or passport) the full, legal name of each wrestler, who almost always was otherwise referred to within the company (including in legacy contracts) by their "ring name."

Proceeds of Personal Performances

The presentation of a personal performance may result in the creation of valuable property, such as audio, visual, or audiovisual recordings of the performance. The unconsented recording, transmission, sale, or rental of copies of live musical performances is a both a civil copyright violation[21] and a criminal offense.[22] However, musicians frequently permit the presenting venue of a performance to record that performance on the musician's behalf and to deliver that recording at the end of the performance in consideration of the reimbursement of the venue's costs. The musician may then use the recording for archival purposes or to offer to their fans. Sometimes, the promoter will want the musician to grant to the promoter the right to record the performance for the promoter's own promotional purposes, and these rights, ancillary to the performance itself, can be crucial to the success of the promoter's business in general, as it seeks to promote itself and its future shows. For this purpose, given that more than one copyright would be involved in exercising such rights, a more lengthy clause would be appropriate. A promoter-friendly example, which actually vests ownership of the resultant footage to the promoter, rather than the artist, is as follows:

> Musician hereby grants to promoter the right to take audio, visual and/or audiovisual recordings of all or any part of musician's performance (all, collectively, "Recordings"). All right, title and interest in and to the Recordings shall vest in promoter, whether embodying sound alone, visual images alone, or sound together with visual images, whether now known or hereafter invented, throughout the universe and in perpetuity. All items created in the course of performance by musician at the show that rise to the level of being protectable intellectual properties have been specially ordered or commissioned by

21. See 17 U.S.C. § 1101(a), implementation of the anti-bootlegging provisions of the Uruguay Round Agreements Act of 1994, Pub. L. No. 103–465, § 512, 108 Stat. 4809.

22. Unauthorized Fixation of and Trafficking in Sound Recordings and Music Videos of Live Musical Performances, 18 U.S.C. § 2319A (2008); see also *Kiss Catalog v. Passport Int'l Prods.*, 405 F. Supp. 2d 1169 (C.D. Cal. 2005) (18 U.S.C. § 2319A enforced against a constitutional challenge).

> promoter and, accordingly, each will be a "work made for hire" (as that term is defined in the Copyright Act of 1976) effective as of the moment each such item is fixed in a tangible medium, whether or not such item is complete; and, in the event that any such item is not a work made for hire and/or there are any rights that do not accrue to promoter as a work made for hire or otherwise, musician hereby irrevocably grants, transfers, sells and assigns, and agrees to grant, transfer, sell and assign, to promoter all right, title and interest, including all copyrights (and all renewals and extensions thereof) in and to each such item. Musician also hereby grants to promoter a non-exclusive and royalty-free license to manufacture copies of, and synchronize with the audio and/or audiovisual recordings authorized by this section all musical compositions underlying musician's performance at the show.

The taking of audio, visual, and audiovisual recordings of a commercially valuable quality may also be managed by controlling access to areas and equipment from which such recordings might be captured (e.g., the physical area immediately in front of the stage, the sound board). Rights to recordings might also be controlled by means of language granting rights in such works to the musician as a condition to the purchase of a ticket, or by means of a waiver signed as a condition to obtaining access to areas and equipment from which such recordings might be captured.[23]

Ticketing

A ticket is generally considered a license to enter a venue at a specific time on a specific date and sit in a specific seat or remain in a certain area to view what is presented at the time, subject to the terms and conditions and policies of the venue. While ticketing is by no means new to the live entertainment industry, it has not always been the method of generating revenue

23. Robert W. Clarida and Robert J. Bernstein, "Aggressive Copyright Positions by Lady Gaga, Burning Man Festival," *Entertainment Law & Finance*, June 2011.

from live performances. It has been said that ticketing (where consumers pay a set amount *before* the performance) was first used in first century ancient Rome, and prior to that only the "pass the hat" method was used (where users pay, if at all, only *an amount they choose*, and only *during* or *after* the performance). It has also been said that Shakespeare's Globe (1599–1644) debuted what is now known as the "box office," where tickets for *future* performances could be purchased. After the existence of the box office, though, ticketing remained largely unchanged for hundreds of years, until 1968, when a company called Control Data launched "Tick-eTron," the first large-scale electronic ticketing service (which later lost its competitive battle with, and was acquired by, the 1976-formed Ticketmaster, which still dominates the ticketing industry today (although it was acquired by Live Nation in 2010)).

Tickets are not a guarantee of subjective satisfaction with that which is presented.[24] Further, tickets can be categorized as either "hard" or "soft." A hard ticket refers to the customary experience of paying for admission to a venue for the purpose of seeing a particular performer. The ticket price reflects primarily the ability of the performer to draw an audience, and ticket prices in such instances are generally determined between the promoter and the performer (assuming the performer is sharing in the overall ticket revenue in some manner). A soft ticket refers to the circumstance in which admission to the performance may be incidental to admission to other activities, such as a fair, festival, or similar event, and the performer is perhaps being used as a draw to attract audiences for such other activities (and revenue streams). In such instances, the ticket price may be unrelated to the actual drawing power of the performer, or even free, and the performer is not typically involved in setting the ticket price.

At least theoretically, the ticket seller for an event may be determined by the promoter, by the venue, or by the musician. Promoters will generally want to select the ticket seller in order to control the terms of the service, including rebates, to retain data concerning the purchasers of tickets, and

24. Brian A. Rosenblatt, "I Know It's Only Rock and Roll, But Did They Like It?: An Assessment of Causes of Action Concerning the Disappointment of Subjective Consumer Expectations Within the Live Performance Industry," *UCLA Entertainment Law Review* 13 (2005): 33.

to keep confidential all information concerning their events from competitors that may own ticketing services. However, since venues often enter exclusive arrangements with ticket sellers, including so-called white label services that permit the venue to brand the ticket service as their own, a promoter may be required to use a specific ticket service as a condition to using a particular venue. It is alleged by the United States Department of Justice that Live Nation controls approximately 60 percent of concert promotions at major concert venues across the United States, owns or controls more than 250 concert venues in North America (including more than sixty of the top one hundred amphitheaters in the United States), and controls at least 80 percent of major concert venues' primary ticketing for concerts and a growing share of ticket resales in the secondary market.[25]

Services such as ScoreBig, Ticketwise, and Convious that offer discounted, "name your own price" sales are used to augment regular sales channels.[26] Services such as Eventbrite and Etix also permit musicians to sell tickets directly to their fans.

The growth of electronic ticketing has created new ways of conceiving the utility of a ticket. Data associated with a ticket purchaser, such as preferences or prior purchases, can be used to value-load a ticket with night-of-performance offers of food, drink, or merchandise purchase credit for redemption at the venue, which become activated when the ticket is scanned at admission. Radio-frequency identification can also be used with wristbands to eliminate the need for cash at an event, to facilitate pre-purchase of products or services to be redeemed at the event, or to track the movement of the wristband wearer within the event to gather marketing information. Paperless tickets have also impacted the secondary market for

---

25. *United States v. Live Nation Ent., Inc.*, No. 1:24-cv-3973-AS, 2024 U.S. Dist. LEXIS 149682, at *3, *16, *28, *30 (S.D.N.Y. Aug. 19, 2024); see also Krista Brown, *The Depth of Live Nation's Dominance: A Data Analysis of the Corporate Capture Behind Top Concert Venues Worldwide* (American Economic Liberties Project, June 2023).

26. Dr. Allison Burnham, *Analytics to Inform Name Your Own Price Reserve Setting* (2015), https://support.sas.com/resources/papers/proceedings15/3497-2015.pdf; S. Cereceda, "Name Your Own Price Just Got a Little Better (and Better)!" *Convious Blog*, https://blog.convious.com/name-your-own-price-just-got-a-little-better-and-better; *Ticketwise*, *Online Ticketing* (2025), https://ticketwise.com/online-ticketing/; *Vivid Seats*, *Name Your Price Tickets* (2025), https://www.vividseats.com/name-your-price-tickets--theater-other-theater/performer/171412.

tickets,[27] as, unlike a physical property, the transferability of an electronic ticket to an entertainment event can be controlled much as the transferability of an airline ticket is controlled. In response, ticket resellers such as StubHub and TicketsNow launched efforts such as the Fan Freedom Project[28] to maintain the secondary market in tickets without interruption and the National Association of Ticket Brokers promulgated a "Ticket Owner Bill of Rights" purporting to espouse rights for ticket owners such as the right to buy or sell tickets in a free and open market and their real value (whether above or below original face value).[29] In turn, many consumer advocacy groups, some states, the Federal Trade Commission, and the Trump administration's executive orders have all mobilized to varying extents to address ticket-selling practices they view as harmful to consumers.[30] Companion

---

27. See generally Laura D. Nemeth, *Secondary Ticket Marketplace, Guide to U.S. Ticket Resale Regulations*, Squire Patton Boggs (2018), https://www.squirepattonboggs.com/-/media/files/insights/publications/2018/10/2018-secondary-ticket-marketplace-guide-to-us-ticket-resale-regulations/2018usticketresalelawguidebrochure.pdf; Eric Schroeder, Josh Fisher, John Orbe, and John Bush, "A Brief Overview on Ticket Scalping Laws, Secondary Ticket Markets, and the Stubhub Effect," *Entertainment & Sports Lawyer* 30 (Nov. 2012): 1.

28. Fan Freedom Project, https://www.facebook.com/FanFreedom/.

29. Ticket Owner Bill of Rights, *National Association of Ticket Brokers*, https://www.natb.org/ticket-bill-of-rights/ (last accessed September 2025).

30. See, e.g., *Federal Trade Commission et al. v. Live Nation, Inc. et al.*, Case No. 2:25-cv-08884 (C.D. Cal. 2025); "Consumer Groups, Venues, and Artists Join to Support the TICKET Act," Energy and Commerce Committee Democrats (December 15, 2023), https://democrats-energycommerce.house.gov/media/press-releases/consumer-groups-venues-and-artists-join-support-ticket-act; Ashley King, "TICKET Act Passes the House by a Resounding 409–15 Vote—Bill Now Headed to Senate," *Digital Music News*, April 29, 2025, https://www.digitalmusicnews.com/2025/04/29/ticket-act-passes-house/; Dylan Smith, "NITO Urges FTC to Expand Concert Tickets Rule—'Does Nothing to Address or Reduce Actual Junk Fees,'" *Digital Music News*, January 24, 2025, https://www.digitalmusicnews.com/2025/01/14/junk-fees-rule-ftc-expansion-request/#:~:text=Though%20a%20larger%20sample%20is,been%20lost%20with%20this%20ruling; Ashley King, "California Bill Banning Speculative Ticketing Gets NIVA Boost," *Digital Music News*, March 25, 2025, https://www.digitalmusicnews.com/2025/03/25/california-bill-banning-speculative-ticketing-gets-niva-boost/; Ashley King, "Trump Signs Executive Order to End Ticket 'Price-Gouging by Middlemen' in the Entertainment Industry," *Digital Music News*, March 31, 2025, https://www.digitalmusicnews.com/2025/03/31/trump-executive-order-price-gouging-entertainment/; Ashley King, "Maine Sets National Standard with Bold Ticketing Law—NIVA & Fix the Tix Hail 'Blueprint for Reform,'" *Digital Music News*, June 20, 2025, https://www.digitalmusicnews.com/2025/06/20/maine-governor-signs-ticketing-law/; Dylan Smith, "FTC Sues Alleged Ticket Scalpers Under the BOTS Act, Says They 'Regularly Circumvented' Ticketmaster Security Measures," *Digital Music News*, August 18, 2025, https://www.digitalmusicnews.com/2025/08/18/bots-act-action-august-2025/.

House and Senate bills have been proposed regarding transparency in ticket pricing (including in the resale market), but as of this writing no such law at the federal level has become law,[31] and the United Kingdom announced the framework of a law that will, among other things, prohibit the resale of tickets for live events above their original cost.[32]

Liability for Mishaps

Given the propensity for danger where live performances are concerned, it is incumbent upon the attorney for any business considering even tangential involvement therein to advise of the potential for liability, should something go awry. For example, in the infamous case of the 2003 fire at The Station nightclub in East Warwick, Rhode Island, in which one hundred people perished, the resulting lawsuits included dozens of defendants, most of whom were not able to extricate themselves at the pleading stage and ultimately were forced to settle for large amounts.[33]

In that case, an investigative reporter for a local television station coincidentally was on-site the night of the fire with a station camera crew, ironically for the purpose of reporting a story on nightclub safety. While the television station was one of the few defendants successful in seeking at

31. The House's bill is the Transparency in Charges for Key Events Ticketing (TICKET) Act (H.R. 3606)—118th Congress (2023–2024) and the Senate's is the Fans First Act (S. 3457)—118th Congress (2023–2024).

32. Department for Business and Trade, Department for Culture, Media and Sport, "Government Bans Ticket Touting to Protect Fans from Rip-Off Prices," November 19, 2025, https://www.gov.uk/government/news/government-bans-ticket-touting-to-protect-fans-from-rip-off-prices.

33. "Rhode Island Judge OKs $176M Settlement in Deadly Club Fire," *Associated Press*, January 11, 2010, https://www.claimsjournal.com/news/east/2010/01/11/106513.htm; see also J. Barylick, *Killer Show: The Station Nightclub Fire, America's Deadliest Rock Concert* (Hanover; London: University Press of New England, 2012), which reports that settlements included six companies in the chain of sale of flammable foam that had been installed in the club as soundproofing ($25 million $18.2 million, $11.25 million, $6.3 million, and $5 million, respectively), the manufacturer of the pyrotechnics ($6 million), broadcasting companies that advertised the show ($22 million), the brewer and distributor of beer sold at the nightclub and promoted the event ($5 million each), the Town of West Warwick and the State of Rhode Island, whose agents arguably did not inspect the premises in good faith ($10 million each), and the owner of the real estate on which the nightclub sat ($5 million).

least partial dismissal at the pleading stage,[34] it was reported to ultimately have later paid $22 million in settlement largely because of an allegation that the presence of its camera operator near the club's exit blocked or slowed the flow of patrons exiting the burning structure.[35]

Fire is no stranger to live entertainment.[36] Yet, fire is not the only potential malady that can strike a live musical performance; stage collapse, crowd crush, terror attacks, and more also make the list.[37] Indeed, the risks of personal injury and death at a live performance means that this is one of the few areas of music law in which material criminal ramifications are perhaps even more important than is civil liability. For example, Dan Biechele, tour manager for the band Great White who, to his great misfortune, both placed and ignited the pyrotechnics that ultimately killed one hundred people in 2003 in West Warwick, Rhode Island, received a fifteen-year prison sentence (four to be served, eleven suspended) when he pleaded guilty to one hundred counts of involuntary manslaughter in connection with the event.[38] Even worse, one nightclub owner who was not even present on the night of his establishment's disaster was sentenced to a term of not less twelve years after having been charged for nineteen of 492 deaths in 1942 after a sixteen-year-old bar boy lit a match to improve his vision in a dark corner and accidentally lit an artificial palm tree.[39]

---

34. *Gray v. Derderian*, 371 F. Supp. 2d 98 (D.R.I. 2005).

35. "WHJY, Clear Channel Offer $22M Station Fire Settlement," *Providence Business News*, February 13, 2008, https://web.archive.org/web/20081120065726/http://www.pbn.com/stories/29721.html.

36. Nightclub Fires Fast Facts, *CNN World*, January 31, 2024, https://ktvz.com/news/national-world/cnn-world/2024/01/31/nightclub-fires-fast-facts-3/.

37. See generally Dean I. Weitzman, "Stage Collapse Incidents: The Show Must Go On But at Whose Expense?" *MyPhillyLawyer Blog*, June 28, 2018 (stage collapse); Claudio Feliciani, Alessandro Corbetta, Milad Haghani, and Katsuhiro Nishinari, "Trends in Crowd Accidents Based on an Analysis of Press Reports," *Safety Science* 164 (August 2023): 106174 (crowd crush); Harald De Cauwer et al., "Terrorist Attacks Against Concerts and Festivals: A Review of 146 Incidents in the Global Terrorism Database," *Prehospital and Disaster Medicine*, February 2023 (terror attacks).

38. "Tour Manager Sentenced in Great White Fire," *Billboard*, May 11, 2006, https://www.billboard.com/music/music-news/tour-manager-sentenced-in-great-white-fire-58470/.

39. *Commonwealth v. Welansky*, 85 N.E.2d 902 (1944); The Cocoanut Grove Coalition, "Legal," web.archive.org/web/20130121134414/http://www.cocoanutgrovefire.org/home/legal (last accessed January 1, 2025).

Insurance

As the preceding section of this chapter should indicate, the personal performance and live event segment of the music industry is perhaps the segment in which there is the greatest potential for liability to arise. Yet, many practitioners do not realize that insurance is available specifically as associated with personal appearances and live events to cover and protect against multiple potential areas of liability. In essence, such insurance can be categorized as general liability (and, as such, should be comprehensible to the general practitioner). However, additional coverages to general liability are available for additional premiums, which can protect against such things as liquor liability, event cancellation, weather, terrorism, and more. While some of the types of insurance available for live events have familiar names and serve the same general purpose as analogous policies purchased for any business (e.g., general liability), some are specific to the live events industry. In any event, the primary types of coverages available, with the ones that should sound the most familiar listed first, are:

- General Liability. Insures against losses due to bodily injury or property damage caused by the promoter's employees or agents. Typically, an unlimited number of the promoter's vendors, and others involved with a live event, can be provided with a certificate of insurance naming them as additional insured in the event of a loss. Occasionally, certain vendors will request waivers of subrogation, which, when given by the insurer (typically in exchange for an extra premium), prevents the insurer from recovering from the vendor for claims due to the vendor's own negligence. Often a medical payments coverage can be specifically included to provide compensation for anyone not covered by workers' compensation (see further down this list) who may be injured, including during load-in, setup, and teardown.
- Property Damage. Insures against loss of or damage to business property, for example from theft, fire, or severe weather. It typically covers the venue itself, gear, sets, and wardrobe.
- Commercial Auto. Insures against liability caused by and/or to vehicles rented or otherwise used by personnel specifically for the live event.

- Workers' Compensation. Insures against injuries to personnel sustained in the course and scope of their work for the promoter (and is mandatory for businesses in all states but Texas).
- Third-Party Damage. Insures against damage to a location while it is under the promoter's control, protecting the promoter from having to pay for repairs.
- Liquor. Insures against losses arising due to the intoxication of a person; the accidental furnishing of alcoholic beverages to a person under the legal drinking age or already under the influence of alcohol; and/or the inadvertent violation of law related to alcohol sales, service, and consumption.
- Cancellation. Insures against cancellation of a live event due to unforeseen situations such as inclement weather; the illness, injury, and/or death of the musician; a damaged or otherwise unusable venue; and so on.
- Ticketing. Insures against ticket-related damages that arise from canceled, counterfeit, lost, or stolen tickets, including printing costs for hard tickets and third-party claims (such as from a disgruntled ticketholder of a ticket that is not honored for entry for one reason or another).
- Terrorism. Insures against damages sustained as the result of an act of terror that affects a live event.

In a society where litigation is increasingly the rule rather than the exception, wise promoters protect themselves from potential worst-case scenarios.[40] Perhaps even more importantly, many venues and vendors will not do business with a promoter that doesn't carry insurance indicative of both solvency and professionalism. Keep in mind that it is possible to procure a one-time, event-specific policy separate from the coverage routinely in place, which can effectively isolate the event at issue, so that any incident that occurs is less likely to affect the regular insurance and insurability of the business venture as a whole.

40. For a discussion of insurance coverages and shortcomings, see Edwin F. McPherson, "Entertainers Beware—You May Have Less Insurance Coverage Than You Think," *Southwestern Law Review* 45 (2015): 333.

Chapter 8
Distribution

Perhaps the most significant changes brought to the music industry by digital technology have occurred in the area of distribution. Although the manufacturing, warehousing, transporting, advertising, and sale of physical goods is still key to making recorded music available to multiple new revenue streams and business models, digital distribution revenue surpassed physical product revenue for record companies as long ago as 2013.[1] Even though actual distribution of physical products is now dwarfed by digital distribution,[2] it still makes sense to first discuss issues involving distribution of physical products and then address digital distribution. Doing so will provide not only historic context and provide guidance for the practitioner representing a client with issues concerning an historic recording agreement, but also aid in understanding how certain digital distribution practices and contract terms originated in the physical distribution world.

1. Recording Industry Association of America, *News and Notes on 2013 RIAA Music Industry Shipment and Revenue Statistics* (2014), https://www.musicbusinessworldwide.com/files/2014/11/RIAA2013.pdf.

2. Recording Industry Association of America, *RIAA 2024 Year-End Revenue Report* (2025), https://www.riaa.com/wp-content/uploads/2025/03/RIAA-2024Year-End-Revenue-Report.pdf.

Distribution of Physical Products

Decades ago, most records were distributed through independent distributors who promoted and distributed recordings regionally to both retail accounts and jukeboxes.[3] With the consolidation of music labels beginning in the 1960s, the major labels each developed their own respective national distribution operations. Independent distributors continued to operate with independent labels, but over time increased their ability to service accounts nationally rather than only regionally.

Today, distribution of physical products is concentrated with the operations connected to the major recording companies. Each major label (Sony BMG, Universal Music Group, and Warner Music Group) maintains a distribution operation for its own respective recordings, together with those of certain independent record labels. Warner Music Group has Alternative Distribution Alliance (ADA), Sony has The Orchard, and Universal has the [PIAS] Group.

A number of independent distributors are also available as distribution options for physical product, including general distributors such as AWAL, CD Baby, DistroKid, Ditto Music, Horus Music, LANDR, TuneCore, and a number of specialty distributors such as Central South Distribution (gospel) or Beatport (dance).[4]

Distribution arrangements for physical products generally take one of two forms. Either the record company delivers finished product to the distributor or the distributor is in charge of manufacturing the product in addition to pressing and distribution (P&D) arrangement.[5] Which option a label selects will depend on the administrative means of the record company and the costs charged by the distribution company for the service of

---

3. For a fascinating history of many of the important independent record labels of the 1950s and 1960s and their distributors, see John Broven, *Record Makers and Breakers* (Urbana: University of Illinois Press, 2009).

4. The American Association of Independent Music maintains a list of its independent distributor members at https://members.a2im.org/member-directory.

5. The rights granted from the record company to the distribution company should include only the right to distribute recordings, and only for the term of the distribution agreement. For the story of a record label that conveyed ownership of its recordings under what it believed was a distribution agreement, see Rob Bowman, *Soulsville U.S.A.: The Story of Stax Records* (New York: Schirmer Books, 1997).

arranging manufacture relative to arrangements made directly. While the record company pays a fee to the distribution company for the manufacturing service, it may be money well spent if the record company does not have the resources or experience to administer the manufacturing process within the delivery, quality, and quantity requirements of the distributor.

Distribution Functions

The functions performed by the distributor of physical products include warehousing the product; producing virtual "catalogs" (in rare cases, perhaps still a physical one) and other sales support material; coordinating marketing efforts such as price and positioning of product within a retail store, e-commerce environment, or co-op advertisement; soliciting and fulfilling sales; processing returns, billing, and collections; preparing regular accounting reports, and, of course, paying amounts due. The distributor generally bears the risk of bad debt because it is the entity with a direct relationship with accounts, it is in the best position to assess the credit risk of the accounts, and it is in the only position to enforce the payment obligation with its contractual counterparties, the accounts. In essence, it is the job of the distributor to get the record into the sales environment that the account represents, and it is the job of the record company to create demand, through marketing and promotion, that will result in a sale of that record from that account.

Distribution Process

The distribution process generally involves the commitment by the record company to a release date for a record, or "street" date,[6] at least three or four months in advance.[7] This permits the distribution company to accomplish

6. The record industry had historically selected Tuesdays of each week as the date new releases will first be made available for sale, but in the mid-2010s that changed to Fridays. See Frannie Kelley, "Why Albums Are Released on Tuesdays in the U.S.," *NPR Music*, September 8, 2010, http://www.npr.org/blogs/therecord/2010/09/08/129725205/why-albums-are-released-on-tuesdays; Other Record Labels, "Why Do We Release Music on Fridays?" https://www.otherrecordlabels.com/why-do-we-release-music-on-fridays (last accessed February 28, 2026).

7. It seems to happen more years than you would guess—it is not unusual for us to be approached around Thanksgiving by someone wanting to know how to obtain distribution of a seasonal recording. The answer is to wait until the following summer.

the tasks just identified. Those special efforts may include favorable payment terms to encourage an account to place an order. Typically, there are specific deadlines for delivery by the record company of finished goods, or, if the distribution agreement is for both pressing and distribution (a P&D deal), artwork and manufacturing parts. Records are then shipped to accounts in anticipation of the release date. The record companies do not want "street date violations," or the sale of records prior to the release date. Such sales will not only cause retailers to be unhappy about perceived lost sales to gun-jumpers, but such sales also fall outside the reporting period for industry sales charts and thus lessen the impact of cumulative first week sales for the benefit of the record company and the artist. Note that in the digital world it is much easier to control street date violations because the record companies provide digital files, the access to which at a retailer can be restricted much more easily and securely than boxes of LPs in the back rooms of thousands of brick-and-mortar record stores.

Billings to accounts are generally payable within ninety days after invoice, and terms can be settled either by cash or by the value of previously distributed product that is returned.[8] The distributor will then in turn pay the label, generally sixty to ninety days after the close of each monthly period, after deduction of its distribution fee (typically a percentage of the receipts). The accounting also will be subject to a reserve for anticipated returns, which should generally be liquidated within nine to twelve months. The distribution company will also charge certain additional costs, such as restickering or otherwise refurbishing returned product, for excess inventory, or for cutting out or scrapping non-moving inventory.[9]

Under the distribution agreement, the record company will typically have its own responsibilities. First, the record company will be required to release a certain minimum number of recordings during each calendar period of the agreement's term. Next, the record company will be required

8. Most physical recorded product is sold on a fully returnable basis. Some products, such as vinyl releases, may be sold on a non-return basis.

9. "Cut-outs" refers to deeply discounted or remaindered copies of physical product typically marked with a physical alteration like a notch, hole punch, or cut corner, to prevent their return to the label for a full refund. See generally Neal Umphred, "The Avid Record Collector #2: 'What Is a Cut-Out?'" *Sixties Music Secrets*, July 7, 2021, https://www.sixtiesmusicsecrets.com/the-avid-record-collector-2-what-is-a-cut-out.

to properly code and package each recording (if the agreement is not a P&D deal, in which case that responsibility will fall on the distributor). The record company will also be required to fund the price and positioning programs and co-op advertisements arranged by the distributor and execute its marketing and promotional programs. The record company will likely also be required to provide periodic financial statements, sales projections, and proof of insurance to the distributor.

Scope of Distribution Agreement

The scope of the distribution arrangement for physical products is one of the principal issues negotiated in a distribution agreement. Generally, distribution rights will be exclusive and for all formats and configurations, including physical and digital. However, carve-outs from the exclusivity provisions may be appropriate in certain situations. This may occur if some recorded products may have commercial appeal in distinct channels of trade that may be serviced by other distributors. For example, the sale of gospel or contemporary Christian releases in the Christian bookstore market is a market that is often carved out of a general distribution agreement. Also, unless the record company has no administrative ability to handle such functions, the record company should reserve the right to directly license its masters to non-retail users of recorded music such as Mood Media, Rockbot, and CloudCover (powered by Pandora) for background music, or TouchTunes, Rockbot, and AMI Entertainment for digital jukeboxes. The record company should also preserve the right to make its products available for premium use or licensing for compilations or synchronization uses.

It is also important to understand how the exclusivity provisions of the distribution arrangement affect the principal owners or officers of the record company, particularly if any such persons may play a creative role in connection with recordings distributed under other arrangements. For example, if a person affiliated with the record company is a recording artist or a producer, must all recordings with which they are involved be distributed under the distribution agreement?

Another issue that is often negotiated in a distribution agreement is whether the record company or distribution company will have any rights to "upstream" a particular recording artist or recording if success is achieved that requires the dedication of resources beyond those of the original record company. The "upstream" conversion may involve moving the distribution of a recording from the independent arm of the distribution company to the major-label equivalent level, or it may even involve moving the artist from the independent label to a major label affiliated with the distribution company, with the original record label retaining a production credit and financial participation. The consequences of any such conversion to a major record label should be carefully considered. While the greater resources brought to a recording or artist may result in a level of success beyond the capabilities of the original, independent record label, the independent label's loss of the artist may have other consequences for the long-term aspirations of the label.

Warranties and Representations

Other significant areas for negotiation are the warranties and representations that the label will be making to the distribution company, the scope of indemnification committed by the record company, and the amount and type of insurance coverage that may be put in place to support such indemnification. Distribution of a copyright-protected work is one of the distinct rights of the copyright holder in and to both a song and a sound recording, and any party in the distribution chain can face liability for distributing infringing product, whether they created it or not.[10] Because the distribution company generally plays no role in the creation of the product that it distributes, yet is in the chain of distribution (and, therefore, the chain of liability that may attach to distribution), it must rely upon its distributed labels to deliver products not subject to adverse claims. A distribution company might also have greater concern about this potential liability when dealing with smaller record companies that may not have the business affairs capabilities enjoyed by larger, more experienced, and fully staffed labels. As a result, most distributors will not make the same mistake one record company made several years ago. It took on distribution of a

---

10. *Columbia Broad. Sys., Inc. v. Scorpio Music Distrib.*, 569 F. Supp. 47 (E.D. Pa. 1983), aff'd, 738 F.2d 421 (3d Cir. 1984); *UMG Recordings, Inc. v. Disco Aztecha Distribs.*, Inc., 446 F. Supp. 2d 1164 (E.D. Cal. 2006).

record company that not only was the subject of multiple IRS liens and garnishment actions, but also whose mechanical licenses with the Harry Fox Agency (HFA) had been terminated for lack of payment. This left the distribution company not only out the advance it had paid to the scofflaw record company, but also in the crosshairs of both the IRS and the HFA and eventually drawn into the record company's bankruptcy proceeding. The recommended practice for a distributor, then, is not only to insist on credit, lien holder, and publishing status checks for potential distributed labels, but also to insist on being named as an additional insured in appropriate insurance policies obtained by and paid for by the record company before committing resources to a new relationship.

Advances

Another important area of negotiation is advances. If an advance is to be paid by a distributor, its amount will generally be based on sales projected from the prior sales experience of the label and the artists expected to be released by the label. Of equal concern is how the advance may be recouped by the distributor. If the distribution company is entitled to recoup an advance from 100 percent of the revenue otherwise payable to the record company, the record company may experience a cash flow problem for operating funds, particularly if the record company was required to expend for funding recording projects a significant portion of any advance it received from the distributor. One solution is to permit the distribution company to recoup an advance from no more than a certain percentage of the revenue otherwise payable to the label, thereby guaranteeing the label with a monthly payment while the distributor still is able to recoup, albeit at a slower rate. For example, the agreement might provide that the distribution company would retain only 50 percent of the revenue payable to the record company, with the record company assured it would receive at least half the sales revenue.

Another issue with advances may be how repayment might be secured by the distributor in the event that recoupment is not sufficient. The record company may have, or may want to seek, an operating line of credit from a bank that would insist on an overall blanket security interest in the assets of the record company. To permit such a line of credit to be extended, the distributor would need to limit its security interest to the label's inventory and receivables, and even as to that, perhaps in a second position to the bank, leaving the remaining assets, including the label's intellectual property rights, available to secure other financing.

DIY Distribution

Artists that elect to self-distribute physical embodiment of their recordings to their fan bases have several options to support that path. Services such as Topspin, CD Baby, DistroKid, and TuneCore facilitate the sale and fulfillment of both physical and digital products from artists. These services can integrate with an artist's own website to fulfill sales generated from the site or simply handle the purchase transaction, with the artist then fulfilling the orders themselves. Most of these services also handle other products on behalf of the DIY artist, such as merchandise and tickets.

Digital Distribution

Having concluded our discussion of physical distribution (historically the only distribution), we can now turn to digital (currently not the exclusive, but the vast majority, of overall distribution).

The development of the means to record, distribute, and transmit sound digitally caused greater disruption and dislocation in the music industry than any other since the advent of recorded sound. Reproduction and distribution of sound recordings is no longer centralized, expensive, detectable, and controlled—it is now ubiquitous and inexpensive, and sometimes undetectable and private. Consumers have the means, and the power, to duplicate, transmit, alter, and compile digital recordings. With this power, consumers have elevated their values and needs, including speed of access, comprehensiveness, reduced costs, portability/ubiquity, and convenience, over the control interests of music owners. Music licensing has also been challenged. For example, territorial limitations have disappeared, content is always accessible, once-secure content can usually be endlessly modified, and channels of distribution and sale have been and continue to be invented faster than transactions can be completed.

As a business matter, most distributors of physical music recording products (as discussed in the preceding section of this chapter) also have the ability to distribute such recordings in digital formats to companies such as online music retailers (e.g., Apple Music and Amazon Music), digital music services (e.g., Pandora and Spotify), mobile devices (e.g., Apple, Nokia, and Samsung), digital cable and satellite television services (e.g., Music Choice and Mood Media), and satellite radio services (e.g., SiriusXM). When the artist requires a distributor for physical product, those distributors of physical music also insist on obtaining exclusive rights to distribute recordings in both physical and digital formats. Issues can arise when the artist has a preexisting obligation to a digital-only distributor, such as Spotify or Apple Music.

Even if a smaller record company or a DIY artist elects to self-distribute recordings to digital music services and retailers, as a practical matter it will need to enter an agreement with a digital music distribution aggregator (e.g., TuneCore, DistroKid, CD Baby, AWAL, and UnitedMasters), since most smaller labels and DIY artists will not have the administrative capabilities to manage the distribution relationships with many digital music users across multiple platforms. Further, most key digital music users will not enter direct agreements with artists or smaller companies but will instead direct them to an aggregator for access to the platform the user provides.

Aggregators assist client artists and labels in the encoding of their recordings and the formatting of the metadata associated with such recordings. The aggregators then deliver the resulting files to the digital music users with which they have entered blanket agreements. Digital aggregators will also work with artists and labels to help promote the artist's and label's recordings within the platforms of the music users. The fee arrangements for aggregators range from set fees to percentages of revenue.

Digital Distribution Revenue

The television series *South Park* has been a cultural touchstone for a broad range of topics since 1997, and of course digital distribution of entertainment content could not escape its attention as long ago as 2008. The following are the thoughts of Kyle Broflovski, one of the principal characters from the show, on the financial rewards of digital distribution:

> You know, I learned something today. We thought we could make money on the internet. But while the internet is new and exciting for creative people, it hasn't matured as a distribution mechanism to the extent that one should trade real and immediate opportunities for income for the promise of future online revenue. It will be a few years before digital distribution of media on the internet can be monetized to an extent that necessitates content producers to forgo their fair value in more traditional media.[11]

In 2008, there was much truth in Kyle's observations, but the range and growth of revenue platforms for digital music have grown beyond what likely could have been his expectations at the time. Worldwide streaming revenues surpassed $1 billion annually more than a decade ago,[12] and currently are reported to be at least twenty times that amount.[13]

Webcasting

Since 1897, the owners of musical compositions have been entitled to compensation when recordings of their composition are publicly performed. Yet, neither the owners nor producers of those recordings, nor the performers featured in the recordings, were able to receive any payment for such public performance until the passage of the Digital Performance Right in Sound Recordings Act (DPRA) in 1995. The DPRA added § 106(6) to the Copyright Act, giving the owners of sound recording copyrights a sixth exclusive right in addition to the five they had held previously, namely, the right to publicly perform such sound recordings by means of digital audio transmissions (which at the time were principally digital cable transmissions).[14] This

---

11. *South Park*, "*Canada on Strike*," Comedy Central television broadcast, April 2, 2008.

12. See generally Paul Resnikoff, "Exclusive: Streaming Revenues Now Surpass $1 Billion Annually in the U.S. . . . ," *Digital Music News*, March 27, 2013, https://www.digitalmusicnews.com/2013/03/27/streamingbillion/; Jeffrey Brabec and Todd Brabec, *Music, Money, and Success* (New York: Schirmer Trade Books, 2022), 1.

13. *Music Streaming—Worldwide, Statista*, https://www.statista.com/outlook/amo/media/music-radio-podcasts/digital-music/music-streaming/worldwide?currency=USD#revenue (last accessed March, 2026); Fabio Duarte, "Music Streaming Services Stats (2025)," *Exploding Topics*, February 21, 2025.

14. *Digital Performance Right in Sound Recordings Act of 1995*, Pub. L. No. 104–39, § 1, 109 Stat. 336 (codified as amended at 17 U.S.C. §§ 106, 114–115).

followed the passage of the Audio Home Recording Act of 1992,[15] which created a royalty system for recording devices and blank digital audio tapes. Three years *after* the DPRA, in 1998, Congress passed the Digital Millennium Copyright Act (DMCA),[16] which among other provisions amended § 114 of the Copyright Act to provide a compulsory license of the sound recording public performance right for non-interactive digital audio transmissions,[17] or webcasting.

With the statutory performance right in sound recordings in place, in 2000, the Recording Industry Association of America (RIAA) created an organization called SoundExchange to act as the central clearing house for the issuance of licenses to digital music users availing themselves of the compulsory licensing provisions of the DPRA and DMCA. SoundExchange was spun off as an independent organization in 2003. Under the authority granted by the Copyright Act, SoundExchange is authorized to participate in rate setting proceedings and conduct negotiations with all interested parties to determine the rates charged for the compulsory licenses provided in the DPRA and DMCA.[18] Rates are ultimately determined by the Copyright Royalty Board,[19] although negotiated settlement agreements between

---

15. Audio Home Recording Act of 1992, Pub. L. No. 102–563, 106 Stat. 4237 (codified at 17 U.S.C. §§ 1001–1010 (1992)).

16. Digital Millennium Copyright Act of 1998, Pub. L. No. 105–304, § 405(a), 112 Stat. 2860 (codified at 17 U.S.C. §§ 101, 104, 104A, 108, 112, 114, 117, 512, 701, 1201–1205, 1301–1332).

17. 17 U.S.C. § 114(d)(2).

18. Amy Miller, "SoundExchange Counsel Faces Royalty Skirmishes," *Entertainment Law & Finance*, December 2008; *SoundExchange, Inc. v. Copyright Royalty Board and Librarian of Congress*, No. 16–1159 (D.C. Cir. 2018), https://law.justia.com/cases/federal/appellate-courts/cadc/16-1159/16-1159-2018-09-18.html; Murray Stassen, "SoundExchange Royalties Dispute with Music Choice to Be Referred to Copyright Royalty Board," *Music Business Worldwide*, December 2, 2021, https://www.musicbusinessworldwide.com/soundexchange-royalties-dispute-with-music-choice-to-be-referred-to-copyright-royalty-board/; "SoundExchange Sues SiriusXM Over Underpayment of Digital Streaming Royalties," *SoundExchange*, August 16, 2023, https://www.soundexchange.com/news/soundexchange-sues-siriusxm-over-underpayment-of-digital-streaming-royalties/; Stuart Dredge, "SoundExchange Sues AccuRadio Claiming Missing Royalty Payments," *Music Ally*, July 23, 2024, https://musically.com/2024/07/23/soundexchange-sues-accuradio-claiming-missing-royalty-payments/.

19. Over the years Congress has tinkered considerably with the mechanism for the setting of royalty rates for mechanical, cable television system secondary transmission, and jukebox compulsory licenses and to distribute and settle controversies over the distribution of compulsory license royalty fees paid by cable television system and jukebox owners. The Copyright Act of 1976 originally established the Copyright Royalty Tribunal as the body to accomplish

SoundExchange and certain groups of webcasters have been authorized and implemented through the Webcaster Settlement Act of 2009[20] and certain subsequent decisions of the Copyright Royalty Board that have corrected rates, formatting errors, and drafting inconsistencies.[21] The service features of the DPRA and DMCA compulsory licenses have been carefully drawn, and SoundExchange may only issue licenses for services that comply with the requirements of such features. For example, services operating under authority of a compulsory license must be non-interactive and must observe limitations on how often recordings by artists or from certain albums may be performed within a particular time period.[22] Music services that are interactive may not obtain a license for such services from SoundExchange but must obtain licenses from the Mechanical Licensing Collective instead.[23] The current rates for webcaster compulsory licenses may be found at 37 C.F.R. Part 381[24] and at SoundExchange.[25]

---

the task. In 1993, Congress passed the Copyright Royalty Tribunal Reform Act of 1993, Pub. L. No. 103–198, 107 Stat. 2304, to replace the Copyright Royalty Tribunal with copyright arbitration royalty panels (or CARPs). In 2004, Congress passed the Copyright Royalty and Distribution Reform Act of 2004, Pub. L. No. 108–419, 118 Stat. 2341, which abolished the system of arbitrators and replaced it with three full-time Copyright Royalty Judges. See 17 U.S.C. §§ 801–805. In 2018, Congress passed the Music Modernization Act, Pub. L. No. 115–264, which left intact the Copyright Royalty Judge positions but established a rotating assignment system for judges from the Southern District of New York to hear rate court cases.

20. Webcaster Settlement Act of 2009, Pub. L. No. 111–36 (amending 17 U.S.C. § 114); 74 Fed. Reg. 34796–34802 (July 17, 2009).

21. See, e.g., David Oxenford, "Webcasting Royalty Decision Developments—Revised Rates and Terms from the CRB, Issues about Performance Complement and Small Webcasters," *Broadcast Law Blog*, December 28, 2015, https://www.broadcastlawblog.com/2015/12/articles/webcasting-royalty-decision-developments-revised-rates-and-terms-from-the-crb-issues-about-performance-complement-and-small-webcasters.

22. 17 U.S.C. § 114(j)(13) (2011). Disputes have also occurred over whether the features of certain digital music services exceed the eligibility requirements for the statutory compulsory webcasting licenses created by the DMCA. See, e.g., *Arista Records, LLC v. Launch Media, Inc.*, 578 F.3d 148 (2d Cir. 2009), cert. denied, 130 S. Ct. 1290 (2010).

23. The Mechanical Licensing Collective (MLC) was established in 2018 pursuant to Music Modernization Act, which designated MLC as the exclusive administrator of blanket mechanical licenses for interactive digital music services (and ensure accurate royalty payments to rights holders). 17 U.S.C. § 115(a)(1).

24. Docket No. 21-CRB-0002-PBR (2023–2027).

25. Commercial Webcaster (CRB), *SoundExchange*, https://www.soundexchange.com/service-provider/commercial-webcaster/ (last accessed September 2025).

SoundExchange distributes license proceeds to copyright owners based upon data it collects concerning the actual usage of recordings in the music services it licenses. After deduction of its service fee, SoundExchange then distributes 50 percent of the revenue directly to the owners of the sound recording copyright in the recordings it represents, 45 percent of the revenue directly to the featured artists appearing on the recordings, and 5 percent to performers' unions for the non-featured musicians and vocalists.[26] The amounts paid to the artists by SoundExchange are not subject to any recoupability provisions that might be included in their respective recording agreements. The amount distributed by SoundExchange over the years has steadily increased. For example, SoundExchange reported that it distributed $426 million in digital performing royalties in 2012, but then by the end of 2024 it had reported an increase to $12 billion.[27]

It is critically important for all recording artists and record labels to register with SoundExchange to obtain their portion of the compulsory license proceeds SoundExchange collects. Once a record label registers, it is also key that it keep registration of its releases current with SoundExchange so that performances of the recordings can be properly logged and allocated. If performances of recordings or featured artists that are reported to SoundExchange cannot be matched to registered parties, SoundExchange will retain royalties for such artists or sound recording copyright holders for up to three years until a match can be found.[28] If no match can be found by the end of the three years, SoundExchange retains them and may

---

26. "Digital Performance Royalties," *SoundExchange*, https://www.soundexchange.com/digital-performance-royalties/ (last accessed September 2025).

27. SoundExchange, "SoundExchange Ends Record-Setting Year with $462 Million in Total Distributions," January 16, 2013, https://www.prnewswire.com/news-releases/soundexchange-ends-record-setting-year-with-462-million-in-total-distributions-187109761.html; SoundExchange, "SoundExchange Surpasses $12 Billion Cumulative Distribution Milestone," February 4, 2025, https://www.soundexchange.com/news/soundexchange-surpasses-12-billion-cumulative-distribution-milestone/.

28. Michael Huppe, "You Don't Know Me, But I Owe You Money: How SoundExchange Is Changing the Game on Digital Royalties," *Entertainment & Sports Lawyer* 28, no. 3 (2010): 3; Glenn Peoples, "SoundExchange Finally Releases Old, Unclaimed Royalties," *Billboard*, January 31, 2014, https://www.billboard.com/music/music-news/soundexchange-finally-releases-old-unclaimed-royalties-5893782/; John Simson, "SoundExchange: Don't Let Unclaimed Royalties Fester," *American Songwriter*, January 11, 2017, https://americansongwriter.com/soundexchange-dont-let-unclaimed-royalties-fester/.

apply them to offset its own administrative costs.[29] As of this writing, it has been more than ten years since SoundExchange last released (i.e., kept for itself) a significant sum of unclaimed royalties.[30] It has been our experience that featured artists who have been unaware of the role of SoundExchange have received significant payments when they have finally registered with the organization. Of course not all parties will receive accrued payments of that amount, but the stakes are significant and increasing. There is no reason not to register to receive payments to which the artists and record companies are entitled.

Music Services

Music services can embrace a range of features but generally are considered to have, as their primary offering, the streaming of recorded music,[31] available downloads of files containing recorded music that may be permanent or that may time out on a subscription basis, or remote storage of files containing recorded music for facilitation of later access across multiple devices and locations.

Many well-known digital music "services" have involved efforts by companies to offer digital music without licensing from the copyright owners. Historically, this led to some equally well-known litigation. Lawsuits involving peer-to-peer offerings—Napster,[32] Aimster,[33] Grokster,[34] and Limewire[35]—initiated within a seven-year span between 2000 and 2006,

29. 37 C.F.R. § 382.5(b).

30. Peoples, "SoundExchange Finally Releases Old, Unclaimed Royalties."

31. Stephen M. Karamarsky, "Internet Music Stream Vs. Download," *Entertainment Law & Finance*, August 2007; Glenn Peoples, "Music Streaming Hits a Tipping Point," *Medium*, October 7, 2016, https://medium.com/@glennpeoples/music-streaming-hits-a-tipping-point-e91f1741afaa; Bill Rosenblatt, "The Short, Unhappy Life of Music Downloads," *Forbes*, May 7, 2018, https://www.forbes.com/sites/billrosenblatt/2018/05/07/the-short-unhappy-life-of-music-downloads/; T. Wagner, M. Rose, C. Baccarella, and K.-I. Voigt, "Streaming Killed the Download Star! How the Business Model of Streaming Services Revolutionizes Music Distribution," *Journal of Organizational Advancement, Strategic and Institutional Studies* VII, no. 1 (2015).

32. *A&M Records, Inc. v. Napster, Inc.*, 239 F.3d 1004 (9th Cir. 2001).

33. *In re Aimster Copyright Litigation*, 334 F.3d 643 (7th Cir. 2003), cert. denied, 540 U.S. 1107 (2004).

34. *Metro-Goldwyn-Mayer Studios, Inc. v. Grokster, Ltd.*, 545 U.S. 913 (2005).

35. *Arista Records, LLC v. Lime Group LLC*, 784 F. Supp. 2d 398 (S.D.N.Y. 2011).

tested the limits of fair use and permissible conduct under the DMCA, and were successful for the copyright owners.[36] Battles continued into the 2010s, with litigation involving music service site Grooveshark[37] and ReDigi,[38] whose services facilitating the resale of digital music files were held to violate the copyright rights of content owners. Those cases resulted in a voluntary shutdown for Grooveshark pursuant to a settlement after its adverse court rulings,[39] and a shutdown for ReDigi after its unsuccessful attempt to use a bankruptcy filing to avoid the consequences of its adverse court rulings.[40]

In addition to pursuing infringement claims against peer-to-peer software providers, the recording industry has not been reluctant to initiate litigation[41] against individual users of such software.[42]

Another example of an unlicensed music service was MP3.com, which offered an unlicensed "locker" service, whereby one could listen to streamed recordings of songs supposedly embodied on CDs owned by the user. The company's fair use defense was rejected because the use was commercial

---

36. See *Arista Records, LLC v. Usenet.com, Inc.*, 633 F. Supp. 2d 124 (S.D.N.Y. 2009) (Usenet operators held liable for infringement occurring within newsgroups); see also *Columbia Pictures Indus., Inc. v. Fung*, 96 U.S.P.Q.2d 1620 (C.D. Cal. 2009) (liability found for operation of site to collect, receive, index, and make available descriptions of content, including so-called dot-torrent files, and to provide access to open-access BitTorrent trackers); see also *Disney Enters. v. Hotfile Corp.*, 798 F. Supp. 2d 1303, 100 U.S.P.Q.2d 1723, 2011 ILRC 2217, 32 ILRD 501 (S.D. Fla. 2011) (criticized Arista Records, saying that ability but refusal to stop infringement was not a sufficient enough volitional act to constitute infringement).

37. *UMG Recordings, Inc. v. Escape Media Group, Inc.*, 37 Misc. 3d 208, 948 N.Y.2d 881 (2012), reversed in party by *UMG Recordings, Inc. v. Escape Media Group, Inc.*, 107 A.D.3d 51, 2013 N.Y. slip op. 2702, 964 N.Y.S.2d 106 (2013).

38. *Capitol Records, LLC v. ReDigi Inc.*, 910 F.3d 649 (2d Cir. 2018).

39. Brittany Spanos, "Grooveshark Shuts Down After Eight Years," *Rolling Stone*, May 1, 2015, https://www.rollingstone.com/music/music-news/grooveshark-shuts-down-after-eight years-74101/.

40. Bill Donahue, "Six Years Later, Capitol Records Is Still Chasing Big Copyright Ruling," *Socast Digital*, March 28, 2022, https://radiox.cms.socastsrm.com/2022/03/28/six-years-later-capitol-records-is-still-chasing-big-copyright-ruling/.

41. See, e.g., *Sony BMG Music Ent. v. Tenenbaum*, 660 F.3d 487 (1st Cir. 2011), cert. denied, 132 S. Ct. 2431 (2012); *Capitol Records, Inc. v. Foster*, 86 U.S.P.Q.2d 1203 (W.D. Okla. 2007); *BMG Music v. Gonzalez*, 430 F.3d 888 (7th Cir. 2005), cert. denied, 547 U.S. 1130 (2006); *Capitol Records, Inc. v. Thomas-Rasset*, 692 F.3d 899, 2012 U.S. App. LEXIS 19040, 104 U.S.P.Q.2d (BNA) 1063, Copy. L. Rep. (CCH) P30,313, 2012 WL 3930988.

42. Robert W. Clarida and Robert Jay Bernstein, "How Courts Are Defining 'Distribution' in Peer-to-Peer File-Sharing Lawsuits," *Entertainment Law & Finance*, May 2008; A. D. Bishop, "Illegal P2P File Sharing on College Campuses—What's the Solution?" *Scholarship@ Vanderbilt Law* (2020), https://scholarship.law.vanderbilt.edu/jetlaw/vol10/iss3/2/.

(first fair use factor), the copied works were creative and, thus, at the core of intended copyright protection (second factor), MP3.com copied entire works (third factor), and the MP3.com service undermined the potential market for the works (fourth factor).[43] The assets of MP3.com were eventually purchased by Universal Music Group for legitimate use. The prior owner of MP3.com returned with a different form of unlicensed "locker" service several years later, and while certain features of the service were found lawful when litigated, liability nevertheless was found against both the company and its founder.[44]

Criminal proceedings have also been commenced against both file storage services and their principals, both in the United States and abroad.[45]

In the aftermath of all the turmoil of all the cases discussed earlier, with the guideposts for lawful behavior that those litigations provided, there have come a number of licensed music services that offer access to millions of musical recordings on a subscription and non-subscription basis, including market leaders Spotify and Apple Music, as well as a number of smaller competitors such as Pandora, Amazon Music, YouTube Music, and iHeartRadio.[46] Unless established through direct licenses with sound recording copyright owners, the rates payable by a music service for the use of musical compositions by means of interactive streaming of sound recordings and conditional, or limited, downloads are described at 37 C.F.R. § 385.21(b). The formula for determining payments is beyond complicated, but it essentially involves alternative calculations based upon revenue, numbers of subscribers, total cost of content (TCC), number of plays, and performance royalties associated with each composition. Payments for the

---

43. *UMG Recordings, Inc. v. MP3.com, Inc.*, 92 F. Supp. 2d 349 (S.D.N.Y. 2000); *Disney Enters, Inc. v. VidAngel, Inc.*, 869 F.3d 848 (9th Cir. 2017).

44. *Capitol Records, Inc. v. MP3tunes, LLC*, 821 F. Supp. 2d 627 (S.D.N.Y. 2011).

45. Ben Sisario, "7 Charged as F.B.I. Closes a Top File-Sharing Site," *New York Times*, January 19, 2012, http://www.nytimes.com/2012/01/20/technology/indictment-charges-megaupload-site-with-piracy.html.

46. The fact that it had obtained licenses for millions of recordings and compositions for its service did not immunize MediaNet from the infringement claims of certain small publishers. See *Appalseed Prods., Inc. v. MediaNet Digital, Inc.*, 2012 WL 2700383 (S.D.N.Y. 2012).

use of master recordings in music services began quite modestly,[47] by 2000 had been reported to have increased to between .12 cents and 1.5 cents per play,[48] and currently are reported to be much lower, with material variances between digital service providers.[49]

In 2024, the Living Wage for Musicians Act was introduced in the House of Representatives proposing to create a new payment system, the "Artist Compensation Royalty Fund," to channel money directly to artists rather than through intermediaries.[50] The bill, though, appears to have died after having been referred to the House Committee on the Judiciary on the day of its introduction.[51]

Permanent Downloads

Permanent downloads, or digital phonorecord deliveries in the nomenclature used in the Copyright Act, were initially the only form of digital music, and Apple and Amazon have long been two of the largest digital retailers of them. Despite the format's dominance in the early years, downloads have lost digital format market share year-over-year for well over a decade, having accounted for just 2 percent of U.S. recorded music revenues in 2024 (as

47. Patrick Smith, "Fair Play? A Million Spotify Streams Earned Gaga $167," *PaidContent*, November 23, 2009, http://paidcontent.org/2009/11/23/419-fair-dos-a-million-spotify-streams-earned-gaga-167/.

48. Ben Sisario, "As Music Streaming Grows, Royalties Slow to a Trickle," *New York Times*, January 28, 2013, http://www.nytimes.com/2013/01/29/business/media/streaming-shakes-up-music-industrys-model-for-royalties.html?_r=0; Paul Resnikoff, "The Most Infamous Music Infographic, Updated for 2012 . . . ," *Digital Music News*, July 30, 2012, http://www.digitalmusicnews.com/permalink/2012/120730infamous.

49. Tom Newman, "How Much Music Streaming Services Pay per Stream in 2025," *RouteNote Blog*, May 22, 2025, https://routenote.com/blog/how-much-music-streaming-services-pay/; "Which Music Streaming Service Pays Artists the Most?" *Soundwave Artist Discussion Forum*, https://www.soundon.global/forum/music-streaming-payments-2025?lang=en (last accessed September 2025); "How Much Do Artists Make from Music Streaming?" *Pandora CloudCover Blog*, https://cloudcovermusic.com/blog/how-much-artists-make-streaming-services (last accessed September 2025).

50. Jazz Monroe, "New Music Streaming Bill Aims to Boost Streaming Royalties for Artists," *Pitchfork*, March 7, 2024, https://pitchfork.com/news/new-music-streaming-bill-aims-to-boost-streaming-royalties-for-artists/.

51. *H.R. 7763–118th Cong. (2024): Living Wage for Musicians Act of 2024*, https://www.congress.gov/bill/118th-congress/house-bill/7763/all-actions.

revenue in other categories hit record highs), hitting just over $150 million in total that year.[52]

On the music publishing side, the mechanical license rate[53] for a permanent download is the same as for a track on a compact disc: the greater of 12.4 cents or 2.38 cents per minute of playing time or fraction thereof.[54]

As mentioned earlier, there are various compression formats used to prepare audio files for sound recordings, as there are various bit rates used to determine the quality of the files. Also, some files sold by digital retailers may be accompanied by digital rights management (DRM) software, which may restrict use of the files in some manner, such as the number of times the file may be used to burn a compact disc, shared with others, or other features.[55] The payment made by digital music retailers for permanent downloads has generally settled at 70 percent of the retail price of the release. The retail price of the permanent download, and thus the amount paid to the label by the retailer, is typically greater for current "hit" product or high resolution files, or less for legacy material.

As also mentioned earlier, there is a significant issue about how royalties are to be calculated for the sale of permanent downloads.[56] Most legacy

---

52. Recording Industry Association of America, *RIAA Mid-Year 2024 Recorded Music Revenue Report* (2024), https://www.riaa.com/wp-content/uploads/2024/08/RIAA-Mid-Year-2024-Revenue-Report.pdf.

53. The performing rights organizations representing the music publishing interests had also argued that downloads of music files implicated the performance right in the songs included in the files and thus claimed license fees were due for download sales. The ASCAP rate court, however, disagreed in (S.D.N.Y. 2007), aff'd, 627 F.3d 64 (2d Cir. 2010), cert. denied, 132 S. Ct. 366 (2011); see also *United States v. ASCAP*, 607 F. Supp. 2d 562 (S.D.N.Y. 2009) (holding that music downloads, which are transmitted at high speeds and cannot be contemporaneously enjoyed, are not public performances requiring a public performance license).

54. Royalty Rates for Making and Distributing Phonorecords, 37 C.F.R. § 385.3(a) (2022).

55. Ali Matin, "Digital Rights Management (DRM) in Online Music Stores: DRM-Encumbered Music Downloads' Inevitable Demise as a Result of the Negative Effects of Heavy-Handed Copyright Law," *Loyola Los Angeles Entertainment Law Review* 28 (2009): 265.

56. Edward F. McPherson, "F.B.T v. Aftermath: Eminem Raps the Record Industry," *Entertainment & Sports Law* 29, no. 1 (2011): 10; Hugh McIntyre, "Universal Music Group Settles with Rick James' Estate for over $11 Million," *Forbes*, April 15, 2015, https://www.forbes.com/sites/hughmcintyre/2015/04/14/universal-music-group-settles-with-rick-james-estate-for-over-11-million/; RNMTEAM, "Eminem Settles Lawsuit with Universal," *Radioandmusic.com*, November 3, 2012, https://www.radioandmusic.com/content/editorial/news/eminem-settles-lawsuit-with-universal.

recording agreements provided that income from the licensing of recordings by the record company to others would be divided equally between the record company and the recording artist. Such licenses typically occurred after a market for a recording had been established through the sale of phonorecords manufactured and sold by the record company for which the recording artist would be paid a much lower percentage of revenue.

The sale of downloads by parties upon license from the record companies caused disagreement about how the relationship between record company and such seller should be characterized. Was the relationship one of wholesaler–retailer or of licensor–licensee? If the former, a royalty rate would be applied to the price paid by the online seller for the download or ringtone, but if the latter the recording artist would be entitled to one-half of the price (license fee) paid by the online seller. Typically, the difference in the amount paid to the artist is significant (e.g., two to three times the amount). Record companies and digital retailers have settled on a wholesaler–retailer model in their own relationships, which is illustrated by the fact that record companies pay the publishing costs for permanent downloads. In turn, artists and record companies have settled on a percentage-of-revenue-to-the-label model, rather than a certain amount per song, album, and so on. However, the interpretation of the relationship between the record companies and their legacy artists, which are subject to legacy contracts that do not fully address the digital age, continues to be less than certain and depends on the contract language, which can differ from contract to contract.

Ringtones and Ringbacks

Although the market for ringtone sales first peaked, then declined, during the 2010s, ringtones remain a source of revenue for sound recording copyright holders and even have resurged in the 2020s.[57] The fee to the music publisher for the composition embodied in a ringtone is 24 cents

57. Robert Dex, "Streaming Success and a Ringtone Revival Help Power the Music Industry to New Heights," *The Standard*, March 10, 2023, https://au.news.yahoo.com/streaming-success-ringtone-revival-help-202051569.html; Jeffrey Brabec and Todd Brabec, *Music, Money, and Success* (New York: Schirmer Trade Books, 2022).

per copy,[58] while the payment for music publishing for a ringback, which is a performance of the embodied composition rather than a download, is licensed through the performing rights organizations ASCAP, BMI, and SESAC.[59] Payments for the use of the master recording in a ringtone are approximately 40 percent of the retail price.[60]

Satellite Radio and Cable Music Services

The royalty rate paid by satellite radio service providers (of which Sirius XM Radio is the only one left) for the use of sound recordings has steadily increased over the years, from 9 percent of gross revenues for 2013 to 15.5 percent of gross revenues currently (and through 2027).[61] The rate is determined through rate proceedings before the Copyright Royalty Board in the Copyright Office[62] and is paid through SoundExchange. However, Sirius XM has sought to obtain direct licenses with record companies for its service due to persistent litigation and other disputes with SoundExchange over the amounts of royalties that should be payable.[63]

---

58. Royalty Rates for Making and Distributing Phonorecords, 37 C.F.R. § 385.11(b) (2024).

59. Publishers also sought without success to establish that the playing by a mobile phone of a ringtone when it received a call was a public performance of the composition featured in the ringtone. See *In re Cellco Partnership*, 663 F. Supp. 2d 363 (S.D.N.Y. 2009); *Arista Records LLC v. Myxer Inc.*, C.D. Cal. No. CV 08–03935 GAF (JCx), 2011 U.S. Dist. LEXIS 109668 (Apr. 1, 2011).

60. See generally Steven Masur and Ursa Chitrakar, "The History and Recurring Issues of Ringtones," *Entertainment and Sports Lawyer* 24, no. 1 (2006): 1; Cornell Law School, "37 CFR § 385.11—Royalty Rates," *LII / Legal Information Institute*, 2025, https://www.law.cornell.edu/cfr/text/37/385.11; Easy Song, "How Cover Song Royalties Are Calculated," January 2, 2024.

61. 37 C.F.R. § 382.21(a).

62. In the Matter of Determination of Rates and Terms for Preexisting Subscription Services and Satellite Digital Audio Radio Services, No. 2011–1 (Copyright Royalty Judges, Feb. 24, 2013), http://www.loc.gov/crb/proceedings/2011-1/rates/Public-Majority-Final-Determination.pdf.

63. Trefis Team, "Sirius XM and SoundExchange Square Off in the Battle over Royalty Rates," *Forbes*, April 10, 2012, http://www.forbes.com/sites/greatspeculations/2012/04/10/sirius-xm-and-soundexchange-square-off-in-the-battle-over-royalty-rates; Dylan Smith, "SiriusXM Swipes Back at SoundExchange's $150 Million Unpaid Royalties Suit, Urging Dismissal and Damages for Counterclaims," *Digital Music News*, August 12, 2024, https://www.digitalmusicnews.com/2024/08/12/sirius-xm-soundexchange-lawsuit-response/; Dylan

Cable music service Music Choice is characterized as a "preexisting" subscription service and may avail itself of a compulsory license to use sound recordings under § 114(d)(2) of the Copyright Act. The compulsory license royalty rate paid by Music Choice, too, has risen steadily over the years, for example from 8 percent in 2013 to the most recent setting of rates by the Copyright Royalty Board in 2022, when it set a phased-in rate over the five-year period from 2023 to 2027 (15.1 percent in 2023, 15.2 percent in 2024, 15.25 percent in 2025, 15.3 percent in 2026, and 15.35 percent in 2027).[64] This royalty is paid through SoundExchange.

Smith, "SiriusXM Voluntarily Dismisses SoundExchange Counterclaims in Ongoing Unpaid Royalties Dispute," *Digital Music News*, October 23, 2024, https://www.digitalmusicnews.com/2024/10/23/siriusxm-soundexchange-lawsuit-counterclaims-dismissed/.

64. In the Matter of Determination of Rates and Terms for Preexisting Subscription Services and Satellite Digital Audio Radio Services, No. 2011–1 (Copyright Royalty Judges, Feb. 24, 2013), http://www.loc.gov/crb/proceedings/2011-1/rates/Public-Majority-Final-Determination.pdf; *Music Business Worldwide*, "Copyright Royalty Board Officially Accepts New Rates That Will See Songwriters Paid More in the U.S. Over the Next 5 Years," December 30, 2022, https://www.musicbusinessworldwide.com/crb-officially-accepts-settlement-that-will-see-songwriters-paid-more-in-the-us-over-the-next-5-years.

Chapter 9

Tax Considerations for the Musician

By Heather Ryan Liberman and Thomas J. Kliebhan

Willie Nelson,[1] Lauryn Hill,[2] Lil Wayne,[3] and Tyga[4] are all world-renowned for their musical talent *and* their tax indiscretions. As illustrated by these musicians' experiences, the consequences of failing to properly file taxes

---

1. Willie Nelson reportedly owed over $6 million in back taxes and $10 million in penalties. Nelson released numerous albums in the effort to pay back the taxes and auctioned off his ranch, which he was eventually able to repurchase. But note that, although Nelson's tax problems were highly publicized, it was the musician Harold Jenkins, professionally known as Conway Twitty, who set tax precedent when Twitty was challenged by the IRS for deductions related to repayment of investors in a failed business, even though he was not obligated to make these payments. In issuing its order, the court concluded with a composition entitled, "Ode to Conway Twitty," which states in part:

   Twitty Burger went belly up
   But Conway remained true
   He repaid their investors, one and all
   It was the moral thing to do.
   His fans would not have liked it
   It could have hurt their fame
   Had any investors sued him
   Like Merle Haggard or Sonny James.
   When it was time to file taxes
   Conway thought what he would do
   Was deduct those payments as a business expense
   Under section one-sixty-two.
   In order to allow these deductions
   Goes the argument of the Commissioner
   The payments must be ordinary and necessary
   To a business of the petitioner.
   Had Conway not repaid the investors
   His career would have been under cloud,
   Under the unique facts in this case
   Held: The deductions are allowed.

   See "Conway Twitty, R.I.P.: Balladeer, Tax Law Hero," *Journal of Taxation* 79 (August 1993): 127.

2. U.S. Department of Justice, *Singer and Actress Lauryn Hill Sentenced to Prison for Failing to File Tax Returns for More Than $2.3 Million in Income*, May 6, 2013, https://www.justice.gov/usao-nj/pr/singer-and-actress-lauryn-hill-sentenced-prison-failing-file-tax-returns-more-23-million#:~:text=NEWARK%2C%20N.J.%20%E2%80%93%20Lauryn%20N.,years%2C%20U.S.%20Attorney%20Paul%20J.

3. Josh Rodgers, "Lil Wayne Once Had $14M in Tax Debt and Jay-Z Came Through—'That Man Helped Me with My Taxes,'" *Yahoo! Finance* via *AfroTech*, January 27, 2023, https://finance.yahoo.com/news/lil-wayne-once-had-14m-163338524.html.

4. Tyga was held to have accrued over $8 million in outstanding liabilities because of chronic tax noncompliance, and ordered to pay $2.3 million for 2019 alone. See Kristen A. Parillo, "Tax Court Tells Rapper to Face the Music on $2.3 Million Tax Bill," *Tax Notes*, 2023, https://www.taxnotes.com/featured-news/tax-court-tells-rapper-face-music-23-million-tax-bill/2023/09/11/7h8xy.

range from financial penalties to imprisonment.[5] Beyond failure to file, improper calculations or inaccurate tax advice can mean the difference between having a surplus or a deficit in the musician's bank account. To avoid such disastrous outcomes, counsel must be sought from accountants who are skilled in various accounting methods[6] and attorneys with specialized knowledge of state and federal tax laws.[7]

A detailed analysis of general tax law and accounting are outside the scope of this chapter. Still, this chapter will examine income, deductions, and choice of entity at length.

A Musician's Gross Income

A musician may derive their gross income from a range of sources. To stay organized, the musician's income should be tracked, recorded, and categorized. This is important because income may be characterized as capital or ordinary, and active or passive. The differences between these tax treatments, as well as other tax concerns, including deferred compensation, foreign income, and emerging income streams are discussed in the following sections.[8]

---

5. Rapper Jeffrey "Ja Rule" Atkins was sentenced to twenty-eight months in prison for failing to pay more than $1.1 million in federal taxes for five years. *Daily Tax Report*, 138 DTR K-1, July 19, 2011.

6. For an overview of accounting methods, including cash basis, accrual, and income-forecast methods, see Pam Gaines and Cathy McCormack, *Financial Management for Musicians* (Intertec Publishing, 2009); see also *ABKCO Indus., Inc. v. Commissioner of Internal Revenue*, 56 T.C. 1083 (1972) (accrual method of accounting improper when contingent royalties too speculative).

7. For an excellent resource to understand the intersection of tax and entertainment law, see Schuyler Moore, *Taxation of the Entertainment Industry* (CCH, 9th ed. 2008).

8. While the musician has a certain set of tax considerations, the entities that support the musician, such as a record label, have another. Although a detailed explanation of these considerations is outside the scope of this chapter, it is worth noting that a record label must capitalize and amortize the costs to record music and create videos, unless the recording or video was created solely for purposes of advertising, in which case the costs can be deducted as an advertising expense. Similarly, it can capitalize advances as recording costs and amortize them using acceptable methods. There have been circumstances where advances have been amortized over the course of recoupment, rather than the life of the license. For a more thorough explanation, see Moore, supra note 7.

Ordinary Income Versus Capital Gains

A musician's income is characterized as either ordinary income or capital gains. The majority of a musician's income is ordinary income, which is taxed at regular income tax rates as high as 37 percent.[9] Some examples of ordinary income are income derived from copyrights in sound recordings such as streaming or synchronization placements and sales of vinyl, and payments from a live performance.[10] In contrast, capital gains income receives lower tax rates when an asset meets certain standards and is held for a specified amount of time, then sold.[11] Capital gains income is realized upon the sale of capital assets, which include assets held for investment, stocks, or real estate. Capital assets do not include inventory or property held for sale in the ordinary course of business, or certain self-created assets.

Specific examples of capital gains and ordinary income are described in the following section.

Capital Gains: Musical Compositions

Although self-created assets are typically excluded from capital assets, the Songwriters Capital Gains Tax Equity Act, which was originally only a temporary tax break for songwriters,[12] was permanently enacted in 2007.[13] The Act allows the taxpayer (songwriter) to elect to receive capital gains treatment on the income derived from the sale of the copyright in a musical composition, if the copyright was owned by them for more than twelve

9. Internal Revenue Service, "Federal Income Tax Rates and Brackets," last modified July 8, 2025, https://www.irs.gov/filing/federal-income-tax-rates-and-brackets.

10. This income stream maintains that characterization even if transferred to another person as a gift. See Capital Asset Defined, I.R.C. § 1221(a)(3) (2010); Basis of Property Acquired from a Decedent, I.R.C. § 1014 (2010).

11. Tax Imposed, I.R.C. § 1(h)(1)–(4) (if the taxpayer is in the 10 percent or 15 percent bracket, the tax on capital gains is zero). Please be aware that tax law is always fluctuating. Exact tax rates should be researched by a qualified professional.

12. Significant lobbying by the Nashville Songwriters Association International convinced Congress to institute the temporary carve-out in § 1221(a)(3) for Songwriters. See Rodney Mock and Jeffrey Tolin, "I Should Have Been a Rockstar: Deconstructing Section 1221(a)(3)," *Tax Lawyer* 65 (2011): 47.

13. Tax Relief and Health Care Act of 2006, Pub. L. No. 109–432, 120 Stat. 2922 (Dec. 20, 2006) (removing the original Dec. 31, 2010, expiration date).

months.[14] Why does this matter? Gain upon the sale of a long-term capital asset (i.e., an asset held more than 12 months) is generally taxed at 0 percent, 15 percent, or 20 percent based on the taxable income rate, rather than regular personal income tax rates which can be as high as 37 percent.[15] This will save the seller a fortune in taxes.[16] To elect the preferential treatment, the taxpayer must include each musical composition sold or exchanged during the taxable year on their Schedule D. The filing is due prior to the date of the income tax return for the taxable year of the sale.[17] Yet, even if a songwriter sells their song catalog and elects capital gains treatment, the ongoing royalty and fee income generated from the copyright in the same musical compositions receives ordinary income treatment.

The Act also allows purchasers of a song catalog to amortize acquisition costs over a five- year period, in lieu of the typical lengthier timeframe, which is based on the life of the income-producing asset. However, this election has limitations that should be reviewed and analyzed prior to purchasing a song catalog.[18]

Ordinary Income: Compensation for Services Rendered Versus Royalties

As previously mentioned, the majority of the musician's income is ordinary income. Ordinary income may be characterized as compensation for

---

14. When the one-year holding period for long-term capital gains treatment begins can be a complicated question. The one-year period begins from creation of the work for a songwriter who has always retained ownership, but what about songwriters or heirs who have been forced to reclaim previously granted copyrights under 17 U.S.C. § 203(a) or other folks who hold future reversion rights? The IRS has not issued a pronouncement on whether the one-year timeframe begins upon notice or actual reversion of copyrights in musical compositions for which the transfer has been terminated under § 203 of the U.S. Copyright Act. For more information, see Michael R. Morris, "Songwriters Continue to Score Tax Breaks," *California Lawyer Daily Journal*, June 21, 2023, https://www.dailyjournal.com/articles/373486-songwriters-continue-to-score-tax breaks#:~text=1221(b)(3)%20provides,for%20elective%20capital%20gains%20treatment.

15. Ibid.

16. Sellers of these rights can elect to write off the purchase price over fifteen years. Ibid.

17. Rules and Regulations, "Time and Manner for Electing Capital Asset Treatment for Certain Self-Created Musical Works," 26 C.F.R. pt. 1 (2011).

18. Depreciation, I.R.C. § 167(g)(8)(E) (2007).

services rendered or royalties. Each of these categorizations impacts the tax treatment of the income.

One way to determine whether the income is compensation for services rendered or royalties is by answering the question: Who has control? When the musician does not have control, as in a work-for-hire relationship, the income is probably compensation for services rendered. In contrast, income is probably deemed royalties when the musician has control, such as merchandising income because it is usually the license of rights owned by the licensor.[19]

Compensation for Services Rendered: Touring Income

Touring income is taxed as compensation for services rendered.[20] In addition to federal taxes, touring may invoke state taxes as well as foreign taxes when the musician is touring abroad.[21] To properly advise the musician client, it is critical to be aware of tax treaties between the United States and the countries in which the musician is accruing income.[22] Many of the treaties include an "artists and entertainers clause" that excludes artists and entertainers from the treaty.[23] Whether the clause exists in the treaty will help to determine whether musician will be subject to local taxes in the country at issue.

---

19. Moore, supra note 7.

20. "Rolling Stones Protest Taxes, Cancel Gigs," *Journal of Taxation* 89 (1998): 64.

21. Income collected in the United States by foreign citizens is outside the scope of this chapter. However, for more information, see Aninda Dhar, "Foreign Music Acts and United States Taxation," 26 *Cardozo Arts & Entertainment Law Journal* 151 (2008); see also Internal Revenue Service, *Instructions on How to Apply for a Central Withholding Agreement* (2025), https://www.irs.gov/pub/irs-pdf/f13930.pdf.

22. Reference IRS Publication 901 for high level summaries of the treaty exemptions on a country-by-country basis. Note that this publication includes only a summary of each treaty (but often includes specific information addressing artists) and that treaties are often updated, so it is wise to check the specific treaty itself before relying on any exemptions. Each tax treaty is available on the IRS website. See IRS Publication 901 at https://www.irs.gov/pub/irs-pdf/p901.pdf and see treaties for individual countries at https://www.irs.gov/businesses/international-businesses/united-states-income-tax-treaties-a-to-z.

23. See Moore, supra note 7.

Royalties: Publishing Income

Unlike touring income or payments under musician recording agreements, a musician's publishing income,[24] whether under a publishing, copublishing, or administration agreement, is typically characterized as "royalties" or "sale proceeds."[25] This distinction is made because musical compositions are typically not works for hire.[26]

Nonqualified Deferred Compensation: Advances

A musician's representatives should also be aware of the existence and impact of nonqualified deferred compensation on a musician's taxable gross income. Nonqualified deferred compensation is prevalent in the recording industry and requires attention by the experienced practitioner to avoid potential pitfalls.[27] Nonqualified deferred compensation occurs when a payment is made to a musician in a tax year after the tax year in which the services were rendered. For example, advances,[28] profit participations, residuals, or other similar payments are usually characterized as nonqualified deferred compensation.[29]

Taxation of nonqualified deferred compensation is very particularized, and changed dramatically under the American Jobs Creation Act of 2004,

---

24. See *Irving Berlin Music Corp. v. United States*, 487 F.2d 540 (Fed. Cir. 1973), cert. denied, 419 U.S. 832 (1974).

25. Importantly, when a payment is considered either a royalty or sale proceeds, rather than regular income, the income is sourced to the location where the work is exploited, for example, if an artist writes a composition in Chicago, that work is subject to U.S. tax law when exploited in the U.S.

26. Note that a PRO typically withholds taxes prior to the distribution of this income.

27. The deferred compensation is nonqualified under § 409A if it does not meet the qualifications for pension or profit-sharing plans.

28. If the record label provides the musician with a recording advance, the musician is only taxed on any excess money not spent on the recording that the musician is authorized to keep. The same principles apply if the record label provides the musician with an advance to create a music video. See Moore, supra note 7.

29. Bradford S. Cohen, "The Taxation of Deferred Compensation in Standard Service Agreements," *L.A. Law*, May 2010, citing Treas. Reg. § 1.409A-03(b); see also James A. McCarten, "Music City Tax-Ache: Avoiding the Heartache of Section 409A's 80 Percent Tax Rate," *Tennessee Bar Association Newsletter* 1 (2009).

which amended several sections of the Internal Revenue Code (the Code).[30] For example, I.R.C. § 409A changed the previous version of the Code by:

(1) requiring service providers to meet deadlines for elections;[31]
(2) limiting events that allow a deferred compensation distribution to be taken;[32] and
(3) prohibiting acceleration of payments.[33]

If any of these requirements are not satisfied, the service provider must pay tax on all amounts deferred for all years at the regular tax rate of up to 37 percent plus penalties at 20 percent and interest on the deferred amount.[34] However, relief for certain inadvertent and unintentional failures to comply with § 409A is available pursuant to IRS Notice 2010–6.[35]

In addition to relief, an independent contractor may be exempt from the requirements of § 409A if the contractor provides services to at least two other unrelated service recipients and the payment from neither service recipient totals more than 70 percent of the independent contractor's revenue for the year.[36] However, a general legal advice memorandum (GLAM)

30. Robert Jason and Olga Loy, "Federal Tax Reform Includes Traps for Deferred Compensation Deals," *Entertainment Law & Finance*, March 2005.

31. The deadlines depend on whether the compensation is performance-based.

32. Deferred compensation distribution may occur upon any of the following: date of the service provider's separation from service, date of service provider's death or disability, a fixed date, date of change in ownership of the employer, or date of the occurrence of an unforeseeable emergency.

33. However, payment thirty days prior to the due date does not constitute an acceleration. See Treas. Reg. § 1.409A-3(d).

34. The service provider may be able to avoid the penalty if they can show a "substantial risk of forfeiture." A substantial risk of forfeiture under § 409A exists if entitlement to the payment is conditioned on either the performance of future services by the service provider or the occurrence of a condition related to a purpose of the compensation, and the possibility of forfeiture is substantial. See Treas. Reg. § 1.409A-1(d)(1). See also Howard Pianko, "Section 409A: Deferred Compensation Tax Rules: Overview," *Thomson Reuters Practical Law Employee Benefits & Executive Compensation, https://content.next.westlaw.com/practical-law/document/I03f4d744eee311e28578f7ccc38dcbee/Section-409A-Deferred-Compensation-Tax-Rules-Overview?viewType=FullText&transitionType=Default&contextData=(sc.Default)* (last accessed September 2025).

35. Internal Revenue Service, *Internal Revenue Bulletin No. 2010–3* (January 19, 2010), https://www.irs.gov/pub/irs-drop/n-10-06.pdf.

36. James A. McCarten, "Music City Tax-Ache: Avoiding the Heartache of Section 409A's 80 Percent Tax Rate," *Tennessee Bar Association Newsletter* 1 (2009).

published by the IRS in December 2022, AM 2022–007, threatened to expand application of § 409A.[37] This thorny situation should be navigated with the guidance of an experienced tax professional.

Emerging Income Streams: Crowdfunded Income

Additional income streams may be available to musicians who follow nontraditional or DIY models. Crowdfunding is one common avenue for musicians to raise financing for use in connection with any number of purposes, including reserving studio time, arranging a tour, or releasing an album.

As discussed in Chapter 4, the crowdfunding companies Kickstarter, Indiegogo, Patreon, PledgeMusic, ArtistShare, and Rocket Fuel are the most widely used platforms for musicians to raise money from the masses. Although crowdfunding is commonly used, its tax implications may not be commonly known by musicians. First and foremost, the pledges from the public are taxable income, unless the pledge is considered a donation and the band has qualified for exemption from federal income tax under § 501(c)(3) of the Code,[38] or if the pledge qualifies as an exempt "capital contribution" under the JOBS Act.[39] Notwithstanding the foregoing exemptions, it is more likely than not that the pledge income is taxable. Further, the

37. The GLAM appears to require any payment of deferred compensation to a professional business arising from its services to be made only by the direct service recipient or client and only if it has with that client a "plan" that sufficiently describes the deferred payment arrangement. That position would significantly limit the independent contractor exception.

To be clear, the GLAM does not represent a formal IRS position on which taxpayers may rely. For more information; see James Earle and Daniel Hogans, "IRS Overreaches in Applying Section 409A to Independent Contractors," *Tax Notes Federal* 186, no. 6 (May 6, 2024).

38. Kickstarter Staff, "6 Essential Tax Tips for Crowdfunders in 2024," February 20, 2024, https://updates.kickstarter.com/6-essential-tax-tips-for-crowdfunders-in-2024/.

39. The Jumpstart Our Business Act "JOBS Act," signed into law on April 5, 2012, provides an exemption from securities registration requirements for crowdfunding and permits companies to sell up to $5 million of securities each year to an unlimited number of investors that may not be accredited. Driscoll R. Ugarte, "Changes to Crowdfunding Rules Open the Door for Real Estate Sponsors," *Duane Morris*, August 10, 2021, https://www.duanemorris.com/articles/changes_crowdfunding_rules_open_door_real_estate_sponsors_0821.html.

musician should be aware that when an album is pre-sold to the purchaser in exchange for a monetary pledge, this is almost certainly taxable income.[40]

There are also issues surrounding crowdfunding and the availability of deductions. Those issues are discussed in the following section.

Taxation of the Musician's Income

Taxes applicable to a musician may include any combination of the following: self-employment tax if they are an independent contractor;[41] payroll tax if an employee;[42] sales/use tax on the sale of merchandise or any tangible medium of sound recordings; personal property tax; franchise and excise tax; and other federal, state,[43] local, and foreign taxes.[44] Further information about tax rates and income brackets are outside the scope of this chapter but are available through the relevant tax authorities.

---

40. This is a bit of a grey area, and what matters most is proportionality. For example, if a musician were to create a crowdfunding campaign where everyone who donates $20 will get a copy of the album once it is complete (i.e., an amount is in keeping with what an album traditionally costs), this type of "rewards based crowdfunding" will be considered taxable income by the IRS. However, if the participants were each required to donate $300 dollars to get a copy of the future album, this would be more akin to a gift (perhaps *not* taxable income). For more information, see Rex Halverson & Associates, "Avoiding Tax Pitfalls When Crowdfunding," https://halversontax.com/avoiding-tax-pitfalls-crowdfunding/ (last accessed September 2025). If crowdfunding contributions are made as a result of the contributors' detached and disinterested generosity, and without the contributors receiving or expecting to receive anything (or anything of meaningful value) in return, the amounts may be gifts and therefore may not be includible in the gross income of those for whom the campaign was organized. See Internal Revenue Service, "IRS Reminds Taxpayers of Important Tax Guidelines Involving Contributions and Distributions from Online Crowdfunding," *FS-2024–28*, August 2024, https://www.irs.gov/newsroom/irs-reminds-taxpayers-of-important-tax-guidelines-involving-contributions-and-distributions-from-online-crowdfunding. The important thing is keeping the "rewards" nominal and disproportionate if the artist is looking to avoid creating taxable income.

41. An independent contractor's income is reported to the IRS on Form 1099 and there are no withholdings. Specific tax considerations surrounding independent contractors are outside the scope of this chapter.

42. An employee receives a W-2.

43. Issues surrounding whether Sheryl Crow's performance in an aircraft invoked state taxes for each state flown through from Chicago to Los Angeles, see "Taxing Sheryl as the Crow Flies," *Journal of Taxation* 101 (August 2004): 128.

44. See Moore, supra note 7.

Deductions

Upon meeting certain thresholds, musicians have unique opportunities to offset their non-W-2[45] income with deductions,[46] such as "qualified creative expenses."[47] This section reviews the hurdles a musician faces in deducting creative expenses, known as the hobby-loss challenge, and provides a non-exhaustive list of those deductions that are available.

---

45. Deductions allowed under I.R.C. 212 (Expenses for Production of Income) or I.R.C. 162 (Trade or Business Expenses) may offset income from other sources, but I.R.C. 183 (Hobby Loss Rule) can limit those deductions. I.R.C. 162 or 212 deductions should not be pursued without consulting a tax expert. The key context is whether the artist is an employee or self-employed. Generally, the Tax Cuts and Jobs Act (TCJA) suspended I.R.C. 212 deductions for the tax years 2018 through 2025 with regard to W-2 employees, even if the artist can meet the threshold proving their career as an artist is professional and not just a hobby. It is unclear if those tax deductions will return in the future for employee expenses. Thankfully for the self-employed musician, some of those deductions that were available to W-2 employees under I.R.C. § 212 are still available to the self-employed musician under I.R.C. § 162. Note also that, while artists (employee or self-employed) generally cannot deduct music business expenses directly against W-2 income, there is a very specific exemption for "qualified performing artists" (QPA) under I.R.C. § 62(b). This section allows a deduction from gross income (even including W-2 income) for expenses incurred by a qualified performing artist in connection with the services they rendered in the performing arts as an employee. However, its adjusted gross income $16,000 per year cap under I.R.C. § 62(b)(1)(C) renders this statute a relic of the past and useless as a practical matter. Nevertheless, if the artist meets the threshold to be a qualified performing artist, the artist can use those qualifying deductions to deduct their expenses from their total gross income (even including their W-2 income) regardless of whether the artistic pursuit is a hobby or business. See Internal Revenue Service, *Activities Not Engaged in for Profit Audit Technique Guide: Internal Revenue Code Section 183, III(A)(4)*, September 7, 2021, https://www.irs.gov/pub/irs-pdf/p5558.pdf.

46. The availability of certain deductions and credits should be analyzed by an accountant and tax attorney. Be aware that certain instances of deductions and credits have constituted "tax shelters." A "tax shelter" can be defined as "an investment which has a significant feature for federal income or excise tax purposes either of the following attributes: (1) deductions in excess of income from the investment being available in any year to reduce income from other sources in that year, or (2) credits in excess of the tax attributable to the income from the investment being available in any year to offset taxes on income from other sources in that year." See *United States v. Music Masters, Ltd.*, 621 F. Supp. 1046 (W.D.N.C. 1985), aff'd, 816 F.2d 674 (4th Cir. 1987) (sound recording lease program was an abusive tax shelter because valuations of sound recordings were grossly overstated, rendering ineligible any deductions and credits to investors).

47. Rules Relating to Property Produced by the Taxpayer, 26 C.F.R. § 1.263A-2(a)(2)(ii)(A)(1) (2012).

Hobby-Loss

Unfortunately, even musicians who are dedicated to writing, recording, and performing their art, and do nothing but music to earn money, may not be able to benefit from certain deductions. This is because the IRS categorizes a musician as either a hobbyist or a professional, because being a "professional" in the eyes of the IRS means more than just making some money, and because only professionals may take most of the available deductions.[48]

Although the IRS acknowledges that a musician is engaged in a business or trade, the musician is presumed a hobbyist unless their activities have yielded a profit during at least three of five consecutive years ending with the tax year at issue.[49] One mechanism to demonstrate profit is to regulate the time and receipt of income and the time and occurrence of expenses.[50] However, this is not recommended without advice from a tax expert.

If deemed a hobbyist, the musician can deduct only the expenses of the hobby up to the amount of income produced by the hobby. For example, if a musician does not yield net profits during three of the consecutive five years leading up to the year in question, and only earned $1,000 in the last year, only $1,000 of expenses can be deducted.

Yet, a musician can overcome the hobbyist characterization if the musician demonstrates a "profit motive."[51] A profit motive is established by the facts and circumstances surrounding a musician's activities, as indicated by assessing the following nine factors:

(1) Manner in which the taxpayer carries on the activity;[52]
(2) Professional expertise of the taxpayer;
(3) Time and effort expended by the taxpayer in carrying on the activity;
(4) The taxpayer's expectation that assets may appreciate in value;

---

48. Moore, supra note 7.

49. See Doak Turner, "Financial Management for Musicians' Author Offers Tax Tips for Songwriters, Workshop Hosted by Songwriters Guild Office, Nashville, TN," *Music Dish*, March 4, 2005, http://intimateaudio.com/article34.html.

50. Moore, supra note 7.

51. *Wesley v. Commissioner*, 2007 WL 968731 (U.S. Tax Ct. 2007), citing *Commissioner v. Groetzinger*, 480 U.S. 23 (1987).

52. Ibid. Musician claiming deductions for installation of recording equipment does not satisfy the profit motive analysis when the musician failed to keep regular records of expenses and presented only a few receipts for studio time from the eight years prior to the year at issue.

(5) Success of the taxpayer in similar activities;
(6) The taxpayer's previous income or losses with respect to activity;
(7) Amount of the taxpayer's earned profits;
(8) Financial status of the taxpayer, for example, wealth and independent income; and
(9) Whether the taxpayer's activities are for personal pleasure or recreation.[53]

If a musician is considered a "professional" after analyzing the factors, there may be deductions available for their ordinary and necessary expenditures beyond the amount of their revenue, which are explained in the following section.

Ordinary and Necessary Business Expenditures

Deductions for ordinary and necessary business expenditures may be available to offset income generated by a self-employed musician filing Schedule C,[54] or an LLC or Corporation. Remember, these deductions are typically not available to offset W-2 income. Further, the 2017 Tax Cuts and Jobs Act repealed all "Miscellaneous Itemized Deductions."[55] Due to this, W-2 musicians can no longer deduct "Unreimbursed Employee Expenses," such as buying an instrument, sheet music, supplies or equipment, required concert clothing, mileage, job search/audition expenses, research expenses (for musicians who are professors), or home office expenses.[56] Keep in mind

53. *Activities Not Engaged for Profit*, I.R.C. § 1.183–2(b); see also Internal Revenue Service, *IRC Audit Technique Guide*, https://www.irs.gov/businesses/small-businesses-self-employed/audit-techniques-guides-atgs.

54. In order to keep track of the musician's expenses, it may be useful to create a worksheet with columns for the following to support claimed deductions: continuing education, such as voice training and rent for rehearsal space; promotional expenses, such as audition tapes, business cards, professional headshots, and website development and hosting; supplies and expenses, such as union and professional dues, insurance, interest on business loans, postage, repairs for instruments, and sheet music; travel to auditions, business meetings, continuing education or other professional activities; and equipment purchases. The worksheet and its supporting receipts will be useful when it is time to file taxes.

55. Scott Stratton, "Big Tax Changes for Musicians in 2018," March 13, 2018, https://internationalmusician.org/tax-changes/; see also Tax Cuts and Jobs Act, Pub. L. No. 115–97, 131 Stat. 2054 (2017), effective Jan. 1, 2018, https://www.govinfo.gov/content/pkg/PLAW-115publ97/pdf/PLAW-115publ97.pdf.

56. Ibid. They also cannot deduct tax preparation fees, investment management fees, memberships to professional organizations, or union membership and work dues.

that, while this does affect only musicians who are W-2 employees, most of these costs are still deductible for self-employed musicians who report their business income on Schedule C.[57]

Ordinary and necessary business expenditures include, but are not limited to, workspace, instruments and equipment, clothing, repairs, travel for business purposes, promotional expenses, and legal and accounting fees.[58] To be deductible, these expenditures must be reasonable.[59] Obviously, the determination of what is reasonable is very fact specific and outside the scope of this chapter.[60] Regardless, the musician and their counsel should be aware of the following non-exhaustive list of possible deductions.

Home Office Workspace

It is not unusual for musicians to teach music lessons out of their home, or allocate space within their home for rehearsals. When done properly, a musician may be able to deduct their home office studio as their principal place of business.[61] A home office could be the taxpayer's principal place of business where:

(1) the office is used by the taxpayer for administrative or management activities of their trade or business; and

57. Ibid. Musicians can still work around this somewhat by adding to Schedule C their "side" income and expenses, such as for teaching private lessons at home studios or offering other self-employment type services. In this way, they can claim some of the expenses no longer available as deductions to W-2 employees via W-2 Schedule A.

58. Although the IRS Market Segment Specialization Program (MSSP) guidelines include fees paid to a musician's managers, Stevie Nicks's attempt to deduct $119,291 paid to her personal manager was challenged by the IRS on the grounds that the expense was not business, but rather, personal. See "Ordinary and Necessary Business Expenses for Entertainers: What's Reasonable," *Journal of Taxation* 87 (1997): 63, citing Docket No. 22733–96, filed October 22, 1996.

59. See *Teschner v. Commissioner*, TCM 1997–498 (U.S. Tax Ct. 1997). The court found that Rod Stewart's backup musician was an employee and not able to deduct expenses for either silk underwear or the costs of meals allegedly paid for as a punishment by Rod Stewart for the musician's late arrival to the tour bus. See also "More on 'Ordinary and Necessary' Business Expenses for Entertainers," *Journal of Taxation* 88 (1998): 126.

60. For example, if the expense is a business necessity, a musician may be able to deduct the cost of using their car to transport musical instruments between home and the business.

61. *Drucker v. Commissioner*, 715 F.2d 67 (2d Cir. 1983) (concert musicians successfully argued that their home office studios used for individual practice became their principal place of business for purposes of deductions).

(2) there is no other fixed location where the taxpayer conducts substantial administrative or management activities of their trade or business.[62]

Instruments and Equipment

Rather than capitalizing and depreciating a musical instrument or other professional equipment, the cost of a certain amount thereof may be deducted during the year of its purchase. Additionally, musicians may deduct the depreciation of musical instruments, even those that have actually increased in value.[63]

Clothing

Musicians may be able to deduct clothing as an ordinary and necessary business expense. The availability of this deduction depends on if the clothing is (1) required or essential in the taxpayer's employment, (2) not suitable for general or personal wear, and (3) not actually worn as general or personal wear.[64] Examples of costumes probably not suitable for general or personal wear are the gown made of meat that Lady Gaga wore to the 2010 MTV Video Music Awards and the chest-bearing jump suit that Harry Styles wore to the 2023 Grammys.[65]

---

62. See *Disallowance of Certain Expenses in Connection with Business Use of Home*, I.R.C. § 280A(c); see also Charles M. Flesch, "Employed Artists' Home Office Deductions in the Aftermath of *Weissman v. Commissioner*: The Second Circuit's New Limited Exception for Taxpayer-Employees," *Cardozo Arts & Entertainment Law Journal* 4 (1985): 337.

63. See *Liddle v. Commissioner*, 65 F.3d 329, *aff'd*, 65 F.3d 329 (3d Cir. 1995); Simon v. Commissioner, 68 F.3d 41 (2d Cir. 1995); Alton A. Murakami, "'Useful Life' Has Outlived Its Useful Life: Tax Depreciation After Simon and Liddle," *New York Law Review* 72, no. 5 (November 1997): 1211, https://www.nyulawreview.org/wp-content/uploads/2018/08/NYULawReview-72-5-Murakami.pdf.

64. Where a musician claims that clothing was for performance in concerts, receipts from department stores for gowns and earrings were insufficient, when such clothing items are typical in women's wardrobes and could be worn outside of performance. See Tilman v. United States, 644 F. Supp. 2d 391 (S.D.N.Y. 2009); see also *Miscellaneous Deductions*, IRS Publications, https://www.irs.gov/publications/p529 (last accessed September 2025).

65. Zack Greenburg, "Lada Gaga's Potentially Meaty Tax Deduction," *Forbes*, April 20, 2011, https://www.forbes.com/sites/zackomalleygreenburg/2011/04/20/lady-gaga-meaty-tax-deduction/; Kevin Huynh, "The 16 Wildest Grammys Looks of All Time," *Instyle*, Jan. 31, 2025, https://www.instyle.com/wildest-grammy-looks-of-all-time-8783617#:~:text=Country%20crooner%20Shania%20Twain%20made,donning%20a%20flaming%20red%20wig.

However, musicians must be careful when trying to deduct clothing and costumes, because the IRS explicitly states:

> Taxpayers in the entertainment industry sometimes may incur expenses to maintain an image. These expenses are frequently related to the individual's appearance in the form of clothing, makeup, and physical fitness. Other expenses in this area include bodyguards and limousines. These are generally found to be personal expenses as the inherently personal nature of the expense and the personal benefit far outweigh any potential business benefit. No deduction is allowed for wardrobe, general makeup, or hair styles for auditions, job interviews, or "to maintain an image."[66]

As with many other IRS inquiries, whether clothing is deductible is very fact specific, and requires sufficient evidentiary support.[67]

Repairs

Musicians may deduct costs associated with the repair and upkeep of their instruments and equipment related to their performances. Musicians may also itemize and deduct any consumable goods they purchase such as rosin for violins or strings for guitars.[68]

Travel for Business Purposes

Travel, lodgings, meals, and attendance fees for industry functions are all deductible.[69] All that matters is that the event is a business expense related to running a music business. Traveling for tour (via car, van, or plane), one-off

66. Internal Revenue Service, *Business Expenses—Entertainment Audit Technique Guide*, IRS Publications VIII (A.3)(2) (March 20, 2023), https://www.irs.gov/pub/irs-pdf/p5774.pdf (hereafter *Entertainment Audit Technique Guide*).

67. Musician's clothing, and maintenance thereof, were deductible as ordinary and necessary business expenses when the clothing was formal evening wear worn only while performing as a lounge singer deductible when he maintained trunks of "off-season" clothing. See *Fisher v. Commissioner*, 23 T.C. 218 (T.C. 1954), aff'd, 230 F.2d 79 (1956).

68. TurboTax, "The Musician's Guide to Taxes: Top Tax Deductions," October 16, 2024, https://turbotax.intuit.com/tax-tips/self-employment-taxes/the-musicians-guide-to-taxes-top-tax-deductions/L3dFXFokF.

69. Ibid.

gigs, lessons, recording sessions, and label meetings are all deductible. Travel tickets, gas, tolls, and parking should all be considered. Deductions often overlooked by musicians are the costs incurred when they attend other musicians' performances. Artists can attend such performances to learn about musical trends, which makes them deductible.

Promotional Expenses

Advertising and promoting is essential for an artist to grow their business.[70] These costs are all tax deductible. Print, digital, and social media advertisements are all costs the artist may deduct. Even fees related to creating business cards or the costs associated with domain and hosting fees for artist websites may be deducted.

Legal Fees and Accounting

Professional services necessary for one's music business such as attorneys' fees and the business portion of tax preparation costs are expenses related to the artist's business. Therefore, they, too, are deductible.[71]

The HITS Act

In 2025, the United States government passed the historic Help Independent Tracks Succeed Act (HITS Act), which gave professional independent artists, producers, and independent record labels significant tax deduction benefits. Prior to the HITS Act, professional artists (not those artists deemed "hobbyists") and labels were able to deduct recording expenses for the creation of sound recordings.[72] However, those expenses had to be amortized over multiple years.[73] The HITS Act will allow deductions of up to $150,000 immediately in the taxable year in which the money was spent.[74]

70. Ankur Bhardwaj, "14 Tax Deductions Every Artist, Writer, and Musician Should Know About," *Doola*, July 9, 2024, https://www.doola.com/blog/14-tax-deductions-every-artist-writer-and-musician-should-know-about/.

71. See Turbo Tax, supra note 68.

72. Dylan Smith, "HITS Act to Become Law Following Mega-Bill Passage—Recording Academy and A2IM Applaud the 'Historic Victory for Independent Music Creators,'" July 3, 2025, https://www.digitalmusicnews.com/2025/07/03/hits-act-passage/.

73. Ibid.

74. Ibid.

Note that this deduction is limited to expenses incurred in the production of sound recordings only. Other expenses such as traveling to record or marketing the sound recordings will have to be deducted through the usual "ordinary business expenditure" routes explained earlier. Expenses that artists should consider for deductions via the HITS Act include studio rental fees, producer fees, engineering fees, session musician fees, songwriter fees, mixing and mastering costs, and equipment rentals.

Passive Loss Deductions

A musician should be aware of the limitations on deducting losses that arise when generating passive income. Passive losses can offset only income[75] that is derived from the conduct of a trade, business, or transaction entered into for profit in which the taxpayer does not materially participate.[76] In other words, passive losses can offset only passive income. Note that material participation is established by regular, continuous, and substantial basis in the operations of the activity.[77] For example, when a musician creates musical copyrights, the royalties collected by the musician for the exploitation of those copyrights constitutes material participation.[78] This distinction highlights the importance of maintaining organized records and seeking counsel from experienced accountants and attorneys.

Charitable Deductions

A musician may claim deductions under I.R.C. § 170(m) if they donate musical copyrights to a charitable organization.[79] This type of donation may be fruitful for the musician, because during the ten years following the donation the musician may deduct a percentage of the income generated

75. See Passive Activity Losses and Credits Limited, I.R.C. § 469 (2005) (hereafter Passive Activity Losses).

76. Ibid. § 469(c)(1); see Reg. §§ 1.1362–2(c)(5)(ii)(A)(2)–(3). But see I.R.C. § 469(e)(1). Certain royalties are considered passive income.

77. Passive Activity Losses, 72 at I.R.C. § 469(h)(1).

78. Schuyler Moore, "Entertainment Industry Affected by Several Tax Developments," *Journal of Taxation* 73 (1990): 176, citing Temp. Reg. § 1.469–2T(c)(7)(i).

79. See generally Bradford S. Cohen and Kyle Neal, "Star Power: Celebrity Involvement in Charitable Causes Raises Both Tax and Business Affairs Issues," *Los Angeles Lawyer*, May 2011.

by the charity for the exploitation of the copyrights.[80] The following table illustrates the percentage of the income generated by the donation that the artist is able to deduct.[81]

Taxable Year of Donor Ending After Date of Contribution	Applicable Percentage
1st	100
2nd	100
3rd	90
4th	80
5th	70
6th	60
7th	50
8th	40
9th	30
10th	20
11th	10
12th	10

Another way that musicians donate to charities is through live performances or lending their name to social causes. Unfortunately, artists are unable to claim deductions for charitable performances. In other words, if an artist has a $5,000 appearance fee, they cannot take a $5,000 deduction by waiving that fee and performing for a charitable cause. Although these activities may benefit the charity, they may be financially detrimental to the musician if the IRS determines that the musician was compensated (directly or indirectly) or if the event is for private inurement. These

80. **Authors' Note:** The authors are aware that while the language of the statute indicates ten years of claimed deductions, the chart that follows shows twelve years of deductions. This chart has been reproduced exactly as it appears in the statute itself. The authors are unable to explain the discrepancy of the language of the statute indicating ten years versus the twelve years of deductions as in the chart, but note that the language and chart have been reproduced exactly as they appear in 170(m).

81. Charitable, Etc., Contributions and Gifts, 26 U.S.C. § 170(m)(7).

questions arise when an insider of the organization benefits from the musician's performance.[82]

Abandoned Property

A deduction may be available to musicians or music-related businesses for losses sustained in connection with the abandonment of intangible assets when the abandonment occurred by an identifiable event.[83] Although relinquishment of legal title is not necessary to support a finding of abandonment, intent and affirmative act of abandonment are needed.[84] A musician may also take a deduction for valueless copyrights, but that is likely much more difficult to demonstrate.[85]

Crowdfunding Considerations

Crowdfunding for creating recorded music raises unique issues related to deductions. First, unlike the usual model where an album is recorded and then sold before the artist earns income, many artists raise crowdfunded income before stepping foot into a recording studio. If the artist does not incur any expenses during the year they receive the crowdfunded income, then they will be foreclosed from taking deductions for those expenses. Therefore, to minimize tax exposure the artist should incur expenses during the year the crowdfunded income is received.[86] However, even if the artist does not do so, deductions still may be available if the artist pre-pays for certain goods or services during the year in which they receive the crowdfunded income, but there are separate pitfalls associated with that practice.[87]

---

82. Blake Behnke and Mark Weinberg, "When Celebrities and 501(c)(3)s Collide—The Perils and the Pathways," *Taxation for the Exempt*, 23 (2011): 12.

83. Bradford S. Cohen and David P. Schwartz, "Accounting: Determining Entertainment Industry Deductions for Creative Properties Deemed Abandoned or Worthless Remains Difficult Despite IRS Guidance," *Daily Tax Report* 135 (2004): J-1.

84. See *Lockwood v. Commissioner*, 94 T.C. 252 (1990) (leaving master recordings on a shelf without preservation constituted abandonment).

85. Internal Revenue Service, *Publication 946 (2023): How to Depreciate Property*, https://www.irs.gov/publications/p946 (last accessed September 2025).

86. A band may elect to use the income forecast method of accounting to depreciate any sound recordings created with Kickstarter financing. See *Kickstarter and Taxes* at https://www.kickstarter.com/help/taxes (last accessed September 2025).

87. Ibid. For example, if a band pre-pays for the services of a producer and that producer is later not used, the band may have wasted its money without the ability to deduct.

Second, if the crowdfunded financing is less than the actual cost of recording, producing, mixing, mastering, and releasing an album, it may be possible to offset all of the crowdfunded income.[88] But bear in mind that when a taxpayer produces or creates a product, including a sound recording, and the taxpayer incurs a large portion of the production or creation expense before the product produces income, the IRS states that "the taxpayer is usually required to capitalize those expenses and recover (deduct) them over the period of time that the product is producing income."[89]

Finally, if the crowdfunded income is greater than the cost of the sound recordings, then the artist may elect to depreciate the crowdfunded sound recordings and deduct a portion of the projected income within the first year of sale.[90]

Tax Credits

Another way in which a musician's tax liability may be reduced is through using tax credits. Although most tax credits provide the same savings regardless of the musician's tax bracket, they may otherwise vary. For example, some are nonrefundable, meaning they do not produce a refund in the event losses exceed payment. The following section describes some of the tax credits available to musicians.

Production Credits

Depending on the state, budget, and type of project, production credits may be available to musicians.[91] For example, in 2007, Louisiana instituted a 25 percent tax refund for in-state expenditures related to the production of sound recordings when a minimum amount of money is spent on the

88. Amy Feldman, "Crowdfunded Business May Owe Taxes, Too," *Reuters*, August 13, 2012.

89. *Entertainment Audit Technique Guide*, supra note 66.

90. Kickstarter and Taxes, supra note 77. To depreciate the sound recordings, the band may choose to follow the income forecast method of accounting.

91. For example, in 2012, the governor of Oklahoma proposed tax reform that would eliminate credits for tourism and film and music facilities. See Nancy J. Moore, *Daily Tax Report State Tax & Accounting, Oklahoma: Governor Proposes Major Cut in Personal Income Tax Rates*, 024 DTR H-3, 2012.

project.[92] In Alabama, there is a 25 percent to 35 percent tax credit for recording a soundtrack with a $50,000 minimum-spending requirement. With the same minimum, Indiana offers a 15 percent refundable credit for audio projects, and Michigan offers a film production credit program that includes a 40 percent refundable tax for sound recordings produced for purposes of scoring films. In Georgia, the production incentives provide up to 30 percent in tax credits for productions, including music videos.[93]

Foreign Tax Credits

In the publication *International Royalties Tax Reporting Guide*, ASCAP provides information that may reduce a musician's tax liability.[94] ASCAP's guide explains that royalties reported on a member's 1099 are "grossed up" to include taxes withheld by foreign affiliated societies. This process may allow the musician to claim the taxes paid to foreign governments as foreign tax credits.[95]

Tax Exemptions

Tax exemptions are yet another way that musicians may reduce their tax liability. For example, in Texas, producers of audio masters receive the benefit of sales and use tax exemptions.[96] The exemption allows the producer to claim a 100 percent exemption from sales and local taxes on certain equipment purchased, rented, or repaired during the studio master recording process. Included in the long list published by the Texas Music Office are acoustic guitars, amplifiers, analog and digital multitrack recorders,

---

92. See Louisiana Economic Development Sound Recording Tax Incentive Program, L.S. R.S. 47: 602, 51:6023.

93. See Georgia Film, Music & Digital Entertainment Office, https://efaidnbmnnnibpcajpcglclefindmkaj/https://georgia.org/sites/default/files/2018-12/tax_incentive_brochure_film_2018.pdf (last accessed September 2025).

94. American Society of Composers, Authors & Publishers, *International Royalties Reporting Guide* (2025), https://www.ascap.com/help/royalties-and-payment/IntlTaxReporting.

95. Foreign tax credits have also been the source of litigation; see *Evans v. Famous Music Corp.*, 807 N.E.2d 869 (N.Y. 2004). In *Evans*, Henry Mancini, Johnny Mercer, and others sued the publishing company Famous Music. Although Famous paid the composers monies actually received from foreign sources, less the taxes paid to foreign governments, Famous did not split the tax credit with the composers. The Court of Appeals of New York held that the publishing company was not obligated to share its tax savings from the foreign tax credits.

96. See Texas Music Office, "Sales and Use Tax Exemptions Available for Producers of Audio Master Tapes," https://gov.texas.gov/music/page/salestax (last accessed September 2025).

analog and digital two-channel recorders, sampling equipment, and studio monitors.

Clearly, this exemption can be extremely beneficial to musicians and producers. Just as with tax credits, it is critical for a musician's representative to stay up to date on the existence of and changing requirements for tax exemptions.

Audit

The IRS is aware of the avenues available to musicians to reduce their tax liability through deductions, credits, and exemptions. Accordingly, IRS agents are provided with examination guidelines specific to the music industry.[97] Those guidelines are split up based on the type of musician or music business being examined, including songwriters, publishers, live performers, producers, managers, and videographers. For each category, an IRS agent is given direction on how to verify whether the claimed deductions are permitted, including what questions to ask to understand the source and amount of the musician's income.

For example, the agents are guided to ask songwriters for PRO royalty statements, publishing agreements, and agency agreements controlling the collection of mechanical and synchronization royalties. In contrast, agents are guided to ask publishers about the sale of copyrights or catalogs and the employment status of performers, producers, nonunion musicians, and arrangers. The IRS also examines live performers as "stars" or "others" depending on the musician's primary source of income. If the musician has multiple jobs to sustain their music career, they will be in the "others" category and examined accordingly.

After an audit, the IRS will determine whether there is a deficiency. If justified, the IRS may file a lien against the musician's assets to secure their interest as a creditor.[98]

---

97. Market Segment Specialization Program, *Music Industry*, Department of the Treasury, IRS Publications, March 1994; see also Market Segment Specialization Program, *Entertainment Industry*, Department of the Treasury, IRS Publications, 1995.

98. See also "Songwriter's Assignment of Public Performance Royalties to Creditors Has Priority Over IRS Tax Lien, Even Though Creditors Did Not Record Assignment in Copyright Office, Federal Appellate Court Rules," *Entertainment Law Reporter* 19 (February 1998), http://elr.carolon.net/BI/v19n09.pdf. But see *Broadcast Music, Inc. v. United States*, 104 F.3d 1163 (9th Cir. 1997) (unrecorded assignments of a taxpayer's rights to receive royalty income

Choice of Entity

Although self-employed musicians may qualify for the deductions, tax credits, and exemptions discussed earlier, the musician may derive those same benefits *and* limit personal liability if they choose to establish a legal entity.[99] Deciding what entity is best for a musician or music-related business requires careful analysis of their assets and applicable taxes.[100]

This section provides an overview of the pros and cons of establishing a sole proprietorship, general partnership, limited partnership, C-corporation, S-corporation, or limited liability company (LLC).[101] The following table is a general introduction to the issues with each entity. Note that under the Corporate Transparency Act, effective January 1, 2024, the vast majority of business owners have been required to submit a beneficial ownership information (BOI) report online to the Financial Crimes and Enforcement Network of the Department of Treasury shorty after their entities are formed.[102] It is essential to advise potential clients of this requirement along with understanding the responsibilities assumed by the individual submitting the required form.

	Formation	**Operation**	**Tax**
Sole Proprietorship	Without a partner or incorporation, the lone musician defaults to sole proprietorship, and the "doing business as" or dba name should be filed with local/state authorities	Unlimited liability	No entity-level tax

from the performance of a copyrighted work are not unperfected and the rights may transfer prior to the attachment of a federal tax lien).

99. When a member of an entity did not create the music copyright, any income from royalties is considered passive income and can only be offset by passive losses.

100. See generally Bradford S. Cohen, "Income, Estate, and Gift Taxation of Entertainment Assets," *Los Angeles Lawyer*, May 2012.

101. Although taxation is a major consideration during the process of selecting an entity, there are additional requirements that must be met if the entity is structured as a tax shelter. For example, the entity must have a profit motive and meet the "at-risk" and investment rules established by the IRS.

102. Justin M. Jacobson, "Entertainers, Creators, Streamers, Influencers, and Service Providers Duties Under the Corporate Transparency Act" (2023), https://jmjesq.com/corporate-transparency-act-duties/ (last accessed September 2025).

	Formation	Operation	Tax
General Partnership	While it can be formalized with a written partnership agreement, with a partner but no incorporation the musicians default to general partnership, and the "doing business as" or dba name should be filed with local/state authorities	Unlimited liability to partners, any general partner may bind the partnership, and partners share in the profits and losses	No entity-level tax, but rather a pass-through of profits/losses to the individual partners for their individual tax returns, and the filing by the partnership of an informational tax return
Limited Partnership	Only by way of a written partnership agreement establishing which partners are general and limited	Limited liability to limited partners but not general partner, and management by general partner (only general partner may bind the partnership)	No entity-level tax, but rather a pass-through of profits/losses to the individual partners for their individual tax returns, and the filing by the partnership of an informational tax return; limited partners must follow the passive income rules
C-corporation	Only by way of filing Articles of Incorporation with the secretary of state in the state of formation	No personal liability as long as corporate formalities are followed, for example, regular meetings, electing directors and officers, issuing stock, opening a bank account, maintaining sufficient capitalization, which are set forth in bylaws; governed by a board of directors, and managed by corporate officers	Corporate income tax (on the entity's profits); corporation then may elect to distribute remaining monies to shareholders as dividends, which must be reported and taxed as personal income; and may be able to deduct more than S-corporation

	Formation	Operation	Tax
S-Corporation	Only by way of filing Articles of Incorporation with the secretary of state in the state of formation, followed by an S-corporation election with the IRS	Similar to C-corporation	Profits and losses flow through to the shareholders who then report on personal income; and taxed at corporate level the same as a C-corporation if it previously *was* a C-corporation
Limited Liability Company	Only by way of signing an operating agreement (the LLC equivalent of both bylaws and shareholders' agreement) and filing Articles of Organization with the secretary of state in the state of formation	Governed by a board of managers, and managed by either members, managers, or corporate officers (as selected by the member(s))	Profits and losses pass through to the LLC members' personal income tax returns, but some states impose a minimum tax on gross revenues

Sole Proprietorship

A sole proprietorship is nothing more than a single musician who has not formalized an entity structure. In other words, it is the default for the situation in which the musician begins doing business (e.g., recording or performing, and earning therefrom) without having done anything else. In this situation, the net profits and losses from the music activities are reported on the individual's income tax returns.[103] It follows that the owner "materially participates" in the operations of the sole proprietorship and is not subject to the passive loss limitations.

103. Brian McPherson, *Get It in Writing: The Musician's Guide to the Music Business* (Rockpress Publishing Company, 1999).

A sole proprietorship may use the accrual or cash basis method of accounting, except with respect to the sale of inventory.[104] If assets are sold by the sole proprietorship, it is deemed as a sale by the sole proprietor themselves, so income received is taxed based on the sole proprietor's individual tax rate.[105]

However, under the sole proprietor structure, the individual musician has unlimited personal liability. In the event they are sued for copyright infringement related to a sound recording or get in a car accident on tour, the musician's personal assets are vulnerable.

Partnership

General Partnership

When two people are doing business together for profit, and they have not formalized an entity structure, a de facto or general partnership is created.[106] In other words, it is the default for the situation in which two or more musicians begin doing business (e.g., recording or performing, and earning therefrom) without having done anything else. A general partnership may also be created when the musicians sign a written partnership agreement, and in such event while they are out of the de facto category the outcome is the same—they have become general partners. Typically, a general partnership may use either the accrual or cash basis methods of accounting.[107] If assets are sold by the general partnership, it is deemed as a sale by the general partners themselves, so income received is taxed based on each general partner's individual tax rate. Each state has its own laws

---

104. General Rule for Methods of Accounting, I.R.C. § 446(d).

105. Moore, supra note 7.

106. It is highly advisable to consult the statute(s) surrounding de facto partnerships in the state where the band is doing business.

107. There is an exception, which requires the accrual method. This exception is known as the Gross Receipts Test. The Gross Receipts Test is met if the average annual gross receipts of such entity for the three taxable year period preceding the current tax year do not exceed a certain threshold. That threshold is indexed for inflation. Therefore, the amount changes from year to year. When using the exception it is imperative to look up the current year's amount. As of this writing, it is $25,000,000. See Limitation on Use of Cash Method of Accounting, I.R.C. § 448(b)(3) and (c).

surrounding partnerships, which should be consulted prior to analyzing a musician's situation.

Generally speaking, musicians working together as a band create a general partnership. Although a partnership may be desirable because it doesn't require any filings with the state, a partnership also has numerous default rules that may be detrimental to one or more of the musician partners in the partnership.[108] First, each musician is an agent of the band and has the ability to bind the partnership. This means that a bassist can book the band for a gig without notifying the remaining band members. This scenario may be problematic when considered along with the next default rule: The partners share in the profits and losses of the band.[109] So, if the drummer cannot come to the gig and the band cannot find a replacement and has to cancel, each musician partner is responsible for any penalties the venue may invoke. To further complicate the relationship, if the bassist repeatedly books gigs the band has to back out of and the band wants to kick out the bassist, there may actually be state default partnership rules that prevent the band from being able to do so.

Moreover, not only is each responsible for liabilities of the partnership, but that liability is joint and several, meaning that if the rogue bass player is destitute and the drummer is not, then as between the band and the disappointed venue, the drummer will be responsible for the entire liability. This also means that if one band member racks up a band credit card purchasing band equipment but forgets to make payments to the credit card, all the members will probably be responsible to pay the debt and accrued interest.

Bands are not the only de facto partnerships, artist–producer development agreements where both the artist and producer jointly share profits from recordings, or joint publishing or distribution deals where a publishing company or record label jointly exploit rights or distribution with bands, are also usually characterized by the IRS as partnerships regardless of

108. John C. Ale and Buck McKinney, "Stumbling into Partnerships: How Bands, Business Owners and Strategic Allies Find Themselves in Inadvertent Partnerships," *Texas Journal of Business Law* 43 (Fall 2009): 465.

109. Ibid.

whether the parties sign a written agreement stating otherwise (e.g., "nothing contained in this agreement creates a partnership between the parties").[110]

If the band insists on establishing a partnership because it does not want to follow corporate formalities or pay filing fees to the secretary of state, the band partnership, or any other music-related business, should definitely create a written partnership agreement. In addition to the general partnership language, the partnership agreement should contain musician-specific clauses, including control, ownership, leaving member, contributions, and amending the agreement.

Limited Partnership

Limited partnerships are similar to general partnerships, except in two ways. First, limited partnerships cannot be formed on a de facto basis—there must be written agreement. Second, formation of a limited partnership generally requires a governmental filing (and the payment of a filing fee) in the state of formation. Limited partnerships also differ from general partnerships in that limited partnerships must have at least one general partner and additional limited partners. Limited partnerships can use either accrual or cash basis accounting methods. If assets are sold by the limited partnership, it is deemed as a sale by the limited partnership. Profits and losses attributable to that sale are passed through to the limited partners in relation to their proportional share of their investment in the sold asset, which is then reported on each limited partner's individual tax return. The general partner(s) in a limited partnership generally control(s) the business decisions of the limited partnership, to the exclusion of the limited partners, and where there are multiple general partners they also share liability in the same manner as the general partnership as described earlier. The limited partners in a limited partnership have not only limited authority and responsibility (typically none) but also limited liability to the extent only of their investment in the partnership. In other words, a limited partner's exposure is typically only the amount they have invested. In addition, passive activity losses by

110. Moore, supra note 7.

the partnership may be offset by passive activity income that is attributable to partners that do not materially participate in the trade or business.[111]

Corporation

C-corporation

Formation of a C-corporation requires a governmental filing (typically called the Articles of Incorporation) and the payment of a filing fee in the state of formation. Written bylaws (which establish how the corporation is run, such as the number of board members that comprise a quorum, the manner in which board meetings may be called) are not required for the formation of a corporation, but are strongly recommended. Similarly, a written shareholders' agreement (which would establish matters between the shareholders, such as what happens when one shareholder wants to sell their shares) is also not required for valid formation but is strongly recommended.

In contrast to sole proprietorships and partnerships, corporations are separate legal entities from the owners and provide limitation of liability to all the owners therein. C-corporations generally are required to use the accrual method of accounting although a C-corporation can use the cash method if its average annual gross receipts for the prior three tax years are $30 million or less. This threshold is adjusted annually by statute for inflation.[112] If assets are sold by the C-corporation, it is deemed as a sale by the C-corporation itself. Income received is taxed based on the amount of profit the C-corporation makes and then, if the proceeds are distributed to its shareholders, those profits are treated as dividends where they are then taxed again to the individual shareholders based on the individual shareholders' tax rates. This "double taxation" is a key characteristic of C-corporations. The shareholders elect the board of directors, who in turn appoint the corporate officers responsible for the day-to-day operation

111. Passive Activity Losses and Credits Limited, I.R.C. § 469.

112. CBIZ, "Mastering Accounting Methods and Periods in 2025," November 7, 2024, https://www.cbiz.com/insights/article/mastering-accounting-methods-and-periods-in-2025 (last accessed September 2025); and see 26 U.S.C. § 448(c)(4).

of the business. When a band establishes a C-corporation, the musicians comprising the band typically elect themselves as the directors and officers of the corporation.

The largest downside of a C-corporation is that it is taxed twice, as just mentioned—once at the corporate level and again at the shareholder level. In addition, while salaries paid to employees are deductible, distributions paid to shareholders are not. To compound that shortcoming, upon the death of a shareholder, their heir receives a stepped-up basis in the stock, but the corporation does not, meaning that the shareholders can sell the stock without realizing gain on the amount up to the stepped-up basis, which is the value of the stock at the time of their devisor's death.[113]

Corporations must also follow corporate formalities and adhere to record-keeping requirements in order to maintain both the tax benefits and the shielding from personal liability that they provide. These regulations make corporations less desirable for musicians or bands that prefer to set up the entity and do as little as possible to keep it running.

S-Corporation

S-corporations are nearly identical to C-corporations, including with respect to their formation, except that one extra form is required for selection of the S-Corporation status for federal tax purposes.[114] If a corporation does not file this form its first tax year between January 7 and March 21, then by default it will be classified as a C-corporation until its next annual opportunity to file the election. S-corporations differ in a few respects from C-corporations. First, S-corporations are not subject to federal income taxes.[115] Instead, the S-corporation passes its taxable income through to its shareholders on a pro rata basis, just like a general partnership, and those shareholders must report that income on their individual returns.[116] In this

113. For a thorough discussion of C-Corporations and S-Corporations, see Cohen, supra note 100.

114. Internal Revenue Service, *Form 2553: Election by a Small Business Corporation*, https://www.irs.gov/pub/irs-pdf/f2553.pdf (last accessed February 28, 2026).

115. Gains on the sales of assets will be taxed at the corporate level if the S-corporation was previously a C-corporation. Ibid., citing Election, Revocation and Termination, 26 U.S.C. §§ 1362(a), 1363(a).

116. Pass-thru Items to Shareholders, 26 U.S.C. § 1366(a)(1).

regard, a clear record of deposits and withdrawals from the S-corporation bank account must be kept to avoid an IRS "bank deposit" analysis of accounts. A bank deposit analysis may reveal that certain withdrawals and transfers do not constitute deductible expenses.[117]

Second, an S-corporation is limited to one hundred shareholders and one class of stock.

Third, an S-corporation generally can use either the accrual or the cash basis method of accounting. However, if the S-Corporation is serving as a tax shelter (discussed earlier), has average annual gross receipts exceeding a certain threshold,[118] or maintains inventory (i.e., if the production and sale of goods is a material income-producing generator for the business) the S-corporation must use the accrual method.[119]

Finally, for the S-corporation both residuals and the sale of copyrights are subject to income in respect of decedent (IRD) rules. The drawback of IRD is that it does not receive a stepped-up basis and must be reported as income to the beneficiary.[120]

---

117. When Larry Johnson, the producer and promoter of the New Kids On The Block attempted to file bankruptcy without filing tax returns for certain years, the IRS analyzed whether payments from ASCAP were properly reported by Johnson's S-corporation and whether certain deductions claimed concerning the S-corporation were actually deductible expenses. See *United States v. Johnson*, No. 1:9-cv-0799-JOF (N.D. Ga. Mar. 30, 2000).

118. This number is $25 million according to I.R.C. § 448(c), however, it is adjusted every year for inflation. For 2024, the threshold sat at $30 million. If the S-corporation's average annual gross receipts for the three prior tax years exceeds this amount, it generally must use the accrual method. See Internal Revenue Service, *Basic Questions and Answers About the Limitation on the Deduction for Business Interest Expense*, December 23, 2025, https://www.irs.gov/newsroom/basic-questions-and-answers-about-the-limitation-on-the-deduction-for-business-interest-expense. Additionally, see CBIZ, *Mastering Accounting Methods and Periods in 2025*, November 7, 2024, https://www.cbiz.com/insights/article/mastering-accounting-methods-and-periods-in-2025.

119. Nikki Nelson, "What Is an S Corp?" *Wolters Kluwer*, December 12, 2022, http://www.wolterskluwer.com/en/expert-insights/what-is-an-s-corp#:~:text=Shareholders%20in%20C%20corporations%20cannot,cannot%20use%20the%20cash%20method; see also Limitations on Use of Cash Method of Accounting, I.R.C. § 448(a)(3), 448(d)(3); General Rule for Taxable Year of Deduction, I.R.C. § 461(i)(3); I.R.C. § 1256(e)(3)(B).

120. Cohen, supra note 100. The recipient of IRD income may deduct part of the estate tax attributable to the IRD income.

Personal Holding Companies

Corporations, both S and C, are deemed by the IRS to be personal holding companies when at least 60 percent of their adjusted ordinary gross income is personal holding company income and more than 50 percent of their stock is collectively owned by five or fewer individuals.[121] Personal holding company income is specifically defined by I.R.C. § 543 and mostly consists of specific types of passive or investment income.[122] Typically, traditional income-producing methods such as sales revenue, service income, or commissions are examples of revenue generating methods that are excluded from personal holding company income for purposes of calculating adjusted ordinary gross income. The musician should be aware that personal holding companies are subject to personal holding company tax in addition to regular income tax.[123] To determine whether these additional taxes apply to the musician client, the Code should be reviewed in greater detail.

Limited Liability Companies

Limited liability companies are very similar to corporations with respect to formation, except they must file an IRS form to elect classification for federal income tax purposes as either a sole proprietorship, general partnership, or corporation.[124] If an LLC elects to be classified as a corporation, it may thereafter (and only thereafter) file the IRS Form 2553 (discussed earlier) to select S-corporation status.

Limited liability companies provide limited liability for their members (the LLC nomenclature for "shareholders") and managers (the LLC nomenclature for "directors") and are generally not subject to taxation at the entity level. As a result, both income and capital gains flow through and are taxed to the members. LLCs can generally use either the accrual or cash basis

121. Personal holding income includes copyright royalties, but not all types of copyright royalties. Additionally, there are a litany of exceptions. See Definition of Personal Holding Company, I.R.C. § 542(a)(4).

122. Ibid.

123. Imposition of Personal Holding Company Tax, I.R.C. § 541 (2012).

124. Internal Revenue Service, *Form 2553: Election by a Small Business Corporation*, https://www.irs.gov/pub/irs-pdf/f2553.pdf (last accessed February 28, 2026).

accounting methods, but as usual there are some instances in which there is no choice.[125] If the LLC has elected classification as a C-corporation, then the C-corporation rules outlined earlier will apply and could potentially require the LLC to use the accrual method. Similarly, if the LLC is considered a tax shelter or has inventory then it will be limited to the accrual method.[126]

The major draw for musicians to establish LLCs is that most creative property, including copyrights, can be contributed to or distributed from LLCs with little to no tax consequence.[127] Unlike corporations, LLCs may also establish disproportionate internal structures allowing artists in multimember groups to define intellectual property ownership, profit sharing, and responsibilities related to the administration of the LLC itself in a way that is disproportionate to each member's ownership interest (e.g., the LLC structure may provide that a member with a 25 percent membership interest in a four-member LLC may receive a lesser or greater percentage interest in ownership of assets, distribution of profits, etc.).

Establishing Multiple Entities

A band may choose to establish multiple entities to separate assets and limit liability. For example, since touring invokes more potential liability than do recording and exploiting sound recordings (e.g., automobile accidents, injuries on stage or in the audience, and destruction of equipment),[128] it is probably wise to create a touring entity that is separate from the primary band entity to insulate certain assets and income streams. It has been reported that the Rolling Stones have four primary corporations, one

125. Justin McGregor Boodram, "Choosing Between the Accrual Method and the Cash Basis for an LLC," *LinkedIn*, July 2, 2024, https://www.linkedin.com/pulse/choosing-between-accrual-method-cash-basis-llc-mcgregor-boodram-ctkfe/.

126. Nelson, supra note 119 & various statutes.

127. See Cohen, supra note 100; see also I.R.C. §§ 721, 731; Bradford S. Cohen, "Income, Estate, and Gift Taxation of Entertainment Assets"; I.R.C. §§ 721, 731.

128. Jeff Brown, "Business Entity for Touring," *Entertainment Law & Finance*, March 2005.

each for publishing, recording/music production, touring/merchandise, and distribution/licensing.[129]

To illustrate more generally on this issue, assume a band maintained one entity housing each of publishing, recording/music production, touring/merchandise, and distribution/licensing, and during a performance the band's stage collapses on the audience. To satisfy the band's liability in connection with the event, all the assets of the one entity, including the intellectual property assets themselves and all the revenue generated therefrom, might be accessed. In contrast, if the same band establishes separate entities, the publishing, recorded music, and licensing income can be protected from any debts or obligations of the touring entity; and the liability could have been further bifurcated if the band had established separate entities for touring and merchandise, instead of just one (for touring/merchandise).

Conclusion

In conclusion, income, deductions, and choice of entity may have a profound impact on the financial success of a musician. Although a tax professional should ultimately advise the client, a working knowledge of the tax law discussed in this chapter will better equip an attorney to provide general advice to their musician client.

129. Andy Serwer, "Inside the Rolling Stones Inc.," *CNN Money*, September 30, 2002, https://ianbell.com/2002/09/18/inside-the-rolling-stones-inc/.

Chapter 10
The Musician's Estate

By Heather Ryan Liberman and Thomas J. Kliebhan

Death does not necessarily end a musician's career. Rather, income streams, goodwill, and performances of video and audio recordings may live on indefinitely. In 2024, Michael Jackson was ranked number one in Forbes Magazine's annual list of the top earning dead celebrities, earning $600 million in that year alone. Also in the top thirteen were Freddy Mercury, Elvis Presley, Ric Ocasek, Prince, Bob Marley, John Lennon, James Brown, and Whitney Houston, earning a collective $459 million.[1]

These musicians attained posthumous financial success due to factors probably not controlled by attorneys. For example, the musician's fame during their lifetime, sensationalized circumstances surrounding the musician's death, the length and depth of the cultural impact of the musician's work, and consumers' ever-changing tastes and trends may all contribute to elevated income. Nevertheless, attorneys should be aware of certain legal

1. Lisette Voytko-Best, "The Highest-Paid Dead Celebrities of 2024," *Forbes*, October 29, 2024, https://www.forbes.com/sites/lisettevoytko/2024/10/29/the-highest-paid-dead-celebrities-of-2024/.

issues surrounding musicians and their estates to prevent unnecessary complications and to avoid common pitfalls.[2]

This chapter provides a general overview of the special estate-related considerations that musicians and their legal representatives should make, but does not provide estate planning guidance that can be broadly applied. How to draft a will, whether to establish a trust or private foundation, how to select an executor or trustee, navigating the probate process and how to avoid it,[3] and other estate planning and estate tax specifics are outside the scope of this chapter. Consult with an estate planning expert to carry out specific legal procedures and to determine what devices fit best for your musician client.

However, this chapter will cover that which comprises a musician's estate:

(1) Inventory (e.g., inventory, including real, tangible, and intangible assets, and existing agreements), as well as approaches to valuation thereof; and
(2) Generating income for the estate, including with respect to copyright, trademark, right of publicity, domain names, digital assets, payors (e.g., SAG, AFTRA, ASCAP, BMI), and tribute bands.

What Comprises a Musician's Estate?

A musician's estate is comprised of all the property the musician leaves after death, including assets and liabilities. Ultimately, the property is liquidated to discharge creditors and pay taxes, and then the remaining assets

2. D. B. Mayoras, "How to Pass on an Inheritance: Celebrity Cases," November 15, 2024, https://daniellemayoras.com/how-to-pass-on-inheritance-celebrity-cases/.

3. The probate process typically begins with the validation of a will or determination that one does not exist. When one exists, it is submitted to the court for supervision of administration to distribute assets in accordance with the will, discharge creditors, and pay taxes. When there is not a will, the estate is subject to the laws of intestate succession, which are determined on a state-by-state basis. Depending on the jurisdiction in which the musician dies a resident, state intestacy laws may provide that the spouse, if any, receives a larger portion of the estate than the children. Note that many musicians, including Prince, Aretha Franklin, and Jimi Hendrix, have died intestate. For all three, this caused significant legal battles; see *In re Estate of Nelson*, 936 N.W.2d 897 (Minn. Ct. App. 2019); *In re Estate of Hendrix*, 134 Wash. App. 1007, 2006 WL 2048240 (Wash. Ct. App. 2006). See also L. R. France, "Aretha Franklin's Family Heads to Court in Estate Battle," *CNN*, July 10, 2023, https://www.cnn.com/2023/07/10/entertainment/aretha-franklin-wills-court/index.html.

are disbursed to the musician's beneficiaries. The musician's debts must be paid first, which means the estate may remain open for a lengthy period of time if the musician amassed sizeable debt during their life.[4]

To begin the process of dividing assets, there must be a determination of whether the musician died with a will, a trust, and/or certain contractual agreements tied to the musician's death. This is important because trusts and certain contractual agreements avoid the probate process. Wills on the other hand go through the probate process, which begins with a determination by the court of the validity of the will. After the will is determined valid, the decedent's personal representative, or executor (usually identified in the will), begins administering the disbursement of assets. When the will does not identify a personal representative or there is no will, the personal representative of the estate is a court-appointed administrator that carries the same duties as the executor.

The administrator's responsibilities include identifying and valuing the musician's property to ensure that all the estate assets are properly allocated.[5] Specifically, valuation of the assets is necessary to facilitate payments to creditors, file as-yet-unfiled federal and state estate tax returns for any period(s) of time the decedent was alive but did not file, determine the step-up (or step-down) in basis for capital gains purposes, make disbursements to

4. Danielle Bacher, "Michael Jackson Was over $500 Million in Debt at Time of Death, New Court Documents Reveal," *People*, June 27, 2024, https://people.com/michael-jackson-was-over-usd500-million-in-debt-at-time-of-death-new-court-documents-reveal-8670327 (Estate of Michael Jackson was faced with over $500 million in debt before the establishment of a complex settlement.); see also J. Blistein, "Liam Payne, Who Died Without a Will, Left $32 Million Estate," *Rolling Stone*, May 7, 2025, https://www.rollingstone.com/music/music-news/liam-payne-will-cheryl-cole-estate-1235333715/ (Payne died with a $38 million dollar estate, but had $6 million of debt to settle before disbursements could begin.); see also "Whitney Houston Heirs Have a Problem: Debt," *New York Daily News*, March 1, 2012, https://www.nydailynews.com/2012/03/01/whitney-houstons-heirs-may-not-receive-any-money-because-of-late-singers-huge-debt/ (Houston's heirs may never see royalty payments due to the $100 million advance and loans she took from Sony Music.).

5. On December 2, 2011, Lisa Simone Kelly, the administrator of the Estate of Nina Simone and the daughter of the late singer, filed a federal lawsuit against her father for wrongfully obtaining and transferring the assets of the Estate, including master recordings, and diaries. See also *Kelly v. Roker*, No. 11-CV-5822 (Cal. Dist. Ct. filed Dec. 2, 2011); see also S. Stathatos, "Nina Simone's Daughter Sues Her Own Father Over Jazz Singer's Estate," *San Francisco Weekly*, July 11, 2012, https://www.sfweekly.com/archives/nina-simones-daughter-sues-her-own-father-over-jazz-singers-estate/article_41ccc930-efec-5a8d-97de-e21acb4fc7e5.html.

beneficiaries, administer future filing dates (such as trademark and copyright renewals), arrange auctions, invest on behalf of the estate, and ultimately close the estate. For purposes of the rest of this chapter, the representative of the decedent's property, be they executor, administrator, or trustee, is simply referred to as a fiduciary.

This section addresses issues surrounding the estate inventory, and identifies approaches for determining its value.

Inventory

An inventory of a musician's assets can be created by speaking directly to the musician during their life, or by relying on secondary sources after the musician's death. Regardless of the approach, a musician's inventory consists of tangible property, both real and personal, intangible property, and digital assets. The tangible personal property may include typical estate property, such as household effects or cars, but may also include unique property such as instruments, recording equipment, notebooks, or clothing. The musician's unique intangible property may include copyrights in musical compositions, sound recordings, and other works of authorship; trademarks; rights of publicity; domain names; and digital assets.

Each of these tangible and intangible assets may be owned by the musician as an individual or as a function of their membership in a band or bands. If the musician was in any band with a formal business arrangement,[6] the partnership or shareholders' agreement of the band entity should outline disbursement of band assets upon the death of a member. When no formal entity exists with respect to a band, or the partnership or shareholders' agreement is lacking in relevant respect, the de facto partnership or corporate laws of the relevant state(s) should be reviewed.[7]

---

6. *Brother Records, Inc. v. Jardine*, 432 F.3d 939 (9th Cir. 2005). The Beach Boys are one band that did formally establish an entity. Their entity, Brother Records, is jointly held by Al Jardine, Mike Love, Brian Wilson, and the estate of Carl Wilson. After Carl Wilson's death, Al Jardine and Mike Love refused to tour together, but the remaining members allowed Love to establish a new group and perform as the Beach Boys, as long as the new band paid royalties to Brother Records. Al Jardine also decided he wanted to tour, but used the name "The Beach Boys Family and Friends." Brother Records brought suit against Jardine for trademark infringement and won because Jardine's use of "The Beach Boys" caused consumer confusion as to the people booking Jardine's band as well as the people who attended Jardine's shows.

7. If bandmembers were residents of different states, and there is no formal entity, it may be open to disagreement as to which state's or states' laws apply.

Whether or not the artist was a member of a band, preparing to handle the rights of their trademarks after death is an important consideration. The first critical step will be determining if the trademark is owned by the artist as an individual or if it is owned by a business entity owned either wholly or partially by the artist.[8] If owned by the business, the trademark will be handled similarly to the other assets owned by the business.[9] Ideally, there will be an operating agreement or another similar business document governing the effect on the business assets of the death of an owner. If an individual owns the trademark, a savvy artist will have addressed the trademark's future in their own will or trust. If no directions are left, then just like any other asset, the rights of the trademark will be addressed in probate court.[10] Keep in mind, whether owned by the individual or a business, the trademark is valid only as long as the owner is using and enforcing the protections afforded by the trademark itself.

It is also important to know whether the musician was married at death and/or divorced during their life.[11] If so, future income streams may be divided amongst spouse and/or ex-spouses and, depending on the separation agreement(s) with the ex-spouse(s), a supported ex-spouse(s) may also be entitled to half of any infringement damages awards[12] or a percentage of the income stream from derivative works.[13] It is important to note that New York and New Jersey recognize "celebrity status" as enhanced earning capacity that is a divisible marital asset in divorce.[14] However, the supported ex-spouse(s) must meet a high threshold to receive any economic benefit for the deceased musician's enhanced financial earnings.

---

8. Another possibility is the trademark owned by the artist, with its use is licensed to the business.

9. A. Butterman, "What Happens to Your Trademark When You Die? Trademark Ownership After Death," *Dunning, Bennett, & Ludwig*, September 20, 2024, https://www.dbllawyers.com/trademark-ownership-and-what-happens-to-your-trademark-when-you-die/.

10. Ibid.

11. See J. L. Poller and E. Warner, "Divorce Distribution of Creative Assets," *Entertainment Law & Finance*, November 2011; see also *Maloy v. Maloy*, 2008 WL 276018 (Tenn. Ct. App. 2008).

12. *In re Marriage of Worth*, 195 Cal. App. 3d 768 (Cal. Ct. App. 1987).

13. *Miner v. Miner*, 2002 WL 33955151 (Tex. Ct. App. 2002).

14. *Elkus v. Elkus*, 572 N.Y.S.2d 901 (N.Y. Sup. Ct. 1991); see also *Piscopo v. Piscopo*, 231 N.J. Super. 576 (N.J. Super. Ct. Ch. Div. 1988).

Valuation of Assets

Once the inventory list is created, the assets should be valued. Valuation of assets can be a very complex process,[15] and is best left up to professionally qualified actuaries (for copyrights, trademarks, or licenses) or professional appraisers (for real or tangible personal property).[16] These professionals will be experienced in the available valuation approaches and will likely keep in mind estate and gift tax considerations.

That being said, valuation is dependent on many factors, including the amount, timing, reliability, and type of income that can be derived from the asset. Additionally, values are influenced by the economy, investor preferences and expectations, the quality of specific industries, and the steadiness of assets.[17]

Valuation will likely follow the market, income, or cost approach or some combination thereof. The market approach considers market transactions for identical or comparable assets. However, the uniqueness of creative assets can make it difficult to find a comparable transaction.

The income approach uses variables to calculate the future expected benefits as expressed in today's dollars. The variables include the income, rate of return, and growth rate. This calculation is typically based on assumptions, so it is not always the best approach. Yet, there are fewer assumptions about the asset's future earnings if it has a steady history of earnings.

The cost approach attempts to estimate the amount it would cost to create anew a comparable asset. This method is, for obvious reasons, less useful for intangible properties, such as copyright and trademark, because of the uniqueness of creative properties and the laws that exist to protect intellectual property rights owners from outright duplication.[18]

---

15. Terry Lloyd, "Valuing Artistic and Creative Works," *PLI Corporate Practice* 1894 (2011): 387.

16. The two largest associations of qualified appraisers are the Appraisers Association of America and the American Society of Appraisers.

17. Lloyd, supra note 15.

18. *Northern Natural Gas v. United States*, 470 F.2d 1107 (8th Cir. 1972), cert. denied, 412 U.S. 939 (1973); see also W. Lockwood, *Estate, Tax and Personal Financial Planning*, vol. 4, § 35:57 (2012). In addition to following one of the valuation approaches, an appraiser must determine what rules they will follow when inserting numerical assumptions into the valuation equation. The purpose for the valuation will dictate which rules to follow. Typically, the IRS follows fair market value, or the value that would be reached between a hypothetical

While valuation may occur posthumously, authentication and appraisal of unusual tangible assets during the life of the musician may make the assets easier to transfer.[19] Such assets may include an instrument played at a famous concert,[20] books,[21] journals, handwritten music, recording equipment, or clothing. Authentication and appraisal are also important to avoid IRS scrutiny of estate and gift tax assessments.[22] A qualified appraisal may also assist the owner of an unusual asset worth more than $50,000 to obtain a "Statement of Value" from the IRS, which can assist in verifying an item's value and potentially avoiding disputes with the IRS in the future when that item is sold.[23] A musician's Statement of Value applies only to the individual requesting the statement and cannot be used by analogy other individuals with comparable assets.

Once valuation is complete, the estate can begin discharging creditors, paying taxes, making disbursements to beneficiaries, initiating investments, arranging auctions, and donating goods to facilities such as the Rock and Roll Hall of Fame[24] or other museums or not-for-profit institutions, subject to any state probate laws.

---

willing buyer and seller. Strategic value is the value to a specific buyer of the asset. Fair value is established by court precedent or statute, which has been used when calculating minority shareholder rights. Fair value is followed by GAAP, or Generally Accepted Accounting Principles, and is a combination of fair market value and strategic value. Going concern is defined as "an intangible that attaches to the tangible assets of some businesses . . . as a value enhancement for the assemblage of a business regardless of a business' profitability." In contrast, goodwill applies only to operating companies, because it is based on earning capacity.

19. The IRS has contested many valuation cases involving unusual assets; see also *Straw v. Commissioner*, 62 T.C.M. (CCH) 1056, (1991) (horses); see also *Estate of Miller v. Commissioner*, 62 T.C.M. (CCH) 997 (1991) (hunting trophies); see also *Sanz v. Commissioner*, 60 T.C.M. (CCH) 1160 (U.S. Tax Ct. 1990), aff'd, 983 F.2d 232 (1st Cir. 1993) (foreign language textbooks).

20. Andy Greene, "Experts: Bob Dylan's Long-Lost Newport Folk Festival Electric Guitar Found in New Jersey," *Rolling Stone*, July 11, 2012, http://www.rollingstone.com/music/news/experts-bob-dylans-long-lost-newport-folk-festival-electric-guitar-found-in-new-jersey-20120711.

21. *The Elvis Presley Collection*, Omega Auctions, 2012, https://www.omegaauctions.co.uk/departments/icons-idols/elvis-presley/.

22. Internal Revenue Service, *Art Appraisal Services*, https://www.irs.gov/appeals/art-appraisal-services (last accessed September 2025).

23. Ibid.

24. The Rock and Roll Hall of Fame Museum has historically sought materials that will tell the stories of Hall of Fame inductees and other significant artists. The museum website

Generating Income for the Estate

Generating income for the estate is critical, particularly when the musician amassed substantial debt during their life. As previously stated, the estate will not close until debts are satisfied and taxes are paid. While an estate may generate income simply due to the musician or their band's (or bands') fame, it may also earn money as a result of the estate's representative successfully performing their duties.

This section does not exhaust all the ways in which an estate may generate income, but will discuss the duties of the estate's representative and the role of income-producing assets, such as copyrights, trademarks, rights of publicity, domain names, digital assets, and other royalty streams.

Fiduciary Duties

An executor is the fiduciary when the decedent left a will, and that individual will need court permission to carry out their duties. When the decedent did not leave a will, the court will appoint an administrator, who will likely be a friend, family member, or attorney of the deceased. In contrast, if the decedent established a trust, the fiduciary is known as a trustee, and they are likely named (along with backup(s)) in the trust document itself. There may be instances when both a trustee and an administrator or executor should coordinate with one another if the decedent did not place all their property in a trust.

A fiduciary is expected to satisfy multiple duties, some of which may seem to conflict with one another. First, a fiduciary has the duty of fair dealing, loyalty, good faith, and to act with integrity.[25] In other words, the fiduciary must administer the estate solely in the interest of the estate and its beneficiaries without letting personal interests conflict with their duty.[26] A fiduciary also has a duty of impartiality.[27] The fiduciary must not favor

provides an artifact donation or loan application. See Rock and Roll Hall of Fame, *Donating Artifacts*, https://rockhall.com/artifact-loan-donation/ (last accessed February 28, 2026).

25. C. Hopper and D. H. Mikeska, "Chapter 5-A: Personal Representatives—Rights, Duties & Powers of Personal Representatives," in *O'Connor's Texas Probate Law Handbook*, § 3, 2025 ed. (Thomson Reuters, 2025).

26. Ibid.

27. Ibid.

one beneficiary over another.[28] The fiduciary has a duty of full disclosure.[29] They must make all material facts known to beneficiaries that may affect the beneficiaries' rights.[30] The fiduciary has a duty to use reasonable care to preserve and maintain estate assets.[31] The fiduciary must use the same care and skill that an ordinarily prudent person would use in dealing with their own property, which includes defending the estate, collecting estate property, and asserting relevant estate-related claims.[32] The fiduciary has a duty to avoid commingling assets and must keep estate property separate from other property.[33] In addition to the preceding, local state statutes or the terms of the distributing instrument may impose additional duties or limit the duties of the fiduciary.[34] Common additional duties can include a duty to keep accurate records for accounting purposes and a duty to make estate property productive, meaning making decisions designed to continue making money for the beneficiaries.

Generally speaking, it is wise for a fiduciary to do the following: stay up to date with changing law; be aware of exceptions or nuances in the law; continue accounting to payees;[35] decide whether to litigate wrongful uses of

---

28. Ibid.
29. Ibid.
30. Ibid.
31. Ibid.
32. Ibid.
33. Ibid.
34. Ibid.
35. Not all estates have been diligent about accounting to payees and as a result have been the subject of litigation. For example, the estate of Merl Saunders sued the estate of Jerry Garcia over rights and royalties associated with a project released by the estate of Garcia entitled "Pure Jerry: Jerry Garcia & Merl Saunders Band, Keystone Berkeley September 1, 1974." The estate of Garcia allegedly failed to account to the estate of Saunders; see also *Mora v. Jerry Garcia Estate, LLC*, No. 08–5772 (N.D. Cal. filed 2008). Additionally, Courtney Love was served with a lawsuit by a management firm, London & Co, over profits from the sale of the rights to songs by Kurt Cobain; see also BBC, "Courtney Love Settles over Nirvana Songs," August 18, 2010, https://www.bbc.com/news/entertainment-arts-11008834.

copyrights,[36] trademarks,[37] or the right of publicity;[38] and review the terms of any agreements executed by the decedent.[39]

Copyright

One type of income-producing asset that the fiduciary may exploit is copyrights the musician owned or transferred during their life. These copyrights

36. Copyright lawsuits cover a range of issues, but notably the James Ambrose Johnson Jr., 1999 Trust filed suit against UMG Recordings, asserting that royalties due to Rick James for digital downloads should be calculated as licenses, applying the holding in *F.B.T. Productions, LLC v. Aftermath Records*, 621 F.3d 958 (9th Cir. 2010) as precedent; see also *James v. UMG Recordings*, No. 11–1613 (N.D. Cal. filed 2011). On a separate issue, Yoko Ono Lennon brought suit against Premise Media over unauthorized use of *Imagine* in a documentary film; see also *Lennon v. Premise Media Corp., L.P.*, 556 F. Supp. 2d 310 (S.D.N.Y. 2008). Additionally, the Estate of Jimi Hendrix was engaged in a forty-year legal battle over rights to sound recordings from two of Hendrix's concerts at Royal Albert Hall in 1969.

37. The Beastie Boys filed suit against Monster Energy Drink for unauthorized use of the band's trademark. Beastie Boys, Michael Diamond, *Horovitz v. Monster Energy*, No. 12 CV 6065 (S.D.N.Y. filed Aug. 8, 2012).

38. Due to his faith as a Rastafarian, Bob Marley died without a will, and his assets passed by intestate succession under Jamaican law. Certain family members allegedly purchased Marley's right of identity for over $11 million and have sought to enforce those rights; see also *Fifty-Six Hope Road Music, Ltd. & Zion Rootswear, LLC v. A.V.E.L.A., Inc.*, 458 Fed. Appx. 892 (Fed. Cir. 2011); Bob Marley's right of publicity is now co-administered by venture capitalist James Salter, and the family continues to establish new business opportunities for exploitation; see also R. Kenner, "The Business of Bob Marley: Billboard Cover Story," *Billboard*, February 4, 2011, https://www.billboard.com/music/music-news/the-business-of-bob-marley-billboard-cover-story-473231/.

39. As technology changes, it is important for the administrators of an estate to be aware of the terms embodying the contracts signed by the decedent. For example, Pink Floyd was victorious over EMI when it invoked language from a 1999 agreement instructing EMI, "Not to couple records delivered hereunder with other master recordings [for example, in compilations] or to sell in any form other than as the current albums." The label was also instructed, "to exploit the albums in exactly the same form as to track listing and timing," and was informed, "There are no rights to sell any or all of the records as single records, other than with [PFM's] permission." This language prevented EMI from selling Pink Floyd's sound recordings on iTunes for individual downloads. Although not an estate issue, this case illustrates the importance of staying informed about signed agreements; see also "Pink Floyd Win EMI Court Ruling over Online Sales," *BBC News*, March 11, 2010, http://news.bbc.co.uk/2/hi/8561963.stm; see also Rodgers & *Hammerstein Organization v. UMG Recordings, Inc.*, 60 U.S.P.Q.2d 1354 (S.D.N.Y. 2001) ("Mechanical License" covered distribution of certain forms of fixed recordings of musical compositions did not cover streaming over the internet.). Moreover, the Estate should be clear on what it actually owns, and only license those rights, not the rights of others; see also D. Porter, "Jimi Hendrix Estate Sued by Former Bandmate," *Billboard*, July 15, 2010, http://www.billboard.com/news/jimi-hendrix-estate-sued-by-former-bandmate-1004104561.story#/news/jimi-hendrix-estate-sued-by-former-bandmate-1004104561.story.

may be in musical compositions, sound recordings, and other works of authorship if the musician was a multidisciplinary artist. As discussed in previous chapters, licensing copyrights can be a substantial source of income.

The copyright for a published or unpublished[40] work of authorship by a lone human author lasts for the duration of the author's life plus seventy years.[41] The existence of a postmortem period of protection means that the successors in interest to the copyright will have substantial rights and responsibilities associated with their inheritance.[42] These rights and responsibilities include the right to terminate a copyright transfer and the responsibility to renew the copyright in certain works.[43] The deadlines associated with these rights and responsibilities should be properly docketed to ensure lasting protection.[44]

---

40. See *Shloss v. Sweeney*, 515 F. Supp. 2d 1083 (N.D. Cal. 2007). Although dealing with the estate of a literary author, *Shloss v. Sweeney* involved the estate of author James Joyce's attempts to restrict Carol Shloss's use of unpublished materials. Works by Joyce that were not published during his lifetime and were not published posthumously at any time before December 31, 2002. They entered the public domain in the U.S. on January 1, 2012. For another examination of a literary author's unpublished materials; see also O. Aderet, "Kafka's Estate Unveiled: Unpublished Works, Personal Letters," *Haaretz*, January 1, 2012, http://www.haaretz.com/print-edition/news/kafka-s-estate-unveiled-unpublished-works-personal-letters-1.261160; *Estate of Martin Luther King, Jr., Inc. v. CBS, Inc.* 194 F.3d 1211 (11th Cir. 1999); *Bartok v. Boosey & Hawkes*, 523 F.2d 941 (2d Cir. 1975) (the 1976 Act followed the definition used in this case); W. Patry, "Posthumous Works and Renewal," *The Patry Copyright Blog*, September 26, 2006, http://williampatry.blogspot.com/2006/09/posthumous-works-and-renewal.html.

41. One very useful resource to track the duration of a particular work's copyright is a chart created by Cornell University and published on its website; see also P. B. Hirtle, "Copyright Term and Public Domain in the United States," *Cornell Copyright Information Center*, January 1, 2025, https://guides.library.cornell.edu/ld.php?content_id=79308166.

42. See *Estate of Brown v. Arc Music Group*, 830 F. Supp. 2d 501 (N.D. Ill. 2011). The estate of the deceased owner of three record labels failed to state a claim for copyright infringement with regard to seventy-seven works when the complaint did not allege that the musical compositions were registered as copyrighted works or that the estate currently owned the copyrights to those works.

43. The process for renewal is not detailed in this chapter. For more information about renewal, see U.S. Copyright Office, *Renewal of Copyright*, May 2021, https://www.copyright.gov/circs/circ06a.pdf.

44. 17 U.S.C. § 302. But see *Capitol Records v. Naxos of Am.*, 4 N.Y.3d 540 (2005) (sound recordings made in the United Kingdom in the 1930s that had entered the public domain there in the 1980s, fifty years after their creation, were still eligible for copyright protection under the common law of the state of New York, even though they were in the public domain in the U.K.).

Termination of Transfer

Since the nuances of the right to terminate a copyright transfer are fairly complicated, they are detailed in this section. The copyright termination right was created to "permit authors, originally in a poor bargaining position, to renegotiate the term of the grant once the value of the work has been tested."[45] That unwaivable[46] right was codified in the Copyright Act, and allows the author of musical compositions or sound recordings to terminate the grant of an assignment or exclusive or nonexclusive license to a third party.[47] However, the termination right does not apply to works made for hire, dispositions by will, or foreign rights.[48]

The termination right is powerful because once the termination is effective, all rights under the original grant revert back to the original author(s) or other person(s) owning the termination interests. After recapturing the copyright, the author(s) or person(s) owning the termination rights may choose to transfer the rights again to the original grantee, but under terms more favorable to the rights holder; or they may retain those rights or assign or license them to a third party.[49]

When the author is deceased, the Copyright Act sets forth explicit rules for who can terminate the transfer, as well as when and how. If the rules are not followed, the original grant will persist for the life of the copyright.

---

45. H.R. Rep. No. 2222, 60th Cong., 2d Sess. (1909); see also, Melville B. Nimmer and David Nimmer, *Nimmer on Copyright* § 9.02 (1989).

46. 17 U.S.C. § 304(c)(5) (2011). Termination of the grant may be effected, notwithstanding any agreement to the contrary, including an agreement to make a will or to make any future grant.

47. See 17 U.S.C. § 101 (2011). A transfer of copyright ownership is defined as an assignment, mortgage, exclusive license, or any other conveyance, alienation, or hypothecation of a copyright or of any of the exclusive rights comprised in a copyright, whether it is limited in time or place of effect, but not including a nonexclusive license; see also 17 U.S.C. § 204 (2011). Transfer is effective by operation of law, or "Instrument of conveyance or note or memorandum of the transfer, is in writing and signed by the owner of the rights conveyed or such owner's duly authorized agent. A certificate of acknowledgment is not required for the validity of the transfer, but is prima facie evidence of the execution of the transfer . . ." based on certain conditions.

48. See *Siegel v. Warner Bros. Entm't Inc.*, 542 F. Supp. 2d 1098, 1140 (C.D. Cal. 2008) (terminating party only recaptures the domestic rights of the grant to the copyright in question).

49. 17 U.S.C. § 304(c)(6)(D) (2011); see also *Bourne Co. v. MPL Communications, Inc.*, 675 F. Supp. 859, 864–65 (S.D.N.Y. 1987), opinion modified, 678 F. Supp. 70 (S.D.N.Y. 1988).

Section 304 of the Copyright Act[50] covers works in their first or renewal term that were transferred before January 1, 1978, and § 203 pertains to transfers that occurred on or after January 1, 1978.[51] The strict requirements to effect the termination under each of these sections are detailed as follows.

Section 304 of the U.S. Copyright Act (Pre-1978 Grants)

Under § 304(c)(2) of the Copyright Act, the termination interest of a deceased author is owned and may be exercised in accordance with the following:

(1) If the author has a surviving widow and surviving children, the widow owns one-half of the author's interest and the children own the other one-half, divided amongst the children per stirpes.
(2) If the author does not have a surviving spouse, then the entire interest goes to the children and vice versa.
(3) In the event that the author's widow or widower, children, and grandchildren are not living, the author's executor, administrator, personal representative, or trustee shall own the author's entire termination interest.
(4) In the case of a grant exercised by more than one author of the work, the termination is only effective if executed by the person or persons entitled to exercise a majority of the total termination interest.[52]

After determining who can terminate the grant, the next considerations are: (1) the timing of the termination, (2) notice to the grantee, and (3) recordation in the Copyright Office.

Termination of the grant may be effected during a period of five years beginning at the end of the fifty-six years from the date the copyright was originally secured, or beginning on January 1, 1978, whichever is later.[53] Additionally, there is a fail-safe for a pre-1978 grant of a copyright transfer or license to be terminated within the five-year termination window

50. *Roger Miller Music, Inc. v. Sony/ATV Pub.*, LLC, 672 F.3d 434 (6th Cir. 2012).
51. 17 U.S.C. §§ 203–204 (2011).
52. 17 U.S.C. § 304(c)(1) (2011).
53. 17 U.S.C. § 304(c)(3) (2011).

beginning at the end of seventy-five years from the date the copyright was secured, if the end of the fifty-sixth year expired by October 27, 1998, and termination was not executed at that time.[54]

Notice of the termination shall be served upon the grantee or the grantee's successor in title[55] during a window of time that is not less than two years or more than ten years before the termination date and must be signed by the owners of the termination interest or their duly authorized agents.[56] The notice must also state the date upon which the termination becomes effective. Finally, a copy of the notice must be recorded in the Copyright Office before the effective date of termination.

Note that a derivative work prepared under authority of a grant of rights may continue to be used under the terms of the original grant even after the termination of that grant. But this privilege does not extend to the preparation of new derivative works based on the copyrighted work after the termination of the grant.[57]

Section 203 of the U.S. Copyright Act (Post-1978 Grants)

The primary difference between § 203 terminations and § 304 terminations are that § 203 terminations cover post-1978 grants. Next, terminations under § 203 must be effected during a five-year window that begins thirty-five years after the date of execution of the grant.[58] If the original grant covers the publication of the work, the five-year period begins at the end of thirty-five years from the date of publication or forty years following the date of execution of the grant, whichever term ends earlier. The remaining aspects of the process are identical to § 304 terminations.

Copyright Termination and Multiple Authors

An exclusive or nonexclusive grant or transfer may be terminated either by a single author (if the work is authored by a single author) or a majority of

---

54. 17 U.S.C. § 304(d) (2011).
55. 17 U.S.C. § 304(c)(4) (2011).
56. 17 U.S.C. § 304(c)(4)(A) (2011).
57. 17 U.S.C. § 304(c)(6)(A) (2011); see also *Mills Music, Inc. v. Snyder*, 469 U.S. 153, 156 (1985); Woods v. Bourne, 60 F.3d 978 (2d Cir. 1995).
58. 17 U.S.C. § 203(a)(3) (2011).

multiple authors.[59] If the author is dead, their termination interest is affected by the majority of their heirs.[60] The author's widow will own the termination right in entirety unless there are surviving children or grandchildren and vice versa.[61] In the event of surviving heirs, the widow will own half of the termination interest while the children (and survivors of dead children) split the other half per-stirpes.[62] If there are no heirs, the estate will retain the termination right.[63]

Another issue to be wary of is loan-out corporations and any rights the author has granted the loan-out corporation. Even if the author granted their loan-out corporation blanket rights, including what they thought were termination rights, the termination rights will be distributed in line with what was described earlier regardless of what was granted to the loan-out corporation. This is because termination rights generally cannot be assigned away in advance.[64] Any upfront agreement doing so will not be legally binding.

Termination of Transfer and Litigation

Although the Copyright Act outlines the procedure for copyright termination, the practical application of termination is complex and still somewhat untested in the courts, notwithstanding that the window for the first terminations for post-1978 grants opened in 2013. This is likely because the parties with the greatest economic interest in such terminations (who are also the parties most likely to possess the resources that would be required to litigate the issue) have largely chosen to negotiate rather than litigate long enough for there to be resultant precedent. For example, musicians such as Bob Dylan, Tom Petty, Loretta Lynn, and Tom Waits famously pursued termination of copyright transfers in their sound recordings quickly after

59. 17 U.S.C. § 203(a)(1) (2011).

60. 17 U.S.C. § 203(a)(2) (2011).

61. 17 U.S.C. § 203(a)(2)(A) (2011) and 17 U.S.C. § 203(a)(2)(B) (2011).

62. 17 U.S.C. § 203(a)(2)(C) (2011). Per-stirpes inheritance ensures that if a beneficiary in one generation passes, the deceased's descendants still receive their share of the inheritance. This is in contrast to per capita inheritance where only the living beneficiaries left at the next generational level can inherit equally.

63. 17 U.S.C. § 203(a)(2)(D) (2011).

64. 17 U.S.C. § 203(a)(5) (2011). "Termination of the grant may be effected notwithstanding any agreement to the contrary, including an agreement to make a further grant."

their windows for termination opened.[65] However, these terminations faced tough scrutiny by record labels that wanted to retain rights. While numerous artists have filed suit over the years, they are consistently met by the record labels with arguments that the sound recordings are excluded from termination as works for hire, compilations, or part of collective works.[66] Unfortunately, the courts have yet to make a ruling on this issue that stands without a remaining appeal in process.

As an example, in January 2011, Victor Willis of the Village People served his § 304 notice of termination for thirty-three musical compositions, including *YMCA*, on Scorpio Music, but the matter plodded on through litigation for years until finally settling without meaningful judicial precedent having been set. More specifically, on July 14, 2011, Scorpio Music S.A. and its administrator in the United States filed a declaratory judgment action challenging Willis's terminations. Although Scorpio originally attempted to argue the works were made for hire, which are not terminable, it withdrew that argument. Instead, Scorpio relied on the argument that Willis's terminations were not effective because he was a joint author and the notices of termination did not reflect the majority of the termination interests. Willis argued that since he originally transferred his rights in separate agreements from the other joint authors, he had the ability to terminate the transfer unilaterally. The United States District Court for the Southern District of California found in favor of Willis and dismissed Scorpio's complaint. Subsequently, there were numerous appeals and Willis and Scorpio Music finally settled in 2017.[67]

New York Dolls singer David Johansen took a different approach, spearheading a class action lawsuit against Sony in 2019 for the same issues, alleging Sony had a policy refusing to approve any termination requests

65. Matthew Perpetua, *Bruce Springsteen, Bob Dylan, and Others May Regain Control of Copyrights*, Rolling Stone (August 15, 2011) https://www.rollingstone.com/music/music-news/bruce-springsteen-bob-dylan-and-others-may-regain-control-of-copyrights-85719/.

66. Id.

67. *Scorpio Music S.A. v. Victor Willis*, No. 3:11-CV-01557-BTM-RBB (S.D. Cal., filed July 14, 2011); see also G. Varga, "Fresh from Out-of-Court Settlement, Victor Willis Set to Rejoin Village People," *The San Diego Union-Tribune*, May 31, 2017, https://www.sandiegouniontribune.com/2017/05/30/fresh-from-out-of-court-settlement-victor-willis-set-to-rejoin-village-people/.

from its recording artists.[68] A similar lawsuit was filed against Universal Music Group by singer John Waite.[69] The labels in both instances argued that the sound recordings were "works made for hire" and thus not subject to the termination rights created by the Copyright Act.[70] Those cases were settled in 2023 and 2024, respectively.[71] It took until October 2024 for an artist to reach a trial court verdict on this issue. 2 Live Crew took their record label Lil Joe Records all the way to verdict in the Southern District of Florida where they scored a major victory for artists as a jury rendered a verdict allowing 2 Live Crew to regain legal control of the majority of their catalog.[72] While many saw this as a victory for artists, the decision was quickly appealed (and that appeal remains pending). Further, the case contains uniquely complex issues regarding the interplay between copyright termination rights and bankruptcy law that could render this an extremely narrow precedent even if the trial court's verdict stands on appeal.

In sum, the termination rights issue remains an ambiguity unresolved by the courts. While artists can use termination notices and the initiation of litigation as leverage to renegotiate old deals, labels continue to fiercely fight with them on the issue, both artists and labels continue to settle, as the major labels in particular seem apprehensive about setting catalog-wide precedent in the courts.

Despite 2 Live Crew's victory, other legal questions surrounding copyright termination still exist.[73] For example, the issue of whether a musician can work around the Copyright Act to prevent his statutory successors from owning the musician's termination interest is illustrated in the following case.

Before his death, Ray Charles created revocable trusts in the amount of $500,000 each for most of his twelve children. The trusts were conditioned

---

68. Bill Donahue, "Sony Music Settles Class Action Lawsuit Filed by Recording Artists over Termination Rights," *Billboard*, February 28, 2024, https://www.billboard.com/business/legal/sony-music-settles-class-action-lawsuit-over-termination-rights-1235617233/.

69. Ibid.

70. Ibid.

71. Ibid.

72. Bill Donahue, "2 Live Crew Wins Jury Verdict to Retake Control of Catalog Rights from Label: 'Justice Served,'" *Billboard*, October 17, 2024, https://www.billboard.com/pro/2-live-crew-jury-verdict-retake-catalog-rights-from-lil-joe-records/.

73. See, *DC Comics v. Pacific Pictures Corp.*, No. CV-10–3633 ODW (C.D. Cal. Order, Jan. 10, 2013).

on the children's waiver of any future interest in the estate.[74] Despite the existence of the trusts, some of Ray Charles's children accepted the money and later served copyright termination of transfer notices on the publishers of roughly fifty musical compositions authored in whole or in part by Charles.

As a result, the Ray Charles Foundation brought suit against Ray Charles's children for a declaration of the Foundation's rights and an injunction to prevent the children or any third parties from representing that they own any rights in and to Ray Charles's compositions, entering into license agreements, or transferring the rights at issue.

On appeal, the Ninth Circuit in 2015 found in favor of the Ray Charles Foundation, stating that the Foundation fell within the "zone of interests" of 17 U.S.C. §§ 203 and 304(c) and that the termination statues created private rights of action intended to protect parties placed in a position similar to the Ray Charles Foundation here.[75]

Clearly, the landscape of copyright terminations is ever evolving and should be closely watched by musicians, their representatives, and their estates.

Trademark

Trademarks are another income-producing asset that should be on the radar of a deceased musician's fiduciary.[76] A musician may have already owned a registered trademark to their name, or all or a partial interest in a registered trademark to a band's name, or the estate may choose to file one or more applications for registration postmortem. Either way, keeping track of a musician's trademark rights is important for the estate, especially in light of the filings required to maintain trademark rights (§§ 8 and 15 filings between the fifth and sixth year after the trademark is registered) and renewing the trademark (§§ 8 and 9 filings required between the ninth and tenth year after registration and every ten years thereafter). To satisfy each of these

74. *Ray Charles Found. v. Raenee Robinson, et al.*, Defendants, No. 12–02725 (C.D. Cal., filed Mar. 29, 2012).

75. Loeb & Loeb, "*Ray Charles Foundation v. Robinson*," *IP/Entertainment Case Law Updates*, July 31, 2015, https://www.loeb.com/en/insights/publications/2015/08/ray-charles-foundation-v-robinson.

76. B. Singer, "Rose by Any Other Name: Trademark Protection of the Names of Popular Music Groups," *Hastings Communications and Entertainment Law Journal* 14 (1992): 331.

filing requirements, the estate must submit an affidavit of use. This means that for trademark rights to exist indefinitely, the estate and the assignee of those rights after the estate closes must not only make the required filings (and pay the required fees) but also continue to use the trademark(s) posthumously so they can truthfully file the required affidavits of use.

As discussed in other chapters, part of using the trademark is enforcing the rights. To enforce trademark rights, the representatives of a musician's estate should stay apprised of what uses in commerce may infringe on the estate's rights. For example, the estates of Lynyrd Skynyrd, Elvis Presley, Notorious B.I.G., Jim Morrison, Bradley Nowell, and others have targeted potential infringers through cease and desist letters or full-blown litigation to ensure that the musician's brand is maintained.[77]

Right of Publicity

Another asset of the estate is the musician's right of publicity. The right of publicity is "the inherent right of every human being to control the commercial use of their identity."[78] Like copyrights and trademarks, these rights can be licensed to accumulate income for the estate. Yet, unlike many other freely assignable assets, rights of publicity cannot be involuntarily sold to creditors.[79]

77. *Grondin v. Rossington*, 690 F. Supp. 200 (S.D.N.Y. 1988); see also *Presley's Estate v. Russen*, 513 F. Supp. 1339 (D.C.N.J. 1981); *Estate of Jim Morrison a/k/a Lou & Pearl Courson v. Rick Sentieri*, Communications Serv. Group, D2009-0334 (WIPO 2009) (rights to jimmorrison.com transferred to complainant); see also *Densmore v. Manzarek*, 2008 WL 2209993 (Cal. Unrep. 2008) (injunction enjoining Raymond Manzarek and Robert Krieger from holding themselves out as the band The Doors); see also S. Ryon, Estate of Notorious B.I.G. Denies Association with *Ready to Die* musical, *HipHopDX*, July 21, 2012, https://hiphopdx.com/news/estate-of-notorious-b-i-g-denies-association-with-ready-2-die-musical/ ; see also M. Belloni, "Judge Blocks Sublime Bandmembers from Using Name," *Hollywood Reporter, Esq.*, November 3, 2009, http://www.hollywoodreporter.com/blogs/thr-esq/judge-blocks-sublime-bandmembers-63444.

78. J. Thomas McCarthy, *The Right of Publicity and Privacy*, § 1:3, 2d ed. (2002).

79. Ron Goldman's father, Fred Goldman, attempted but failed to transfer O.J. Simpson's right of publicity to satisfy a debt; see also L. Rosenthal, "Celebrity Rights of Publicity: For Sale, but Not Necessarily Available for Creditors," *Intellectual Property & Technology Law Journal* 19, no. 3 (2007): 7; see also B. R. Villalva, "Courtney Love Sued by Lawyers: Sent Love but No Money," *Christian Post*, June 25, 2012, http://www.christianpost.com/news/courtney-love-sued-by-lawyers-for-500000-sent-love-but-no-money-77210/ (Courtney Love accepted a loan in exchange for Kurt's publicity rights); see also rights of publicity have been used to satisfy judgments for federal taxation and divorce purposes; see also *Estate of*

Although every individual has a right of publicity during life, postmortem rights of publicity vary depending on the state in which the musician dies. In New York, the right of publicity is extinguished upon death of the individual possessing the right.[80] In contrast, other state legislatures have gone to great lengths to establish and extend a postmortem right of publicity. For example, in California, the legislature created a statutory right of publicity pursuant to the California Celebrities Rights Act.[81]

Similarly, after the Sixth Circuit decided in *Memphis Development Foundation v. Factors, Etc., Inc*, that there was no descendible right to Elvis Presley's right of publicity,[82] the legislature changed the law in Tennessee. The new law changed the right of publicity to begin for a period of exclusivity for ten years and to continue for however long the image or likeness is used continuously.[83] Other jurisdictions have also analyzed the question of postmortem publicity rights through case law.[84]

The following chart details the duration of the postmortem right of publicity by state:[85]

State	**Duration of Postmortem Right**
California	Seventy years
Florida	Forty years
Illinois	Fifty years
Indiana	One hundred years
Kentucky	Fifty years
Nevada	Fifty years

Andrews v. United States, 850 F. Supp. 1279 (E.D. Va. 1994); *Piscopo*, 555 A.2d 1190; *Golub v. Golub*, 527 N.Y.S.2d 946 (N.Y. Sup. Ct. 1988); *Elkus v. Elkus*, 572 N.Y.S.2d 901 (N.Y. App. Div. 1991).

80. *Milton H. Greene Archives, Inc. v. Marilyn Monroe*, LLC, 692 F.3d 983 (9th Cir. 2012); see also *Pirone v. MacMillan, Inc.*, 894 F.2d 579 (2d Cir. 1990).

81. Celebrities Rights Act, CAL. CIV. CODE § 3344.1.

82. *Memphis Dev. Found. v. Factors, Etc., Inc.*, 616 F.2d 956 (6th Cir 1980).

83. Protection of Personal Rights, TENN. CODE ANN. § 47–25–1101.

84. *McFarland v. Miller*, 14 F.3d 912 (3d Cir. 1994) (the estate of George McFarland, the actor who played "Spanky" in *The Little Rascals*, maintained a postmortem right of publicity); see also *Martin Luther King, Jr. Ctr. for Soc. Change v. American Heritage Prods.*, 694 F.2d 674 (11th Cir.1983) (Georgia recognized a postmortem right of publicity).

85. Alexander Lindey, *The Right of Publicity*, 1 *Lindey on Entertainment, Publishing & the Arts* § 3, 3d ed. (2013).

State	Duration of Postmortem Right
New York	Forty years
Oklahoma	One hundred years
Tennessee	Ten years of initial exclusivity, then the right continues for however long a person's name, image, and likeness are used continuously
Texas	Fifty years
Virginia	Twenty years

In addition to ranging durations, different states have varying registration requirements to maintain the right of publicity. For example, in Texas,[86] California,[87] Oklahoma,[88] and Nevada,[89] registration and a fee are required to enforce a decedent's right of publicity during the first year following death. After that first year, the right can be exercised with or without registration.

While most would agree the images of celebrities and artists are inherently valuable, placing a numeric value on a deceased figure's rights of publicity can be another story. For example, Michael Jackson's executors placed a value of only $2,105 on his rights of publicity due to a diminishment in value from the child molestation allegations against him during his life, while even the IRS valued those rights at only around $434,264.[90] Case law on the valuation issue is slim. Ultimately, the attorneys should be considerate of issues such as fair market value of the artist's name and image based on contracts they (or the estate) have recently entered. Contracts for anything speculative such as book publishing, music publishing, or recording are typically too unpredictable to consider in this valuation unless the musician has a long history of consistent revenue from the contract at issue (or one(s) like it).

Just as the administrators of the musician's estate should be aware of potential infringers of a musician's copyright and trademark rights, the administrators should also stay informed of potential breaches of a

86. Tex. Prop. Code Ann. § 26.010 (1999).
87. Celebrities Rights Act, Cal. Civ. Code § 3344.1 (2000).
88. *Okla. Stat.* tit. 12 § 1448 (1999).
89. *Nev. Rev. Stat. Ann.* §§ 597.770–597.810 (2000).
90. J. T. Ashe, S. D. Lassar, and D. R. Roche, "Issues in Valuing Celebrity Estate Publicity Rights," *Entertainment Law & Finance Journal Newsletter* 30, no. 3 (June 2014). ALM.

musician's right of publicity to determine whether litigation is an appropriate avenue to enforce those rights. To illustrate, on October 18, 2012, the estate of Marlon Brando filed an action for trademark infringement and breach of Marlon Brando's right of publicity against Madonna for her use of Brando's image on tour during her performance of "Vogue."[91] The matter settled outside of court, but still illustrates the need of an estate to enforce rights of publicity. More recently, Australian pop singer Kylie Minogue and socialite Kylie Jenner have been waging trademark war over their shared first names for the majority of the 2010s. The dueling Kylies have been duking it out in a variety of trademark spaces including cosmetics, advertising services, toiletries, live entertainment, jewelry, toys, and music/sound recordings among others.[92] Just to highlight one example, Jenner attempted to trademark the name "Kylie" for her cosmetics line in the United States.[93] Minogue argued that Jenner's trademark would create confusion in the marketplace with her existing "Kylie" brand, which was associated with fragrances, furniture, and other products.[94] Minogue was successfully able to block Jenner from being granted a trademark in this space.[95] While the two Kylies have settled some trademark battles, Minogue has ruthlessly protected her "Kylie" trademarks and has successfully won the war in most spaces. What's in a name? Minogue and Jenner seem to think there's quite a bit of value and surely have the attorney fees to show for it.

It is also worth noting that artists' rights of publicity is an area likely to be heavily affected by artificial intelligence and holograms. Litigation is already well underway in this space. Tech company OpenAI had been in negotiations with actress Scarlett Johansson to use her voice for their GAI

91. CMG Worldwide and the Estate of Marlon Brando settled a dispute over whether a valid agreement existed between the parties for use of Marlon Brando's name and likeness during Madonna's performance of the song *Vogue*. See *CMG Worldwide, Inc. v. Brando Enters., LP*, No. 12–01384 (S.D. Ind., filed Sep. 26, 2012). Note that Madonna need not license the rights from the estate of Marilyn Monroe in connection with her performance of *Vogue* because Monroe does not have a protectable right of publicity; see also *Milton H. Greene Archives, Inc. v. Marilyn Monroe, LLC*, 692 F.3d 983 (9th Cir. 2012).

92. "The Kylie Minogue Vs. Kylie Jenner Trademark Battle," *BBC*, February 7, 2017, https://www.bbc.com/news/world-australia-38877658.

93. Ibid.

94. Ibid.

95. Ibid.

voice assistant features to power ChatGPT with a human voice.[96] Negotiations ultimately fell through.[97] When OpenAI released their GAI voice assistant feature, one of the voice options named "Sky" sounded similar to Johansson, bringing the company under scrutiny. Johansson[98] sent OpenAI a cease and desist letter.[99] Although OpenAI claims Sky was not trained with Johansson's voice, they removed Sky from their platform.[100] Johansson wrote a letter stating that she believes the similarity was intentional after OpenAI CEO Sam Altman tweeted the word "her" at the time of the launch, "a reference to the film in which I voiced a chat system, Samantha, who forms an intimate relationship with a human."[101]

The brief legal spat between Johansson and OpenAI sparked lengthy debate regarding technology's intersection with right of publicity issues that drew commentary from tech personalities as well as SAG-AFTRA. Many experts noted that the case had a striking similarity in many respects to the *Midler* case mentioned in Chapter 2. The estate of legendary comedian George Carlin was involved in a similar case, suing a podcast company called Dudesy in the U.S. District Court for the Central District of California in early 2024, claiming the company used artificial intelligence to generate a comedy special that impersonated Carlin's voice and likeness without permission.[102] The matter was settled out of court.[103]

---

96. K. García, "OpenAI v. Scarlett Johansson? Georgetown Law Professor Answers Legal Questions on AI-Generated Content," *Georgetown University*, June 4, 2024, https://www.georgetown.edu/news/ask-a-professor-openai-v-scarlett-johansson/.

97. Ibid.

98. Ironically, in 2013 Johansson "appeared" in the science fiction drama film *Her* where she voiced an artificially intelligent operating system with whom the main character Theodore Twombly falls in love.

99. Winston Cho, "Scarlett Johansson's AI Legal Threat Sets Stage for Actors' Battle with Tech Giants," *The Hollywood Reporter*, May 21, 2024, https://www.hollywoodreporter.com/business/business-news/scarlett-johansson-ai-legal-threat-1235905899/; L. I. Alpert, "Scarlett Johansson's Fight with OpenAI Isn't the Star's First Legal Battle over Artificial Intelligence," *MarketWatch*, May 21, 2024, https://www.marketwatch.com/story/scarlett-johanssons-fight-with-openai-isnt-the-stars-first-legal-battle-over-artificial-intelligence-667ec7b4.

100. Ibid.

101. Ibid.

102. Ross A. Lincoln, "George Carlin Estate Settles Lawsuit with Podcasters Behind Purported AI Comedy Special," *The Wrap*, April 2, 2024, https://www.thewrap.com/george-carlin-estate-settles-lawsuit-over-purported-ai-comedy-special/.

103. Ibid.

This was not Johansson's only legal fight with an artificial intelligence company. Likenesses of Johansson's image and voice "appeared" in a twenty-two-second ad posted on X by artificial intelligence image-generating app company "Lisa AI."[104] Fine print under the advertisement read: "Images produced by Lisa AI. It has nothing to do with this person."[105] Johansson once again sent a cease and desist and the company removed the advertisement from all platforms.

For more information on artificial intelligence and rights of publicity, see the Chapter 2 discussion regarding current litigation as well as the following for more information on holograms and their intersection with rights of publicity.

Domain Names

While social media accounts have become the primary tool for artists to communicate with fans, domain names still have their utility in the artist's toolbox. Domain names can be a central hub for artists to post announcements, list tour dates, sell merchandise, and post contact information. The need to police domain names for imitators, scammers, squatters, and other cheats remains necessary. It can even be used to bolster arguments in your trademark dispute like Kylie Minogue did in her multiple spats with Kylie Jenner before the United States Patent and Trademark Office.[106] Fortunately for U.S. trademark owners, there are two options for stopping others from using your mark in their domain name: the Anticybersquatting Consumer Protection Act (ACPA) and the Uniform Domain-Name Dispute-Resolution Policy (UDRP). The ACPA, codified under 15 U.S.C. § 1125(D), was created to address cybersquatting.[107] Artists can file a federal civil lawsuit against anyone who, in bad faith, registers, traffics in, or uses a domain name that could confuse consumers with your trademark or dilute the distinctiveness of your mark.[108]

104. Ibid.
105. Cho, "Scarlett Johansson's AI Legal Threat."
106. "The Kylie Minogue Vs. Kylie Jenner Trademark Battle," *BBC*.
107. Eric Estadt, "What Do You Do When Discovering Somebody's Domain Name Includes Your Brand Name?" *Carlile Patchens & Murphy LLP*, August 2, 2024, https://www.cpmlaw.com/what-do-you-do-when-discovering-somebodys-domain-name-includes-your-brand-name/.
108. Ibid.

The UDRP is an international administrative procedure to resolve disputes about domain names.[109] The UDRP is administered by several different international bodies, primarily the World Intellectual Property Office (WIPO).[110] UDRP proceedings are often more friendly to trademark owners for a number of reasons: they're cheaper, they avoid jurisdictional issues, they are conducted via email, there are no formal court proceedings (motions, evidence, discovery, hearings, etc.), and the panelists are experienced in intellectual property law.[111] Keep in mind that the trade-off for all these benefits is that there are no monetary damages available.[112] The only remedy is the transfer, forfeiture, or cancellation of the infringing domain name.[113] If you're dealing with a highly motivated scam artist, expect a game of whack-a-mole. The standards for "bad faith" are also more rigid than an ACPA matter.[114] Generally speaking, for more complex domain issues or cases with large potential monetary damages, an ACPA claim is likely more appropriate than the simpler UDRP claim.

Digital Assets

The musician's estate is also composed of digital assets,[115] which may be an additional source of income. Note that cryptocurrencies are outside the scope of this book and thus ignored for what the authors are referencing as "digital assets." According to a 2011 survey conducted by McAfee, "U.S. consumers value their digital assets, on average at nearly $55,000."[116] Presumably, this figure has only increased as technology has improved and become ever more pervasive. These digital assets include content such as digitally stored music, videos, e-books, and other entertainment, and all internet-based accounts, including email, blogs, Instagram, Facebook, TikTok, and X (formerly Twitter).

109. Ibid.
110. Ibid.
111. Ibid.
112. Ibid.
113. Ibid.
114. Ibid.
115. Dennis Kennedy, "Of Sound Mind: Make Plans for Your Digital Estate," *ABA Journal Magazine*, August 2012.
116. Kelly Greene, "Passing Down Digital Assets," *Wall Street Journal*, August 31, 2012, http://online.wsj.com/article/SB10000872396390443713704577601524091363102.html.

For each digital asset that may be a part of the musician's estate, a determination should be made as to who owns the copyright. In certain instances, such as digitally stored music, the estate is probably not the copyright owner, unless the musician downloaded their own, wholly owned music.[117]

Next, it is useful to have access to the decedent's online accounts, passwords, usernames, and answers to security questions.[118] Unfortunately, if this information is not known by the fiduciary or family members, certain digital accounts may not be accessible without a court order (and, of course, getting a court order, even when the evidence showing an entitlement therefor is strong, can be expensive). Due to this hurdle, a musician should create a chart during their life that lists passwords, accounts, and so on, and save that information in a safe place. Ideally, this chart is created physically to prevent hackers from accessing these accounts. Refraining from emailing this information is also advised. A copy of this chart should be kept with the musician's estate planning attorney or another trusted party. Indeed, many estate planning attorneys include a request for, and secure memorialization of, this information in the estate planning packages they create and maintain for their clients.

Even if the digital account information is known, a digital platform's terms of service may address and control whether a digital asset passes to the decedent's successors. If the decedent accepted terms of service that prohibit assignment, the personal representative is bound by the terms of that agreement.[119] Of course, and again, a fiduciary could bring suit against a particular website to compel access to an account or seek declaration of the estate's right to access the account, but there would be a cost associated.

For example, the terms of service for Google, Gmail, LinkedIn, YouTube, TikTok, and X do not allow personal user accounts to be transferred or assigned. For META platforms such as Facebook and Instagram, only an authorized representative of the organization or public figure may administer

117. 17 U.S.C. § 106A (2011). The Visual Artists Rights Act (VARA) may also be a consideration when determining digital assets.

118. Dennis Kennedy, "Of Sound Mind: Make Plans for Your Digital Estate," *ABA Journal Magazine*, https://www.abajournal.com/magazine/article/of_sound_mind_make_plans_for_your_digital_estate.

119. See Transactions Authorized for Personal Representatives, Uniform Probate Code § 3–715(3).

the page. Even if digital assets the musician acquired (rather than created, then uploaded) are transferred to a device, such as a tablet, computer, or smartphone, and the device is put in a will, the musician should be aware that companies such as Apple or Amazon may actually have the right to take the digital content away from the estate.[120]

However, case law has not always been clear-cut on implementation of these terms of service. To facilitate consistency, the Uniform Law Commission drafted the Revised Uniform Fiduciary Access to Digital Assets Act (RUFADAA) in 2015 for legislators to enact concerning rights of a fiduciary to manage and distribute digital assets.[121] Most states passed this Act or a similar version of their own by 2020, allowing power traditionally given to the executor of an estate or a trustee when managing someone's tangible assets to include their digital assets as well.[122] The businesses that make, store, or provide digital assets, like Google and Facebook, are known under RUFADAA as custodians.[123] To limit their role in the settlement of an estate, custodians may request court orders before turning over access to an account. They may also only provide access to "reasonably necessary" information for settling an estate.[124] Custodians cannot provide access to deleted assets or joint accounts.[125]

Custodians have also created online tools to facilitate account transitions to fiduciaries or family members after death. Google allows users to designate a "trusted contact" on accounts so that those designated persons can gain access after a certain period of inactivity. The user can also choose to have that inactivity result in a permanent deletion of their accounts instead. Facebook allows users to designate a "legacy contact" they trust to manage their account after death. The legacy contact has most of the features of a normal user, but cannot read a user's private messages, remove old

120. Quentin Fottrell, "Who Inherits Your iTunes Library?" *MarketWatch*, August 23, 2012, https://www.marketwatch.com/story/who-inherits-your-itunes-library-2012-08-23; see also Imposition and Rate of Tax, I.R.C. § 2001. Digital assets may be subject to estate and gift tax if the asset generates income and can be transferred by the decedent.

121. Craig Parker, "What Is RUFADAA—Everything You Need to Know," *Trust&Will*, https://trustandwill.com/learn/what-is-rufadaa (last accessed May 11, 2025).

122. Ibid.

123. Ibid.

124. Ibid.

125. Ibid.

posts, or remove "friends." If a custodian does not offer similar online tools, RUFADAA states that the next course of action is reviewing the legal instrument distributing assets and rights.[126] Should that fall silent, the individual custodian's terms of service will dictate.[127] It is imperative that the attorney review their individual state's RUFADAA law for any unique provisions that could impact individual estates.[128]

Updating Payors: SAG, AFTRA, ASCAP, BMI, and Others

If a musician is affiliated with a performing rights organization (PRO) during their life, then the information provided to the PRO must be updated to reflect the federal employer identification number (FEIN), bank account information, address, and executor of the estate. Accounts with other organizations, such as SAG, AFTRA, and SoundExchange should also be updated to ensure that payors of royalties or other income will know where to send payment.

Tribute Bands

The fiduciary should also be aware of the existence of tribute bands. Tribute bands may violate a deceased musician's right of publicity, trademark rights,[129] and even copyrights.[130] These violations may occur because tribute bands publicly perform and/or record the songs of a specific musician and attempt to recreate that musician's shows.[131] For example, Apple Corps Ltd. sued the tribute band Beatlemania. A California court held that the

---

126. Ibid.

127. Ibid.

128. Luftman provides links to numerous states' RUFADAA laws.

129. *Herb Reed Enters., LLC v. Florida Entm't Mgmt., Inc. & Larry Marshak*, No. 12–00560 (N.D. Nev., filed Apr. 4, 2012) (lawsuit for unauthorized use of the trademark THE PLATTERS in connection with entertainment services); see also "MJ Tribute Band—The Battle Over Neverland," *TMZ*, March 9, 2010, http://www.tmz.com/2010/03/09/mj-tribute-band-the-battle-over-neverland/ (estate of Michael Jackson pursued legal action against a tribute band using the registered trademark NEVERLAND); Jason A. Sanford, "Which One's Pink? The One Suing Local Tribute Band!," *San Diego Reader*, May 23, 2011, http://www.sandiegoreader.com/weblogs/jam-session/2011/may/23/which-ones-pink-the-one-suing-local-tribute-band/.

130. Suzanne Lynn, "Rock Stars Sue 8150, Van Halen, Jimmy Page and Others Allege Copyright Violations by Vail Business Owner," *Vail Daily*, February 22, 2007; see also Stephanie Butler, "Rock Band's Lawsuit Takes Aim at Videogame," *Reuters*, December 8, 2007, http://www.reuters.com/article/2007/12/09/us-romantics-idUSN0842944420071209.

131. See Mark Newman, "Imitation Is the Sincerest Form of Flattery, but Is It Infringement? The Law of Tribute Bands," *Touro Law Review* 28 (2012): 391.

tribute band violated the Beatles' right of publicity and was not protected by fair use or the First Amendment.[132] The court also held that Beatlemania caused unfair competition and consumer confusion. While the Beatlemania case dates back to the 1980s, it's hardly dead law. In 2024, Earth, Wind & Fire sued Substantial Music Group for violations of the Earth, Wind & Fire trademarks. The band sued the promoters of a tribute show featuring musicians who previously played in the legendary 1970s R&B group.[133] The core issue was whether the marketing of the tribute show was misleading to fans, implying an official connection to Earth, Wind & Fire.[134] A Miami federal judge sided with the band claiming that the tribute act was "deceptive(ly) misleading consumers" by using the name "Earth, Wind & Fire Legacy Reunion."[135] In particular, the judge cited angry social media posts and emails from fans who attended the "reunion" shows because they thought it was the original band—proof of the kind of "actual confusion" in the marketplace that is crucial in a trademark lawsuit.[136]

Another example of enforcement of copyright and trademark rights against tribute bands is illustrated by the representative of Frank Zappa's estate, Gail Zappa. Specifically, the attorneys for the Zappa Family Trust sent numerous cease and desist letters to Zappa tribute bands and venues alleging that public performance blanket licenses do not cover tribute shows and such performances violate dramatic rights.[137] The trust has also asserted that advertisements for tribute shows violate Frank Zappa's trademark rights and cause consumer confusion.

Gail Zappa's crusade to protect Frank's rights has proven to be an effective blueprint. More recently, Pearl Jam sent a cease and desist letter to U.K.

---

132. *Apple Corps Ltd. v. Leber*, 229 U.S.P.Q. 1015 (Cal. App. Super. 1986) (*Estate of Presley v. Russen*, 513 F. Supp. 1339 (D.N.J. 1981)) ("entertainment which merely imitates, does not have a creative component of its own and is not protected by the First Amendment").

133. Brian Donahue, "Earth, Wind & Fire Wins Trademark Lawsuit Against 'Reunion' Tribute Act: 'Deceptive and Misleading,'" *Billboard*, March 4, 2024, https://www.billboard.com/business/legal/earth-wind-amp-fire-wins-trademark-lawsuit-reunion-tribute-act-1235621205/.

134. Ibid.

135. Ibid.

136. Ibid.

137. O. J. Sloan, "Letter from Berger Kahn, A Law Corporation, Attorneys for Zappa Family Trust," January 20, 2009, https://www.killuglyradio.com/wp-content/uploads/2009/01/paul-green689.pdf.

tribute act "Pearl Jamm" requesting they refrain from using that name as it was infringing on trademarks and causing confusion in the marketplace.[138] In addressing the allegation that they were causing confusion in the marketplace, a Pearl Jamm member responded rather cheekily stating, "No one's ever come to a show, got to the end of the show, came to us and demanded money back because they were expecting to see Pearl Jam."[139] The U.K. imitators ultimately complied, changing their name to "Legal Jam."[140] If there are any lessons to be taken from Beatlemania, Earth, Wind & Fire, and "Pearl Jamm" it is that a tribute band must be clear in its advertising and carry a distinct name that is unlikely to cause confusion. However, some rights owners may say this still is not enough.

Holograms

Various estates raised concerns after Digital Domain Media used technology to project the image of Tupac Shakur, a deceased rapper, on stage at the Coachella Valley Music and Arts Festival in 2012. Although Digital Domain Media had plans to do the same for Marilyn Monroe, Elvis, Jim Morrison, and Jimi Hendrix, it reportedly filed for bankruptcy before completing the projects.[141] There have been numerous estates and companies willing to pick up where Digital Doman Media and Tupac Shakur's estate left off. Since then, the estates of Michael Jackson,[142] Whitney Houston,[143]

138. Daniel Kreps, "Pearl Jam Ask Tribute Band Pearl Jamm to Change Name for Obvious Reason," *Rolling Stone*, January 21, 2021, https://www.rollingstone.com/music/music-news/pearl-jam-cover-band-legal-jam-1117018/.

139. Ciara Breathnach, "After Receiving Cease and Desist Letters from Pearl Jam, U.K. Tribute Band Pearl Jamm Change Their Name to Legal Jam," *Guitar.com*, January 20, 2021, https://guitar.com/news/music-news/pearl-jam-peal-jamm-cease-and-desist/.

140. Ibid.

141. "Maker of Tupac Shakur Hologram Files for Bankruptcy," *Rolling Stone*, September 12, 2012, http://www.rollingstone.com/music/news/maker-of-tupac-shakur-hologram-files-for-bankruptcy-20120912.

142. Lisa Respers France, "Michael Jackson's Hologram: Creepy or Cool?" *CNN*, May 19, 2014, https://www.cnn.com/2014/05/19/showbiz/michael-jackson-hologram-billboard-awards/index.html.

143. Ryan Reed, "Whitney Houston Hologram Tour Plots First 2020 Dates," *Rolling Stone*, September 17, 2019, https://www.rollingstone.com/music/music-news/whitney-houston-hologram-tour-2020-dates-image-885666/.

Roy Orbison and Buddy Holly,[144] Maria Callas,[145] and Ronnie James Dio,[146] among others, have each licensed their rights of publicity as well as the copyrights underlying the songs they control to various tech companies for hologram one-off performances or even tours. Hologram performances are an excellent way for artists to posthumously monetize their legacy. Though the money could be tempting, there are undoubtedly artists who would rather take their performances to the grave with them. Addressing the artist's willingness to appear as a hologram after death and in what context(s) is going to be essential as this technology only gets better as well as more common. Holograms are an intellectual property minefield of issues that intersects estate planning, rights of publicity, and both composition and sound recording copyrights. There is also an obvious and inherent emotional weight in their creation for the artist's family and the owners of the estate. The ethics of hologram performances are still hotly debated. Navigating these issues carefully and considerately is imperative.

Conclusion

A musician's legacy may prosper after the musician dies and the possibilities are expected to grow as time passes. As technology for metaverses/virtual reality and holograms improve, newly available methods of exploiting artist copyrights belonging to artists' estates are expected to develop. If estate planning experts are consulted, the inventory is created, the relevant filing deadlines are met, and the estate enforces the musician's copyright, trademark, and publicity rights, the estate may generate enough income to timely discharge its creditors, pay taxes, and thereafter make disbursements to beneficiaries for years to come.

144. Amanda M. Yglesias, "Roy Orbison & Buddy Holly Hologram Tour Dates Are Here," *The Recording Academy*, June 18, 2019, https://www.grammy.com/news/roy-orbison-buddy-holly-hologram-tour-dates-are-here.

145. Anthony Tommasini, "What a Hologram of Maria Callas Can Teach Us About Opera," *New York Times*, January 15, 2018, https://www.nytimes.com/2018/01/15/arts/music/maria-callas-hologram-opera.html.

146. Craig Harding, "Holograms Hit the Road: Will Fans of Frank Zappa, Ronnie James Dio and Others Show Up for Their Virtual Versions?" *Billboard*, May 19, 2018, https://www.billboard.com/pro/hologram-artists-tour-frank-zappa-ronnie-james-dio-roy-orbison/.

Chapter 11
Music and the General Business Client

Music law issues do not always involve musicians, music producers, or distributors. Most general businesses will encounter music-related issues in one form or another at some time, which is the topic of this chapter.

Advertising and Music Branding

Few radio or television advertisements are prepared without the use of music in some fashion. Music can set a mood or environment, conjure an emotion, or punctuate text or an image. When attention must be grabbed and a message delivered unambiguously in a very short period, music helps get the job done.

Music can also play a role in helping brand a business. The NBC chime is a classic example of a sound trademark that has identified NBC programming to listeners since the late 1920s. Anyone who ever spent time watching television or listening to the radio in Chicago after 1977 will hear familiar music in their head when they read the telephone number 588–2300. The "Yahoo! yodel" will be familiar to anyone who lived during the internet boom. Music has tremendous mnemonic power that can be engaged to create brand identity. This is recognized by the fact that sounds may be registered on the Principal Register of the United States Patent & Trademark Office when they are "arbitrary, unique or distinctive and can be used in a manner so as to attach to the mind of the listener and be awakened on later hearing in a way that would indicate for the listener that a particular product or service was coming from a particular . . . source."[1]

If a company is seeking to acquire original music to associate with its advertisements as part of its overall branding strategy, it is likely to engage a production company, sometimes referred to as a jingle house, to compose the music and produce the musical recording that will be used in the advertisement. This is sometimes done directly by the company, or sometimes through the company's advertising agency. In the end, it will be critical for the company to own all rights in and to both the composition and the recording being produced. In order to ensure that occurs, each agreement in the series of agreements—the composer(s) and musician(s) with the production company, the production company with the advertising agency and the advertising agency with the client company—will need to be in writing and contain language that both identifies the deliverables under the agreements as works made for hire (if the material is intended for inclusion in an audiovisual commercial) and alternatively assigns all right, title, and interest in and to them as a whole. Without such language, the rights actually lodged with the company to use the composition and/or recording going forward may be unclear, which could impair the company's adoption of the material for branding purposes. One right the composer might preserve is the right to receive their portion of any performance income generated by the public performance of the composition in broadcast commercials (which would be payable under § 106(4) of the Copyright Act).[2]

Use of preexisting music for commercial and promotional purposes, including user-generated content for social media sites to boost brand engagement and increase customer loyalty, requires consent of the owners of the works being used, whether that is a composition being rerecorded by

1. *In re Vertex Grp. LLC*, 89 U.S.P.Q.2d 1694, 1700 (T.T.A.B. 2009).
2. 17 U.S.C. § 106(4) (2002).

the company producing the commercial or both the composition and the recorded master if the use of an existing recording is being sought. There is no statutory compulsory license for any such uses. The copyright owner has the absolute right to deny any such use, and, if they are inclined to grant the right, to set the terms under which any such use might be made. The fee for use of an iconic song in a national television campaign can exceed $1,000,000,[3] while a local commercial featuring a more modest, regionally successful song will be much less. Variables that will likely affect both the yes/no answer to the request for permission and the price (if the request is granted) include the territory of the advertisement,[4] channel(s) of use of the advertisement, duration of use of the composition and/or sound recording, changes to the composition and/or sound recording (if any), scope of exclusivity, and options to extend. Also, as noted in the discussion about trademark rights and individuals' rights of publicity, if the client company wants a new recording of a composition to be used in a commercial to sound like a preexisting recording, consent of the performers in the original recordings may need to be obtained. While the Copyright Act permits the production of "soundalike" recordings of musical compositions that are independent fixations of sound,[5] the use of such recordings in commercials may create liability for claims that the identity of the performer in the original recording has been wrongfully used or the trademark rights of such performers have been violated if listeners are likely to believe that the original performer is the performer in the recordings used in the advertisements.

Several services exist to facilitate the connection between owners of sound recordings and those seeking music to use in advertisements and other audiovisual works. These services provide indexing, search, and sampling access to a range of recorded works whose producers and composers they represent and further process the purchase and delivery of material that is selected. These services include Deep Sounds, Taxi, Getty Images,

3. Jeffrey Brabec and Todd Brabec, *Music, Money, and Success* (New York: Schirmer Trade Books, 2022), 336.

4. Note that the territory provision of the agreement may provide for permitted "spillover" outside the specified territory, particularly where technological limitations are either unavailable or cost-prohibitive for strict territory maintenance (e.g., terrestrial radio and television broadcast from within some specified territories may often be heard outside that territory).

5. 17 U.S.C. § 114(b) (2011).

Jingle Punks, Rumblefish, Soundstripe, and Songtradr. While such services have not been without some criticism from within the production music community,[6] they are a viable alternative for companies seeking music for use in advertising that do not require "hit" songs or recordings or exclusive, long-term rights. Human-composed and recorded sound recordings are also available for commercial uses from archives such as Getty Images and through platforms such as SoundCloud, ALIBI Music, Artlist, Musicbed, and Epidemic Sound.

Newer among the services that exist for those seeking music to use in advertisements and other audiovisual works are those that offer music created by artificial intelligence, such as Suno AI, Udio, Empress Lyric Lab, Voicify, Stable Audio (and seemingly countless others, with the number regularly growing). The GAI offered by those services generates musical compositions and sound recordings based upon narrative text prompts input by the user. While these services tend to be more affordable than those described and listed in the preceding paragraph that facilitate the connection between owners of human-composed/performed sound recordings and those seeking music to use in advertisements and other audiovisual works, the services that offer GAI-composed/recorded works pose their own, unique set of positives and negatives. To the positive, and aside from the potential cost benefit already mentioned, since GAI is "fast," the available libraries of prerecorded GAI music are rapidly growing, and GAI has the ability to quickly create multiple, new sound recordings for "pick-and-choose" availability to any given customer's own, unique specifications. To the negative, critics argue that GAI music still lacks the emotional depth and nuance often found in human-composed music, which they say is crucial to a connection between advertiser and audience. Critics also note, rightly, that GAI music raises questions about both infringement and copyrightability, in other words, *both* whether the GAI music infringes a third party's

6. Leah E. A. Solomon, "Potential Pitfalls When Using Music in Social Media Marketing," *National Law Review* (2022), https://natlawreview.com/article/potential-pitfalls-when-using-music-social-media-marketing; David Hesmondhalgh, "Is Music Streaming Bad for Musicians? Problems of Evidence and Argument," *New Media & Society* 23, no. 12 (2020): 1–23, https://doi.org/10.1177/1461444820953541; L. G. Craton and G. P. Lantos, "Attitude Toward the Advertising Music: An Overlooked Potential Pitfall in Commercials," *Journal of Consumer Marketing* 28, no. 6 (2011): 396–411, https://doi.org/10.1108/07363761111165912.

rights *and* whether the GAI music, even if non-infringing, is itself subject to copyright protection. To the former point (infringement), litigation has begun. For example, three major record labels, acting under the auspices of the Recording Industry Association of America (RIAA), quickly sued online music GAI generators Suno and Udio for copyright infringement after those services launched, based upon an allegation that the services reproduced the labels' artists' music in the content creation process;[7] both a lone and relatively unknown country artist and a small consortium of Chicago-based independent artists of varying genres have each filed purported class actions on behalf of thousands of independent-musician class members against those same companies;[8] and an aligned group of music publishing companies has sued GAI company Anthropic for copyright infringement based upon similar allegations and theories of infringement.[9] The U.S. Copyright Office (USCO), for its part, has provided its analysis of fair use in the context of GAI training, emphasizing that GAI training is at the very least not categorically fair use, and that whether a use qualifies as a fair use is a matter of context and degree.[10] Interestingly, and of course,

---

7. *UMG Recordings, Inc. et al. v. Suno, Inc.*, Civil Action No. 1:24-cv-11611 (D. Mass. 2024); *UMG Recordings, Inc. et al. v. Uncharted Labs, Inc.*, d/b/a Udio.com, Civil Action No. 1:24-cv-04777 (S.D.N.Y. 2024). As of this writing, Universal Music Group and Warner Music Group have settled with Udio on terms including license agreements while the labels' litigation remains pending against Suno, and Sony Music Group's litigation remains pending as against both GAI operators; and the pending litigation against Suno did not keep it from closing a Series C funding round of $250 million at a $2.45 billion valuation. See generally Ethan Millman, "Universal Music Group Settles Major AI Lawsuit with Udio After Song Theft Claims," *Hollywood Reporter*, October 30, 2025, https://www.hollywoodreporter.com/music/music-industry-news/universal-music-group-announces-settlement-with-udio-1236414023/#:~:text=More%20Stories%20by%20Ethan&text=Universal%20Music%20Group%20is%20settling,music%20generation%20and%20streaming%20platform; Ethan Millman, "Warner Music Group Settles AI Infringement Lawsuit with Udio," *Hollywood Reporter*, November 19, 2025, https://www.hollywoodreporter.com/music/music-industry-news/warner-music-group-settles-lawsuit-udio-1236431207/; Dylan Smith, "Suno Raises $250 Million at a $2.45 Billion Valuation, Says It's 'Proud to Be at the Forefront of This Historic Moment for Music,'" *Digital Music News*, November 19, 2025, https://www.digitalmusicnews.com/2025/11/19/suno-series-c/.

8. See, e.g., *Justice et al. v. Uncharted Labs, Inc.*, Case No. 1:25-cv-05026 (S.D.N.Y. 2025); *Woulard et al. v. Suno, Inc. et al.*, Case No. 1:25-cv-12684 (N.D. Ill. 2025).

9. *Concord Music Group Inc. v. Anthropic PBC*, Case No. 3:24-cv-03811 (N.D. Cal. 2023).

10. *Copyright and Artificial Intelligence: Part 3 Generative AI Training* (U.S. Copyright Office, 2025), https://www.copyright.gov/ai/Copyright-and-Artificial-Intelligence-Part-3-Generative-AI-Training-Report-Pre-Publication-Version.pdf.

it is not the USCO that will decide whether any given use of copyright-protected material is (or is not) fair use—that issue is for triers of fact to decide. Finally, as of this writing, legislation has been introduced (but not progressed very far) in the United States Senate that would create a new federal tort for the unauthorized use of an individual's copyrighted works (or personal data) for GAI training, requiring express prior consent and disclosing third-party use.[11]

The USCO has also weighed in on copyrightability of works generated in whole or in part with the use of artificial intelligence, having stated that works of authorship qualify for copyright protection only when they have a human author (although that author may be aided by GAI, provided there is a "sufficient" amount of human expression in their (the human's) contribution).[12] At least one court has already agreed.[13] This, in turn, would mean a catchy, GAI jingle popularized by one advertiser could potentially be used by others without exposure to a copyright infringement claim (although it still might give rise to a trademark claim).

---

11. AI Accountability and Personal Data Protection Act (S.2367).

12. *Copyright and Artificial Intelligence: Part 2 Copyrightability* (U.S. Copyright Office, 2025), https://www.copyright.gov/ai/Copyright-and-Artificial-Intelligence-Part-2-Copyrightability-Report.pdf.

In its Report, the USCO considered multiple different examples of GAI usage and stated its position on each.

- With respect to *using prompts to get a particular result from a generative GAI engine*, the USCO said definitively that the output is unprotectable (and the corollary to this is, of course, once it exists it can't be infringed). The rationale provided by the USCO was that prompts themselves are ideas, and if the human's only contribution to a creation is an unprotectable idea, they cannot claim copyright. The USCO left open that there may come a time when prompts can sufficiently control expressive elements in GAI outputs to reflect human authorship.
- With respect to *inputting a human-created work, and asking the GAI to alter it in some way*, the USCO said that only those parts of the work that a human created are subject to copyright protection (and those parts created by GAI are not).
- With respect to *modifying or arranging GAI content*, the USCO said that the output is subject to copyright protection if the human creator has modified those elements "in a sufficiently creative way" (without further definition as to what is meant by "sufficiently creative").

13. *Thaler v. Perlmutter*, 687 F. Supp. 3d 140 (D.D.C. 2023).

Sponsorships and Endorsements

Celebrities have allure. They can gather an audience, or enhance the commercial prospects of one's products or services when associated with their resonant values. Whatever the reason, companies frequently call upon celebrities, including musicians, to associate themselves in some way with the companies and their products or services in a range of arrangements.

It is important to distinguish between a sponsorship and an endorsement. Sponsorship simply means that a company has given consideration for the right to associate itself in some manner with a performer. It may be as basic as the purchase of an advertisement in an event's program booklet or as comprehensive as an international tour. Although an endorsement by an artist might be implied by the circumstances of the sponsorship, an actual endorsement of a product or service is a specific action that must be bargained for in any agreement for the artist's services. For example, a sponsor of a performance might receive a "presented by" credit in the announcements for the performance, but to quote the performer as recommending the sponsor's product or service will require additional, specific authorization (and, likely, payment). The following are some key issues that are important in sponsorship and endorsement agreements, in addition to the amount of the artist's fee, expenses, and hospitality requirements.

What the Artist Will Be Required to Do

The range of activities and deliverables for a sponsorship or endorsement agreement is broad. At its simplest, an artist may be engaged to appear at a particular event meant to mark a company's business development (a store opening or significant sale) or perhaps to attract customers to aid inducement of product sampling. In such cases, a description of what the artist is required to do may include speaking; signing autographs or memorabilia (though some performers refuse to sign memorabilia on the grounds that the purpose of the request is simply to increase the value of an item intended for sale and not for its keepsake value); posing for pictures; performing; making a presentation; being interviewed; participating in a broadcast or other recording of the even; making a certain number and/or type of social media posts on one or more of their branded platforms; facilitating a contest, drawing, or other activity; or interacting with others.

The scope and other terms of an expanded sponsorship arrangement with an artist can be quite broad and will be driven principally by the marketing goals of the company engaging the artist. The sponsorship could include a range of activities specific to the company engaging the artist or could be in association with a more general event, such as a performance tour. Some of the deliverables required by an artist under such circumstances could include appearing at so-called meet and greet events, press conferences, private performances, creation of special material such as recordings or videos, interviews, voiceovers for advertisements, recorded outbound telephone greetings, blogs, social media postings, participation in or judging of contests, words of endorsement, receptions, autographs, autographed property or memorabilia, the prominent use in public of a product or service, links between the artist's and the company's respective websites, and event tickets.

Artist's Identity and Trademark Rights

Fundamental to a sponsorship or endorsement agreement is the company's ability to use the artist's identity and trademarks in connection with the activities contemplated by the agreement. The identity includes not only the artist's name and likeness but also the artist's biography, voice, and other items that personally identify the artist. The artist's trademarks could include logos, names, or such things as distinctive costuming. The two principal issues to negotiate concerning these uses are (1) approval by the artist of specific proposed uses and (2) how and where the identity and marks may be used. Artists will generally have the ability to approve their biography and how they are depicted and quoted (particularly if an endorsement is to be provided). Once approved, consent is generally not required for how the approved image or quote may be implemented, although approval of overall ad copy, advertisements, and other forms of messaging may be negotiated as well. Use may also be generalized for the company and its products and services or keyed to a specific campaign, such as a new product launch.

Creation of Special Material

Sponsorship relationships with musical artists frequently involve the development of creative works, such as compositions, recordings, or videos, which are used to help deliver the sponsoring company's commercial message. A sponsor may want to permit streaming or downloading of exclusive recordings from the company's website, or use such recordings in the soundtrack of commercials. A sponsor may also want to record a special performance given by the artist under the auspices of the sponsor and permit streaming or downloading of the recording. This may create issues if the artist is a party to an exclusive recording agreement with a record label that would bar the artist's involvement in the production of sound recordings or videos with a third party. Similarly, an exclusive songwriter agreement could bar the delivery of a musical composition to a third party. In such instances, each record or publishing company will have its own requirements for granting consent. In some cases, the consideration given for the artist's participation in the sponsor's recording activities may be to either permit the record company to use the recordings in certain ways after the sponsor's promotional period has passed, or to assign the recordings to the record company, with a reservation by the sponsor of the right to continue using the recordings in certain ways.

Scope of Exclusivity

Sponsoring companies will generally want to have the exclusive right to the artist's association during the period of the sponsorship relationship and for a term thereafter. The company does not want to expend resources to exploit the goodwill associated with the artist and find that the association is being diluted with other related products or services. Even worse, the company does not want a competitor to piggyback on the attention created by the company. The scope of this exclusivity implicates product categories, territories, and time periods. From the company's point of view, the product category should be defined as generally and broadly as possible, which may conflict with an artist's existing or anticipated agreements with others.

The territory of exclusivity could reasonably be broader than the actual territory where the sponsorship relationship will be promoted. Media in which a competing sponsoring relationship is promoted might not observe territorial limitations and could be likely to surface in the licensed territory, particularly if the sponsored products or services are directly competitive. Finally, it is reasonable for a sponsor to obtain an extension of the exclusivity provisions of the sponsorship agreement for a period following the actual period of sponsorship activity to protect the residual effect of such association and prevent a competitive sponsorship from causing confusion with an immediate follow-on promotion.

Morals Clause

It is the nature of celebrity that an individual, once well regarded by the public, can fall into disrepute. When that happens, the goodwill bargained for by a sponsoring company to associate with its products or services disappears. A so-called morals clause in a sponsorship agreement permits a sponsoring company to terminate an agreement with an artist in the event the artist engages in any activity that causes them to be held in lesser regard by the public. Given that misconduct can also be committed by business organizations, which can fall into disrepute by reason of a variety of legal or ethical violations, some artists have begun negotiating so-called reverse morals clauses in sponsorship agreements, which permit them to disassociate themselves from organizations in the event the organization experiences a fall in public regard and the artist believes they would be harmed by seeming to support the organization.[14]

For a full discussion of morals clauses, see the material under the heading "Terminations for Immoral Behavior" in Chapter 7. The considerations raised therein apply to promotion and sponsorship agreements as well.

Non-disparagement

As a counterpart to the express or implied endorsement obtained by a sponsoring company from the artist under the sponsorship agreement, the company will want to obtain a commitment by the artist not to publicly comment upon the artist's experience in participating with the company without the company's consent or in a manner that is "off message" from the promotion. The sponsoring company will of course want to receive

14. For an example of reputational harm, and potential liability, that can arise for an endorsing musician based upon the actions of the endorsed product or service, see Ashley King, "Drake Faces Class Action Lawsuit for 'Glamorizing' a 'Deeply Fraudulent' Gambling Platform," *Digital Music News*, October 28, 2025, https://www.digitalmusicnews.com/2025/10/28/drake-lawsuit-gambling-app/.

as much coverage of its sponsorship as it can, but comments in news stories, articles, publicity, and social media platforms in any form (other than unalloyed praise) can derail the commercial message a company may be seeking to convey. Further, comments that are disparaging of the experience or revealing of the "inside" story of the experience can erase the value bargained for by the sponsor.

From the artist's perspective, the language of the non-disparagement clause should be as objective as possible to avoid subjective interpretation resulting in either an unintended claim for damages or right of termination, since agreeing to not take actions that are objectively determinable by reference to applicable statutes and case law (e.g., to not defame, to not portray in a false light) is a different matter entirely than agreeing to more subjective terms. An example of a non-disparagement clause that would present higher risk for the artist due to its subjectivity is:

> Artist shall not: (i) employ deceptive, misleading or unethical practices that are or might be detrimental to the Product, Company and/or the public, including, without limitation, disparagement of either the Product or Company; (iii) make any false or misleading representations with regard to either Company or the Product; or (iv) publish or employ or cooperate in the publication or employment of any misleading or deceptive material. Artist shall provide the Services in a manner that reflects favorably at all times on the good name, goodwill and reputation of Company.

Music at the Workplace

Music has become almost ubiquitous in our lives. Its use and consumption do not stop at the workplace entrance. This has implications in several circumstances.

Performance of Music in Customer Environment

As mentioned earlier, the public performance of musical compositions is one of the enumerated rights of the copyright owner under the Copyright Act. It has long been held that performance of music in such places as hotels[15] and restaurants,[16] on radio and television,[17] by means of the playing of musical recordings,[18] and staging karaoke performances[19] constitutes a performance for which the copyright owner is entitled to compensation. On the other hand, playing a radio broadcast to the public in a commercial establishment by means of "a single receiving apparatus of a kind commonly used in private homes" is not a performance of music for which payment is due under an ASCAP, BMI, or SESAC license unless there is a charge to see or hear the transmission or the transmission is retransmitted.[20]

In 1998, Congress passed the Fairness in Music Licensing Act,[21] essentially expanding the exemptions available to restaurants and other establishments from the requirements of obtaining public performance licenses from ASCAP, BMI, and SESAC for the retransmission of regular broadcast, cable system, or satellite carrier signals. No license is required in the case of establishments other than food service or drinking establishments where the establishment either has less than 2,000 square feet of space or, if more space, the performance is communicated by no more than six loudspeakers (no more than four of which are in any one room) and no more than four audiovisual screens having a diagonal screen size no greater than fifty-five inches (no more than one of which is in any one room). The same requirements apply to food service and drinking establishments, but the triggering space size of the establishment is 3,750 square feet.[22]

15. *Remick Music Corp. v. Interstate Hotel Co.*, 58 F. Supp. 523 (D. Neb. 1944), aff'd, 157 F.2d 744 (8th Cir. 1946), cert. denied, 329 U.S. 809 (1947).

16. *Leo Feist, Inc. v. Lew Tendler Tavern, Inc.*, 267 F.2d 494 (3d Cir. 1959).

17. *Buck v. Jewell-LaSalle Realty Co.*, 283 U.S. 191 (1931).

18. *Associated Music Publishers, Inc. v. Debs Mem'l Radio Fund, Inc.*, 141 F.2d 852 (2d Cir.), cert. denied, 323 U.S. 766 (1944).

19. *Morganactive Songs v. K&M Fox Inc.*, 77 U.S.P.Q.2d 1064 (S.D. Ind. 2005). However, there is a division of authority about whether karaoke discs are audiovisual works. See *Leadsinger, Inc. v. BMG Music Publ'g*, 512 F.3d 522 (9th Cir. 2008); *ABKCO Music, Inc. v. Stellar Records, Inc.*, 96 F.3d 60 (2d Cir.1996) (karaoke discs are audiovisual works). But see *EMI Entertainment World, Inc. v. Priddis Music, Inc.*, 505 F. Supp. 2d 1217 (D. Utah 2007) (karaoke discs are not audiovisual works).

20. 17 U.S.C. § 110(5) (2011).

21. Fairness in Music Licensing Act of October 27, 1998, Pub. L. No. 105–298, 112 Stat. 2827 (1998).

22. 17 U.S.C. § 110(5) (2011).

Businesses that use music within a customer environment, whether in the form of live performances or recorded music, are advised to obtain appropriate agreements with the performing rights organizations if they are not exempt by reason of the criteria mentioned in the preceding paragraph. There are two strong reasons for this advice. First, while the performing rights organizations in the United States hold only nonexclusive rights to the compositions whose rights they enforce and it is possible for a company to obtain permission to perform compositions directly from the owners of the compositions, the effort to do so is inefficient, at best. The performing rights organizations issue blanket licenses of their full catalogs, which guarantee access to all compositions and reduce transaction costs.

Second, the performing rights organizations are diligent in the enforcement of the rights of the publishers and songwriters they represent[23] and enjoy a strong history of success in litigating when faced with recalcitrant unlicensed music users.[24] As an alternative to obtaining direct licenses from performing rights organizations, businesses may elect to subscribe to certain background music services such as Mood (formerly Muzak), DMI, MTI Digital, and Tuned Global, which obtain performance rights in the material that they distribute to their client users so that the music user is only responsible for paying a single fee for the bundle of rights required for their music use.

Unfortunately, there arises a sticky issue with respect to whether the business owner should obtain appropriate agreements with multiple performing rights organizations, or with just one. This issue arises because of the fact that many songs are written by multiple songwriters, each of whom with respect to any particular song may be affiliated with a different performing rights organization. If a business uses, within its customer environment,

---

23. See, e.g., John Bowe, "The Music-Copyright Enforcers," *New York Times*, August 6, 2010; Cassandra Day, "CT Venue Among 15 in U.S. Sued for Alleged Music Copyright Violations," *The Middletown Press*, March 7, 2025, https://www.middletownpress.com/news/article/sicily-middletown-ct-copyright-music-suit-ascap-20206201.php. For further evidence, a real-time internet search for "BMI sues restaurants," "ASCAP sues nightclubs," or the like (choose your business premises type) will typically result in pages of returns of recent news coverage of such enforcement activity.

24. Certain state statutes regulate the licensing practices of performing rights organizations. See, e.g., Music Licensing Fees Act, 815 ILCS 637.

songs written by an ASCAP-affiliated writer and a BMI-affiliated writer, for example, then having a license from only ASCAP or only BMI, instead of both, would be exposed to a claim from the other (i.e., from the performing rights organization from which the business had not procured a license). This is because each performing rights organization would have the right to grant only its fractional interest in the song at issue, and the business would need licensing from both.[25] As you may have already surmised, this issue grows in correlation with the number of songwriters on a particular song (which, of course, is likely unknown to the business using music within its customer environment—at least not without research).

Other Workplace Use of Music

Copyright infringement is a tort, and liability for infringement of copyright, as with any other tortuous acts, may extend to persons other than the direct performer or publisher of the infringing work. The infringing acts of a company's employees will create liability for the company.[26] Further, under the concepts of vicarious or contributory liability, where the company is in a position to control the activities of the primary infringer and has a direct financial interest in the activities, liability can be extended to the company. For example, the operator of a flea market where infringing material is sold was found liable for the acts of the client sellers at the market.[27]

As a result, companies should take care to establish and enforce policies with respect to the use of music in the workplace. Companies cannot afford the blinkered view that unauthorized internal uses of music will remain undiscovered.[28] The following are some examples of workplace use of music outside the customer environment.

25. See generally David Oxenford, "Court of Appeals Upholds BMI Decision Allowing Fractional Music Licensing—What Are the Issues?" *Broadcast Law Blog*, December 20, 2017, https://www.broadcastlawblog.com/2017/12/articles/court-of-appeals-upholds-bmi-decision-allowing-fractional-music-licensing-what-are-the-issues/.

26. *Famous Music Corp. v. Bay State Harness Horse Racing & Breeding Ass'n, Inc.*, 554 F.2d 1213 (1st Cir. 1977).

27. *Arista Records Inc. v. Flea World Inc.*, 78 U.S.P.Q.2d (D.N.J. 2006).

28. Note the effort by the Business Software Association to solicit confidential information concerning software misuse from disgruntled ex-employees. See *Business Software Association*, https://reporting.bsa.org/r/report/add.aspx?src=us&ln=en-us (last accessed September 2025).

Employee Downloading or Subscribing to Music Services

Use of company computers or systems to either upload or download music files through the use of file-sharing software or sites should be barred in a document that each employee signs (e.g., employee handbook). There is little ambiguity about whether such activity is wrongful, no matter how urgent the arguments in support, but communicating and requiring employees' signatures on such a policy is nevertheless recommended.

Companies should also remain mindful that music subscription services such as Spotify, Apple Music, Amazon Music, YouTube Music, SoundCloud, and others may be used in a commercial environment only if the company has entered an appropriate agreement with such service. An individual employee who is an authorized user of a service only has the right to use that service for personal purposes, which does not extend to broader deployment and transmission within the workplace. An individual employee who uses their company email address for purposes of subscribing may be giving the provider of the service an argument that the employee has bound the company.

Music on Hold

Playing music through the company's telephone system to callers who are placed on hold constitutes a public performance of that music that must be authorized.[29] Companies are advised to avoid retransmission of broadcast, cable, or satellite signals through their telephone systems and to use only recordings of compositions for which they have obtained the right to use in an on-hold feature.

Office or Warehouse Performance of Music

Under clause (1) of the definition of "publicly" in § 101 of the Copyright Act, a performance or display is "public" if it takes place "at a place open to the public or at any place where a substantial number of persons outside of a normal circle of a family and its social acquaintances is gathered."[30] The House Report that accompanied the passage of the Copyright Act

29. *Prophet Music, Inc. v. Shamla Oil Co., Inc.*, 1993 WL 300204 (D. Minn. 1993).
30. 17 U.S.C. § 101 (2011).

of 1976 stated that "Routine meetings of businesses and governmental personnel would be excluded because they do not represent the gathering of a 'substantial number of persons.'"[31] However, in one case, a group of twenty-one members of a private club and their respective guests who were in the audience for a performance of music were found to constitute a "substantial number."[32] Moreover, music performed for the benefit of a company's employees is also subject to licensing.[33]

Based on the foregoing, companies are advised that use of music performed in routine meetings within a non-customer environment would not create liability if not licensed. However, music regularly performed, for example, throughout a warehouse or within all or a large portion of an office environment generally, or at overall company meetings, may create liability if the music is not a retransmission of a regular broadcast, cable system, or satellite carrier signal. If so, the company's sound system and space size exceed the limits of the Fairness in Music Licensing Act described earlier.

Trade Shows and Conventions

Music is often a feature at trade shows and conventions, either as a form of entertainment for attendees, to attract an audience, or to enliven a presentation. Courts have been divided as to whether the organizers of professional trade shows are liable for the actions of trade show participants that violate the rights of music rights holders.[34] However, organizers of such shows and/or the facilities in which they are held are generally licensed themselves for their own activities that involve the performance of music.[35]

Companies are advised to carefully review the terms and conditions of the agreement with the organizer of any trade show at which they intend to use music as a feature of their exhibit, or any facility in which they intend to

31. H.R. Rep. No. 1476, 94th Cong., 2d Sess. 64, reprinted in 1976 U.S.C.C.A.N. 5659, 5677–78.

32. *Fermata Int'l Melodies, Inc. v. Champions Golf Club, Inc.*, 712 F. Supp. 1257 (S.D. Tex. 1989).

33. *Merrill v. County Stores, Inc.*, 669 F. Supp. 1164 (D.N.H. 1987).

34. *Compare Artists Music, Inc. v. Reed Pub'l (U.S.A.), Inc.*, 31 U.S.P.Q.2d 1623 (S.D.N.Y. 1994), and *Polygram Int'l Publ'g, Inc. v. Nevada/TIG, Inc.*, 855 F. Supp. 1314 (D. Mass. 1994).

35. Jeffrey W. King, "Music Licensing at Trade Shows and Conventions: Who Pays the Band?" *Licensing Journal* (Nov./Dec. 2007).

use music as part of a planned activity (such as a hotel), to understand the extent of their responsibility for obtaining any public performance agreements required by their plans. Companies will save fees if their intended activities fall within the scope of the licenses already in place through the event organizers or facilities. Alternatively, the event organizers or facilities may seek to shift responsibility for obtaining the proper licenses to the exhibitors, who would likely be responsible for indemnifying the event organizer or facility for any failure for having done so.

Reproductions of Recordings

The ease with which preexisting music may be sourced and incorporated into a sales presentation, an electronic press kit, a website, or a social media post is a powerful tool. However, unless any such use may be excused as a fair use, as explained in Chapter 2, using music in any of these ways will require the consent of the appropriate rights holders. This could involve the owner of the composition, the owner of the recording, and the artist whose performance is featured in the recording. The exact nature of the rights necessary to be licensed may also require expert review. Alternatively, companies are advised to avail themselves of such services as Getty Images or Corbis as a "one-stop shop" to license recordings for their particular requirements, to obtain public domain recordings from such places as MusOpen.org., or to obtain rights through Creative Commons.[36]

Creation of Music in the Workplace

In some circumstances, workers involved in the business of the company will create music that the company then uses. This possibility raises its own unique issues with respect to ownership and usage rights.

As discussed more broadly in Chapter 2, ordinarily the human creator of a musical work (in this case, the worker) will be the copyright owner, but there are circumstances under which someone other than the human creator (in this case, possibly the company) will be considered the author

36. *Creative Commons*, http://creativecommons.org/about (last accessed September 2025).

and, therefore, own the copyright and be considered the "author" thereof from its inception. Those circumstances occur when a work is created in what is called a "work-for-hire" situation, which can occur either when musical works created within the scope of a person's employment (in which cases the person's human or entity employer is deemed to be the creator (i.e., the author) of those works) or when an independent contractor who is commissioned to create a musical work by way of an agreement in writing signed by the contractor and the work that is created falls within one of the categories of works enumerated by the work-for-hire statute.

Obviously, who owns a musical work that is used in the business of the company is a critical issue, since the business's use of a work that it neither owns nor has a license to use can create significant liability for the company, particularly after the passage of time during which relations between the business and the worker may erode and/or the musical work grows in value as attached to the business of the company. See Chapter 2 for more on these scenarios and ways to assist a business client in avoiding the pitfalls.

Jukeboxes

The Copyright Act of 1976 eliminated the prior statutory exemption from copyright liability for music played on jukeboxes and established a compulsory license for jukebox operators.[37] Operators pay an annual fee for each machine to the Register of Copyrights, and operation of a jukebox without paying this fee is a copyright infringement.[38] The current annual rate for jukebox royalties may be found at 37 C.F.R. § 388.3. The collected jukebox royalties are distributed to ASCAP, BMI, SESAC, and any person unaffiliated with a performing rights society that proves entitlement.

37. 17 U.S.C. § 116 (2011).
38. *Broadcast Music, Inc. v. Fox Amusement Co.*, 551 F. Supp. 104 (N.D. Ill. 1982).

Chapter 12
Representing the Musician

The relationship between artists and attorneys has at times been marked by mistrust and misunderstanding. Finding the balance between the aesthetic creativity of the artist's mindset and order of the attorney has never been easy.

Attorneys have been historically stereotyped by artists as persons "whose avarice is exceeded only by [their] monkey-like cunning,"[1] or akin to the nameless man from Porlock who interrupted Coleridge as he wrote *Kubla Kahn* to just get in the way and spoil everything. Attorneys on the other hand often disdain the antithetical artistic world for its ambiguity and nonconformity. It was the view of Oliver Wendall Holmes that "the law is not the place for the artist or the poet. The law is the calling of thinkers."[2] More recently, Glenn Frey and Don Henley channeled William Shakespeare to

1. David Apatoff, "The Unhappy Relationship Between the Lawyer and the Artist," *Paideia: A Journal of Legal Experience* 1 (1975): 8.

2. Oliver Wendell Holmes, "The Profession of the Law," in *The Mind and Faith of Justice Holmes: Their Speeches, Essays, Letters, and Judicial Opinions*, ed. M. Lerner (Piscataway, NJ: Transaction Publishing, 1988), 31 (originally delivered February 17, 1886, at the conclusion of a lecture to undergraduates of Harvard University).

proclaim, in their 1994 song *Get Over It*, that "The more I think about it old Billy was right; Let's kill all the lawyers kill 'em tonight."[3]

For an attorney, becoming engaged with the creative community is enlightening and fun, and it makes a difference that matters. It also is not unusual for friendships and long-term client relationships to develop from this arrangement. Creative artists are grateful for the assistance they receive for problems that can seem quite overwhelming to them. In return, they enthusiastically acknowledge those who help them by sharing access to the creative process in sometimes singular experiences.[4] Sometimes, they even publicly display their affection.[5]

In one sense, representing musical talent is like representing any other client: You are engaged to provide your legal services to solve a problem, or to provide your best judgment and experience to give advice. And musicians want you to do what they cannot or do not want to do. The matters they will entrust to you will be very dear to them. They are not looking for something they can find elsewhere, such as more fans or critics. Like many individual clients, they quite often may feel overwhelmed by the need to deal with the legal system without succumbing to its afflictions. However, musicians do present some unique issues for practitioners that one should be mindful of to enjoy a successful relationship, both personally and professionally.[6]

---

3. Don Henley and Glenn Frey, "Get Over It," recorded by Eagles, on *Hell Freezes Over* [album] (Geffen Records, 1994).

4. Of course, matters do not always follow a smooth course. For some interesting examples of where it seems to all go wrong between attorneys and artist clients, see Stan Soocher, *They Fought the Law: Rock Music Goes to Court* (New York: Schirmer Books, 1999); Bill Donahue, "Sublime Hits Top Music Law Firm with Legal Malpractice Lawsuit," *Billboard*, February 1, 2024, https://www.billboard.com/business/legal/sublime-music-law-firm-legal-malpractice-lawsuit-1235595635/; Annie Youderian, "Lil' Kim's Attorney Accused of 'Intentionally Sloppy' Work," *CourthouseNews.com*, March 11, 2013, https://www.courthousenews.com/lil-kims-attorney-accusedof-intentionally-sloppy-work/.

5. Chris Williams, "Young Thug Rolls Out New Music with Brian Steel Merch," *Above the Law*, April 17, 2025, https://abovethelaw.com/2025/04/young-thug-rolls-out-new-music-with-brian-steel-merch/.

6. For an excellent discussion of ethics and entertainment law generally, see Kenneth J. Abdo and Jack P. Sahl, *Entertainment Law Ethics* (2012), https://lommen.com/wp-content/uploads/2016/03/Entertainment-Law-Ethics-1.pdf.

Popularity Contest

It often happens that a musician will receive recommendations for, or have otherwise heard of, several attorneys to consider for representation. The artist will then meet with those attorneys to determine whether there is a "fit" professionally and personally before engaging them. There will be a temptation by the attorneys in such "popularity contests" to prove their expertise and perhaps provide some advice as an example of the kind of insight and value they could bring to the relationship. Attorneys frequently find themselves in such circumstances when trying to win new clients, but there is a special sensitivity that should be brought to the development of a relationship with artists, who may not be experienced consumers of legal services. Even though the attorney may not believe that an attorney-client relationship is being formed during the initial interview process, the artist may not understand that to be the case and may rely upon the advice given during such initial interviews. In a well-known case involving the singer/songwriter Jim Croce, an attorney representing a production company seeking to sign Croce for his recording and composing services was introduced to Croce and his wife as "the attorney," who then proceeded to provide explanations of the proposed relationship to Croce and his wife. When Croce later sought to extricate himself from these agreements, the attorney was successfully sued for breach of his fiduciary duty to Croce for having not advised him to obtain independent counsel to assist him concerning the agreements when the Croces reasonably believed they could rely upon his advice.[7] Counsel should also be mindful under such circumstances of Rule 1.18 of the ABA Model Rules of Professional Conduct concerning prospective client obligations.[8] Rule 1.18 bars the use or revelation of information

7. *Croce v. Kurnit*, 565 F. Supp. 884 (S.D.N.Y. 1982).

8. Model Rules of Professional Conduct, r. 1.18 (2020). Note that California is the only state that has not adopted the ABA Model Rules in some form, but Rule 1.8.6 of California's Rules of Professional Conduct provides essentially the same on this issue as does ABA Model Rule 1.8(f); see generally American Bar Association, *Alphabetical List of Jurisdictions Adopting Model Rules* (2018), https://www.americanbar.org/groups/professional_responsibility/publications/model_rules_of_professional_conduct/alpha_list_state_adopting_model_rules/ (last accessed September 2025); The State Bar of California, *California Rules of Professional Conduct* 1.8.6 (2023), https://www.calbar.ca.gov/Portals/0/documents/rules/Rules-of-Professional-Conduct.pdf.

learned during a consultation with a prospective client and can further bar representing a client with interests materially adverse to those of a prospective client in the same or a substantially related matter if the attorney received information from the prospective client that could be significantly harmful to that person in the matter.

Payment of Fees

It is often the case that a musician may present themselves as having modest resources for the payment of fees, but that there are others who are supporting the musician, such as parents, managers, or investors, who will pay the fees on the musician's behalf. It also sometimes occurs that the party on the opposite side of a transaction with an artist client, such as a record company, is willing to pay an amount to the attorney for the attorney fees to the artist. Such arrangements are ethically permissible, as long as certain criteria are met. Rule 1.8(f) of the ABA Model Rules of Professional Conduct provides as follows:

> (f) A lawyer shall not accept compensation for representing a client from one other than the client unless:
>
> (1) the client gives informed consent;
> (2) there is no interference with the lawyer's independence of professional judgment or with the client-lawyer relationship; and
> (3) information relating to representation of a client is protected as required by Rule 1.6.[9]

Compliance with Rule 1.8(f) can be reflected in the engagement agreement with the client. Compliance in practice may require some diligence, particularly if the party paying the fees is the artist's manager and most material communications concerning the artist's professional matters take place through the manager.

9. Model Rules of Professional Conduct, r. 1.8(f) (2004).

Dealing with Representatives

As noted earlier, the entertainment industry is based on intermediaries, such as managers, agents, and business managers. Because of this circumstance, the attorney may find themselves dealing principally with a manager or an agent rather than the client artist. This can present problems.

First, the attorney should always understand the full extent of the intermediary's authority to act on behalf of the artist. That authority should not be presumed as to either scope or duration. Confirmation may be as simple as reviewing the management agreement. No matter what the understanding of authority may be, the attorney should be sensitive to certain requests that an intermediary might make that should raise suspicion. Requests to change payment directions, for example, or to register trademarks or other intellectual property in the name or co-name of the intermediary or third party rather than the artist, should alert the attorney to confirm such requests with the artist.[10] If the artist is not available to discuss the terms of a proposed agreement and seeks to rely upon the attorney and the artist's representative to finalize the agreement, the attorney may need to memorialize any advice concerning the agreement that is addressed to the artist to ensure that their own exposure is not compromised. Finally, unless the document requiring the artist's signature is of only minor consequence and the intermediary's signature on the artist's behalf is acceptable, the artist should sign such documents themselves to ensure enforceability.

It is not uncommon for an artist's attorney and representative to develop a close working relationship, particularly if most communication to and from the attorney concerning the artist is conducted through the representative. It is not unusual under such circumstances for the representative to view the artist's attorney as a source for legal advice that pertains to the representative personally or with respect to matters not directly concerning the artist. Unless the advice is of the most general type, such as factual information about resources that might assist the representative, the artist's attorney should generally resist providing legal advice under such circumstances and should instead refer the representative to other counsel. While

10. See, e.g., *Reznor v. J. Artist Mgmt., Inc.*, 365 F. Supp. 2d 565 (S.D.N.Y. 2005).

arrangements might be documented in accordance with Rule 1.7 of the ABA Model Rules of Professional Conduct between the attorney and their artist client to waive the conflict in the representation of both the artist and the representative, the highly personal relationship between the artist and the representative, particularly personal managers, and the sometimes frequent volatility of such relationships creates additional tensions that disfavor representing both parties even in unrelated matters.[11]

Counsel should also be mindful of maintaining the attorney-client privilege in connection with communications with agents and personal managers. The attorney-client privilege generally extends to those serving as an agent of either the attorney or the client.[12] However, to be protected, the communications must be intended to facilitate the provision of legal services by the attorney to the client. Agents and managers generally will be considered agents of their clients, but the exact nature of the relationship between a representative and the talent may not always be clear.[13] Further, the privilege may be lost if communications occur in the presence of third parties that are not characterized as agents.

Dealing with Groups

Musicians often perform as groups, and it is as a group that the musicians will approach the attorney for representation. The issues that arise under

---

11. Given the highly relational makeup of the music industry, some attorneys have promoted their multiple representations of parties in transactions as a desirable and value-adding practice. See, e.g., *Joel v. Grubman*, No. 261–55–92 (N.Y. Sup. Ct. 1992).

12. *Robert V. Straus Prods. v. Pollard*, 734 N.Y.S.2d 170 (N.Y. App. Div. 2001).

13. Public relations agents have been deemed both subject and not subject to the privilege. See Roy Simon, "The Attorney-Client Privilege and Third-Party Consultants: An Update," *The New York Professional Responsibility Report* (2010), https://www.newyorklegalethics.com/the-attorney-client-privilege-and-third-party-consultants-an-update/; Lisa Baird, Colleen Davies, and Andrew Stillufsen, "Attorney-Client Privilege and Communications with Third-Party Consultants," *LawFuel.com*, August 23, 2015, https://www.lawfuel.com/attorney-client-privilege-and-communications-with-third-party-consultants/; Brian Spahn, "Privilege and Work Product Considerations When Engaging Third-Party Consultants," *Godfrey Kahn Government Investigations, White Collar & Compliance Update*, July 26, 2017, https://www.gklaw.com/Insights/Privilege-and-work-product-considerations-when-engaging-third-party-consultants.htm.

such circumstances are the same as those presented when multiple people elect to start a venture and seek the services of an attorney to organize and represent that venture.

The first question that needs to be answered is "Who is the client?" If the group is organized as a separate legal entity, or seeks such organization, the client generally would be the entity. If a separate entity is not formed, then the question of how the group is organized should be resolved. Is the group really a sole proprietorship of one of the members with everyone else an employee, are the group members a general partnership, or is the answer somewhere between (e.g., two general partners and three employees)? If the group members are unincorporated joint owners of the group, it is advisable to obtain waivers of conflict of interest from each of the group members in accordance with the requirements of Rule 1.7 of the ABA Model Rules of Professional Conduct.

When representing multiple members of a musical group, communication between one member of the group and the attorney is not treated as confidential vis-à-vis the attorney and the other members of the group (i.e., the attorney may—indeed, even may be required to—discuss with other members of the group the contents of the conversation between the one member and the attorney). The group members may not understand that—they may believe they can conduct communication with the attorney that is not sharable with other members. Therefore, it is a good practice to advise the group members in either the engagement agreement or the conflict-waiver agreement that communications between individual group members and the attorney cannot be kept from the others.

The makeup of a musical group can be fluid, with people leaving and joining for a variety of reasons. When representing multiple members of a group, the attorney should not be drawn into discussions concerning the replacement of band members. The attorney cannot be an advocate for one or several of the group members against any other(s).[14]

14. See, e.g., *Adler v. Manatt, Phelps, Phillips & Kantor*, BC O5307 (L.A. Sup. Ct., filed Apr. 1992) (former member of group Guns N' Roses sued the group's law firm for malpractice in connection with group settlement agreement).

While the attorney cannot be the advocate of one group member against any other(s), the attorney may ask for written instruction from the group as a whole as to how decisions are made within the group and whose authority the attorney can rely upon to undertake action on behalf of the group.

Shopping Groups

The music industry is highly competitive, and although the paths to public appeal have expanded greatly over the years, there are certain traditional opportunities performers seek to achieve for themselves to improve their chances for success. Access to these opportunities, whether recording agreements with major record labels, song publishing agreements with influential music publishing companies, or agreements with powerful managers or agents, is sometimes restricted given the great number of people seeking entry through the same doors. As a result, attorneys are often sought out by artists to open those doors and help present the artists and the results of their talents to decision makers with the hope that the favorable inroad will make the difference. This door opening is often referred to as shopping the artist, and it is often the service beginning performers want the most.

Shopping an artist to important decision makers is often the way an attorney begins developing a practice representing artists. If an attorney is successful in such efforts, it becomes a powerful practice development tool—the attorney demonstrates they can advance an artist's career in a material way. It is also a way for an attorney to meet others in the industry, which may also lead to productive business development from those contacts. However, it is also an activity that often has for its fee structure a contingent arrangement based upon the success of the effort. To be effective, and as required by Rule 1.5 of the ABA Model Rules of Professional Conduct, such fee agreements should be in writing, should be reasonable in the manner in which the fee is determined, and should be independently reviewed on behalf of the artist by another attorney to ensure reasonableness as to the amount of the fee and its other terms.

The reasonableness of a fee for seeking to secure a recording or publishing agreement for an artist will turn on the amount of time involved, the level of success of the effort, and fees customarily charged by others for similar services. Given that the customary fees for agents is in the range of 10 percent to 15 percent and the customary contingent compensation arrangement between attorneys and entertainment clients for handling general entertainment business matters is 5 percent, a fee of 10 percent for shopping an artist would seem reasonable.[15] In the event of a termination, the attorney is still entitled to recover in quantum meruit the value of their services prior to discharge.[16]

Among the practical risks for an attorney shopping a band are that the group could become unstable or break up for any number of reasons, leaving the attorney without a transaction from which to collect their fee. Also, the act of shopping a band may spark interest in some of the members of the group but not all, which could create a conflict or problem for the attorney if a member is pushed out or otherwise left behind.

Alternative Fee Arrangements

It is not uncommon for some attorneys representing musicians, particularly successful, high-income performers, to charge the musician on a percentage basis rather than hourly. The customary amount is 5 percent, which is usually applied to the musician's income from contracts entered during the course of the attorney's representation.

As with respect to shopping, as already discussed, and Rule 1.5 of the ABA Model Rules of Professional Conduct, a contingent-fee agreement should be in writing, and an attorney is best advised to have their client obtain independent advice concerning entering such an agreement. Two key issues that should be addressed in such an agreement are the scope of services to be provided in exchange for the contingent fee and what is the contingency that must be met in order for the fee to be payable. Negotiation and drafting of the agreements upon which the fee will be calculated

15. See, e.g., Donald E. Biederman et al., *Law and Business of the Entertainment Industries*, 5th ed. (Westport, CT: Praeger, 2007), 22–28.

16. *Musburger v. Meier*, 394 Ill. App. 3d 781 (1st Dist. 2009).

will certainly be included, but what about real estate transactions, tax planning, litigation, or corporate transactions? Another key issue is the length of time the commission will be payable. Unlike management agreements, which generally provide that the management commission will be payable on all income derived from an artist's contract entered during the term of the management agreement (whether the payment occurs during or after the term of the management agreement), payment of contingent attorney fees after the attorney-client relationship has ended may not be enforceable.

In the case of *Hirsch Wallerstein Hayum Matlof & Fishman v. Hirsch Jackoway Tyerman Wertheimer Austin Mandelbaum & Morris*,[17] a law firm sought to enforce contingent-fee arrangements, both oral and written, with former clients who followed a partner who left the firm to start another. The first law firm took the position that the fee arrangement bound the former clients to pay that firm in perpetuity for any revenue derived from agreements that had been entered while the former clients were clients of the firm. That position was rejected by the trial court as unconscionable and unenforceable for several reasons, including that such an arrangement would conflict with a client's absolute right to discharge an attorney at any time and select another.[18] More recently, in a six-year legal battle between rapper Lil Wayne and his former attorney, the artist contended both that a 10 percent fee was unconscionably large and that the alleged oral contingent-fee contract that provided for it was unenforceable. The court held that the purported agreement that provided for the 10 percent fee was unenforceable for having been oral, and that the attorney was entitled to only a reasonable fee under a quantum meruit theory (the court did not

17. *Hirsch Wallerstein Hayum Matlof & Fishman v. Hirsch Jackoway Tyerman Wertheimer Austin Mandelbaum & Morris*, BC 320128 (L.A. Super. Ct., filed Aug. 13, 2004); see also *Mandel v. Liebman*, 303 N.Y. 88 (1951).

18. Michael I. Rudell and Neil J. Rosini, "Block to Perpetual Attorney Fees," *Entertainment Law & Finance*, September 2007; Brad Graham and Jason Robles, "Attorney Fees in Repeated Relationships," *Journal of Economics* 127, no. 2 (2018): 99–124, https://doi.org/10.1007/s00712-018-0633-1; Ashley Hollan, "Music Lawyers Taking the Rap: The Musicalization of Legal Ethics," *Denver Sports & Entertainment Law Journal* 4, no. 1 (2008): Article 7, https://digitalcommons.du.edu/selj/vol4/iss1/7; Anthony J. Sebok, "Selling Attorneys' Fees," *University of Illinois Law Review*, October 20, 2018, https://illinoislawreview.org/print/vol-2018-no-4/selling-attorneys-fees/.

opine as to whether 10 percent was reasonable, but rather, remanded for discovery and determination on that issue).[19]

The fact that a perpetual fee arrangement may not be enforceable, however, does not necessarily mean that an attorney is without a remedy for the payment of fees that may have been earned. In the Illinois case of *Musburger v. Meier*,[20] an attorney who represented radio talent on a contingent fee basis was discharged during the course of a negotiation with a radio station. The attorney's fee arrangement with the radio talent had previously been in written form, but that agreement had not been renewed at the time of the negotiation at issue. While the court in *Musburger* noted that an attorney may be discharged at any time by a client, with or without cause, the attorney is still entitled to recover in quantum meruit the value of their services prior to discharge. Musburger was able to reconstruct the time he devoted to representing the radio talent in the negotiation and was thus able to recover their fee on that basis. The lesson for attorneys generally from the case may be to maintain time records of their services, even when the matter they are handling is on a contingent fee basis.

Multiple Roles

Occasionally, an attorney may desire to enter into a relationship with an artist in which the attorney is acting as a contractual counterparty, not as a lawyer (or perhaps not *entirely* as a lawyer, but rather, as both lawyer and in another capacity). For example, the attorney may actively seek to manage the career of an artist they represent for legal services, or the attorney may desire to license or purchase from the artist rights in and to some artist-owned songs and/or sound recordings. The attorney and/or the artist, too, may desire that the attorney procure performance engagements for the artist.

In any such case, Rule 1.8(a) of the ABA Model Rules of Professional Conduct will apply unless the attorney proves that, while they *do* possess

19. Sweeney v. Carter, et al., Case No. 2:2021cv01689 (C.D. Cal. 2021).
20. *Musburger v. Meier*, 394 Ill. App. 3d. 781 (1st Dist. 2009).

a license to practice law, they and the artist are not, in fact, attorney and client. Rule 1.8(a) provides as follows:

(a) A lawyer shall not enter into a business transaction with a client or knowingly acquire an ownership, possessory, security or other pecuniary interest adverse to a client unless:
  (1) the transaction and terms on which the lawyer acquires the interest are fair and reasonable to the client and are fully disclosed and transmitted in writing in a manner that can be reasonably understood by the client;
  (2) the client is advised in writing of the desirability of seeking and is given a reasonable opportunity to seek the advice of independent legal counsel on the transaction; and
  (3) the client gives informed consent, in a writing signed by the client, to the essential terms of the transaction and the lawyer's role in the transaction, including whether the lawyer is representing the client in the transaction.

Where an attorney is considering entering any transaction with an artist, the conservative path for the attorney is to either confirm in writing with the artist that the attorney and artist are not attorney and client, or, if they *are* attorney and client, comply with Rule 1.8(a).[21] Other ethical issues, too, can arise for the attorney in these instances, because of other ethics rules that apply to attorneys but not to others, for example, rules concerning advertising, client solicitation, jurisdictional limits on the practice of law, and communication with third parties (e.g., venue owners or record labels who may themselves be represented by counsel).[22]

---

21. See generally *Viper Publishing, LLC v. Bailey*, Civil Action No. 3:17-CV-00314-GCM (W.D. N.C., Charlotte Div. 2018), in which an artist and their licensed attorney acting as manager disputed whether the attorney's services were management services or legal services (and, thus, whether the artist's contingency payment obligation could last beyond the end of the executory relationship between the attorney and the artist, as discussed earlier in the section of this chapter headed "Alternative Fee Arrangements").

22. For a good discussion of such ethical issues, and some thoughtful proposals on how to solve them, see Jeremy M. Evans, "Lawyers, Agents, and the Blurred Lines Regulating Talent Representation," *Entertainment & Sports Law Journal* 34, no. 2 (2018): 27.

Where the attorney and/or the artist desire that the attorney procure performance engagements for the artist, an additional issue arises as to whether the attorney, despite their law license, also needs a talent agent license.[23] In *Solis v. Blancarte*, the California labor commissioner held that an attorney cannot procure performance engagements for an artist without also being a licensed talent agent (and, consequently, loses their right to enforce the payment of a fee). In that case, the commissioner even went so far as to hold that the attorney cannot even handle a live performance contract for an artist because that act comprises procuring employment (although note that the artist in that case did not have a separate, licensed agent, leaving open the question of the attorney's ability to negotiate a live performance contract when the artist *does* have a separate agent).[24]

Practical Issues

Relating to a musician client may involve a certain amount of simpatico. Unless you are handling something that will not involve much direct contact with a musician client, it is generally not enough to be a good tactician. As with all creative individuals, artists' talents, and the results of their talents, are very important to them on a highly personal basis. Those results are not just their livelihood, but a reflection of their identity. Your respect for that talent is key to a successful long-term relationship. We are not suggesting a fawning approach or the mustering of an insincere enthusiasm for their work, as musicians are no less capable of detecting such expressions than anyone else. Indeed, they are usually better since they may encounter it more often than others. The best approach is consistent with the role you are actually being engaged to fulfill, which is the advocate of the musician's interests and the protection of their rights. You do not need to understand the musician's work, or even enjoy it. If you do, that is a bonus. The most important thing is that you respect the work, the talent, and the effort the musician is bringing to their career and the process of creating that work.

23. See generally discussion in Chapter 6 regarding licensure requirements for talent agents.

24. *Solis v. Blancarte*, TAC-27089 (2013).

It has been our experience that this support is the most appreciated—that creative artists most value the trust they have in the attorney's commitment to their interests, much more than they care whether the attorney likes everything they do.

Respect may take many forms. It may mean understanding when the creative process leads to unexpected changes of direction or decisions and being prepared to accommodate those changes within the deal-making process. It may mean giving appropriate weight to intuitive analysis when you might otherwise strictly insist upon reason. It may mean exercising greater patience to bring an understanding of a situation to a musician client without condescension when that musician turns out to be a less-sophisticated purchaser of legal services than one customarily works with. It may also mean reminding yourself of the strength you summon when seeking the positive judgment of one or a small group of judges, then multiplying that group by the many hundreds or thousands from which a musician risks rejection whenever they perform—that is a special strength worthy of much respect.

Appendix A

Recommended Further Reading

Weston Anson, *Right of Publicity: Analysis, Valuation, and the Law* (ABA 2025).

Jeffrey Brabec and Todd Brabec, *Music, Money and Success* (8th ed., Schirmer Trade Books 2022).

David Byrne, *How Music Works* (McSweeney's Books 2012).

Xavier M. Frascongna Jr. & H. Lee Hetherington, *This Business of Artist Management* (4th ed., Hal Leonard Corporation 2004).

Steve Gordon, *The Future of the Music Business* (3d ed., Hal Leonard Corporation 2011).

Barry Irwin and Adam Reis, *Band Law for Bands* (Lawyers for the Creative Arts 2013, 2016).

Martin Kamenski, *Minding Your Business: A Guide to Money and Taxes for Creative Professionals* (Hal Leonard Corporation 2018).

Al Kohn and Bob Kohn, *Kohn on Music Licensing* (5th ed., Wolters Kluwer 2021).

William Krasilovsky and Sydney Shemel, *This Business of Music* (10th ed., Billboard Books 2007).

Cecil C. Kuhne III, *The Little Book of Elvis Law* (ABA 2013).

Schuyler M. Moore, *Taxation of the Entertainment Industry* (10th ed., CCH 2009).

Kevin Parks, *Music & Copyright in America* (ABA 2014).

Donald S. Passman, *All You Need to Know About the Music Business* (11th ed., Simon & Schuster 2023).

Mary Hutchings Reed, *IEG Legal Guide to Sponsorship* (International Events Group 1989).

Julie Ross and Michael J. Huppe, *Music Law: The Changing Landscape in the Music Industry and the Law That Governs It* (West Academic Publishing 2021).

Ray D. Waddell, Rich Barnet and Jake Berry, *This Business of Concert Promotion and Touring* (Billboard Books 2007).

Appendix B

List of Dispute Resolution Service Organizations

California Lawyers for the Arts
12304 Santa Monica Boulevard
Suite 304
Los Angeles, CA 90025
Phone: (310) 207-0001
Email: losangeles@calawyersforthearts.org
Web: calawyersforthearts.org

Judicial Arbitration and Mediation Services, Inc. (JAMS) Entertainment and Sports Group
555 West Fifth Street
32nd Floor
Los Angeles, CA 90013
Email: nmoreno@jamsadr.com
Web: nmoreno@jamsadr.com

Lawyers for the Creative Arts

161 North Clark Street
Suite 4200
Chicago, IL 60601
Phone: (312) 649-4111
Web: https://law-arts.org/

National Arbitration and Mediation (NAM)

122 East 42nd Street
Suite 803
New York, NY 10168
Phone: (800) 358-2550
Email: customerservice@namadr.com
Web: namadr.com

United States Copyright Office Copyright Claims Board

101 Independence Avenue, S.E.
Washington, D.C. 20559–6000
Email: asktheboard@ccb.gov
Web: ccb.gov

Volunteer Lawyers for the Arts

729 7th Avenue
New York, NY 10019
Phone: (212) 319-2787
Email: registrations@vlany.org
Web: vlany.org

World Intellectual Property Organization (WIPO) Arbitration and Mediation Center for Film and Media

34, chemin des Colombettes
CH-1211 Geneva 20, Switzerland
Phone: +41 (22) 338–8247 or +41 22 740 3700
Email: arbiter.mail@wipo.int
Web: wipo.int

Index

Table of Cases